# No Grid Survival Projects

## How to Produce Everything You Need on Your Property

Michael Major | Amber Robinson
Claude Davis | James Walton

© 2021 Global Brother SRL

All rights reserved. No part of this book may be reproduced or used in any manner without the prior written permission of the copyright owner, except for the use of brief quotations in a book review.

# Disclaimer

This book is designed only to provide information about do-it-yourself projects for survival and self-sufficiency. **No Grid Survival Projects** is sold with the knowledge that the publisher, editor, and authors do not offer any legal or other professional advice regarding this or any other subject. In the case of a need for any such expertise, you should always consult the appropriate professional, whether that is an electrician, plumber, or other.

This book does not contain all the information available on the subject of these DIY projects.

It has not been created to be specific to any individual's or organization's situation or needs. While the authors, editor, and publisher have made every effort to make the knowledge inside this book as accurate as possible there may still exist typographical and/or content errors that have made it through. Therefore, this book should serve only as a general guide and not as the ultimate source of information on the subject of DIY projects.

The foods described in this book do not comply with FDA, USDA, or FSIS regulations or local health codes. Dehydrating meat products does not reduce the health risks associated with meat contaminated with Salmonella and/or E. coli O157H7. The authors, editor, and publisher cannot and will not guarantee the shelf-life of any of the food products described in this book. Eating the foods will be done at your own risk and it will be your responsibility to test them for microbes, bacteria, viruses, or germs before consuming them.

The authors, editor, and publisher shall have no liability or responsibility to any person or entity regarding any losses or damage incurred, or alleged to have incurred, directly or indirectly, by the information contained in this book. The instructions provided have not been reviewed, tested, or approved by any official testing body or government agency; you agree that by using them you waive any right of litigation.

The authors and editor of this book make no warranty of any kind, expressed or implied, regarding the safety of the final products or of the methods used. Building and operating any of the projects described in this book will be done at your own risk. This includes but is certainly not limited to any physical injury which may occur to yourself or others by incorrectly or unsafely using the knowledge inside this book.

By reading past this point you hereby agree to be bound by this disclaimer, or you may return this book within the guarantee time period for a full refund.

# Table of Contents

**Disclaimer** .................................................................**02**
**Table of Contents** ...................................................**03**

**PROJECTS RELATED TO WATER............... 09**

**DIY Sink To Save Water** .......................................**09**
   Materials Needed ................................................09
   The Building Process .........................................09

**How To Build A Rainwater Catchment System** ...**12**
   What to Use for Rain Barrels.............................12
   Placement of the Rainwater Catchment
   System......................................................................12
   Building the Frame..............................................12
      Tools ....................................................................12
      Materials ............................................................12
      Instructions ......................................................13
   Plumbing the Barrels..........................................15
      Tools ....................................................................15
      Materials ............................................................15
      Instructions ......................................................16
   Variations ...............................................................17

**How To Build A Water Tank For Long Term
Storage** .......................................................................**18**
   How Much Water?...............................................18
   Container Options...............................................18
      Food Grade 55 Gallon Plastic Drums............18
      Jerry Cans..........................................................19
      Soda Bottles......................................................19
      Disposable Water Bottles .............................20
   Designing a Water Storage System..................20
   Preparing Containers for Long Term Water
   Storage ...................................................................20
   Sanitizing Containers.........................................21
   Vertical Placement of 55-gallon Drums............21
   Horizontal Placement of 55-gallon Drums......22
   Filling a 55-gallon Drum....................................22
   Using Your Water Stores ...................................22

**How To Build Your Own Water Filter** .................**23**
   Step 1: Affixing the Valve ..................................23
   Step 2: Prepping Buckets ..................................23
   Step 3: Adding Filtering Materials ..................24
   Step 4: The Charcoal ..........................................24
   Step 5: Assembly .................................................24
   Step 6: Using the Filter .....................................25
   Step 7: Care and Maintenance ........................25

**How To Make A Hand Pump** .................................**26**
   The Check Valve ..................................................26
   Parts List................................................................26

   Build the Plunger Assembly..............................27
   Build the Valve Assembly .................................27

**How To Make Drinkable Water Out Of Air** ........**28**
   Safety of Dehumidifier Water .........................28
   Choosing a Filter ................................................28
   Building Your Project .........................................29
      Tools ...................................................................29
      Materials ..........................................................29
      Instructions .....................................................30
   My Test Run..........................................................31

**PROJECTS ON GUNS AND AMMO ................. 32**

**Ammo For Long Term Storage** ............................**32**
   Protecting Ammo ................................................32
   Additional Practices for Long Term Ammo
   Storage ..................................................................33

**Hidden Gun Storage Shelf** ....................................**34**
   Covert Locations for Firearms.........................34
   Building a Set of Covert Shelves ....................34
      Materials (Makes 2 Shelves).........................34
      Procces..............................................................34

**How To Build A Ghost Gun** ....................................**36**
   What Is a "Ghost Gun"?.....................................36
   Use an 80% Lower Jig .......................................36

**How To Make Black Powder** .................................**38**
   Methods for Making Black Powder.................38
      The Dry Method..............................................38
      The Wet Method .............................................39
   Safety When Making Black Powder ...............39
   Tools .......................................................................39
   The Process ..........................................................39
   Testing Black Powder ........................................41

**How To Recycle Ammo** ...........................................**42**
   Safety Equipment and Procedures.................42
   Components and Cost .......................................42
   Process ..................................................................43
      Installing Your Press......................................43
      Reloading Dies.................................................44
      Preparing Your Charge..................................45
      Measuring Case Length ................................45
      Adding Your Charge.......................................46

**PROJECTS RELATED TO ELECTRICITY ..... 47**

**DIY Bicycle Generator** ............................................**47**
   Materials Needed ...............................................47
   Building the Bicycle Generator .......................48

**How To Build A Faraday Cage**..............................**52**

What Is a Faraday Cage?.................................52
Microwave Faraday Cage...............................53
Ammo Can Faraday Cage ..............................53
Using a Faraday Cage ......................................55

## How To Build A Hydroelectric Generator............56
How to Use a Hydroelectric Generator.............56
Building a Basic DIY Hydroelectric
Generator..........................................................57
   Tools ..................................................................57
   Materials ............................................................57
   Instructions .......................................................57
   Testing ...............................................................59
Considerations and Modifications....................60

## How To Charge Your Phone When There Is No Electricity...............................................................61
Materials Needed..............................................61
The Step-by-step Process..................................61

## How To Get Power Out Of Dead Batteries ...........63

## How To Make Your Own Solar Panel System.......65
Why Choose Solar?..........................................65
Basic Electrical Terminology ..........................65
Essential Components of a Solar Power
System..............................................................66
   Batteries ............................................................66
      Lead Acid Batteries ...................................66
      Lithium Batteries ......................................66
   Solar Panels ......................................................66
   Charge Controller ............................................67
   Inverter..............................................................67
   Battery Monitor................................................67
   Cables and Wiring ...........................................67
Designing a Solar Power System .....................68
Building the Battery Bank ...............................70
   Tools Required .................................................70
   Materials ...........................................................70
   Construction of the Battery Bank..................71
   Considerations..................................................73
Installation and Wiring of the Solar Panels ....73
   Deployment of Solar Panels...........................73
   Ideal Solar Panel Placement...........................73
   Realistic Solar Panel Placement .....................73
   Wiring Solar Panels ........................................74
Deploying a Portable Folding Panel ................78
Connecting the Solar Power System to the
Power Grid.......................................................79
Putting Your Solar System to Use...................79

## How To Make Your Own Wind Turbine................80
Materials Needed .............................................80
Building Your Wind Turbine ..........................80

## How To Protect Your House Using An EMP Shield .....................................................................84
How it Works...................................................84

How to Install an EMP Shield .........................84
   Tools Needed....................................................84
   Instructions .......................................................84

## How To Turn A Car CB Radio Into A Powerful Transmitter............................................................87
How Powerful Are CB Radios?........................87
The Best Way to Increase the Reach of Your
CB Radio..........................................................87
Building a CB Base Station Ground Plane
Antenna............................................................87
   Tools Needed....................................................87
   Materials Needed.............................................88
Building the Antenna .......................................89
How to Establish Your CB Base Station .........92
Putting it All Together.....................................93
Tuning the Antenna.........................................93

## How To Use A Ham Radio In A Blackout ...........95
Get Licensed....................................................95
Get Equipped ..................................................95
   Mobile Radio....................................................96
   CB/FRS/GRMS..............................................96
   Receivers...........................................................96
Preparing for Emergency ................................97
   Frequencies.......................................................97
Use During a Blackout....................................98
   Declaring an Emergency ................................98
   Check-in on Your Neighbours!......................98

## PROJECTS YOU CAN MAKE TO KEEP INTRUDERS OFF YOUR PROPERTY ........... 99

## Backyard Lights With Sensors That Turn On Automatically When Someone Walks On Your Property ................................................................99
How These Motion Activated Lights Work....99
Building the Motion Activated Lights.............99
   Materials ...........................................................99
   Instructions .....................................................100
   Bench Test ......................................................100
   Placement........................................................101

## Backyard Traps Against Property Intruders......102
DIY Razor Wire.............................................102
   Tools Needed..................................................102
   Materials .........................................................102
   Instructions .....................................................103
   Variations........................................................103
Spike Traps.....................................................103
   Tools ................................................................103
   Materials .........................................................103
   Construction ...................................................103
   Placement........................................................104
Lights and Cameras .......................................104
   Lights...............................................................105
   Cameras ..........................................................105

**How To Build A Trip Wire Alarm** .......................107
  What to Use as a Tripwire.............................107
  Clothes Pin Silent Alarm..............................107
    Tools ...................................................107
    Materials .............................................108
    Instructions ..........................................108
    Placing the Clothes Pin Tripwire Alarm .......109
  Sound Grenade Trip Wire Alarm...................110
    Tools ...................................................110
    Materials .............................................110
    Instructions ..........................................110
    Notes ..................................................110
  Cans and String Trip Wire Alarm .................110
    Materials .............................................111
    Instructions ..........................................111

## PROJECTS ON FOOD ..............................................112

**Bean And Rice Survival Soup** ........................112
  Here's What You Need.................................112
  Putting Together the Beans and Rice
  Survival Soup ............................................112

**Canning Amish Poor Man's Steak** .................114
  Ingredients Needed....................................114
  The Recipe................................................114

**How To Dry Meat And Turn It Into Powder** ......117
  Preparing the Marinade ...............................117
    Ingredients:..........................................117
  Preparing the Meat ....................................117
  Drying Your Jerky ......................................118
  Making the Powder ....................................119

**How To Make 2400 Calorie Emergency Ration Bars Designed To Feed You For A Full Day** ......120
  Materials and Ingredients Needed.................120
  Making Your Own Ration Bars......................120

**How To Make Dandelion Bread** .......................122
  Ingredients ...............................................122
  The Step by Step Recipe.............................123
  Taste Test ................................................124

**How To Make Hardtack (Emergency Survival Bread)** .......................................................125
  What You Will Need....................................125
  The Step by Step Recipe.............................126

**How To Make Lard** ........................................129
  What You Will Need....................................129
  The Step by Step Process ...........................129

**How To Make Pemmican**..................................131
  Meat Preparation........................................131
  Let's Make Pemmican .................................132
  Cost and Nutritional Value...........................133

**How To Preserve Eggs**....................................134
  Preserving Eggs with Mineral Oil..................134
  "Waterglassing" Your Eggs with Pickling
  Lime........................................................135
  Preserving Eggs with Isinglass.....................136

**Meal In A Bag: Hamburger Gravy And Mashed Potatoes** .........................................138
  What You Will Need....................................138
  The Step by Step Recipe.............................138

## PROJECTS ON TRAPS YOU CAN MAKE FOR ANIMALS AND BIRDS..................................140

**Automatic Traps For Animals** .........................140
  DIY Wire Snare..........................................140
    Materials .............................................140
    Tools ...................................................141
    Constructing the Snare............................141
    Placing the Snare ..................................142
  Twitch Up Snare.........................................142
    Tools ...................................................142
    Materials .............................................143
    Constructing the Trap.............................143
    Construction of a Twitch Up Snare............143
    Placement of a Twitch Up Snare...............144

**Automatic Traps For Backyard Pests** ..............145
  Bucket Trap for Rats And Mice ....................145
    Tools ...................................................145
    Materials .............................................145
    Construction ........................................146
    Placement ............................................147
  Wasp\Hornet Trap and Mosquito Trap..........147
    Tools ...................................................147
    Materials .............................................147
    Construction ........................................147
    Bait for Wasps/Hornets ..........................148
  Fruit Fly Trap ............................................149
    Materials .............................................149
    Construction ........................................149
    Placement ............................................149

**Automatic Traps For Fish** ...............................150
  Gill Net....................................................150
    Making a Gill Net...................................150
    Materials .............................................150
    Instructions for Making a Gill Net.............151
    Loading the Needle ................................151
    Weaving the Net....................................151
    Deploying the Gill Net ............................153
  Trot Line .................................................153
    Materials .............................................153
    Making a Trotline...................................154

**Automatic Trap-System For Birds** ..................156
  How This Automatic Trap for Birds Works ....156
  Building the Automatic Bird Trap .................156
    Tools Required ......................................156
    Materials .............................................156

Instructions ..............................................157
Using the Automatic Bird Trap...............158
Variations ...............................................159

## OTHER PROJECTS TO DO IN YOUR BACKYARD ..............................................160

### DIY Air Conditioner.....................................160
How Effective Is the DIY Air Conditioner? ...160
Building the DIY Air Conditioner................161
  Tools Required ......................................161
  Materials................................................161
  Instructions ...........................................162
Testing the DIY Air Conditioner...................163
Variations and Improvements .....................164

### DIY Charcoal Briquettes To Have In Case Of Emergency .................................................165
Here Is What You Need ...............................165
Here Is the Process ....................................165

### DIY Dollar Store First Aid Kit.........................169
Basic First Aid Kit Supplies.........................169
Individualized Items and Why You'd Need Them .........................................................170
Putting Your Kit Together...........................171

### DIY Rocket Stove ........................................172
What Is a Rocket Stove?...........................172
Materials Needed ....................................172
Instructions .............................................172

### DIY Smokehouse In A Barrel .......................174
1. Building Your Basic Smokehouse ..............174
2. Building a Custom DIY Smokehouse .........175

### DIY Stove Made From Used Tire Rims ............177
Materials Needed ....................................177
Building the Stove ...................................177

### EMP Proof Cloth: Easy EMP Protection For Your Car And Generator...............................179

### How To Build A Fuel Storage And How To Preserve It ..................................................181
Where to Store Gasoline and Diesel................181
Fuel Storage Containers ...............................181
How Much Fuel to Store ..............................182
Preserving Gasoline and Diesel .....................182
  Fuel Stabilizers ......................................183
  Rotating Fuel Stores ..............................183
Building Your Long Term Fuel Storage.........183
  Materials................................................183

### How To Build A Greenhouse..........................185
Tools Required........................................185
Materials................................................185
Instructions .............................................186
  Getting the Dimensions .........................186
  Building the Sloped walls ......................186
  Building the Straight Walls ....................187

Putting it All Together ..............................187
Putting on the Roof .................................188
Make the Door and Window ...................188
Finishing the Greenhouse .......................188
Things to Consider ..................................188

### How To Build A Hinged Hoophouse For A Raised Bed..................................................189
Tools ......................................................189
Materials ................................................189
Process ...................................................190

### How To Build A Raised Bed .........................193
Tools ......................................................193
Materials ................................................193
Process ...................................................193
Filling Your Raised Bed ............................194

### How To Build A Small Storage Shed From Pallets ........................................................195
Tools and Materials Needed .....................195
Building the Small Storage Shed..................195

### How To Build A Smokehouse .......................199
Building a Smokehouse ...........................199
Smokehouse Construction .......................200
  Tools Required ......................................200
  Materials................................................200
  Instructions ...........................................201
Operating the Smokehouse ......................204

### How To Build A Solar Dehydrator ......................205
Tools.......................................................205
Materials ................................................205
Building the Dehydrator ...........................207
  Building the Heating Box ......................207
  Building the Storage Box ......................208
  The Last Few Steps ..............................208
Drying Times...........................................209

### How To Build A Solar Oven .........................210
Building Your Own Solar Oven .................210
  Tools ....................................................210
  Materials and Cost................................210
  Process.................................................211
5 Great Foods to Cook in a Solar Oven ........212

### How To Build A Water Heater......................213
How Does this Water Heater Work?................213
The Wood Stove ......................................213
  Tools ....................................................214
  Materials ..............................................214
  Instructions ...........................................214
The Heater ..............................................216
  Tools ....................................................216
  Materials ..............................................216
  Instructions ...........................................217
Using the Water Heater ...........................219

### How To Build An Indoor Greenhouse ................220

| | |
|---|---|
| Determining the Size .........................221 | Bicycle-Powered Washing Machine .............236 |
| Tools Required ...............................221 | Tools ........................................236 |
| Materials ....................................221 | Materials ....................................236 |
| Building the Indoor Greenhouse .........222 | Instructions ................................237 |
| Building the Shelf ..........................222 | How to Use the Bicycle Operated Washing ..239 |

## How To Build An Off-Grid Shower.................225
Tools .........................................225
Materials .....................................225
Building the Shower Head Assembly ............227
Building the Shower ..........................228
   Construction of the Base.....................228
   Building the Frame ..........................228
Using the Off-Grid Shower ....................229
Variations ....................................229

## How To Build An Off-The-Grid Stone Grill Oven ..........................................................230
Planning Oven Size ...........................230
Materials Needed .............................230
Tools Needed .................................231
The Building Process .........................231
   Step 1: Prepare the Mortar..................231
   Step 2: Start Building the Base of the Oven .........................................231
   Step 3: Keep Adding Bricks Over the Base Until We Reach the Fire Base Level ............232
   Step 4: Place the Metal Sheet as the Base for the Fire Spot ...............................232
   Step 5: Cut the Corners of the Bricks and Place Them Over the Metal Sheet ...............232
   Step 6: Add a Few Extra Rows of Bricks Before Placing the Stainless-Steel Grill........232
   Step 7: Cut the Corners of the Bricks and Place the Grill in the Channel ......................233
   Step 8: Adding the Metal Sheet as the Base of the Kitchen Countertop ..........................233
   Step 9: Add Mortar Over the Bricks Covering the Metal Sheet ..........................233
   Step 10: Add a Few More Brick Rows on Sides and Bottom of the Oven.....................234
   Step 11: Clean the Extra Mortar While it Is Still Not Too Dry .............................234

## How To Build An Off-The-Grid Washing Machine..................................................235
The Plunger Washing Machine.......................235
   Tools ........................................235
   Materials ....................................235
   Instructions ................................236
   How to Operate the Plunger Washing Machine .....................................236

## How To Build Your Own Aquaponics System ....240
Quick Setup Aquaponics Tip........................240
Materials and Cost ..............................240
Process .........................................241
   Assembling the PVC System...................241
   Starting Seeds ...............................242
   Adding Fish ..................................243

## How To Hide From Thermal Vision ..................244
Hide Behind Things..............................245
Block Your Body Heat ...........................245
Match Your Background .........................245
Use the Crossover ..............................246
A few Don'ts ....................................246

## How To Make A Mini Root Cellar In Your Backyard ..................................................247
How the Root Cellar Works .....................247
   Materials ....................................247
   Process......................................247
How Long Will Food Keep in the Root Cellar ..........................................................248

## How To Make Bio Fuel At Home From Leaves And Manure ..............................................249
Materials Required .............................249
Tools Needed ..................................249
Making Your Own Bio Fuel .....................249
The Process of Making Gas.....................251

## How To Make Your Own Toilet Paper .............253
Materials Needed ..............................253
Making Your Own Toilet Paper ................253

## PROJECTS ON SEEDS, HERBS, AND NATURAL REMEDIES ...................................256

## DIY Mason Jar Soil Test....................................256
Understanding the Basic Components of Soil..256
The Mason Jar Soil Test........................256

## DIY Survival Garden........................................258
Why You Should Grow a Survival Garden......258
Design Your Survival Garden...................258
Important Crops for Your Survival Garden ....259

## DIY Wall-Hanging Herb Garden .....................260
What to Plant in a Hanging Herb Garden......260
How to Use Herbs from Your Garden...........261
Building the Hanging Herb Garden ..............261
   Tools ........................................261
   Materials ....................................261
   Instructions ................................262
Variations .....................................263

**How To Make Cabbage Bandages To Treat Inflammation And Joint Pain..........................264**
    What You'll Need ..........................264
    How to Make Cabbage Bandages ..................264

**How To Make Moringa Powder......................266**
    Step-by-Step Guide on How to Make Moringa Powder..........................266

**How To Make Your Own SHTF Medicinal Garden..........................269**
    How Much Space Do You Need? ..................269
    Materials Required ..........................269
    Plants Required..........................270
      1. Medicinal Plants to Have at Hand for Your Circulatory System ..................270
      2. Medicinal Plants to Have at Hand for Your Digestive System ..................271
      3. Medicinal Plants to Have at Hand for Your Endocrine System..................272
      4. Medicinal Plants to Have at Hand for Your Integumentary System..................273
      5. Medicinal Plants to Have at Hand for Your Immune System ..................274
      6. Medicinal Plants to Have at Hand for Your Muscular System ..................275
      7. Medicinal Plants to Have at Hand for Your Nervous System ..................276
      8. Medicinal Plants to Have at Hand for Your Renal System..................277
      9. Medicinal Plants to Have at Hand for Your Reproductive System ..................278
      10. Medicinal Plants to Have at Hand for Your Respiratory System ..................278
      11. Medicinal Plants to Have at Hand for Your Skeletal System ..................279
      12. Medicinal Plants to Have at Hand for Infections ..................280
      13. Medicinal Plants to Have at Hand for Pain Management ..................281
    Estimated Cost ..........................282
    How Much Work to Put Into it ..................284
    How to Tend Your Garden in Winter and How to Use Plants in Winter ..................284

**How To Stockpile Seeds..........................285**
    Why You Should Stockpile Seeds Now ..........................285
    The Best Way to Stockpile Your Seeds ..........................286
    Seed Shelf Life ..........................286
    The Best Seeds to Stockpile ..........................287

**Natural Remedies To Make At Home Using Local Plants..........................288**
    1. Natural Remedies to Fight Viruses ..........................288
      Japanese Honeysuckle, *Lonicera japonica* 288
      Elderberry, *Sambucus nigra* or *Sambucus canadensis* ..................288
    2. Natural Remedies to Treat Wounds ..........289
      Yarrow, *Achillea millefolium* ..................289
      Witch Hazel, *Hamamelis vernalis* ..........289
    3. Natural Remedies to Treat Allergies ..........289
      Purple Deadnettle, *Lamium purpureum* ...289
      Stinging Nettle, *Urtica dioica* ..................290
    4. Natural Remedies to Treat Sore Throat ......290
      Echinacea, *Echinacea* spp. ..................290
      Bee Balm, *Monarda fistulosa* ..................290
    5. Natural Remedies to Treat Ear Infections ..291
      Mullein, *Verbascum Thapsus* ..................291
      Oregano, *Origanum vulgare* ..................291
    6. Natural Remedies to Treat Bronchitis and Respiratory Ailments..........................291
      Mullein, *Verbascum Thapsus* ..................291
      Pleurisy Root, *Asclepias tuberosa* ..........292
    7. Natural Remedies to Treat Urinary Tract Infections ..........................292
      Oregano, *Origanum vulgare* ..................292
      Aloe Vera ..........................292
    8. Natural Remedies to Treat Gastrointestinal Issues..........................292
      Mints, *Mentha* spp. ..........................292
      Agrimony, *Agrimonia eupatoria* ..................293
    9. Natural Remedies to Treat Pain..................293
      Willow, *Salix* spp. ..........................293
      Poplar, *Populus* spp. ..........................293
    10. Natural Remedies to Treat Circulation/Heart Ailments..........................294
      Motherwort, *Leonurus cardiaca* ..................294
      Hawthorn, *Crataegus laevigata* and *Crataegus pruinose* ..........................294
    11. Natural Remedies to Treat Liver Issues ....294
      Dandelion, *Taraxacum officinale* ..........294
      Yellow Dock, *Rumex crispus* ..................295
    12. Natural Remedies to Treat Kidney Issues..........................295
      Cleavers, *Galium aparine* ..................295
      Goldenrod, *Solidago* spp. ..................295
    13. Natural Remedies to Treat Insomnia, Depression, and Anxiety..........................296
      St. John's Wort, *Hypericum perforatum* ..296
      Skullcap, *Scutellaria lateriflora* ..............296

**The Only 7 Seeds You Need To Stockpile For A Crisis..........................297**
    A Staple Since the Dawn of Times ..................297
    A Nutrition-Packed Root Vegetable ..................298
    The Two Great Grains..........................298
    The Grandiose Greens ..........................299

PROJECTS RELATED TO WATER

# DIY Sink To Save Water

MATERIAL COST  $ 99.00     EASY  DIFFICULTY     30 MINUTES

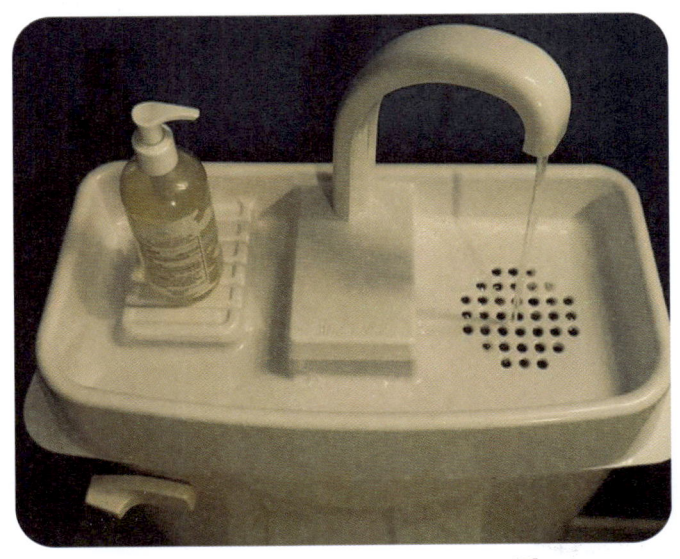

www.amazon.com/Twice-gloss-expander-larger-measured/dp/B08DJC9WN1/ref

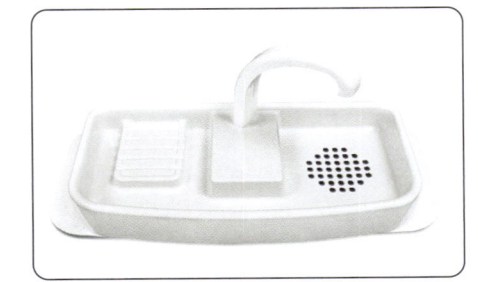

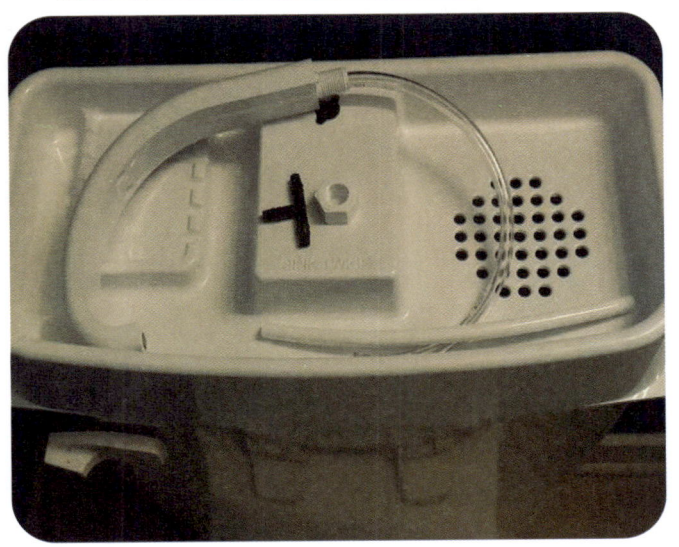

Your off grid water supply is precious. The amount of water you have on hand depends on what kind of water catchment system you have and the type of area you live in. No matter how much water you store conservation of water is always important.

Off grid water might come from the rain, a creek, or even a well. If you are using toilets that flush rather then composting toilets, then you need water to flush them. Modern toilets use around 2 gallons of water every time you flush, while older toilets can use as much as 7 gallons per flush!

This simple DIY project will allow you to turn your toilet into a sink on every flush. By running the water to fill your toilet both into the bowl and up through this simple faucet, you will be able to wash your hands with the same water you use to fill your toilet bowl.

There will be no water lost handwashing after using the bathroom. Every drop of water used will pour over your hands and right backdown into the reservoir that will flush your toilet the next time. Even better, the soap you use will also be rinsed off into that reservoir and when you flush your toilet next the bowl will be flushed with soapy water. This helps keep your toilet clean, too!

## Materials Needed

In order to put together this project, you will need:
- Sink Twice Sink Fixture $99.00
- Included Tubes and Faucet Attachment
- Extender for Better Fit

## The Building Process

1. Measure your toilet before ordering your Sink Twice fixture. There are a couple of different models depending on the size of your toilet. This is an important step because you could waste a lot of money if you buy the wrong size and it doesn't fit.
2. Once you have received your Sink Twice, you are going to remove the porcelain top from your toilet and check the fit.
3. If you bought the extenders or bought a unit that includes them, you will be able to install those now too. That is an easy process of just slipping both sides inside the unit.
4. Now that you know the unit fits properly, you can begin the work to reroute the water that fills your toilet after every flush to run up through the Sink Twice, too.
5. Start by assembling the faucet by feeding the faucet tube through the hole in the sink basin.

6. Slide the included hex nut over the faucet tube on the underside of the sink and screw it, tightly, into the facet tube.
7. At this point we are going to move into the toilet tank and find our refill tube, refill valve, and overflow tube.
8. We are going to take our fill cycle diverter or this black T shaped part and insert a clear flow modifier. This will divert the water to your sink faucet. The flow modifier should be in the downward position and the short end of the fill cycle diverter should be pointed towards your refill tube.
9. Attach the refill tube to the short end of the diverter and then attach the sink faucet to the tube to the diverter end that is pointing up. You may need to trim the faucet tube. It should be straight. Any crimping will affect water pressure to the sink.
10. Be sure the fill cycle diverter is pointing its lower prong into the overflow tube. You could even attach a small length of tube to this part of the diverter and feed it into the overflow tube for stability of the entire setup.
11. Check all your connections and then place the sink basin over the toilet tank.
12. Check that the unit is levelled. This is required for the water to properly drain back into the tank.
13. This is where the expanders can come in handy. In some models of the Sink Twice these are not included, but I did find one where they were included.
14. At this point you should be ready to give the toilet a flush and test out the whole system.
15. It is recommended that you use sea mineral soap or unscented foam soap as other may have an affect on the toilet bowl over time.
16. Your DIY water saving sink is now installed and you should give it a try.

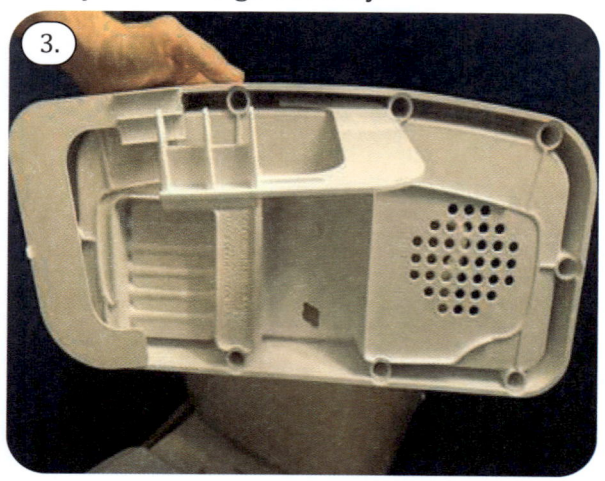

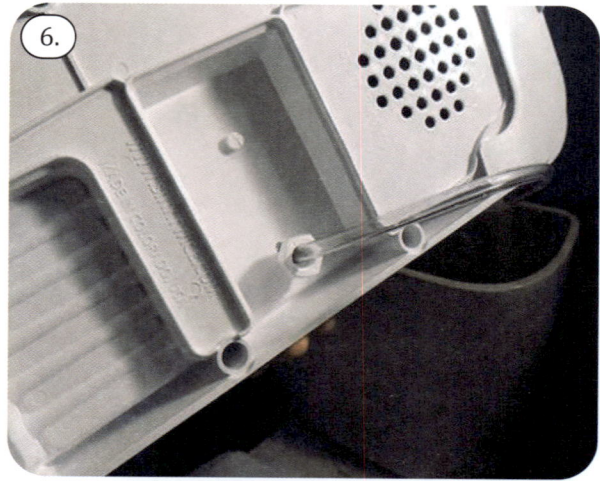

9.

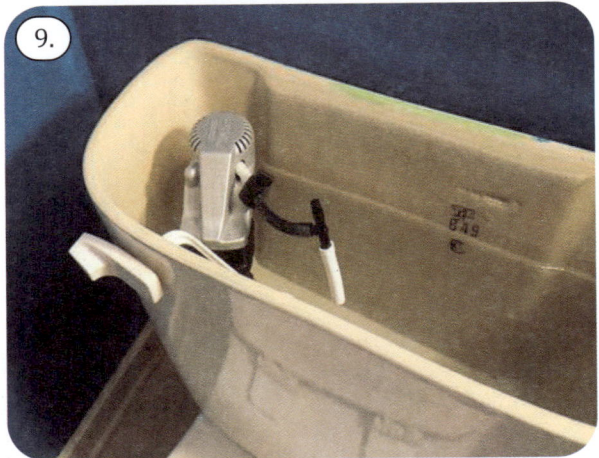

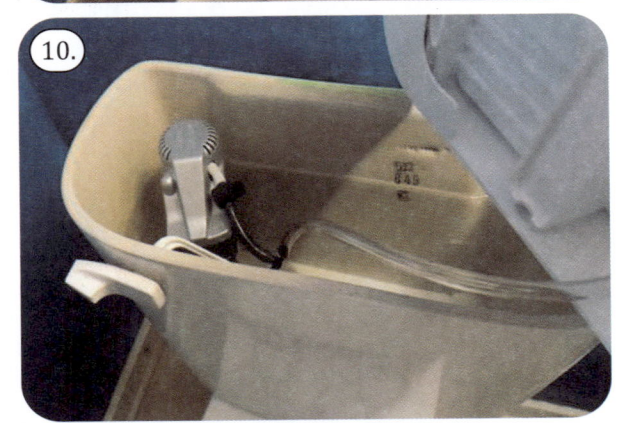

9.

10.

11.

14.

The more effectively you can manage your water resources the better life you will have off grid. This build is incredibly easy and practical, too. While the design might seem strange or awkward at first, it won't be long before you use this faucet as your defacto handwashing after using the bathroom.

The water you will save just from handwashing will make a massive difference over time. Not to mention the benefits to the planet of not wasting water.

PROJECTS RELATED TO WATER

# How To Build A Rainwater Catchment System

**MATERIAL COST** $ 411.56    **COMPLEX DIFFICULTY**    **3 HOURS**

Fresh water falls from the heavens every so often, but normally this water flows through our gutters and into the ground. In an off-grid or grid-down scenario, we can not afford to let this resource slip away; we can and should harvest this rainwater to help us. Harvesting rainwater from our roof is as simple as catching it in barrels, but there is a way that we can use the space by our downspouts more efficiently.

## What to Use for Rain Barrels

The best option for a rain barrel is a 55-gallon drum. While you can use steel drums, plastic drums are easier to handle and often easier to obtain. The drums designed for industrial use will be far stronger and made of higher quality plastic than the barrels often sold as rain barrels in big box stores. While you can purchase new drums, you may find some used plastic drums at a lower price, but you should try to lonely buy used food-grade drums.

## Placement of the Rainwater Catchment System

Unless you want to drill holes into your gutters, you'll be placing your rainwater catchment system in very close proximity to an existing downspout. Try to put the system at a point that collects the most water from your roof.

Ultimately, you will have to determine the best way to attach this system's plumbing to the downspout or the connection in the gutter itself.

## Building the Frame

When full, this frame is going to support almost 1500 pounds of water. Do not cheap out on materials for a build like this purchase the best wood and fasteners that you can. Also, take your time and make sure that all the joints are solid and the frame is square and level.

## Tools

- Drill and drill bits and drivers
- Level
- Square
- Saw

## Materials

- Three 55 Gallon Plastic Drums can be found at Home Depot for $90.00USD each.
www.homedepot.com/p/55-Gal-Blue-Industrial-Plastic-Drum-PTH0933/205845768

- Thirteen 2x4x8' boards are found at Home Depot for $6.55USD each.
www.homedepot.com/p/2-in-x-4-in-x-96-in-Prime-Whitewood-Stud-058449/312528776

- Three 1x4x8' boards which are $6.43USD at Home Depot.
www.homedepot.com/p/1-in-x-4-in-x-8-ft-Premium-Kiln-Dried-Square-Edge-Whitewood-Common-Board-914681/100023465

- #8 - 2 ½" Screws, which are $5.97USD a pound at Home Depot.
www.homedepot.com/p/Grip-Rite-8-2-1-2-in-Phillips-Bugle-Head-Coarse-Thread-Gold-Screws-1-lb-Pack-212GS1/100128995

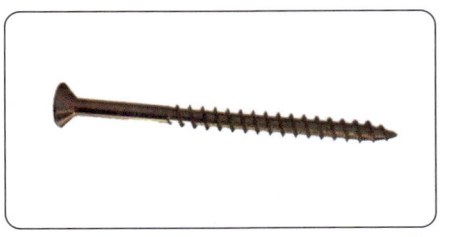

- #8 – 1 ½" Screws, which are $7.98USD for a pack of 100 at Home Depot.
www.homedepot.com/p/Everbilt-8-x-1-1-2-in-Zinc-Plated-Phillips-Flat-Head-Wood-Screw-100-Pack-801842/204275487

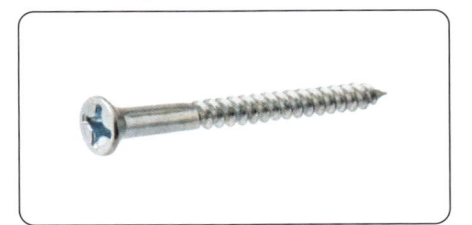

### Lumber Cut List
**2 x 4 x 8' Lumber**
- 4 pieces @ 84 inches.
- 12 pieces @ 32 inches.
- 6 pieces @ 29 inches.
- 24 pieces @ 10 inches (45-degree angle on one end).

**1 x 4 x 8' Lumber**
- 6 pieces @ 35 inches.

## Instructions

1. Cut all of your material as per the above cut list. If you need to modify the design to fit your space, sketch it out before cutting to determine your true dimensions.
2. Layout and screw together the frame for the shelf on which the barrels will rest.
3. Attach two inside braces about 13 inches in from the outside edges.
4. Build the other two shelves on top of this one to make things easier.
5. Take one of the shelves and place a barrel on top of it, centring it. Place two of the angled 2x4s with offcuts of 1x4s up against the barrel as shown above.
6. Determine how far the 2x4s should be off the centre line of the shelf. This is the dimension that you will use to place all eight 2x4's on each shelf.
7. You will need to drill some holes to accommodate the screws about halfway through the boards.
8. Secure these 2x4's to the shelf, placing them at the dimension you determined in step 6.
9. Secure the 1x4s, drilling pilot holes to avoid splitting. Align the 1x4s as shown above and secure with 1 ½" screws to each angled 2x4.
10. Confirm that the barrel sits appropriately in the cradle.
11. Repeat for the next two shelves.
12. Take the bottom shelf to the location where it will be installed.
13. Prop the shelf up to the height that you want and level it.
14. Stack the remaining shelves on top.
15. Attach the 84" legs to the bottom shelf.
16. Lay the rack on its side to make spacing and securing the remaining shelves to the legs easier. In this case, I used an inside spacing of 24 ½".
17. Stand the rack up and slide in the drums.

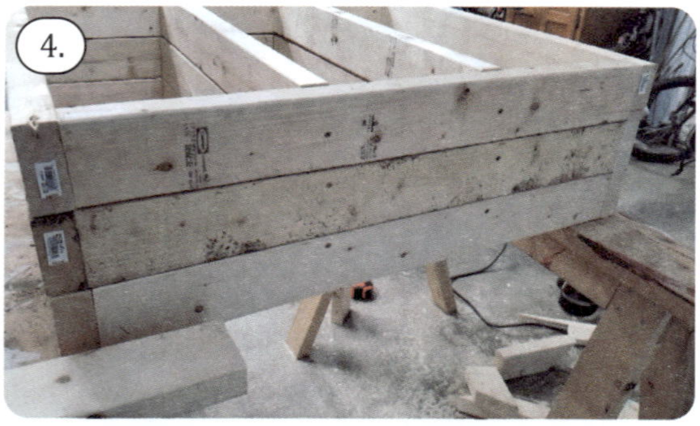
4.

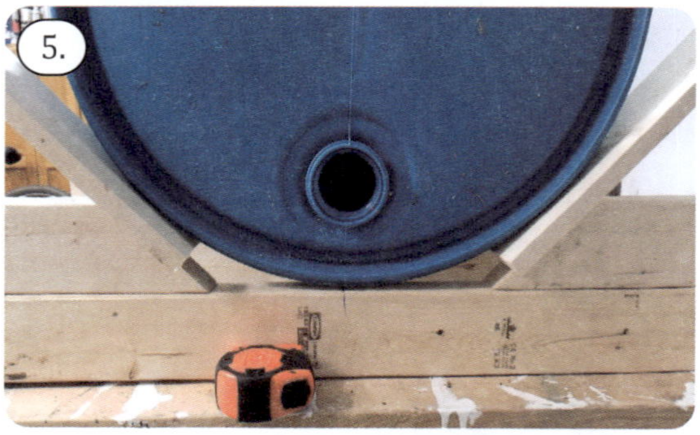
5.

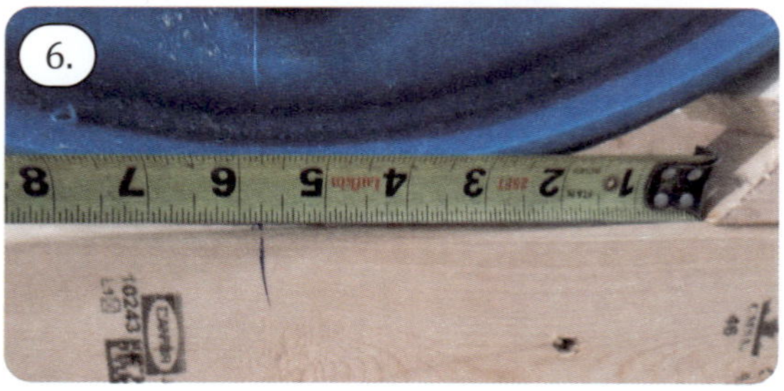
6.

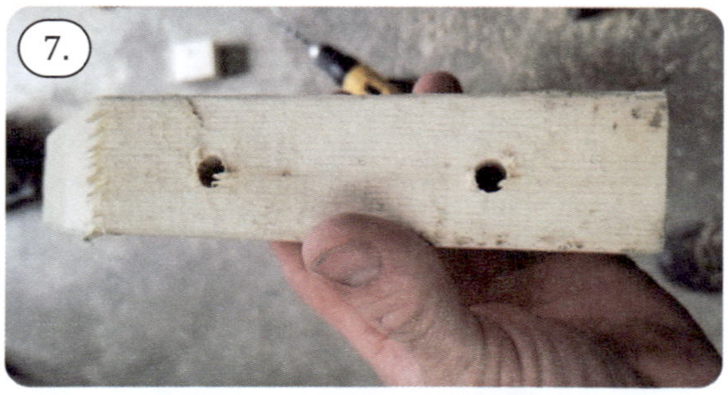
7.

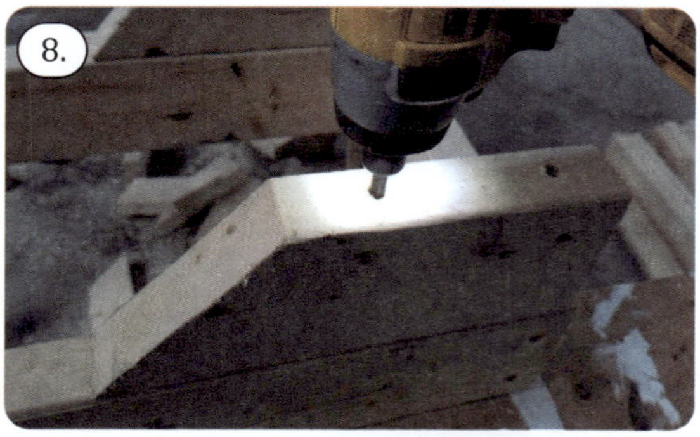
8.

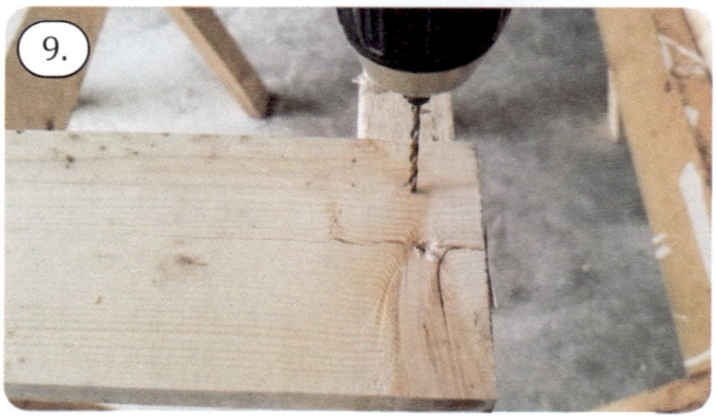
9.

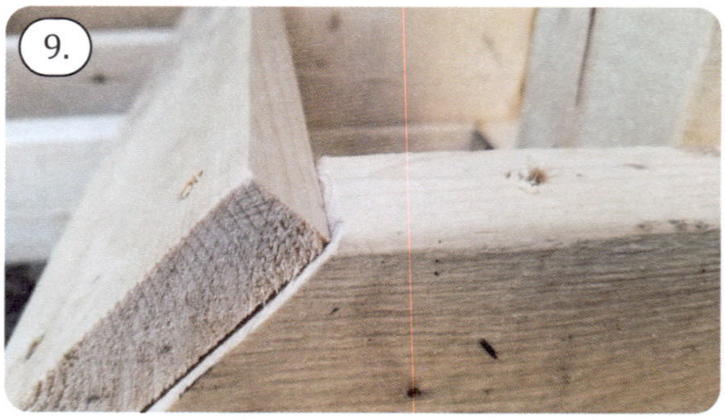
9.

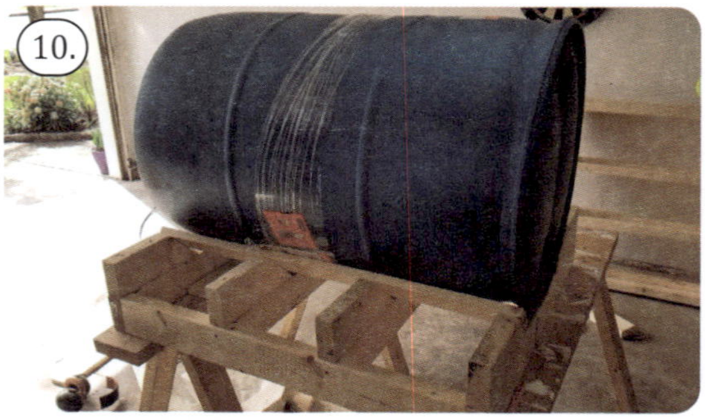
10.

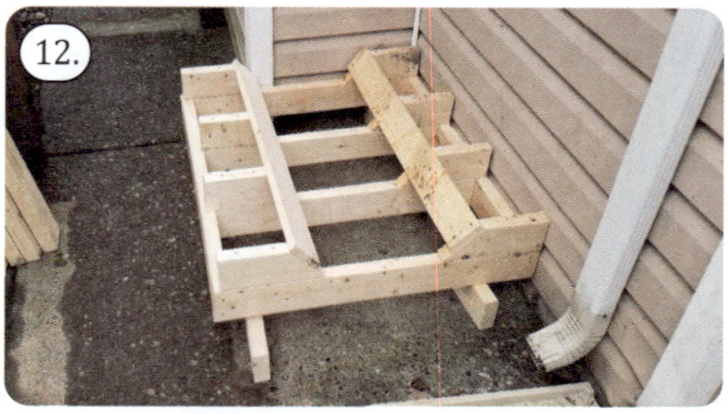
12.

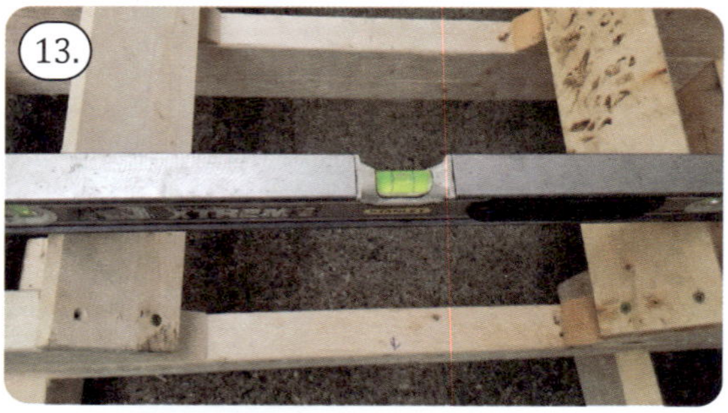
13.

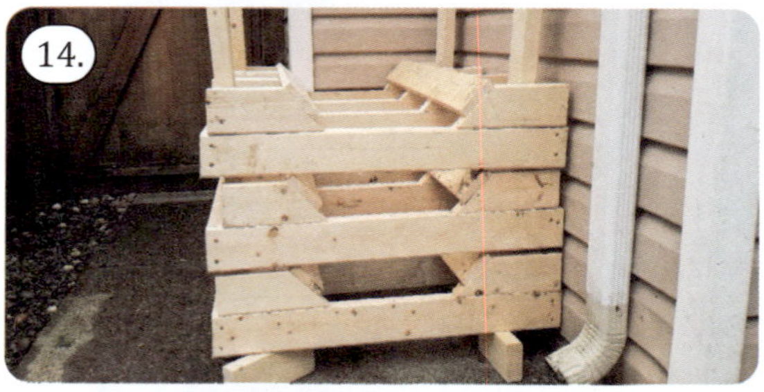
14.

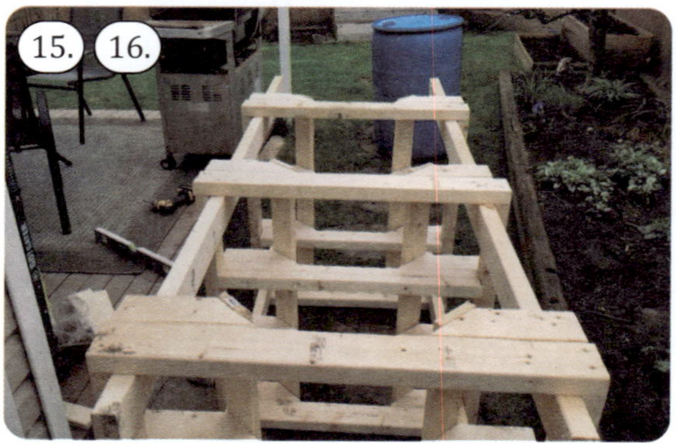
15. 16.

## Plumbing the Barrels

With the rack built and the barrels installed, it is time to plumb the system. There are a few different ways that you can go about moving water between the barrels. In this case, I used the ¾" NPT threaded knockouts in the barrel bung caps. If you can find larger fittings feel free to do so.

## Tools

- Bung Wrench
- Saw
- Wrenches

## Materials

- Two feet of 1" Sch 40 PVC pipe which is $2.34USD at Home Depot.
www.homedepot.com/p/VPC-1-in-x-24-in-PVC-Sch-40-Pipe-2201/202300506

- Ten feet of ¾" Sch 40 PVC pipe which is $3.56USD at Home Depot.
www.homedepot.com/p/Charlotte-Pipe-3-4-in-x-10-ft-PVC-Schedule-40-Plain-End-DWV-Pipe-PVC-04007-0600/100348472

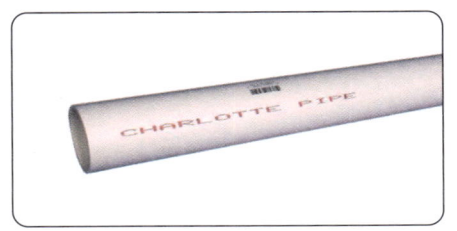

- One threaded hose bib, which Home Depot sells for $7.73USD.
www.homedepot.com/p/Everbilt-3-4-in-Heavy-Duty-Brass-MIP-x-MHT-Hose-Bibb-VHBCON-F4EB/312029306

- Five ¾" NPT to ¾" PVC Slip-on adapters can be found at Home Depot for $0.52USD each.
www.homedepot.com/p/DURA-3-in-x-4-in-Schedule-40-PVC-Reducing-Male-Adapter-MPTxS-436-341/203225030

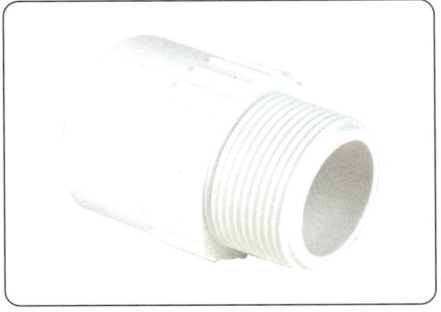

- Six ¾" PVC 90 degree elbows are sold at Home Depot for $0.52USD each.
www.homedepot.com/p/Charlotte-Pipe-3-4-in-PVC-Schedule-40-90-S-x-S-Elbow-Fitting-PVC023000800HD/203812123

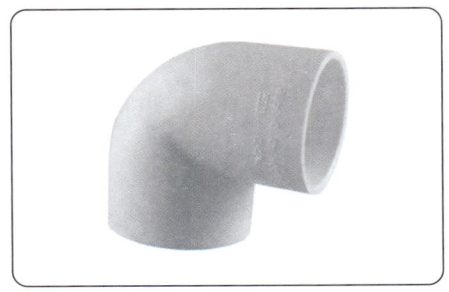

- One ¾" PVC slip-on tee can be found at Home Depot for $0.89USD each.
www.homedepot.com/p/Charlotte-Pipe-3-4-in-Schedule-40-S-x-S-x-S-Tee-PVC024000800HD/203812197

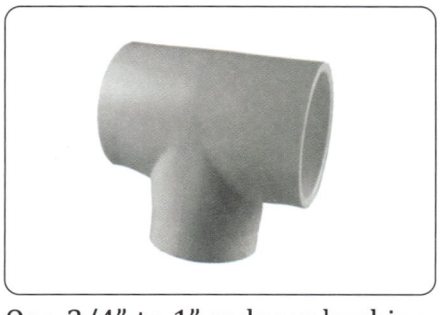

- One 3/4" to 1" reducer bushing, which Home Depot sells for $0.89USD.
www.homedepot.com/p/Charlotte-Pipe-1-in-x-3-4-in-PVC-Sch-40-SPG-x-S-Reducer-Bushing-PVC021070800HD/203811449

- Two 1" PVC 45-degree slip-on elbows are sold at Home Depot for $1.02USD each.
www.homedepot.com/p/DURA-1-in-Schedule-40-PVC-45-Degree-Elbow-C417-010/100345015

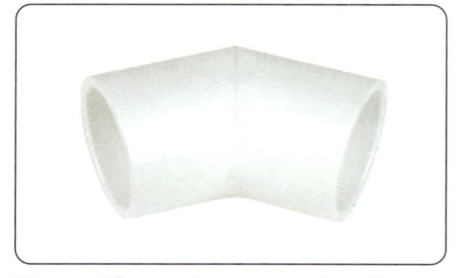

- You will need some miscellaneous fittings to adapt your downspout to the intake of the rain barrel system.

## Instructions

1. Cut out the knockouts on each of the bung caps.
2. Install the bung caps into the drums.
3. To the bottom bung cap threaded hole attach the spigot.
4. To the rest of the bung caps, attach the ¾" PVC adapters and a 2-inch section of ¾" PVC pipe.
5. Install the 90-degree elbows and measure to determine the cut size for the ¾" pipe that will join the drums together.
6. Cut and install the pipes between the bottom and middle drum and the center and the top drum.
7. From the top bung cap, run a small length of PVC up above the drum's top and connect the tee joint.
8. Run another short line off this tee joint perpendicular and connect a 90-degree elbow.
9. Run a line from this elbow down to the ground. This is your overflow line.
10. You will have to run pipes to either the downspouts or the gutter from the tee's open end. In my case, I used a 1" to ¾" reducer to widen the line to 1" PVC, then using lengths of 1" PVC pipe and two 45 degree elbows, I was able to make a run of pipe from the gutter to the drum.
11. I then used a 1 ½" to 1" reducer to widen this pipe system's inlet. You may have to use a different set of fittings to achieve the goal of moving water from your gutters to the rainwater catchment system.

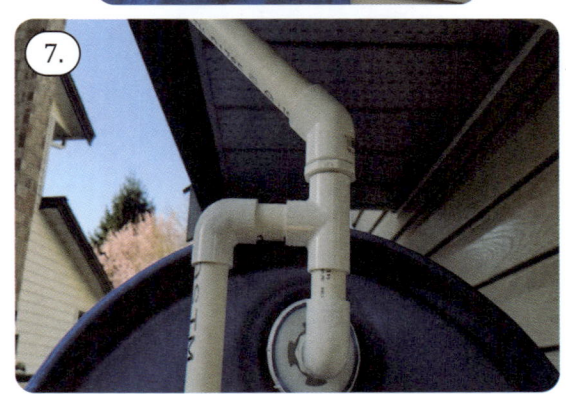

## Variations

You may want to consider a few variations when designing your own three-barrel rain catchment system.

- If you can locate elbows with a hose barb instead of a slip-on fitting, you can use a clear plastic hose instead of PVC pipe, which will act as a sight glass and give you a visual of the water level in the drums.
- Instead of joining the drums with a PVC pipe section, you can have a continuous run of pipe from the lowest bung cap to the highest bung cap. Each of the bung caps connects to this run of pipe through PVC tees. Since all the drums and bung caps connect to one pipe run, the drums will vent air easier. This variation is good if you have a significant volume of water that runs through your gutters and downspouts.
- You should consider installing some mesh on the inlet to the rainwater catchment system to prevent dirt and debris from entering your barrels. The downside of this is that this mesh will become clogged and need to be checked and cleaned regularly.
- Rainwater has various uses around the garden and the house, both in a grid-down situation and in daily life. Three 55-Gallon drums stacked atop each other will give you access to 165 gallons of freshwater that you can use in your garden and around the home instead of using your drinking water stores. In a dire emergency, this water could be used as drinking water as long as it is filtered appropriately.

PROJECTS RELATED TO WATER

# How To Build A Water Tank For Long Term Storage

EASY DIFFICULTY

Water is the most critical element to survival besides air and shelter, so it must be one of our chief concerns when prepping for any emergency or disaster. The average human will not survive longer than three days without access to this precious resource, but our water requirement comes at a high price in terms of space and weight to store it.

## How Much Water?

The average adult human needs about 1 gallon of water per day, and this is what we base our estimates on. Fortunately, the measurement of most water storage containers is Gallons so figuring out how many days a given container will supply us is very straightforward.

Start by forming a realistic view of how long you will need to live off your stored water. In my case, the most realistic scenario is a massive earthquake which would knock out services for at least a couple of weeks. My family has four people, so that would be four gallons of water per day. Right? Wrong. We can not forget about our pets, and my crazy chocolate lab also needs water to survive. To make matters easy, account for your pet's water needs the same as your own. In my case, I need to have five gallons of water on hand each day.

Five Gallons multiplied by 14 days equals 70 Gallons of clean and potable water. With each gallon weighing around 8.34 pounds, this means that two weeks of water for a family of four and a dog will equal about 584 pounds.

That is a lot of water that we need to find containers to hold it.

## Container Options

There are a lot of options for vessels to store your emergency drinking water. Regardless of the type of container, the procedures for cleaning, sanitizing and storing remain very similar.

## Food Grade 55 Gallon Plastic Drums

The best bang for your buck is a food-grade 55-gallon drum filled with water. You can store eleven days' worth of water for a family of five in a relatively small footprint. While these drums are great for water storage, they suffer from a couple of issues. If the drum ruptures or the water inside becomes contaminated, the result is a massive loss of clean drinking water. Also, a full 55-gallon drum of water is nearly 500 pounds, making it nearly impossible to transport effectively.

◆ You can purchase one at Amazon for $ 103.50 USD
www.amazon.com/Gallon-Plastic-Barrel-New-Factory-Fresh/dp/B07B6B2JP7/ref=mp_s_a_1_3?dchild=1&keywords=55+gallon+drum&qid=1616678249&sprefix=55+g&sr=8-3

## Jerry Cans

Water jerry cans come in various capacities, with the five-gallon size being common and a size that is not too heavy when full of water. Storing water in jerry cans is much the same as in the 55-gallon drum, but the size and shape of these cans mean that you can not keep the same water volume in the footprint of a 55-gallon drum. Jerry cans have the distinct advantage of being portable, and if you needed to bug out, they are much easier to take with you.

◆ Five-gallon jerry cans are available at Amazon for as low as $24.99USD I own a few of these, and I like that they are easy to manage and can be thrown into the back of the truck easily.
www.amazon.com/Scepter-04933-Water-Can-5-Gallon/dp/B000MTI0GA/ref=mp_s_a_1_3?dchild=1&keywords=5+gallon+water+jerry+can&qid=1616678393&sprefix=5+gallon+water+je&sr=8-3

◆ A 7 gallon Jerry can with a spigot is found on Amazon for $14.97USD. This one is nice because it is square and will not tip over. It can be laid over on its side, giving good access to the spigot.
www.amazon.com/Reliance-Products-Aqua-Tainer-Gallon-Container/dp/B001QC31G6/ref=mp_s_a_1_17?dchild=1&keywords=5+gallon+water+can+with+spout&qid=1616678715&sr=8-17

## Soda Bottles

Soda or any other beverage bottle is not the ideal container to use, but if you are on a budget or have a surplus of them around, they can be an acceptable option. Soda bottles are good for people that are short on space, such as condo and apartment dwellers. Cleaning these bottles is difficult, and the water stored inside of them should be rotated regularly.

## Disposable Water Bottles

You can get a flat of water at your local Costco for around six dollars, so it would seem like a good idea to have water stores of individual 500ml bottles of water. The problem with flats of disposable water bottles is that they were never designed to store water long term, and while the water inside of them will never expire, the plastic will break down over time.

That being said, rotating a flat or two along with your water stores is a good idea for use as barter items or to give to needy neighbours.

## Designing a Water Storage System

It is important not to put all our eggs in one basket when it comes to long-term water storage. While 55-Gallon drums are an effective and efficient means of water storage, you need to have several different types and sizes of containers and store them in multiple locations.

Suppose you are going to base your water storage around 55-Gallon drums. In that case, it is imperative that you also have an assortment of smaller containers to allow for easier water movement from the drums to the locations inside your home that you require water. Using five-gallon jerry cans as your primary day-to-day water source and then refilling them from the 55 Gallon drums allows for easier access to water throughout the home. It also gives you the ability to take water with you during a bugout.

Think about how you will be accessing the water stores. If you store water in an outbuilding, you need to be very mindful of what scenarios might cut off your access to that water. In these situations, you'll need to take extra care to maintain a water supply where it is necessary to minimize the need for resupply.

## Preparing Containers for Long Term Water Storage

When it comes to 55-Gallon plastic drums, you will need to purchase a few items along with them to clean, sanitize and fill effectively.

- Bung wrenchs are on Amazon for $16.98, and you will need this to remove and tighten the bung caps on a 55-Gallon drum.

www.amazon.com/Duda-Energy-dwrench-Aluminum-Standard/dp/B00950CICE/

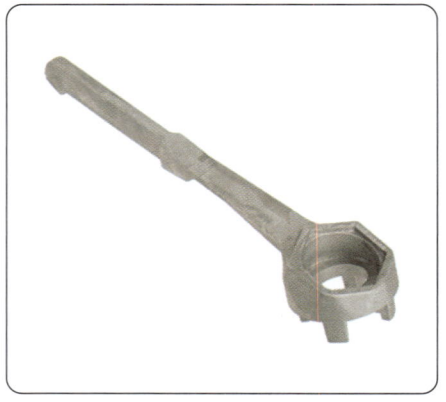

- Regular unscented bleach with between 5.25% and 8.25% Chlorine you can find at your local grocery or big box store.
- Any dish soap will do for cleaning a new container.
- Food safe tubing is found on Amazon for $ 19.85 USD for 50 feet of tube.

www.amazon.com/50-ID-OD-Vinyl-Tubing/dp/B01LY3LSPE/

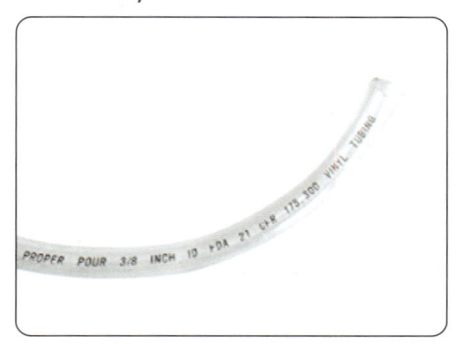

- Baking soda and vinegar are also available at your local grocery or big box store.

Even if you purchased brand new drums or jerry cans, you would still need to clean them inside and out. In the case of new containers, simply filling the container about a quarter of the way full with warm water and adding a generous squirt of dish soap is going to be more than adequate to clean it.

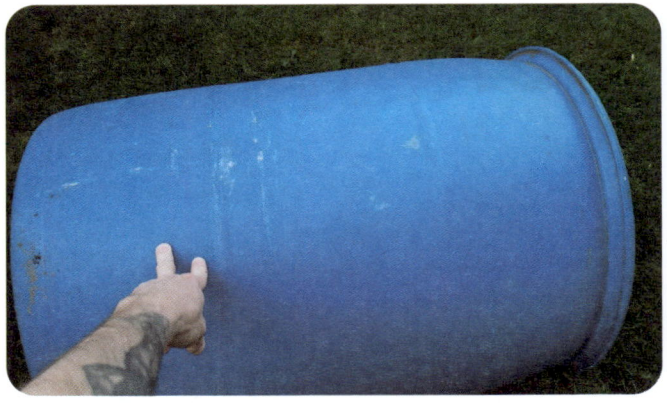

Seal up the container and roll it around, allowing the soapy water to cover the entire interior of the drum or jerry can.

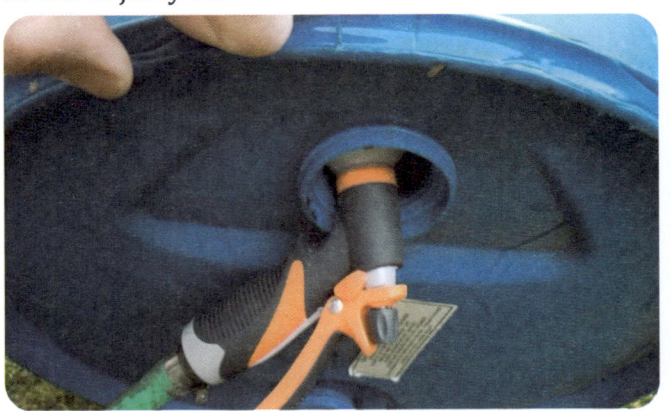

You will then need to rinse it out with clean water repeatedly until all the water you dump out of it runs clear and free of any soap or bubbles. This process will take a lot of time, do not rush it. Since we have not sanitized the container yet, it is ok to use a garden hose to rinse out the soap.

If there have been other substances stored inside the drum and dish soap is not doing a good enough job of cleaning the inside or there is an unpleasant ordor, you may need to use another cleaning method. Pour half a gallon of vinegar and a box of baking soda into a 55-gallon drum filled a quarter of the way with clean water. Allow this solution to work over every surface, rolling the drum around slowly, tipping upside down and letting it sit in various positions for long periods. You may want to let the solution work overnight.

Then rinse thoroughly and check for cleanliness. If this method does not work, the drum is probably not worth your effort, and you should consider using it as a rain barrel instead.

## Sanitizing Containers

Once you have cleaned the container, you need to sanitize it before filling it. In the case of a 55-Gallon drum, add ¼ of a cup of unscented fresh bleach to the drum and then fill about a quarter of the way full of fresh, clean water.

Roll the drum around slowly, allowing the bleach to cover every surface of the container. This is a process that you need to take your time doing; it is better to be sure the entire inside is sanitary than sorry that eleven days' worth of water is spoiled.

After sanitizing, dump the bleach water out as best that you can. It is virtually impossible to remove every drop of water, but it is not a big deal if a little bleach water is left over.

Your drum is now ready for placement and filling.

## Vertical Placement of 55-gallon Drums

The easiest way to store these drums is vertically, but this poses one significant issue. To get the water out of the drum, you will need to either siphon or pump the water out. When storing water vertically, consider the possibility that your pump will break and that you'll be forced to siphon.

No matter what, no water container should sit on the ground. There should always be a separation between the ground and the bottom of the container.

## Horizontal Placement of 55-gallon Drums

To lay a drum horizontally, you allow for easier access to the water if you install a spigot. Since 55-Gallon drums have two ports and two bung caps, you can orient the drum so that one is at the bottom and the other is at the top. However, you also lose some water storage capacity since the fill port at the top will leave some headroom filled with air instead of water.

The best way to fill the drum is to install a fitting into the top bung cap with a short section of PVC pipe to fill the drum until it is as full as it will allow. Orienting the drums horizontally means that you need to build a stand for the drum that will elevate the drum high enough so that it can be used to fill any container that you need to fill and be strong enough to support 500 pounds of weight.

## Filling a 55-gallon Drum

Once you have placed the drum in the location that you will store it, you'll have to fill them with clean water. Under no circumstances should you use a garden hose to fill any water container. Always use food-grade tubing to fill a container that will hold drinking water. If you do not have access to food-grade tubing or it is not practical, use your five-gallon jerry cans to ferry water to the 55-gallon drums.

To treat the water, you can use the same bleach that you used to sanitize the drum. If your local water supply is chlorinated, you do not need to treat your water. However, if you are unsure as to the condition of the city water, simply follow these guidelines:

- ¼ tsp. bleach per gallon for cloudy water.
- ⅛ tsp. bleach per gallon for water that is clear.

Once your drum, jerry cans, or bottles are filled, and treated seal them up and keep them away from extreme temperatures or sunlight.

## Using Your Water Stores

When the time comes to use your water stores, it is a good idea to run the water through a filter in case something went wrong during the sanitization process leading to microorganisms running amuck through your water supply.

Even though water has no expiration date, you should habitually drain sanitizing and refill your water storage containers every six months. I use the interval for changing batteries in my smoke detectors for changing out my water. Every January and June, I empty, sanitize and refill all of my water stores which is a big job but will pay off when I need it.

Water storage is the least exciting prep but also is the most critical. With a little planning, a few containers, drums, and minimal supplies, you can secure your family's water needs through whatever disasters are on the horizon.

# How To Build Your Own Water Filter

**MATERIAL COST** $ 50.00    **EASY** DIFFICULTY    **3 HOURS**

If the American water system were ever crippled, we would see panic that would make 2020 flinch. Our tap water resources are taken for granted and most of us simply cannot imagine life without a limitless supply of clean water to waste, bath, and drink. What would you do if the tap water was contaminated or stopped flowing?

Rain barrels and rain catchment systems are great, but you still want to filter much of the water that you catch and store in outside containers. However, straw filters or even a hand pump style filter could make this an arduous task.

Instead, you should make your own large scale water filter that can be used to filter 5 gallons of water at a time! These are simple to make and dirt cheap! For under $50 you can be filtering water from local creeks and rain barrels, in the event of a disaster.

**WARNING:** Be sure to boil any water that you have filtered, using any kind of filter, just as a precaution.

### TOOLS
- Razor Knife
- Silicone or Epoxy
- Drill
- Drill Bit

### MATERIALS NEEDED
- 5 Gallon Buckets
- Shemagh
- Lids
- Screen
- Sand
- Gravel
- Charcoal
- ¾ CPVC Valve
- ¾ inch CPVC Pipe

## Step 1: Affixing the Valve

Starting with one of your buckets, you are going to cut a hole that is just big enough to fit your pipe and feed it through.

Drill some holes in your pipe so the water can get to the valve.

Use your pipe cement to affix the valve to the pipe. I also sealed around the opening of the valve and bucket on both sides.

This takes about 2 hours to cure completely.

## Step 2: Prepping Buckets

One bucket is outfitted with a valve now. The next two must be outfitted with holes and screen to filter. Flip a bucket upside down and using your drill begin to drill holes into the bottom of the bucket. Drill about 10 holes in the bottom of the bucket, starting in the center and spreading out from the center. This will be the way that water makes its way from one tier of buckets to the next.

Next, cut a piece of screen that is large enough to fit the bottom of the bucket. If you need two squares that overlap, that is fine, too! You do not need to adhere these pieces of screen in any way. The weight of the ingredients in each bucket will hold the screen down in place. Prep the next bucket in just this way!

## Step 3: Adding Filtering Materials

I am not sure where you are getting your gravel and sand. We will source ours from a local creek. Here we will fill our sand and gravel bucket to assure that we have plenty of tight spaces to filter the water through.

We will start by taking a few scoops of sand and gently placing them into the bottom of the bucket. These first few scoops are important because they will keep the mesh screens in place, and we want them secure to begin. From there we are going to fill this bucket up ½ way with sand.

Once you have plenty of sand in this bucket, we are going to add gravel. Now, if you are sourcing from a creek you can simply go do the water's edge of a sandy bank and you will find plenty gravel there. Or you can buy both the sand and gravel from a hardware store.

Mark this bucket SAND/GRAVEL.

Fill another quarter of the way with gravel. This bucket is going to be very heavy! If it is too heavy for you to carry, simply separate the gravel and sand up into another bucket.

## Step 4: The Charcoal

Charcoal is highly absorbent. Activated charcoal is even more absorbent, so you should use a combination in this build to get the most out of the charcoal bucket.

Start by covering your mesh screen with a folded shemagh. This will be another layer of filtering for the finer bits of charcoal.

I find it best to add a little water to this first layer, so you don't lose the majority of it over through your mesh and holes in the bottom of the bucket. Then add some activated charcoal and you should be ready with your charcoal layer.

Mark this bucket CHARCOAL.

## Step 5: Assembly

Start with your valve bucket at the bottom. This is going to be the final place the water will pool after being filtered.

Next slide your charcoal bucket down inside of the valve bucket.

Do the same think with the heavy sand and gravel bucket/buckets. You can keep a lid on top of this whole contraption until you are ready to filter water.

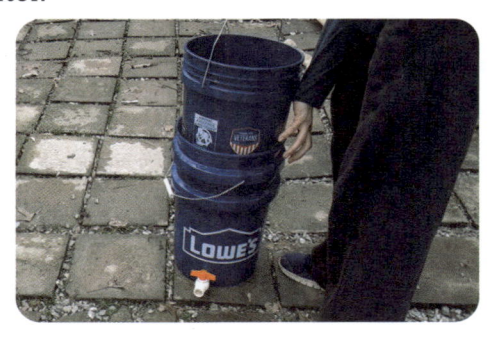

## Step 6: Using the Filter

Before you use the filter to turn bad water into better water you are going to need to soak the filter and all its layers thoroughly. The best way to do this is to settle a hose on low inside the top bucket and let it run.

As you check the water you will see sediment and maybe even charcoal bits in the filter. Just keep running the hose until the water is clear. Then you know you are ready.

Gather another 5-gallon bucket of water from a water source, creek, lake, rain barrel or somewhere else that needs to be filtered.

Turn the valve on and place a clean 5-gallon bucket underneath the valve to catch the water. Dump a quarter of your water into the filter and let it start to seep through. Now, add the rest slowly so you don't overflow the filter.

If this is your first dump of water, then take your time and you may want to run the water through one more time. A good tell is if you are getting specks of charcoal in your water. That means the charcoal has to get wetter and settle into place.

After the water is filtered, you will still need to boil it to make it safe to drink.

## Step 7: Care and Maintenance

After you are done filtering water, you should leave the valve open so that residual water can be left to dry out.

Separate your buckets and allow each to drain thoroughly, too! You can pit the lids on these and stack all the buckets in the corner of a shed until they are ready for the next use. Just make sure you marked them, as instructed so they are easy to identify.

This simple filter will improve the visibility and taste of water that you catch or source from around your home. It is a great build that is easily repeatable as long as you do not destroy the buckets. As I mentioned, you can literally gather the gravel and sand from a creek bank, and you can get the charcoal from a fire!

If you keep these buckets stacked up in your shed, you will be able to filter water on a large scale. If you have a couple nice big pots to boil water in than you will be able to quickly filter and boil water in large quantities which will have tremendous value in any kind of disaster or SHTF situation.

PROJECTS RELATED TO WATER

# How To Make A Hand Pump

**MATERIAL COST** $ 17.50    **EASY** DIFFICULTY    **2 HOURS**

One of the most important parts of any off-grid lifestyle is the well. Water can sometimes be a huge burden for those living off grid.

Well pumps make life even more convenient as water can be pumped directly into the home, or at least gathered at a well location with that pump.

A small solar array can assure that your electric well pump works even when there is a power outage!

However, you should still consider a hand well pump, in case all else fails. A simple DIY hand water pump for your well is easy to make if you have the rights parts and pieces.

This pump can be something you put away in case of emergencies, or it can be part of your system full time. The choice is yours.

## The Check Valve

This project all hinges on the use of check valves. These are valves that allow air or water to go in one direction only. It "checks" the flow in one direction.

This is incredibly important for this project. When you pull your plunger, the left check valve will suck water in but will not allow it to drain back out. When you push the plunger back down, the opposite check valve will allow the water to come rushing out.

During the build you are going to have to pay very close attention to the check valve flow direction. The flow should be in the same direction across the entire valve assembly.

In other words, it should enter the valve going one direction and leave the opposite end in the same direction.

If the check valves are pointing in the opposite direction, it will either not allow any water in or it will allow water in but never let it back out! So, take your time with this part of the build.

THIS WILL NOT WORK IF YOU DO NOT MAKE OR BUY CHECK VALVES!

## Parts List

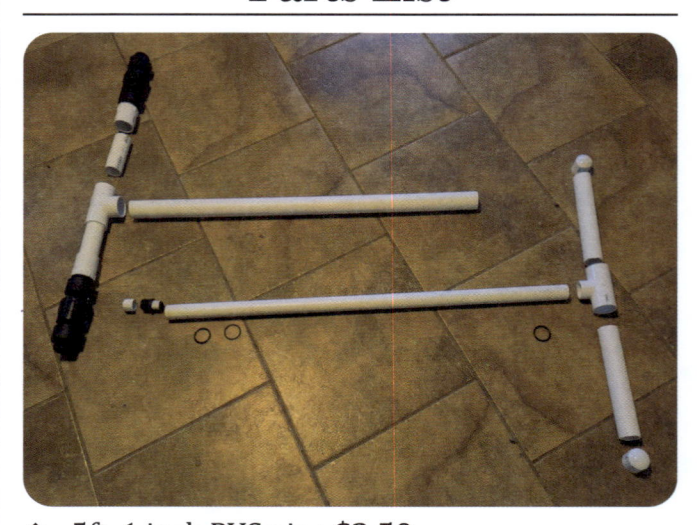

- 5ft. 1 inch PVC pipe **$3.50**
- 5ft. 1 ¼ inch PVC Pipe **$3.50**
- 1 ¼ inch T Fitting **$0.50**
- 1 ¼ to 1 inch T Fitting **$0.50**
- ¾ inch Threaded Reducer to ½ inch **$0.50**
- ½ inch Threaded Cap **$1.00**
- 2 Check Valves that fit 1 ¼ inch pipe **$7.00** each
www.amazon.com/Superior-Pump-99555-Universal-Plastic/dp/B005MKGQGA/ref=sr_1_8?dchild=1&keywords=check+valve&qid=1615224092&sr=8-8

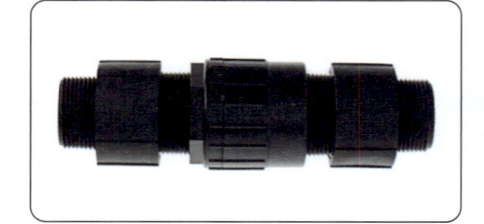

- 2 1 ¼ Thread Fittings $1.00 each
- OPTIONAL: 2 - O Rings for Plunger Assembly

## Build the Plunger Assembly

1. Begin by cutting your 5ft. of PVC pipe down into a 3ft. length.
2. Using a hacksaw, cut a shallow trench all the way around your pipe for the O Rings (optional).
3. Add the O Rings.
4. Use pipe cement to attach the threaded reducer.
5. Cement the threads and then screw on the ½ inch threaded cap.
6. Allow this to dry for an hour.
7. Attach the plunger into the 1 ¼ - 1inch T fitting.

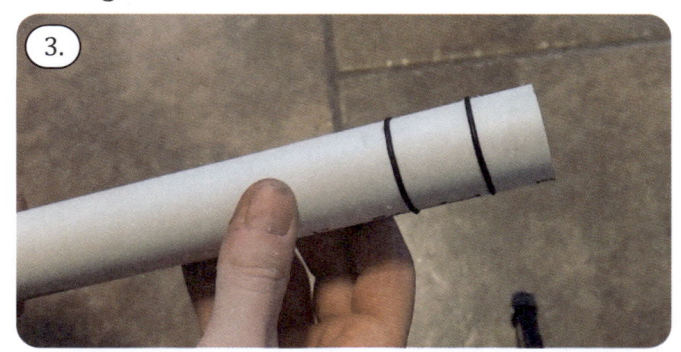

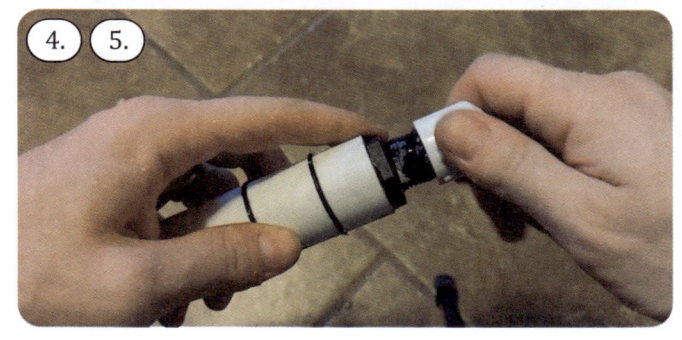

You will also add 2 segments of 1 ¼ inch PVC pipe to the T fitting to create handles but that will be cut in the valve assembly directions.

Once all the cement is dried your plunger assembly is finished.

## Build the Valve Assembly

1. Cut your 5 ft of 1 ¼ inch PVC into a 3ft length.
2. Attach the 1 ¼ inch T assembly.
3. Cut your remaining length of PVC into pieces of 6 inches each.
4. Use two pieces to create the handles for your plunger.
5. Cement the other two into either side of the 1 ¼ inch T fitting.
6. Screw your check valves onto your 1 ¼ in thread fittings
7. PAY CLOSE ATTENTION TO THIS STEP BECAUSE THE VALVES MUST BE PROPERLY AFFIXED.
8. The pump's function depends entirely on the direction of your check valves. Pay attention here.
9. When assembled the arrows of flow on your valves must just be pointing in the same direction along the valve assembly.
10. Once your Valve Assembly is complete you, can insert the plunger and you are ready to start pumping some water.

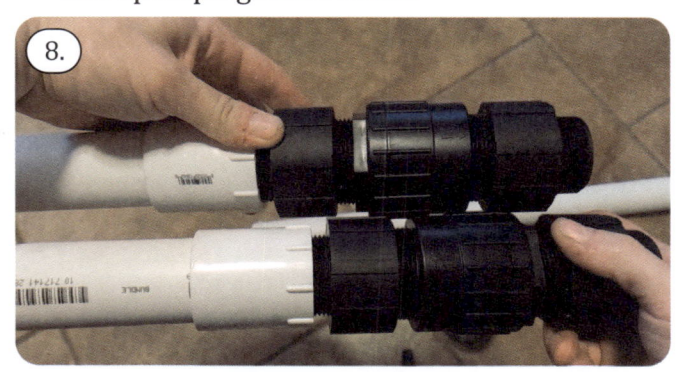

This pump system means that you can now dig your own well, run pipe down into the water and hand pump it back up to the surface. You can also use this pump design to pump air from one place to another, too.

The O Rings did not work out on this build so I removed them before inserting the plunger. This is great news because the build still worked! That means with properly sized and fitted O Rings you are going to be able to get an even more efficient pump!

Have fun!

PROJECTS RELATED TO WATER

# How To Make Drinkable Water Out Of Air

**MATERIAL COST** $ 129.27    **EASY** DIFFICULTY    50 MINUTES

Water is such a critical resource that human beings are hard-pressed to survive more than three days without it. Storing water is vital to our long-term survival and we should all have significant water stores. However, we also need to have other freshwater sources to round out our water preps. A creek, lake, or natural spring is ideal, but with a few easily obtained items, you can also extract fresh water from the air.

The humidity in the air around us is freshwater waiting for us to extract it. To do this, we are going to use an average household dehumidifier and a water filter. The dehumidifier fan pulls air into the unit and over coils that cool the air. The result is that the water in the air condenses on the coils forming water droplets. These drops of water are collected, and cool, dry air blows out of the dehumidifier. These drops of water collect in a tank that we empty when full.

Dehumidifiers are available in several sizes, from small tabletop units to larger ones requiring wheels to move around. When selecting a dehumidifier, our first consideration needs to be the power requirements to run them. Making drinkable water out of air in an SHTF or grid-down scenario only works if you have an excess supply of electricity to power them.

Consider using several smaller dehumidifiers rather than just a large one for this project. The reason for this is two-fold: a smaller unit draws less power, and with several of them in operation, you can decide which unit to power on and which to turn off depending on available power.

Another advantage to using several smaller units is that they often run on 12 volts of electricity. These units get electricity through a transformer plug that steps down the 120 volts of AC power from the wall outlet to 12 volts of DC power. If you are running your home on 12 volts DC power, you could, with a little ingenuity, power these units straight from your battery bank.

A major benefit of this project is that the machine constantly runs and draws water from the air without any input or effort from yourself. The device will work for you twenty-four hours a day as long as it has power and the air is humid.

The largest issue with devices like this is that they require electricity to operate and in an SHTF or grid-down situation, electricity will be an invaluable resource. As I stated before, it is a good idea to consider using several smaller units instead of one large unit.

The volume of water that these units produce versus the power you need to provide them may not make sense for your home during an SHTF or grid-down scenario. However, if you find yourself with excess capacity in your power system, then this project may be worthwhile to have running and to top up your water stores.

The final drawback is that its operation is very dependant on the weather and the levels of humidity in the air. If you live in a moist environment, then these units will work quite well, but if you live in a desert environment, then the amount of produced water will be significantly less. Also, the changing of the seasons will affect the amount of water these units produce. In the dryer months, the levels of water production will be noticeably less.

## Safety of Dehumidifier Water

Water from a dehumidifier is not ready for human consumption. Since dehumidifiers pull water out of the air, any mould, viruses, bacteria, or other contaminants can tag along with the water drops. While the water in the tank seems essentially the same as distilled water, since the water was not exposed to heat high enough to kill pathogens, we must filter the water before drinking.

## Choosing a Filter

There are many filters available on the market, but the filter we need for this build needs to filter water without a pump or suction. We want gravity to pull the water down through the filter and into whichever container we will store it in.

Any filter that can adequately filter water rendering it safe to drink out in the bush will work well. If the filter you use does not filter viruses and this is a concern for you, you should boil the water after filtering as an added precaution

## Building Your Project

The construction of this project is very simple and requires only a couple of easily obtained materials.

## Tools

- Saw
- Cordless drill with bits and drivers
- Sharp knife

## Materials

- Dehumidifier, which I bought off Amazon for $39.99USD
  www.amazon.com/dp/B09CFTBBX1/ref=redir_mobile_desktop?_encoding=UTF8&%2AVersion%2A=1&%2Aentries%2A=0

- Water Filters, like these filters that I found on Amazon for $24.95USD
  www.amazon.com/Sawyer-Products-SP128-Filtration-System/dp/B00FA2RLX2/?th=1

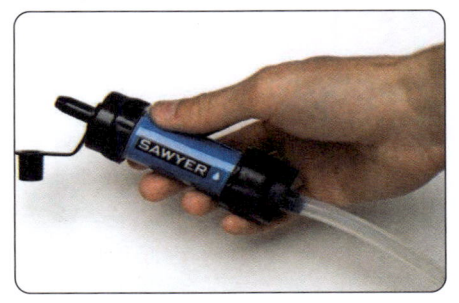

- Water Jerry, which I bought off Amazon for $ 31.65 USD and holds seven gallons
  www.amazon.com/Reliance-Products-Jumbo-Tainer-Gallon-Container/dp/B000GKDFH4

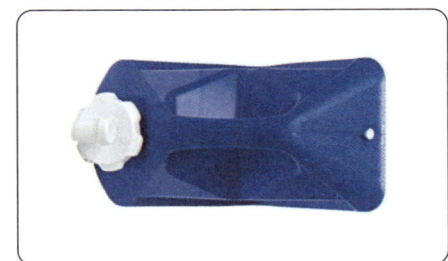

- ¾" PVC Pipe is available at Home Depot for $ 1.60 USD for a 24-inch length
  www.homedepot.com/p/VPC-3-4-in-x-24-in-PVC-Sch-40-Pipe-22075/202300505

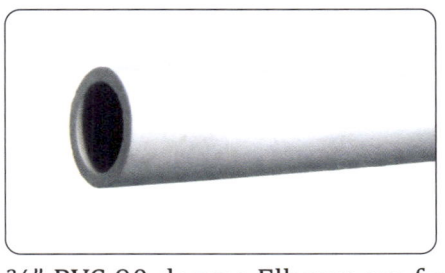

- ¾" PVC 90 degree Elbows are found at Home Depot for $ 0.59 USD each
  www.homedepot.com/p/Charlotte-Pipe-3-4-in-PVC-Schedule-40-90-S-x-S-Elbow-Fitting-PVC023000800HD/203812123

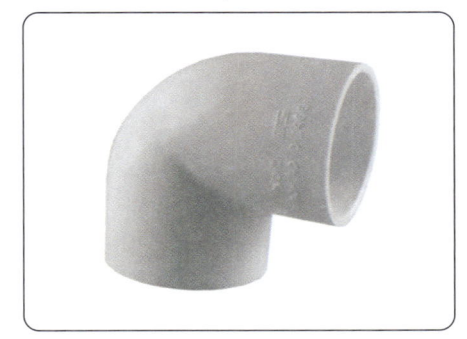

- #8 – 1 inch screws are found at Home Depot for $ 5.28 USD per pack of 100
  www.homedepot.com/p/Everbilt-8-x-1-in-Zinc-Plated-Phillips-Flat-Head-Wood-Screw-100-Pack-801822/204275495

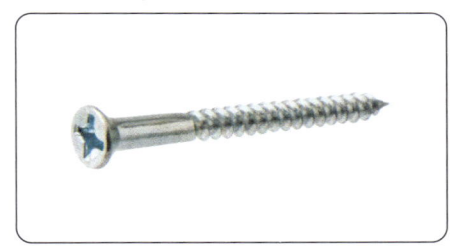

- Metal strapping can be found at Home Depot for $ 16.58 USD for a 100-foot roll
  www.homedepot.com/p/Master-Flow-Perforated-Metal-Hanger-Straps-3-4HS/100396917

- 1x6 lumber is available at Home Depot for $ 8.04 USD for a six-foot boar
  www.homedepot.com/p/1-in-x-6-in-x-6-ft-Premium-Kiln-Dried-Square-Edge-Whitewood-Common-Board-1X6-6FT/315221928

## Instructions

1. Remove the tank from the dehumidifier and locate the port where the water flows into the tank. Most of these units have a switch that turns the unit off when the tank is full. This switch may need to be deactivated or avoided altogether to allow your build to work properly.
2. Cut a piece of ¾" PVC that is long enough to get water from the dehumidifier to a position above the jerry can or tank that the water will end up.
3. Attach a 90-degree elbow to each end of the ¾" PVC pipe.
4. Secure a length of ¾" PVC long enough to reach the jerry can or water tank below.
5. Align the open elbow with the water discharge port on the dehumidifier. You will probably have to fashion a device to hold this pipe straight and in position so that the water flows out of the dehumidifier and through the PVC piping. In my case, I used some metal strapping and a scrap piece of 1x6 lumber to secure and lift the pipe, aligning it with the port.
6. I had to use a couple of small screws as levelling feet so that my pipe holder did not rock when in the dehumidifier.
7. For my filter assembly, I cut the bottom off a one-litre water bottle.
8. I then screwed it onto my Sawyer mini filter, creating the filter assembly.
9. I then placed the filter assembly into the mouth of my water jerry can and activated the machine.

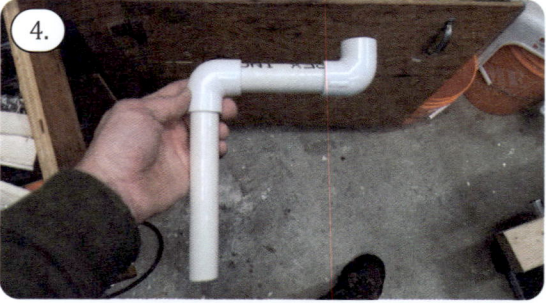

6.

6.

7.

7.

8.

9.

## My Test Run

I set one of these units up in my garage and let it run for over 24 hours, producing about a quarter of a litre of clean filtered water. The problem is that the weather was fairly dry, so there was not a lot of humidity to work with. Had I placed the device indoors in a room that sees higher humidity, such as a bathroom, I would expect the device to work more effectively.

I taste-tested the water and found it to have virtually no taste whatsoever.

This project is an effective way of pulling water from the air we breathe but suffers the significant drawbacks of requiring electricity to operate and depending on weather conditions. In no way should these devices be counted on as your sole water source, but you can find a place for one supplementing your water stores.

# Ammo For Long Term Storage

The price and availability of ammunition has been a serious concern for many gun owners lately. Ammunition that once cost mere cents per round is now breaking the $1 mark per round, and beyond!

Paying this kind of money for ammunition is bad enough; but you can also wait MONTHS at a time before that ammo is delivered.

Firearms and ammunition are one of the cornerstones of any preparedness plan. This ammo is needed to both develop proficiency with your firearms and add a layer of lethality to your security plans.

It only makes sense to both conserve and protect your current ammunition stores. We are talking about long term storage for ammunition. We have long term storage methods for things like food and fuel. So, why not for ammunition?

There aren't many enemies of long-term ammo storage but the conditions that can corrode casings and ruin primers have to be accounted for.

## Protecting Ammo

Well, it's important to understand that the simple primer is an incredibly efficient and effective invention. The success rate is astounding! Consider this from Glen Weeks, Winchester ballistician:

*"Based on the SAAMI-specified drop test, statistics will tell you that our primers are 99.9997 percent reliable. That means that when struck with sufficient energy and properly centered, they will go off 99.9997 percent of the time. A lead-styphnate primer is probably one of the oldest and most reliable devices on the planet."*

Understanding that ammo is usually not the culprit when it comes to misfires is important, but poor ammo storage can turn something that is a marvel of man's ingenuity into something worthless.

## Humidity

Storing Ammo in humid areas can both affect the brass itself and the primer inside. This is a characteristic of an awfully bad environment for long term storage of any ammunition. Corrosion is what will follow if your ammo is stored in a humid location. If the brass starts turning green then you mustn't shoot it, it is now unsafe. It's useless at this point.

## Moisture

Moisture is even worse than humidity. Direct contact with moisture is going to ruin ammo in a hurry. Most often you are going to have to worry about moisture when you do things like cache ammunition in the ground. If water gets into your container and your ammo is not protected it will be ruined.

The same corrosion mentioned above will set in on your ammo.

## Oil

Though it is often overlooked, oil is a more effective enemy against the long term well being of your ammunition. Oils have a better chance of getting on your ammo from handling. Your hands are covered in oils, and it can easily transfer to your ammunition.

## Russian Lacquered Ammo

For long term storage eastern European nations and Russian nations sealed primers with lacquer. This was a practice for storing ammunition long term. In fact, this surplus ammo is still available for those who are interested in buying it. Some say it's no good while others actually enjoy shooting it and prefer the lacquered coating that protects the ammo for the long term.

## Spam Can Ammo

The Russians also created something that was referred to as spam can ammo. This ammo garnered its name because of the cans that it is sold in. The ammo comes in a tin that looks like some kind of sardine or Spam can.

These rounds come to you prepared for long term storage and you merely need to find the proper place to store them in your home or an alternate location.

## Vac Seal

A more modern take is to gather up your ammo and vac seal it. The vacuum sealer is going to protect it from moisture and if you are smart about where you store it, you will not have to worry about things like humidity, extremes or temperature or oils from touching and moving the ammunition.

The vac sealer is for much more than just sealing up food!

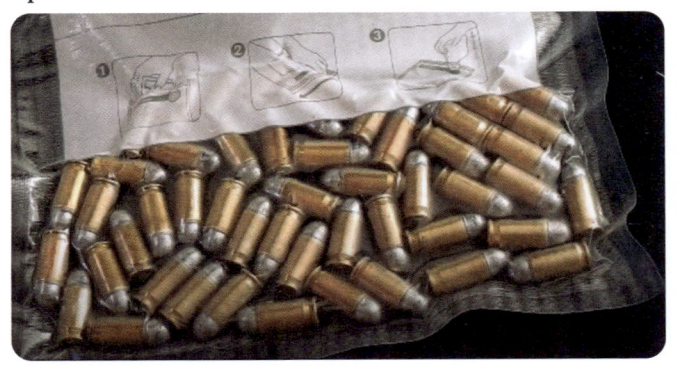

## Additional Practices for Long Term Ammo Storage

There are a couple things that you can do to your stored ammo to be sure you get the most out of that big ammo purchase.

## Date and Label

Just like your food storage, you are going to want to rotate your ammo. This way you use the oldest first and eliminate the greatest possibility of ammo going bad.

Simply use a black magic marker and put a date on the container you choose to use.

If you are vac sealing ammo, I would recommend dating each pack of ammo. You should even include the caliber and quantity of each package to make counting easier.

This will also help if you send someone to retrieve ammo that doesn't know a lot about guns and ammunition.

## Silica

No matter what package you decide to use for long term ammo storage, you should also include a silica pack inside along with the ammo. Remember, humidity is no good for your ammunition. The silica pack adsorbs, not absorbs, water because it has a porous surface on which the water molecules like to adhere.

These can be tossed into ammo cans or even sealed up with your vac sealed ammo. These are especially important if you do things like bury ammo for caching.

The price of ammo is out of control but if you wanna remain proficient with your firearm you've got to, well, bite the bullet. If you started stockpiling ammo years ago, then you have really made good on that investment.

Of course, how you store that ammo will decide the shelf life of that investment. If you understand the enemies of long term ammo storage than you can easily take the steps required to avoid them.

In all honesty, storing ammo for the long term is not that hard if you keep most of it at home. If you do decide to cache ammo, I would recommend it, then you will need to take care to use proper containers and include silica gel to deal with the changes of humidity.

If you are going to buy ammo today for long term storage, than you are going to make a serious investment. Protect that investment to assure that you have the ammo you need if, God forbid, you should ever need to use it.

PROJECTS ON GUNS AND AMMO

# Hidden Gun Storage Shelf

**MATERIAL COST** $ 77.00    **MEDIUM** DIFFICULTY    2 HOURS

When people are allowed to own firearms, they empower a nation. This might seem counterintuitive to what is being preached to us on a daily basis. Radical anti-second amendment culture and legislation are putting us all in danger. At best it will create an even larger black market for untraceable guns in the US. At worst it will have people forced to surrender their weapons or police and civilians facing off in a battle for their God given right to keep and bear arms.

Having guns close by but, having them hidden is always beneficial. It can be. We can talk about the safety of hiding firearms in plain sight. We can also talk about the importance of not having all of your guns locked away in a safe.

## Covert Locations for Firearms

### PVC PIPE

A great way to hide firearms in plain sight is to create a PVC cache that is similar to the pipes under your home. This could be cut to fit a space in the top of your crawlspace. To the untrained eye it will look like another pipe running under the house. Be sure you buy a pipe that is big enough to hold the gun you want to store. You can also cap either end or seal with pipe cement to bury these pipes.

### HOLLOWED OUT BOOK

If you own or have access to a bandsaw, you can clamp the cover of any book open, sketch a compartment on the pages and then cut that compartment out using the saw. These books are very easy to make, and cheap ones can be had at flea markets or yard sales.

### POWERFUL GUN MAGNETS

One of the easiest means of concealing a weapon is to install a gun magnet. These can be screwed into almost anything and they hold onto your weapon and keep it in place. The more creative you get with where you install the magnet, the more covert that firearms storage can be.
- Bedside Table
- Behind Headboard
- Inside the Top of a Drawer
- Under a Table
- Behind a Toilet
- Inside a Closet

## Building a Set of Covert Shelves

Below we have a build for a pair of covert shelves that use concealed door hinges to create the look of decorative floating shelves. The build and materials are designed to make two that can be hung one over the other.

This will maximize storage space but also give them more of an unassuming decorative look. Remember to sit something interesting on these shelves to divert attention away from the shelving and focus it more on what is sitting on top.

## Materials (Makes 2 Shelves)

- 6 – 2ft .5x6's $20.00
- 1 – 2ft 1x6's $10.00
- 2 – 2ft .5x1.5" lengths $8.00
- Sandpaper $4.00
- Wood Stain $5.00
- Brad Nails $2.00
- Wood Glue $3.00
- 2 Pairs of Concealed Door Hinges $20
- Screws $5.00

## Procces

1. Cut and smooth the edges of your lumber. You can also buy precut lumber. No matter which way you go, you are going to spend plenty of money on the wood for this project. Cut your 1x6s into 6 inch lengths. These will become the caps for your shelves.
2. Wipe the wood with a dry cloth and use one or two different stains to coat the wood. Allow to dry completely before moving onto the next step.
3. Before assembling the shelves lay two of your .5x6s next to one another to start building your concealed door. Place your hinges a few inches inside by screwing one side to each piece

of lumber. Build the door for the 2nd shelf the same way.

4. Glue and nail the .5X1.5 length of wood to your 1x6 that is going to face downward. This is going to be how you hand the shelves on the wall. It should be flush with one side of the 1x4. Set this aside to dry.
5. Now using your caps, nails and glue begin to assemble the shelves. Glue and nail each cap so it's flush with the concealed door. DO NOT CLUE OR NAIL IT TO THE CONCEALED DOOR.
6. Allow to dry completely before hanging the shelves.
7. Depending on the type of walls you have gather the appropriate hanging hardware. You will be sinking 2-3 screws into your walls for each shelf.
8. Use a scrap piece of 1x6 to space the shelves if you are going to hang them over one another. It's a pretty nice look if you do this.
9. Don't forget to put some things on the tops of these shelves. Small plants, books, and décor. To the passerby you want them to see shelves not a covert storage space. Put something dazzling on those shelves to divert attention away from the shelves.

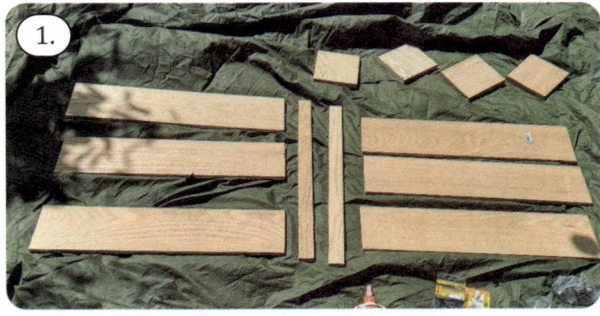

During the great depression, a lot of effort was put into hiding things and storing things away from prying eyes. There are some real benefits to this practice. As we enter this new phase in America you will find value in a more covert approach to how you store important things. Moreover, you might want to have a firearm or weapon at close reach but out for the world to see. If this is the case, these shelves will serve you well.

PROJECTS ON GUNS AND AMMO

# How To Build A Ghost Gun

MATERIAL COST  $ 424.00   MEDIUM   DIFFICULTY   2 HOURS

As the scope of our 2nd Amendment tightens, Americans are facing numerous challenges. Obstacles like new laws, price, and availability have changed the landscape for gun owners. Despite the resounding calls for "common sense gun laws", the demand for overpriced firearms is still off the charts.

The powers that be assume that by tracking, registering, and limiting firearms in any way possible will prevent Americans from owning the types of guns they do not like. However, this seems to be backfiring.

Right now, there are calls for legislation that would help eliminate ghost guns. The irrational fear around these guns is that they can be purchased and milled into a working firearm without any kind of background check.

If only they had the same vigor to prevent illegal firearms from crossing our border! It is estimated that as many as 2,000 illegal guns cross the border each day! This study comes from the Mexico's governmental research service.

While there is not matching American research data to back this up, we do know that astounding levels of firearms are confiscated by agencies like ICE each year.

## What Is a "Ghost Gun"?

So, what is an American creating when they build the infamous Ghost Gun?

To understand this, you have to first understand what an 80% lower is. An AR15 is made of many parts. The two major parts are the lower and upper receivers. The lower receiver houses the magazine, trigger, and the firing mechanism. The upper receiver is basically the barrel.

In the eyes of the law the lower receiver is considered the gun portion. When you buy a lower receiver, you have to go through a background check. When you buy an upper receiver, you do not.

An 80% lower looks like a lower but has not been machined enough to be considered a gun. There is no area for the trigger or the firing mechanism. It is simply just a block of metal with a mag well and threaded stabilizer ring.

There is no way you can use an 80% lower to fire a round in the form that it is delivered to you. In order for it to work, you have to literally machine the 80% lower another 20% with a variety of drill bits and some skill.

The good news is I am going to show you exactly how to do this.

## Use an 80% Lower Jig

Your 80% lower is a little more than a paperweight until you start to drill and machine it. However, this can be a risky proposition if you do not know what you are doing. This is why it is very important that you get your hands on an 80% lower jig for this purpose.

These jigs will fit around your 80% lower and show you exactly where to mill and drill to get the 80% lower to 100% and have it ready to take a lower parts kit. You can drill and mill with confidence, if you have one of these jigs.

**MATERIAL COST**
◆ BILT HARD 13-inch floor Drill Press $269.00
www.amazon.com/BILT-HARD-16-Speed-Benchtop-Certified/dp/B09G2J5HCJ

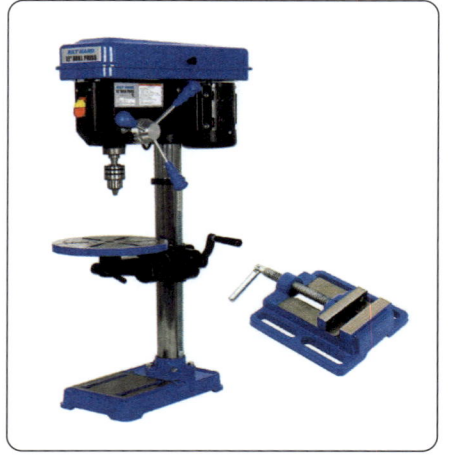

◆ Hybrid 80 Liberator AR15 polymer 80% Lower and Jig – FDE $75.00
www.midwayusa.com/product/1020069561

◆ AR15 Lower Parts Kit $60.00

www.ar-15lowerreceivers.com/products/ar-15-lower-parts-kit-butt-stock-and-buffer-tube-assembly/

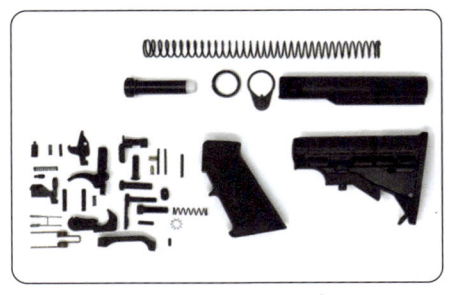

- Milling Bits: 3/8. 5/32 $20.00
www.amazon.com/Cutter-Drill-Aluminum-Titanium-Straight/dp/B07PFT7PQS

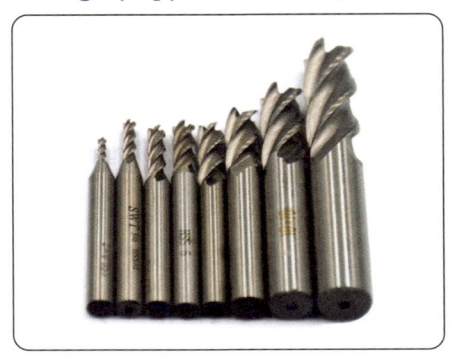

**PROCESS**

1. Begin by securing your 80% lower into the jib with the included screws.
2. Take the lower/jig combo to your workspace and place it in the vice of your drill press. The BILT HARD comes with a vice so that is why I recommend this budget model.
3. Start with the 5/32 and the 3/8 holes on the side of the lower first. Secure the jig/lower combo on its side in the vice.
4. If you have never used a drill press before, raise the jig as close to the drill as possible and then add light pressure to start gradually taking away material. Take your time and you will have great results.
5. After your three holes are drilled, lower the platform and flip the jig/lower upright so you can see the larger portion to be milled out. You will want to remove the trigger jig portion at this point. That is the little cap that covers the larger part to be milled out. Set this aside but do not lose it!
6. Since the BILT Hard is small, you may need to put your 3/8 milling bit higher into the spindle. You can adjust it once you get your jig/lower in place.
7. Begin milling holes out of your lower. I drilled to a depth of 1 ½ inches. Measure and mark your bit with a marker. Make sure the holes are tight and side by side. This will make the milling easier later.
8. Using your milling bit you are now going to mill out the sections. I loosened up my lower/jig in the vice and move the bit around inside to mill out the pieces that are left over.
9. Once the inside is completely milled out, you can add your trigger jig cap. This cap will give you all the area to mill out for your trigger to fit through. Mill the area out by pushing your drill be all the way through the lower. This should be just a small area that is drilled all the way through.
10. You can sand or smooth out the inside of the jig from here. A Dremel tool works really well. Then you are ready to add the lower parts.
11. Add the lower parts kit to your build and you will have completed your first ghost gun. Now all you have to do is add an upper and you will have a completed rifle build.

PROJECTS ON GUNS AND AMMO

# How To Make Black Powder

MEDIUM DIFFICULTY

Black powder is an ancient implement of much contested origin. Nearly all of the major societies around the 13th century have laid claim, in written form, to the use and creation of black powder. Lots of evidence points to 10th century China and its use of black powder as an explosive in fireworks and signals.

Even the Arabs threw their hat in the ring with a 13th century "gun" that was the first of its kind. This was a length of bamboo that was reinforced with iron and used black powder charge to throw an arrow. Around the same time the Chinese were hurling rocks from bamboo poles using the same method.

No matter where it originated, black powder was and still is the combination of three basic ingredients:

- Potassium Nitrate
- Sulfur
- Charcoal

This combination creates a highly volatile powder that burns and smokes when touched with direct heat. When combined, thoroughly, using a very simple ratio, you get black powder.

What is the ratio?

75-15-10. That is 75% Potassium Nitrate, 15% Charcoal, and 10% Sulfur.

**IS IT GUNPOWDER?**

Black powder was the original gunpowder, but we have come a long way in how we shoot projectiles. Gun powder has changed and today it is a much more powerful substance. You will notice that when you light your black powder it burns fast and puts off a lot of smoke.

Modern day gunpowder is smokeless and way stronger than the black powder that you're making. Still, a black powder rifle gets the job done on an annual basis all across this nation. It can still be used to fire projectiles with deadly force.

However, modern gunpowder is what is used in all modern ammunition. It is just a more powerful and effective chemical reaction.

## Methods for Making Black Powder

The process of making black powder is, basically, all about the ration and the thorough mixing of these ingredients. The better the integration, the more effective your black powder will be. So, we are going to look at the two methods that are most commonly used to make black powder.

The first is the dry method that is pretty straightforward mixing but requires some diligence. The second is the wet method which, in my opinion, is the best method for newbies and it yields the best results.

## The Dry Method

This is a method that requires that you keep the mix dry and can be done by hand. I find it best to take a page from the baker's book and sift the powders together in the same way you would with sugar and flour for a cake.

You can also mix by hand but that takes time and diligence. The most effective and pretty cool method for making black powder with the dry method is to use a ball mill. A ball mill is a metal or PVC container that is large enough to house the necessary ingredients and also a 3-4 marbles. These mills are often connected to some kind of motorized spinning device that will cause the mill to turn.

As the contents are rolled over themselves and smacked by the marbles, there is a serious integration that happens. You can mill each ingredient first before milling them together in the appropriate ration.

## The Wet Method

In the wet method you have to addition of 70% isopropyl alcohol which will further combine the ingredients and also allow you to granularize them. The wet method is just a couple of steps longer than the dry method, but it opens up a lot of possibilities

We are going to explore the wet method of making black powder. We are going to granulize and dry the black powder because there are benefits to both.

## Safety When Making Black Powder

Black powder burns at around 1400 degrees Fahrenheit! One mistake can be very costly.

So, before we get rolling with this process, we have to talk about safety and some precautions. Black powder is an explosive and incendiary that can afflict serious and even life-threatening burns. Things like sulfur and potassium nitrate are also not things you want to be inhaling for a long period of time either. So, be sure you do this in a well-ventilated area.

This was the same stuff used to hurl musket balls at the British. While it might seem like no big deal because you can buy the ingredients yourself, mishandling black powder can land you in the ER if you are not careful.

**PPE OR PERSONAL PROTECTIVE EQUIPMENT**

Be sure that you are using the following safety equipment when you are working with all or any of the components of black powder.
- Protective Eye Wear
- Rubber Gloves
- Respirator
- Work Gloves for Testing

## Tools

You will need the following:
- Wood Spoon
- 70% Isopropyl Alcohol
- Fine Sieve
- Large 4 Cup Mason Jar
- A Few Large Plates
- Ceramic Bowl
- Sieve or Screen for Granulating

## The Process

1. Start by gathering your ingredients and tools and bring them to a workbench outside or in a well-ventilated area.
2. Get your PPE or personal protective equipment on.
3. Begin by opening the three ingredients and preparing to fill the mason jar. Remember the ratio is 75-15-10.
4. You can measure these ingredients by weight with a scale, but I have made black powder many times and you can do it with a simple 4 cup mason jar.
5. Start with the potassium nitrate. We need 75% of this stuff so that means we need 3 cups worth. Using your scoop simply fill the mason jar up to the 3 cup line. That is 75% of the 4 cup container.
6. You are left with 1 cup of space in the jar. Note the markers. Every three markers on the glass is a cup. The last cup is to the upper most taper

on the bottle. In this last space you have to get 15% charcoal and 10% sulfur. To do this, fill a little over half of that small section with your charcoal.
7. Some people use charcoal they breakdown themselves. I buy activated charcoal because it is already powdered fine. It is also a great prep to have around the house for a number of things.
8. After you have filled a little over half of the remaining space with charcoal now you can finish it off with the sulfur. Fill just to the top of the taper! Your charcoal is dark and fine so it may absorb the sulfur. That is fine. As long as your ingredients reach that topmost taper.
9. Dump the entire mason jar into your ceramic bowl now that it is measured. Mix this, first, with a wooden spoon. Combine it all thoroughly. You might have to seek out pieces of sulfur that clump together. Its best to use a rubber gloved hand to crush these.

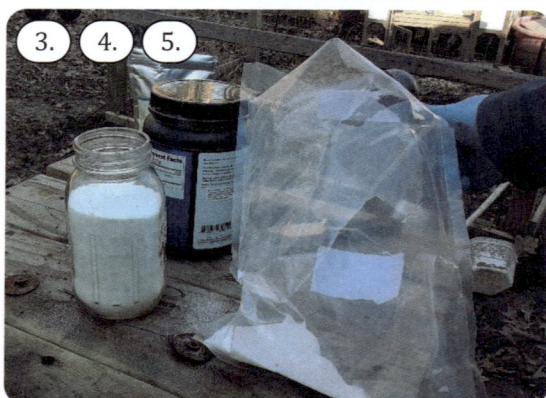

### ADDING ALCOHOL FOR THE WET METHOD
1. Now, pour enough 70% isopropyl alcohol into your mix so that you can create a paste or almost a "dough" that can be packed together.
2. Pack the mix up into a few balls and set them aside.
3. From here you can push this paste through a fine sieve or something bigger to granulate the powder in larger granules.
4. Using the wooden spoon press all the wet mix through sieves and onto your plates to dry. This mix will dry fast and when it is done you have granules of black powder that are ready to burn.

## Testing Black Powder

At this point you have mixed together a substance that will create a chemical reaction when it is lit on fire and will burn at 1400 degrees Fahrenheit! It is no laughing matter. Be incredibly careful how you deal with this substance.

If you are going to test it, you can place some on a hard surface, outdoors, that will not catch fire. Using a long lighter or some punk to light from a distance add direct flame to your granules.

BE SURE YOU ARE STILL WEARING PPE!

As soon as the powder catches, back away quickly. It will be very bright, hot and give off a lot of smoke. You don't want any of that on or in you! If you see the fireworks show, than you know you have done it correctly!

You can also remove the contents of an egg before filling it up with black powder and taping it back up. A simple toilet paper 'fuse' can be made to light the egg. This will create an incendiary that shoots fire in one direction.

Black powder is something we use each and every year when we shoot off fireworks. While it is not the war powder that it once was, there is still some real romance in knowing how to make and use it. There are a number of projects that you can undertake with your new black powder.

You know, we have entire hunting seasons devoted to the use of this substance!

However, at its core is basic chemistry. It is a great fire starter that can be used as such.

It was often carried around in leather bags so there is no reason why it couldn't make an appearance in your own fire kit. Whatever you decide on when it comes to how you use your homemade black powder just do it carefully and responsibly.

PROJECTS ON GUNS AND AMMO

# How To Recycle Ammo

**MATERIAL COST** $ 440.00    **COMPLEX** **DIFFICULTY**

It's no secret that the cost of ammo has gone way up. The demand has risen, production is down, and now we have decided to no longer important ammo from Russia which will affect these markets, too. Keeping ammo prices up and supplies low is a great way to affect the 2nd Amendment without directly attacking a person's right to bear arms.

Learning how to reuse ammo gives you options. That is what you want in this age of things like shortages, inflation, and ransomware attacks.

This skill will allow you to make ammunition for much cheaper than the price of buying. It's an involved process but once you understand the components and process, you have a means of stretching your ammo stores and perhaps helping others stretch their own!

### THE IMPORTANCE OF PRECISION AND SAFETY

Look, we are not talking about canning jams here. We are using explosives and creating something, that is designed to kill. You have got to get this right or you could hurt yourself very badly when firing reused ammo.

With every component and every step that we discuss there is a collection of information out in the world about it. If you are going to seriously get into reloading ammunition, then you need to study the process and the components.

TAKE YOUR TIME AND IF SOMETHING DOESN'T LOOK RIGHT DON'T FIRE IT.

## Safety Equipment and Procedures

- Wear safety glasses;
- Tidy up a reloading area;
- Keep primers and powders away from heat;
- Use a proper reloading scale;
- Use gloves to avoid lead exposure;
- Follow reload data instructions;
- Use a reloading handbook for your recipes.

## Components and Cost

The components of this ammo and dies were specific to 9 mm. Buy the components and dies for your desired caliber.

- Lee Value Turret Press Kit (scale, powder measure, all pieces for setting up a press) $160.00

www.midwayusa.com/product/1013016267

- Lee Carbide Set (for desired caliber) $40.00

www.amazon.com/Lee-Deluxe-Carbide-4-Die-Set/dp/B078S7XJKN

- Reloading Handbook $35.00
  www.midwayusa.com/product/1023637228

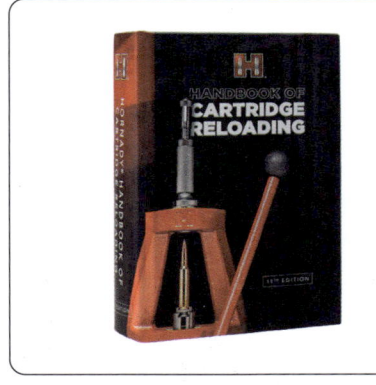

- 9mm Bullets $25.00
  www.midwayusa.com/product/1023839753

- Brass $65.00
  www.midwayusa.com/product/941136131

- No.7 Accurate Powder $35.00
  www.midwayusa.com/product/2183542088

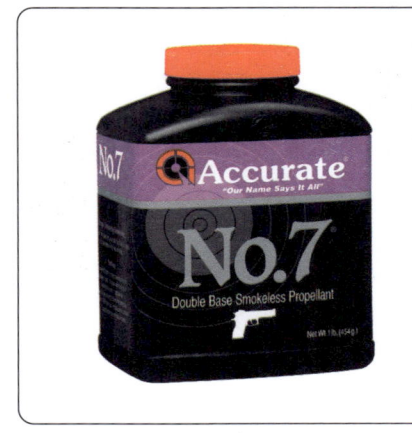

- Primers (1000) $80.00
  www.evergladesammo.com/cci-500-primers-1000.html

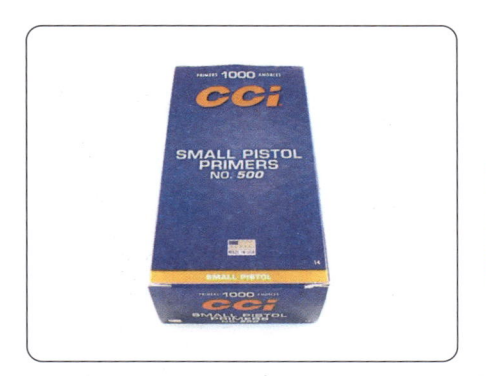

## Process

This is a very involved process that takes time and patience to set up. I cannot stress the importance of safety and accuracy when reloading ammo. Take the time to tweak each step so that it is working just the way it should based on your recipe.

### YOUR RECIPE

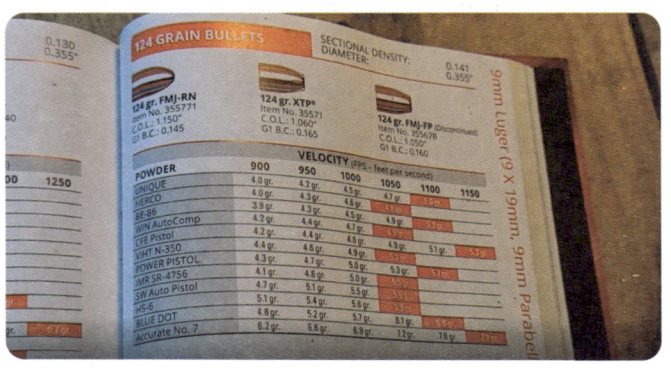

Before you start any reloading of ammo you need to first look through your reloading handbook. This handbook is essential to reloading ammo safely. In this book you will be able to identify some very important information.

- Caliber;
- Bullet Type and Grain;
- Powder Type;
- Charge Amount;
- Desired FPS (start low).

You will need all of this information before you get started. You can write down this recipe but keep the book close by just in case.

## Installing Your Press

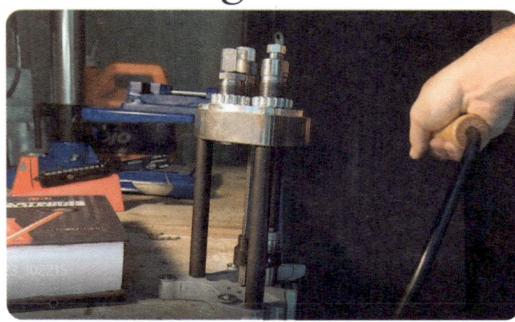

The Lee Press drills down onto your bench, or you can buy another piece to attach the press to. The installation of the rest of the press is laid out in your manual and is pretty simple stuff.

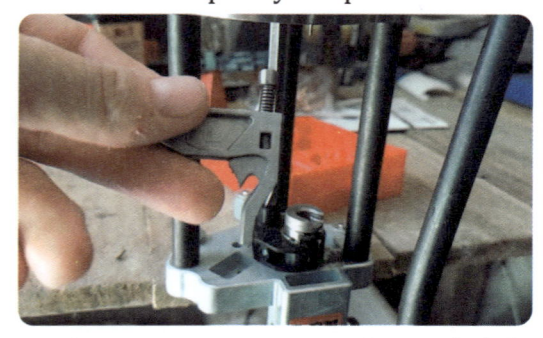

You can also raise your press a bit and slide your primer down into the press. This looks like a little trigger shaped piece of metal with a spring. It just slides down into the open area beneath your shell holder.

The primer holder should be facing up and move into the shell holder as you drop the arm of the press.

## Reloading Dies

The reloading dies are specific to the type of caliber that you are reloading. You will need dies for each caliber that you plan on reloading.

You are going to need 3 different dies to execute the reloading process. When you buy a pack of reloading dies it will come with the three dies you need.

### Decapper
The first die you will use is the decapper die. This die uses a thin post to push the old, used primer out of the casing. It helps to clean that primer area out if you are not using cleaned brass already.

### Resizing
The next die will resize the shell casing to receive the bullet. This die will also be where you attach the hopper of gunpowder. It will add your gunpowder as it resizes the casing.

### Bullet Seating and Crimping
The final die is going to seat your bullet into the casing that is primed and filled with gunpowder. After you use this die your process will be completed.

### INSTALLATION OF DIES

1. To begin installing the dies you are going to screw your decapping die into the press. Raise the press to its max and then continue screwing the decapping die until it touches the shell holder. Next you are going to tighten the nut on the die until the die is secure in place.
2. After that you are going to install your resizing die. This die is going to screw in until it touches the raised shell holder. Then you are going to give it one full counterclockwise turn before tightening down the nut.
3. Finally, you are going to install the bullet crimping die. This die will be screwed in to touch the shell holder and then you will give 3 full counterclockwise turns before tightening the nut down.

4. The best way to manage these turns is to mark a small line or dot on the top of the die so you can see where the dot starts and stops on a full turn.

### SETTING YOUR SCALE
1. With all your dies set you are now going to have to set up the scale and prepare your

charge. Your goal here is to weigh the charge coming from each pull of the press and to be consistent to your recipe.

2. The Lee scale is a weight scale that can be harder to manage. A digital scale will work but I use the provided scale and find it is very accurate if you know how to use it.
3. First you need to find a level place on your workspace or create one. Then you are going to install the arm by balancing it on the indentation in the arm.
4. Roll your ball to the 0 position and make sure your grains measure is at 0, too. Hang the small metal pan to the end of the scale and it should balance.
5. Now you refer back to your recipe and set the scale to the number of grains that it calls for. There is a small plastic post that, when pushed, will lock the small sliding grain scale in place.
6. At this point you are ready to start weighing charges.

## Preparing Your Charge

1. Each time you pull the arm down on your resizing die and insert a shell casing you will drop a charge of powder from the hopper.
2. Be sure you prime the casing first or the powder will just leak out of the hole in the bottom.
3. After you drop a charge into a casing you can simply dump the contents out into the pan that is hanging from your scale.
4. If the charge balances the scale, then you know you're dumping the right amount of powder from your powder measure each time you resize a round.
5. If the charge is high you are going to use the provided key and turn it clockwise to reduce the amount of charge.
6. If it's too light, then you can turn the key counterclockwise and it will increase the charge.
7. Play with your powder measure until your charge is just right before you start reloading any ammo.

## Measuring Case Length

We are using the 9mm round as an example here. Using a pair of digital calipers, you are going to measure the case length of the brass to assure it is 0.744 inches. That is the desired case length for 9mm.

If you are buying prepared brass, it will likely be at that length but measure a few of the cases just to be safe.

REMEMBER CASE LENGTH WILL VARY FOR EVERY CALIBER!

### REMOVING AND ADDING A NEW PRIMER

1. The reloading process begins by first removing and adding a primer to your shell casing. If the casings are cleaned, then they might not have a primer. If you are reusing ammo that you already fired, then you can clean the casing and remove the primer.
2. Place your shell into the shell holder and then raise the press allowing the post to push out the old primer.
3. Then you are going to add a new primer to the priming arm under your shell holder. Be sure the concavity in the primer is facing up.
4. Raise the shell holder about halfway up and then place the casing into the shell holder, then push the arm of the press upward and it will drive the casing down onto the priming arm and insert the primer.
5. Make sure the shell and the priming arm line up as you do this.

6. If you do this properly the primer will be flush with the bottom of the casing.

## Adding Your Charge

1. When you pull the press arm down all the way the turret will rotate to the next die. Next you are going to use the resizing die to resize and charge your primed casing. 
2. At this point your charge should be measured so you should be dropping the right amount. You may still want to verify it with the scale on the first few rounds.
3. Place the casing in the shell holder and raise it into the resizer. Lower the arm and you should have a casing with powder inside of it and the rim of your casing should be flared a very little bit.
4. If a bullet drops into the casing easily then your resizer will need to be unscrewed a bit more. It's going to deep.
5. If the bullet sits in the top of the casing just barely, then you are in business. It's time to seat and crimp.

**SEATING THE BULLET**

- With your shell casing still in the shell holder you can now gently sit your bullet to the flared opening.
- Slowly raise the press and allow the bullet to press up into the die.
- When you let it down you will see your finished round of ammunition.
- Check the bullet and see how it is seated. Sometimes they can be seated too low. Most of the time this means your resizer is off.

If all of these steps have gone well then you are now prepared to fire rounds of ammunition, gather your brass, and reload the ammunition. After lots of use, you might need to tighten dies and check your powder reloader to assure everything is still on point.

In the meantime, it would be wise to begin storing the kinds of powder, primers, dies, and bullets that you want to reload on a regular basis. Having these things in stock is a great idea because none of them really have a shelf life.

As long as you keep powders sealed and dry, you are going to be able to store all of your ingredients for the long haul. Also, protect your reloading manual. This is the only way you can get your weights and measures right.

Reloading ammo is a skill that will benefit your personal ammo inventory, but you can barter this skill or charge for it to make ammunition for others. You can turn it into an income stream!

PROJECTS RELATED TO ELECTRICITY

# DIY Bicycle Generator

**MATERIAL COST** $ 410.00    **MEDIUM DIFFICULTY**    **2 HOURS**

Making your own bicycle generator is a good addition for those who are interested in going off the grid and finding a way to live on their own terms. It not only generates electricity but also provides you with a great cardio workout, which could be an alternative to going for a run and a good addition to anyone's life.

## Materials Needed

Building the generator is simple if you have the motivation, creativity and, of course, the items necessary to build it:

- Two 50-inch x 6-inch x 2-inch wooden planks $ 20 USD
- One 24-inch plank (or a height that would be enough to lift up the back wheel of your bike when the plank is cut in two) $ 10 USD
- A short plank that will connect the two 50-inch planks $ 10 USD
  www.lowes.com/pd/Severe-Weather-Common-2-in-x-6-in-x-12-ft-Actual-1-5-in-x-5-5-in-x-12-ft-2-Prime-Treated-Lumber/4564620
- A saw $ 10USD
  www.lowes.com/pd/Severe-Weather-Common-2-in-x-6-in-x-12-ft-Actual-1-5-in-x-5-5-in-x-12-ft-2-Prime-Treated-Lumber/4564620

- A saw $ 10USD
  www.lowes.com/pd/CRAFTSMAN-15-in-Medium-Cut-Hand-Saw/1000595443

- Nails of different sizes $ 5 USD
  www.lowes.com/search?searchTerm=nails

- A Phillips screwdriver $ 7 USD
  www.lowes.com/pd/CRAFTSMAN-Bi-Material-Handle-2-Phillips-Screwdriver/1000596447

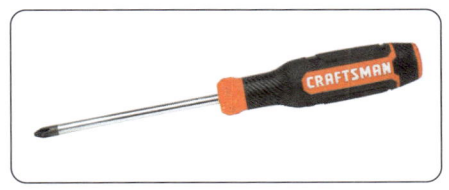

- Screws $ 6 USD
  www.lowes.com/search?searchTerm=screws
- Hammers $ 6 USD
  www.lowes.com/pd/Kobalt-16-oz-Smooth-Face-Steel-Head-Fiberglass-Claw-Hammer/4776985

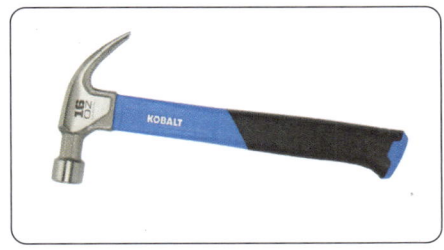

- A nail puller $ 12 USD
  www.lowes.com/pd/Estwing-9-in-Steel-Moulding-Pry-Bar/1000402797

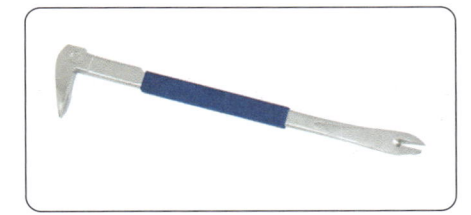

- Metal L corner braces in two different sizes $ 8 USD
  www.lowes.com/pd/ReliaBilt-RB-4-IN-GALV-CORNER-BRACE-4-CT/5001634687

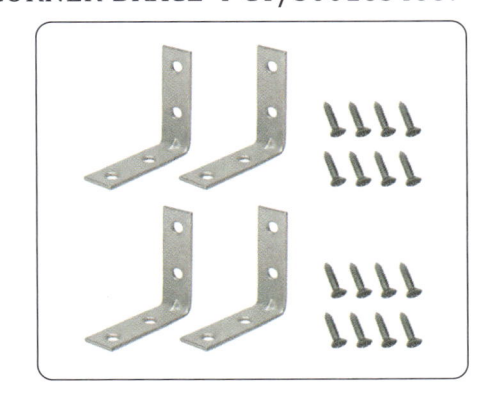

47

- A fan belt $ 16 USD
www.amazon.com/Dayco-15450-Fan-Belt/dp/B000C0ULIO/

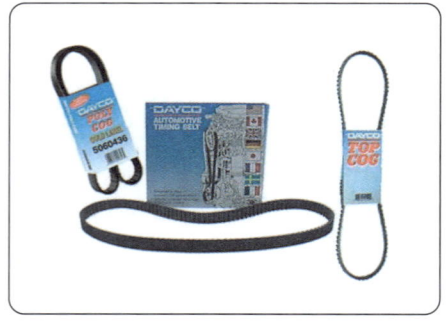

- A car alternator $ 100 USD
www.amazon.com/DB-Electrical-AFD0103-Alternator-Excursion/dp/B007Y87WDO/

- A battery $ 185 USD
www.amazon.com/Weize-Battery-System-Camping-Trolling/dp/B07SW353M8/

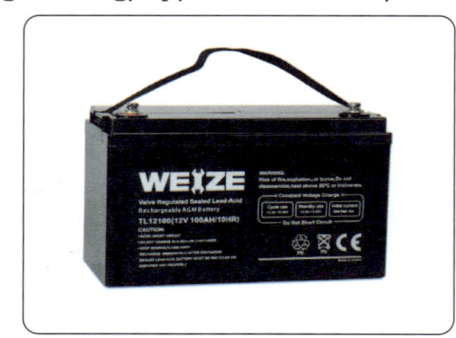

- A voltage regulator $ 17 USD
www.amazon.com/Voltage-Regulator-Converter-Waterproof-Transformer/dp/B07V9D6SF2/

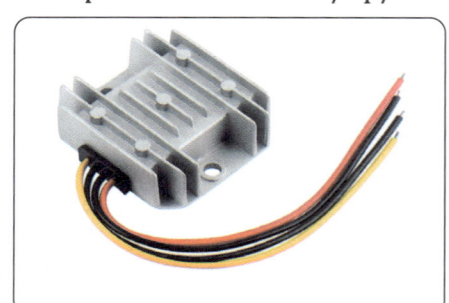

- A switch $5 USD
www.lowes.com/pd/Hillman-Single-Pole-Metal-Toggle-Light-Switch/1000882102

## Building the Bicycle Generator

First, we need to set up the base of the generator. Start with the two 50-inch wooden planks and put them next to each other. Saw the 24-inch-long plank down the middle into two pieces. Nail these planks to the 50-inch-long wooden plank at the top and bottom, creating the base.

Place the bike onto the base, and draw a line at the bike's cassette sprocket onto the boards. Cut the 24-inch wooden plank into two, and cut a triangle onto one end of each. With screws and the corner braces, fix the planks vertically each side of where you marked the sprocket.

You should end up with something similar to mine:

Put some sort of lock at the front of the base that will stop the front wheel from moving. I found some bendable metal braces that I used to secure the front wheel.

To try it out, I put the bike onto the base with the front wheel locked tightly in place.

The front wheel was locked tightly. The back wheel was sitting firmly on the stand, slightly above the base, which made it able to spin.

The next step was to take apart the hub of the back wheel to release it from the frame of the bike, put the fan belt onto the wheel then reattach the wheel to the bike frame. Find a way to attach the alternator to the wooden base. I found a piece of metal that I cut to size and drilled holes into.

Put the fan belt onto the alternator and see how far you can pull it out to make the belt tighter.

After finding the perfect spot, draw a line so you can see where to screw the piece of metal.
Next, I attached the alternator to the piece of metal then attached the fan belt with the motor.

To make the belt tighter or looser, I attached a piece of metal that looked similar to a clamp and connected it to the motor with a bolt and a nut.

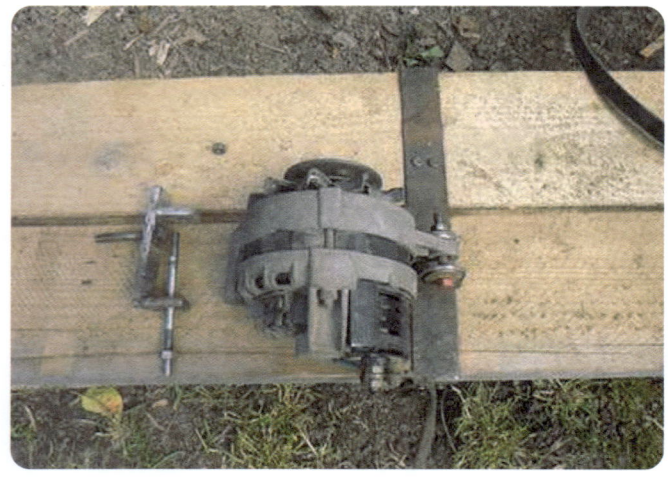

I drilled a hole into the ground to make a place for the other bolt. I also attached another piece of metal to the wood where I made the hole in order to make the bolt stronger. Now I was able to make it tighter or looser.

Because I want to show that this system really works, I prepared two light bulbs; one of them was a 12-volt, 8-watt bulb, while the other was a 110-volt 20-watt bulb. For this, I needed an inverter because of the higher voltage needed.

To set it all up I got an inverter, the battery, a soldering iron and solder, and a multimeter.

Install the voltage regulator to the alternator to add the switch. This way the alternator can be turned off and won't steal the electricity inside the battery while it's out of use. Attach the positive (red) wire to the motor.

1. Connect the negative (blue) wire to the voltage regulator.
2. Connect the switch (white wire) to the system with one end attached to the same spot on the alternator where the positive wire went. Connect the other one to the B+ (the right one) on the voltage regulator. Connect the motor to the regulator, and attach the wire to the DF on the regulator.
3. Now the button should be functioning.
4. Attach the positive and negative wires to the battery to finish.
5. To try out the system, I grabbed my soldering gun and the 12-volt light bulb. I first started out by wrapping the positive wire around the light bulb.
6. Using the solder gun, I attached the negative wire to the bottom of the bulb.

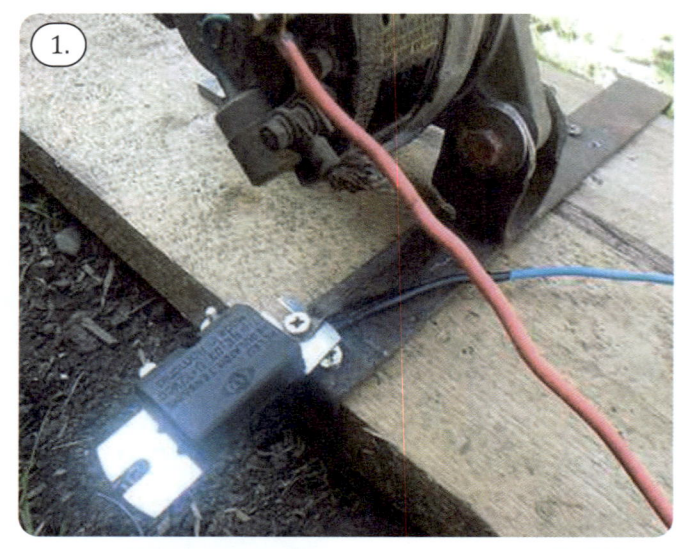

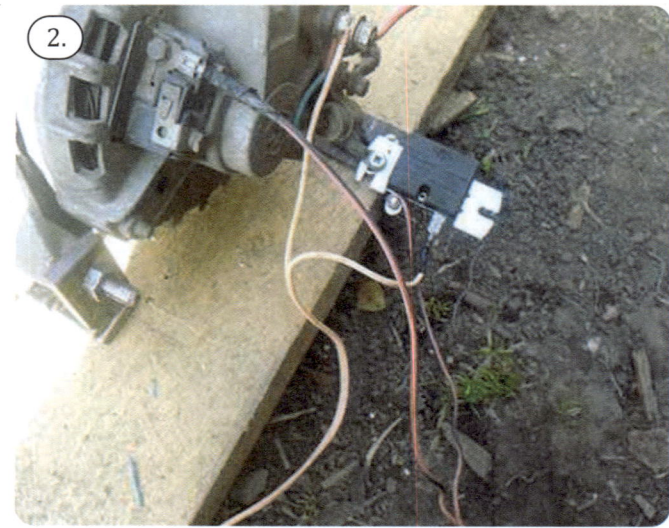

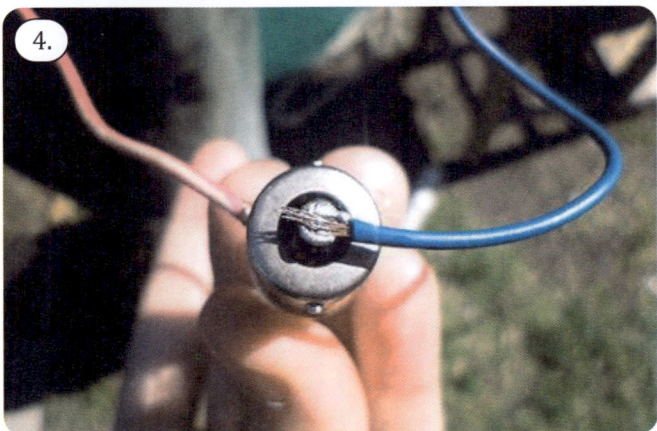

I started pedaling the bike.

The light bulb lit up with ease. You can see that the light bulb isn't attached to the battery. It is connected to the clamps of the inverter (which was turned off) and the multimeter to measure the amount we can make.

Depending on how hard you pedal, how strong the alternator is, and how big the bike wheel is, you could get different readings. I consistently got around 14–15 volts out of it.

I then put the clamps back onto the battery and turned the inverter on to see if I could light up the 110-volt light bulb.

You can see the light bulb on the ground and that the inverter is on.

# How To Build A Faraday Cage

**PROJECTS RELATED TO ELECTRICITY**

MATERIAL COST $ 44.78    EASY DIFFICULTY    30 MINUTES

Electronics have become an integral part of our lives, so much that we can hardly imagine a world without them. Unfortunately, these miracles of engineering can be taken away from us. Fortunately, there are some DIY protective measures that you can take to prevent an Electromagnetic Pulse (EMP) or a Coronal Mass Ejection (CME).

Before building a Faraday cage, we need to understand against what we are defending our sensitive electronics.

### Coronal Mass Ejection

A Coronal Mass Ejection (CME) is an eruption of magnetized plasma which occurs several times a day. Occasionally a CME will be strong enough to reach Earth. The resulting geomagnetic storm disrupts the magnetosphere when interacting with our atmosphere, compressing the day side and extending the night side. What happens is that as the magnetosphere returns to normal, a lot of energy is released towards Earth.

The result is disruption of radio communications, satellites damaged, and power transmission lines damaged. We have a few historical examples of the effects of a CME.

- The Carrington Event of 1859 resulted from a CME and profoundly affected the telegraph network in the United States and Europe, which was only a few years old. Many telegraph operators received electrical shocks, and there were reports of fires and sparks coming from the telegraph lines. In some cases, telegraph operators were able to transmit and receive messages despite the power being disconnected.
- In 1989 a CME knocked out power to large areas of Quebec for a week in some places.
- There have also been several near misses. One notable example was in 2012 when a potentially damaging CME missed the Earth. Some other CME's have delivered glancing blows to the Earth's magnetosphere, which caused brilliant auroras.

Fortunately, the current thinking is that CME's will not be a significant threat to complex electronics such that you would want to put inside of a Faraday cage. That being said, the possibility still exists that a CME may pose a threat to your electronic devices, and it is worth protecting them.

### Electromagnetic Pulse

An Electromagnetic Pulse (EMP) is a sudden burst of electromagnetic energy. This is caused by charged particles undergoing sudden and rapid acceleration. As far as preparedness is concerned, the primary source of concern regarding an EMP is a high-altitude nuclear detonation.

The United States discovered the possibility of using a nuclear bomb to generate a destructive EMP in July 1962 during the Starfish Prime test. After detonating the weapon, significant electrical damage was reported in Hawaii, which was 898 miles away. Since then, many tests have been conducted by most nuclear powers who have successfully weaponized the concept of EMP.

If there is an EMP attack, the initial effects will probably be similar to a CME in which the power grid will be disabled. In addition to this, an EMP will induce a high voltage and current in modern electronic components. The longer the conductors within electronic devices, the greater the EMP effect may be on those devices, including the cables and cords plugged into them. Essentially, if the device has electrical circuits inside, it will be vulnerable to the effects of an EMP.

## What Is a Faraday Cage?

A Faraday cage is an enclosure coated in conductive material. Equipment sensitive to electromagnetic fields is placed inside the cage to protect them from possible damage or interference from electromagnetic radiation. Faraday cages can be as simple as a foil-lined wallet to shield the RFID tags in your credit card to the copper lining in an MRI room.

A simplistic explanation of how a Faraday Cage works is that the conductor outside the cage dissipates electrostatic energy that comes in contact with it. The result is shielding of the interior of the enclosure from the effects of electromagnetic energy. As long as the electronics within the cage are insulated from the conductive exterior, they will be protected from damage.

You will want to put sensitive electronics into a

Faraday cage that you would need after a CME or an EMP attack. Some examples of equipment to store inside a Faraday cage are:

- Amateur radios
- Flashlights and headlamps
- Shortwave receivers
- Power banks
- Rechargeable Batteries and Chargers.

There is no one size fits all solution to protecting our sensitive electronics, and depending on the situation, you may want to employ different methods. These are two methods, the first being less effective but more field expedient and the second requiring some more preparation but offering a higher level of protection.

## Microwave Faraday Cage

One of the easiest Faraday cages you probably already have in your home is a household microwave oven. Microwaves have a Faraday cage built into them to protect us from the radiation that the magnetron produces. Not all microwave ovens are created equal, and before you think that yours will be an effective Faraday cage, you will need to conduct a couple of tests.

To test your microwave's effectiveness as a Faraday cage:

1. Unplug the microwave, place a cellphone inside, and close the door.
2. Call the phone, and if the call goes to voicemail, you know that the microwave is successfully blocking electromagnetic radiation.
3. You can do the same test with a radio by placing it inside the microwave. Position it so that you can see the display. If the microwave door is not transparent, put a camera inside to record the radio display during the test.
4. Close the door and transmit on another radio set to the same frequency.
5. If the radio inside the microwave does not receive the signal, you know that the microwave blocks radio frequencies.

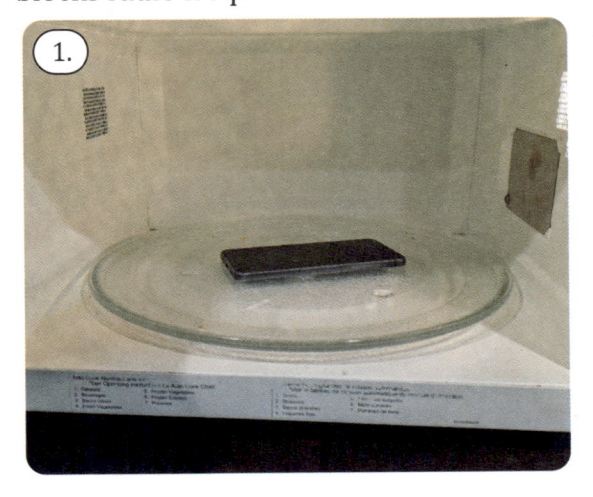

1.

3.

## Ammo Can Faraday Cage

One of the Faraday cages that I use to protect a collection of VHF ham radios is the ammo can Faraday cage. Making a Faraday cage from an ammo can is almost as easy as using a microwave and requires only a few items to construct. It is also very cost-effective, and the materials are widely available. This concept can also be adapted to any type of metal container that you may want to use.

**TOOLS:**
- Sharp knife
- Sandpaper or emery cloth

**MATERIALS:**

- One ammo can, which can be found on Amazon for $24.80USD

www.amazon.com/Box-Military-Long-Term-Waterproof-Magazine-Storage/dp/B08T7C6NX7/

- Cardboard or another material that will insulate from electrical fields
- Electrical Tape which I found on Amazon for $ 4.99 USD

www.amazon.com/Wapodeai-Electrical-Temperature-Resistance-Waterproof/dp/B07ZW-C2VLX/

- Metal Tape which you can find on Amazon for $14.99USD per roll

www.amazon.com/Professional-Grade-Aluminum-Foil-Tape/dp/B0778PTNHK/

**INSTRUCTIONS:**

1. Find a metal ammo can that is appropriate for holding the equipment you want to protect.
2. Sand the area around where the lid and the body of the ammo can meet.
3. Cut cardboard to line the interior of the ammo can.
4. Line the interior with the cardboard taping the seams with electrical tape as an added measure of insulation.
5. Place whichever items that you want to protect into the ammo can.
6. Place insulating material on top of the equipment.
7. Replace and close the lid.
8. Seal the outside seam with metal tape.
9. If you want to access the gear inside the Faraday cage quickly without having to tape the seams, you will have to remove the gasket from the lid of the ammo can. After this, you will need to line where the lid and the body contact with a conductor. The goal is to make this connection tight and electrically conductive.

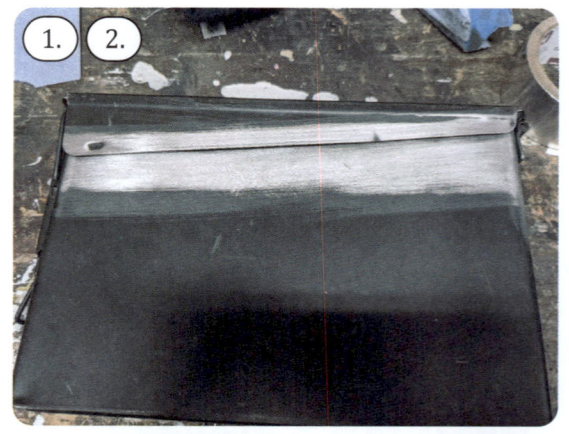

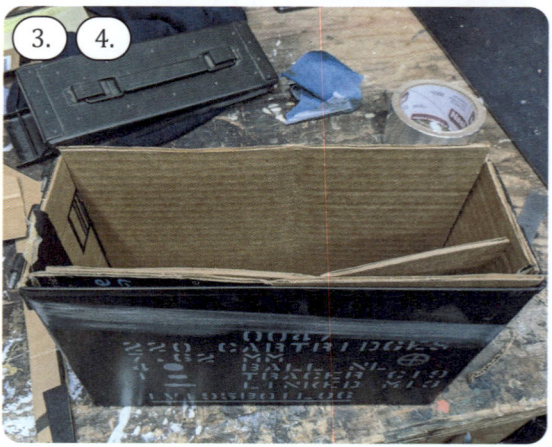

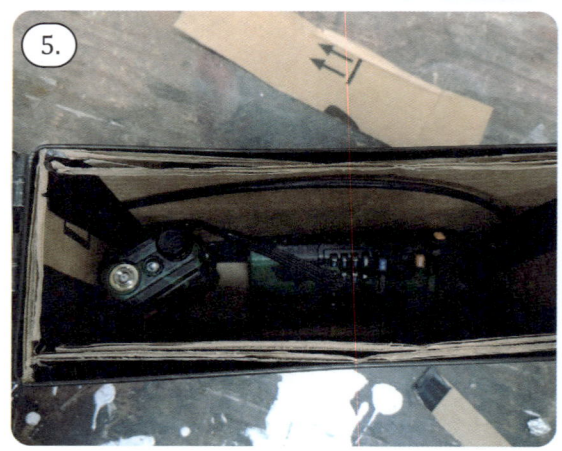

## Using a Faraday Cage

The problem with a CME or EME is that there will be no warning when they occur. If there is any equipment that you wish to protect, then they need to be stored inside of a Faraday cage all the time. Doing this is very inconvenient, especially when the seams get taped with metal tape. One option is to purchase electronic devices specifically for storage in a Faraday cage for use after a CME or EMP.

While a Faraday cage is not a perfect solution for protecting your electronics from a CME or EMP, it is a great insurance policy against possible damage or destruction of your most sensitive electronics. Since these enclosures are so cheap and easy to build, it is a good idea to have a Faraday cage or two available to keep a few radios or battery banks safe from damage.

PROJECTS RELATED TO ELECTRICITY

# How To Build A Hydroelectric Generator

**MATERIAL COST** $ 58.17    **COMPLEX** — **DIFFICULTY**    **3 HOURS**

Hydroelectric power is in wide use throughout the world, for a good reason. It is a truly renewable resource since as long as the water is flowing, you have energy that you can turn into electrical power. Most designs for DIY hydroelectric power plants involve a DC motor or a vehicle alternator, but this build will demonstrate the mechanics of how a hydroelectric generator functions imparting some knowledge in the meantime.

### How Is Hydroelectric Power Made?

Water moves through a turbine which spins, creating mechanical energy. This mechanical energy is converted to electrical energy by way of a generator. We are left with a few options for those of us who wish to DIY our hydroelectric generators. In some cases where there is a significant water flow, you can use a car alternator or DC motor attached to the turbine. The water will turn the turbine which spins the shaft of the alternator or DC motor, which will convert that mechanical energy into electrical energy.

In this build, we will construct a generator from scratch. While it may be easier to use a DC motor or alternator, preppers and survivalists need to understand the inner workings of devices like these. Only by understanding how they work, can we modify and repair our power sources when they inevitably require servicing.

### How a DIY Hydroelectric Generator Generates Electricity

The generator we will be building uses coils of magnet wire and some strong rare earth magnets to turn the mechanical energy into electrical power. How this works is that the magnets will be fixed to a disc attached to the turbine's shaft (the rotor). This disc spins over a stationary disc (the stator) that holds the coils of wire. What happens is that the magnetic fields are picked up by the coils of wire which in turn generates an electrical current in those coils of wire. This is a dramatic oversimplification, but it is basically what is happening when the magnets spin over the coils.

### Benefits and Issues with Hydroelectric Power

No method of generating electricity is without drawbacks or benefits, and hydroelectric power generation is no exception.

The main benefits of hydroelectric power are that it is clean and renewable. The process generates zero emissions and will generate power as long as the water is flowing. Hydroelectric power is also very quiet since the only sounds are the spinning of the turbine.

Some drawbacks are that when the water freezes, you lose your source of power. Along with freezing, the water source may dry up or have an insufficient flow to generate any usable power. Another issue is that your water source may be a significant distance from your home, in which case you will need to run power lines from the generator to your home. This means that there will be some loss of power along the way.

While a gas or diesel generator can produce several thousand watts of power and 120 or 220 volts of AC power, a homemade hydroelectric generator will not see high wattages like a gas generator. With some experimentation and ingenuity, you can use a generator like the one I describe to generate voltages around 12 volts.

## How to Use a Hydroelectric Generator

Powering anything directly from the generator is never a practical solution. Instead, you'll need to set up a battery bank that uses the hydroelectric generator to keep the batteries charged. To do this, you will need to determine how large a battery bank you will need to power the devices and how much input power you will need to keep the batteries topped up.

Then you can build a hydroelectric generator, after which you need to test it and come up with a baseline level of power that you can expect it to generate. Remember that these generators are running 24 hours a day, effectively charging your batteries while you sleep. If you find that the power generated by one of these generators is too low, then consider installing multiple units, all delivering power to your battery banks.

As for batteries, there are far too many options to cover here effectively, but you will need to look into charge controllers and transformers to convert AC power into DC power when setting up your off-grid power system.

## Building a Basic DIY Hydroelectric Generator

This is a very bare-bones hydroelectric generator but will serve as a fantastic foundation to build on when considering hydroelectric power. While the generator shown here does not produce a significant amount of voltage, with a few additions and modifications, you can achieve voltages of more than 12 volts.

### Tools

- Saw
- Soldering iron
- Square
- Tape measure
- Side cutters
- Razorblade or emery cloth
- Glue

### Materials

- 22AWG magnet wire is sold on Amazon for $20.98USD per one-pound spool.
www.amazon.com/BNTECHGO-AWG-Magnet-Wire-Transformers/dp/B07DYMMYSK/

- Rare earth magnets are sold on Amazon for $16.99USD per package of eight.
www.amazon.com/Super-Strong-Neodymium-Magnets-Powerful/dp/B072KDBJWC/

- 3/16" Hardboard panels are sold at Home Depot for $17.29USD a sheet.
www.homedepot.com/p/Hardboard-Tempered-Panel-Common-3-16-in-x-4-ft-x-8-ft-Actual-0-175-in-x-48-in-x-96-in-832780/202404545

- ¾" PVC pipe is available at Home Depot for $1.60USD for a 24" length.
www.homedepot.com/p/VPC-3-4-in-x-24-in-PVC-Sch-40-Pipe-22075/202300505

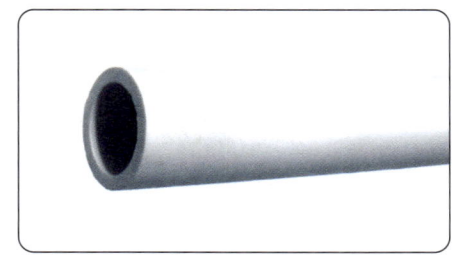

- ½" PVC pipe sold at Home Depot for $1.31USD for a 24" length.
www.homedepot.com/p/VPC-1-2-in-x-24-in-PVC-Sch-40-Pipe-22015/202300504

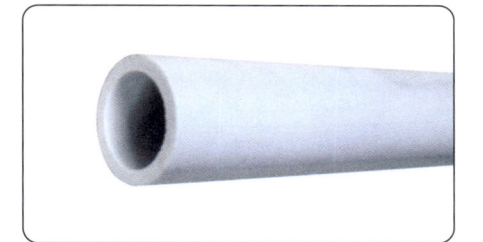

### Instructions

**BUILDING THE STATOR**

1. Wind coils of 22AWG magnet wire around a form such as ¾" PVC pipe. Leave a tag end of a few inches to accommodate joining to another coil. Wrap the wire 200 times, leaving a tag end of a few inches. Scrape the enamel off the free ends of the wire so they can be soldered together later.
2. Cut two discs from the hardboard of a diameter that will accommodate the number of coils and magnets you have chosen to use.
3. Drill a hole in the disc centre that will hold the coils large enough to accommodate the ¾" PVC pipe. This disc is what is known as the stator.
4. To attach the coils to this disc, drill holes in the disc on either side of the coil and in the centre of the coil. These holes should be appro-

priately placed and sized to thread zap straps through.
5. Arrange the coils so that the electron flow will alternate between clockwise and counter-clockwise as it moves through the coils. This is a very important step. Trace the direction that the wires are coiled from the input wire to the output wire to determine whether the coil is clockwise or counterclockwise.
6. Solder the free wires of the coils together, joining input and output wires. Leave the last set of wires free.
7. Drill two holes into the stator and install a couple of machine bolts to attach the loose wires.
8. Connect wires to the opposite side of the stator to the machine screws.
9. Test the resistance of the coils through the machine screws. You should see a reading of fewer than 10 ohms.

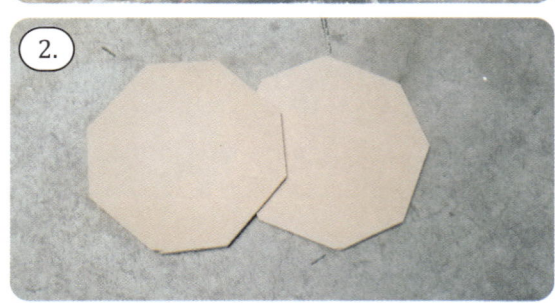

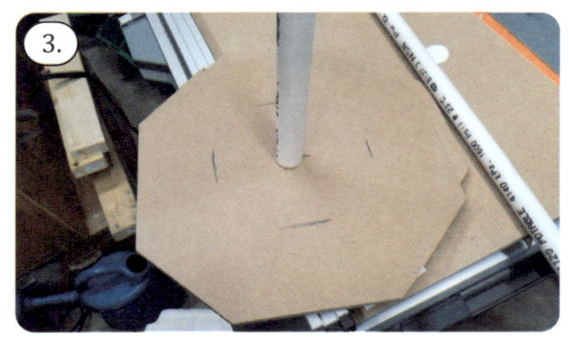

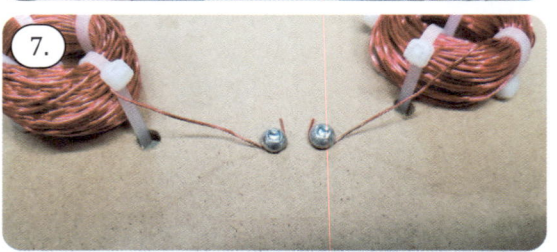

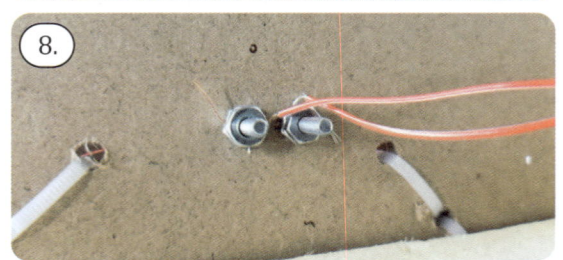

**BUILDING THE ROTOR**
1. Drill a hole in the centre of the disc that will hold the magnets sized to accommodate the ½" PVC pipe.
2. Glue or use double-sided tape to attach the magnets to this disc. Arrange them so that the North and South poles will alternate. Since my package of magnets contained eight magnets, I used all eight on my rotor.
3. Slide the disc onto the ½" PVC pipe and glue it in place. This pipe will be the axle of the generator, so make the length long enough to slide into the section of pipe attached to the stator and leave enough on the other side to accom-

modate the water wheel that we are about to construct.

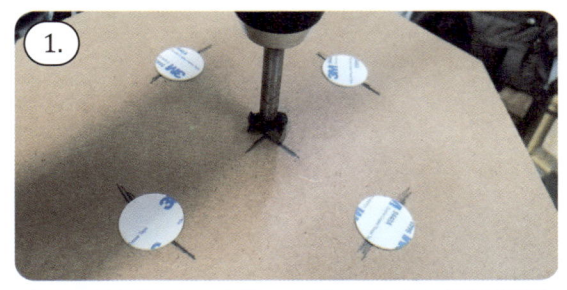

## WATER WHEEL CONSTRUCTION

1. Use the remainder of the hardboard to cut at least six rectangles three inches by five inches and two discs around 7 inches in diameter. If you want to build a larger water wheel, adjust your dimensions accordingly.
2. Cut a piece of ¾" PVC to six and a half inches.
3. Drill a hole to accommodate the PVC pipe that you just cut in the centre of each disc for your waterwheel.
4. Slide the discs onto the PVC pipe.
5. Glue and secure the rectangle pieces to the PVC pipe and between the discs to form the paddles of the water wheel.
6. Slide the water wheel onto the axle and secure it to the axle using a screw.

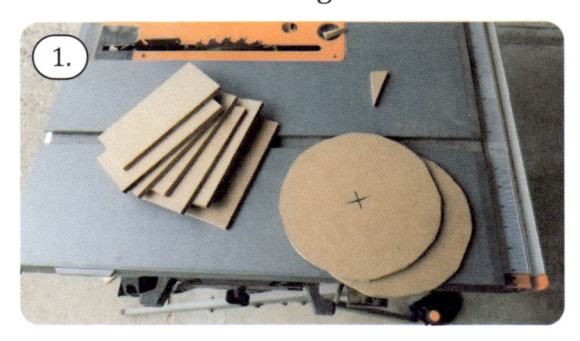

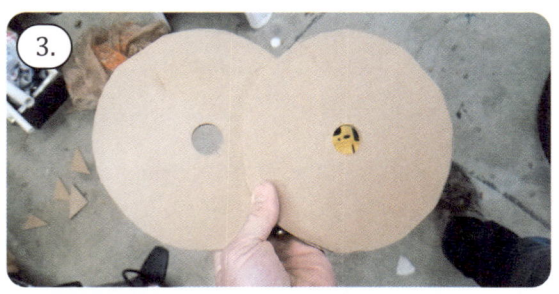

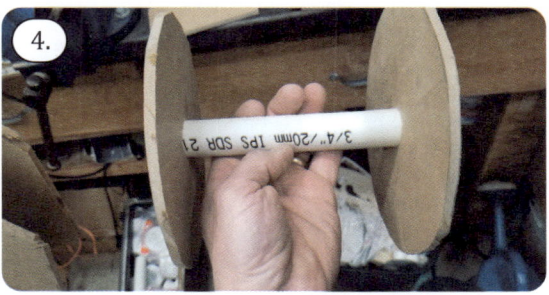

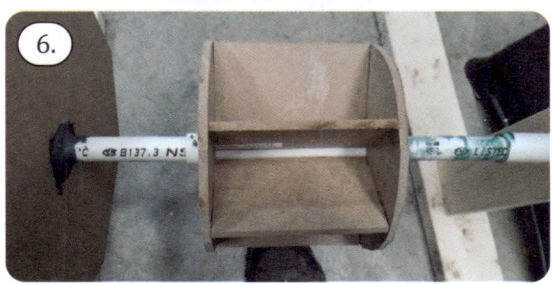

## Testing

1. Putting this device into operation depends on where the water source is and how you intend to position the generator. Before placing it in operation, test the generator to make the necessary tweaks and modifications to achieve the voltage you want.
2. I built a test jig out of old 2x4's with a hole in either side to fit a 1" PVC pipe.
3. On one side, attach the stator by sliding it onto the PVC pipe, leaving only enough sticking out to cause the rotor's magnets to be as close as possible to the coils as they spin.
4. Slide the axle into this same pipe so that the rotor's magnets are facing the coils.
5. Slide the other end of the axle into the PVC pipe on the other end of the jig.
6. Connect a multi-meter to the leads on the stator.
7. Set the multi-meter to AC voltage and use a

hose or other water source to spin the water wheel.
8. Check the voltage and make any adjustments as required.

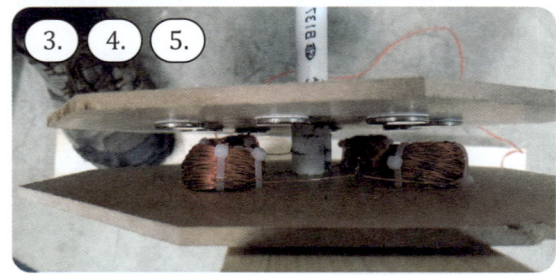

## Considerations and Modifications

- ◆ You will need to use a transformer to switch the current from AC to DC. It is possible that the charge controller that you use to control the charging of your batteries may do this for you.
- ◆ Adding coils and magnets will increase the voltage of your generator.
- ◆ Consider using bearings and grease to reduce friction, and this will increase the efficiency of the generator.
- ◆ Instead of a waterwheel, you could design a turbine or something similar along with directing the water to the best position to achieve the highest RPMs.

While this style of hydroelectric generator will not produce a lot of power, it can be adjusted, modified, and designed to be a constant source of power fed into your battery bank. The knowledge of how this generator works will potentially become very useful in a prolonged grid-down scenario allowing you to design and build your hydroelectric powerplant from materials that will be littered around a post SHTF world.

PROJECTS RELATED TO ELECTRICITY

# How To Charge Your Phone When There Is No Electricity

EASY DIFFICULTY

What would you do if the power was out and your phone battery was dead, but someone's life would depend on you being able to make a call?

You can charge your phone from another battery. Gone are the days of our grandparents. The modern society we all live in now seems to be unable to function without certain commodities. Among these, electricity seems to be at the top of the list. Electricity is something almost all of us take for granted now. It seems that, no matter what you plan on doing, you will need electricity. Whether you want to clean your house, watch a movie, read a book at night or just charge your phone, you will need electricity.

This chapter will show you how to charge your phone when no power is available - whether you want to prepare yourself in case of a power outage, a storm, or a possible EMP, or you just want to test it for yourself out of curiosity to see if it really works.

## Materials Needed

Apart from your phone and its charging cable, you will only need these four items:

- a 9V Alkaline battery
- a spring (you can take one out of a pen)
- a car charger
- some tape

## The Step-by-step Process

1. The first step is to take out the spring from a pen. Once it is out, you need to connect it to the negative terminal of the battery (The negative terminal is the bigger one.)
2. The spring will also need to touch the metal part of the car charger's side nub. Use some tape to hold the spring in place, making sure the spring is touching both the negative terminal of the battery as well as the metal nub of the car charger.
3. The next step is to connect the car charger to the positive terminal.
4. Then you need to connect your phone to the car charger using the phone's cable.

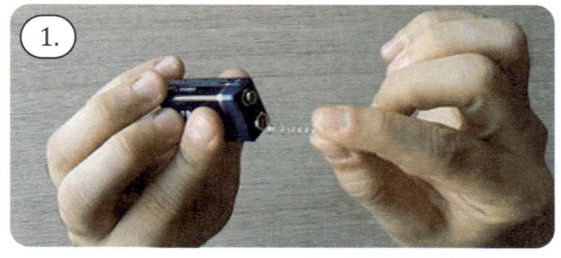

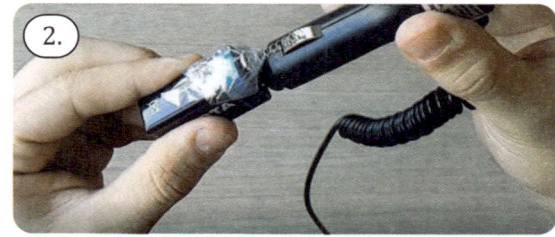

At this moment, the green light of the car charger should be on. This means your phone is being charged.

On average, a 9V battery has about 550 milli-Ampere hours (mAh), while a mobile phone's battery has 2000 mAh. This means your phone's battery will not be fully charged by using only one 9V battery. You would need about four 9V batteries to fully charge your phone, depending on what type of battery you use and what mobile phone you have. But you'll surely make a LOT of phone calls with one battery. Please see the table below for more details:

- Samsung Galaxy S6: 2,550 mAh
- Samsung Galaxy S7: 3000 mAh
- Samsung Galaxy S7 Edge: 3600 mAh
- Samsung Galaxy S8: 3000 mAh
- Apple iPhone 6s: 1715 mAh
- Apple iPhone 7: 1960 mAh
- Apple iPhone 8: 1821 mAh

Who knows, maybe this simple trick can save someone's life by allowing you to make a 911 call.

| Type | | IEC name | ANSI/ NEDA name | Typical capacity in mAh | Nominal voltages |
|---|---|---|---|---|---|
| Primary (disposable) | Alkaline | 6LR61 | 1604A | 550 | 9 |
| | | 6LP3146 | 1604A | 550 | 9 |
| | Zinc-Carbon | 6F22 | 1604D | 400 | 9 |
| | Lithium | | 1604LC | 1200 | 9 |

PROJECTS RELATED TO ELECTRICITY

# How To Get Power Out Of Dead Batteries

EASY DIFFICULTY

With so many electronic devices in our daily lives, anyone who doesn't have a good stockpile of common sized batteries is asking for trouble. While it is still possible to live without those electronic devices, we've become so accustomed to using them, and the convenience that they provide, that it would be difficult to get by without them, especially in the event of an emergency.

But there are more types of batteries today than ever before. So, between the increased types of batteries and the increased number of devices we all have, it can be challenging having all the batteries we need. If only we could make our batteries last longer; that would save us money, as well as allow us to use our survival devices longer in a crisis.

What if I were to tell you that you could? What if I were to say that "dead batteries" weren't really dead?

Let's talk a little battery theory for a moment. Small batteries fall into two basic categories: rechargeable and single use. Obviously, you can recharge batteries that are designed for it and continue using them. That's not what I'm talking about. What I'm talking about are the batteries designed for single use. We usually throw them away, once they are dead. But what is dead?

For simplicity sake, let's just talk about AA and AAA batteries. These are the most common sizes and whatever applies to them will also apply to all other single use batteries. These battery sizes, as well as C and D cells, are rated at a nominal 1.5 volts DC. I say "nominal" because new batteries actually have a higher charge, typically somewhere around 1.6 volts DC.

The devices we use generally have (use) a number of these batteries, as there is little that actually runs off of 1.5 volts (although there are some devices that do). To get more voltage, the batteries are connected in series. That means that the positive end of one battery (the one with the nipple on it) is connected to the negative end of the next (the flat end). Whenever we do that, the voltage of the batteries is added, increasing the voltage. So, we'll put two batteries in to have a nominal 3 volts or 4 batteries to have a nominal 6 volts.

Batteries produce this electrical power by chemical reaction. As the device is used, it draws power from the batteries, gradually lowering the amount of available chemicals. As this level diminishes, the voltage that the battery produces drops as well.

So, that battery which started out somewhere around 1.6 volts, will keep dropping its voltage until it hits about 1.3 volts. At that point, the device usually stops working. This is the point at which we normally say that the battery is "dead." But it really isn't. The battery just has less power than it needs to have, in order to power our device. But perhaps it can be used for something else.

**GETTING MORE OUT OF THE BATTERIES**

Okay, so if those batteries still have some power in them, all we need is some way of getting it out. To do that, we're going to do the exact same thing that we did inside the device; we're going to connect the batteries in series. The only difference is, we're going to connect more of them together, than we usually do. By doing this:

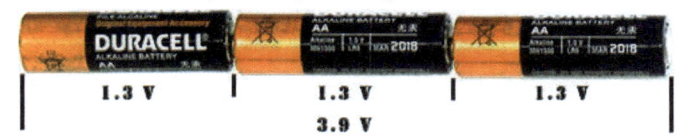

- 4 batteries provide us with 5.2 volts (1.3 x 4)
- 6 batteries provide us with 7.8 volts (1.3 x 6)
- 8 batteries provides us with 10.4 volts (1.3 x 8)
- 12 batteries provides us with 15.6 volts (1.3 x 12)

Obviously, these batteries can't be put in the device this way, because there isn't enough physical space for them inside the device. But many electronic devices have an external power connector, which we could connect to.

Many of today's electronics are designed to be able to be recharged by a computer; connecting it to the USB connector. The USB connector on your computer provides 5 volts. So do the USB chargers that plug into the wall. The main difference is that the ones which plug into the wall will provide a lot more 5 volt power than you can pull out of a USB connector on your computer. That's why some devices won't charge when connected to a computer. If you look at the battery in many of these devices (cell phones are a great example), it's actually not a 5 volt battery, but a 3.6 to 3.8 volt battery. So, as long as we are providing more than 3.6 volts to the device, it will work. We can get more than that much power out of 4 dead AA batteries.

All we need, is a way of hooking all this up together; some sort of a battery pack that will allow us to connect the batteries together, along with a connector to attach to our electronic devices.

This battery pack holds 4 AA batteries. If we put in 4 dead AA batteries, that means we've got a total of 5.2 (1.3 x 4) volts available to us. There's an intermediate connector that I've attached to it, in order to allow the same battery pack to provide power through a variety of connectors. Finally, since that's enough to run those devices that charge off of a USB connector, I've added a USB connector.

This device will now work to charge or power a cell phone, tablet or digital camera; amongst a host of other devices. All I need is a USB to micro USB adapter, something that is quite common. So, I can continue using those batteries, until their output voltage drops to 0.867 volts each. Then the batteries will have to be replaced.

## BUT THEY ARE STILL NOT DEAD

Granted, 0.867 volts doesn't sound like much, but it's still a bit over half the battery's nominal rating. So, we should be able to continue using them a while longer, just by using more batteries connected together in series, than what we had before.

If we connect six of these batteries together in a battery pack, we'll be producing 5.2 volts. If we connect eight of them together, we'll be producing 6.936. Either of these would work for powering those same USB devices. Since battery packs to hold six batteries are not that common, but battery packs for four and eight batteries are fairly common, we might be better off using the eight batteries.

Even though this sounds like too much power for the devices, it's not. All electronic devices have a voltage regulator in them. They have to, as the amount of power the batteries provide isn't constant. We've seen how it goes down. So, the "extra" voltage will be cut off, only allowing the amount of voltage that the device needs to pass through.

In real terms, there are limits to how much voltage we can give a device, before the voltage regulator can't do its job. But that's not a worry here, as we're not going over that limit. Were we to hook 12 volts to a 5 volt device, however, it would probably be too much.

So, there you have it, a great way to save money on batteries, but more importantly, a great way to get more mileage out of your batteries in an emergency survival situation.

PROJECTS RELATED TO ELECTRICITY

# How To Make Your Own Solar Panel System

**MATERIAL COST** $ 2.475   **COMPLEX** DIFFICULTY   **6 HOURS**

One of the key components to becoming self-reliant is to have the ability to produce electricity outside of the traditional power grid. However, there is a good reason why most people do not exercise energy independence. It is because generating enough renewable energy to power a home is no easy task. However, it is possible to set oneself up with an off-grid power option that will power critical components within the home, such as a refrigerator.

## Why Choose Solar?

The Sun is our constant companion during its daily transit across our sky. Since the Sun is guaranteed to rise and set each day and has predictable amounts of daily sunlight, it makes sense that we should convert some of that solar energy into electrical energy.

However, not all areas of the globe are equally suited to use solar power as an off-grid power solution.

Those who live in arid environments can expect to see an unobstructed Sun daily. Therefore, solar power is a very good option since the generous amounts of sunlight will provide maximum output from solar panels. However, suppose we travel further North to above the arctic circle where the Sun's angle is very low with protracted periods of darkness. In that case, solar power can still be used but requires other forms of renewable energy to pick up the slack.

### Pros and Cons of Solar Power

Solar power is currently in wide use as an alternative to the traditional means of generating electricity, and like all the other methods, it has its pros and cons.

### PROS

- It does not rely on mechanical or moving parts to generate power, which means less maintenance and breakdowns.
- In some areas, electricity can be sold back into the power grid, generating some income to offset the costs of setting up the system.
- Solar panels have a long lifespan.
- Modern systems have become efficient enough to generate electricity on overcast days.

### CONS

- Generates no power at night.
- The panels need to be oriented to take full advantage of the Sun's transit across the sky to optimize the system for maximum efficiency.
- Solar panels can be covered in snow or damaged by hail.

Solar power should not be relied on as your only means of off-grid power. Instead, you should have another method of generating enough electricity to recharge your system's battery bank. Ideally, this alternate power should be renewable energy, but a gas or diesel generator is acceptable.

### SAFETY

Before continuing, you need to educate yourself about the risks of setting up a solar power system, like the one I will describe here. The amperages involved throughout the system can deliver electrical shocks, which have the potential to be fatal. Exercise extreme caution in all aspects of installing and using this system, and make yourself aware of all the rules, regulations, and building codes in your area before constructing your solar power system. Also, exercise caution in all aspects of installing and using this system, and make yourself aware of all the rules, regulations, and building codes in your area before constructing your solar power system. Also, exercise extreme caution when installing panels on your roof, as a fall can result in serious injury or death.

## Basic Electrical Terminology

This chapter will use a lot of technical jargon when describing the components of the solar power system. A basic overview of these terms and what they represent is useful at this point.

**Volt (V)** - Voltage is the measure of electrical force to produce current.

**Amp (A)** - An ampere is the measure of the flow of current through the conductor.

**Watt (W)** - A watt is a way we measure electrical

power. To find the wattage, we only need to multiply the Volts by Amps.

**Ampere-Hour (Ah)** - A unit of measurement used to represent battery capacity. For example, a 10Ah battery will provide 10A of power for one hour.

**Watt-hours (Wh)** - A watt-hour is the number of watts of energy used in one hour.

**Direct Current (DC)** - Direct current is an electric current that flows in one direction only. DC power is often associated with electrical circuits powered by batteries.

**Alternating Current (AC)** - Is an electrical current that reverses direction multiple times a second. Most household appliances operate on AC power.

# Essential Components of a Solar Power System

Solar power systems can become very complex, but when we break it down to the basics, they all have a few basic components: solar panels, a charge controller, an inverter, and a bank of batteries.

## Batteries

The battery bank is the heart and soul of your solar power system, along with probably being the most expensive component. Batteries come in a wide variety of voltages, but since 12 volts is the most common voltage for a small solar power system, I will be using this voltage throughout this chapter. Of course, there are many reasons you would want a higher or lower voltage battery bank, but to keep this instructional as basic as possible, I will stick to describing a simple 12-volt solar power system. There are many battery choices, but I will speak to the most commonly used battery types and their strengths and weaknesses.

### Lead Acid Batteries

Lead-acid batteries are a popular choice for solar battery banks mainly because they are more affordable than lithium. Lead-acid batteries are also the oldest form of rechargeable battery, and chances are there is a lead-acid battery under the hood of your car.

Lead-acid batteries come in two main types: Flooded Lead Acid (FLA) and Absorbent Glass Mat (AGM).

#### a) FLA Batteries

FLA batteries are filled with liquid electrolytes that are responsible for storing and delivering electricity. This means that FLA batteries need to be stored upright and require good ventilation since they release toxic gasses. FLA batteries also require regular maintenance and are large and heavy. They are, however, cheaper than both lithium and AGM batteries.

#### b) AGM Batteries

AGM batteries, on the other hand, have fibreglass inside of them to suspend the electrolytes. Storing the electrolyte in this way means that the batteries do not have to remain upright. Also, they require no maintenance and do not release any toxic gasses.

Regardless of the type of lead-acid battery, **DO NOT** discharge them below 50 percent of their capacity. This means a lead-acid battery bank that is 600ah will only have 300ah of usable capacity, so keep this in mind when designing your system.

### Lithium Batteries

Lithium batteries are available in many types, but the one most commonly used in solar power systems is Lithium Iron Phosphate (LiFePO4). These batteries are far lighter and smaller than SLA batteries, as well as being more efficient. These batteries have a few advantages over their SLA counterparts, most notably that they are safer and more stable. In addition, lithium batteries are designed to be discharged much deeper than SLA batteries, up to 80% of their capacity.

One significant disadvantage is that lithium batteries are far more expensive than SLA batteries, which often financially put them out of reach.

## Solar Panels

Eventually, your battery bank will need a recharge, and in a grid-down situation, you will need to seek renewable power sources. For example, solar panels harness the Sun's energy and convert it into electric current through the photovoltaic effect. What happens is that photons from the Sun get absorbed by the solar cells in the panel, which causes electrons to excite and become free. These free electrons are what creates the electrical current. Solar panels come in various shapes and sizes. When we talk about the size of a solar panel, we usually refer to the number of watts they produce under full and direct sunlight. Solar panels can be flexible, with some models which can be rolled up or folded.

## Charge Controller

A charge controller does more than regulating the flow of current from your panels to the battery bank. They prevent the battery bank from both over and undercharging. They also distribute power to any DC loads that you have connected to the charge controller. This component is one of the most important to install since it protects the most costly part of your solar power system.

Charge controllers come in two types: Pulse Width Modulation (PWM) and Maximum Power Point Tracking (MPPT).

**PWM controllers** turn on and off rapidly, acting as a throttle for the power coming from the solar panels to the batteries. These charge controllers are an older technology and require that the nominal voltage of the solar panels match the voltage of the batteries. As a result, PWM charge controllers are less efficient than their MPPT counterparts, but they are often better for smaller solar power projects since they are less expensive.

**MPPT controllers** can be up to 30% more efficient than PWM controllers and can handle higher voltages from solar panels. These charge controllers will continuously monitor the power levels generated by the panel and automatically adjust to find the best combination of voltage and current to deliver the most power to the batteries.

## Inverter

Solar power systems produce direct current (DC), which is incompatible with household appliances that use alternating current (AC). The device that we use to convert DC to AC is an inverter. Manufacturers classify their inverters based upon the number of output watts. When selecting an inverter, we need to choose one that can produce greater wattage than the number of watts we expect our appliances to consume. It is important to buy an inverter that delivers enough power to handle the momentary power surge when some devices start; in the case of a fridge, that surge of power can be 1500 Watts!

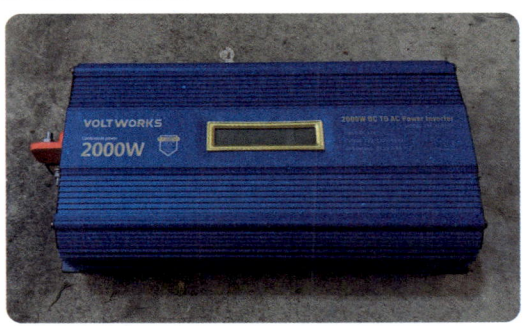

Inverters are classified not only by their output wattage but also classified by how they convert power. Most inverters that you will find are going to be either pure sine wave or modified sine wave. **Pure Sine Wave** inverters produce a waveform that most closely resembles the grid's AC power. Pure sine wave inverters are needed if you want to tie your solar power system into grid power or if you plan on running complex electronics from solar energy. They are also preferred for larger systems.

**Modified Sine Wave** inverters don't produce the clean sine wave that a pure sine wave inverter does. Instead, the waveform is more choppy, and while this is ok for some devices, any complex or delicate electronics should not be connected to a modified sine wave inverter.

## Battery Monitor

Battery monitors are not required, but they can help you track and monitor the usage and state of your battery bank. In addition, they can help you to get a better understanding of the capacity left in your battery bank instead of simply monitoring the voltage and making an educated guess as to how close to 50% of capacity your SLA batteries are. Try to find charge controllers of inverters that include a battery monitor.

## Cables and Wiring

To tie all of this together will be a mess of cables and wires, with every wire and connection being a possible failure point. It is very important to select the proper wire size for each part of the system and ensure that the appropriate connectors are in

the correct places.
- Wires that run from the solar panels to the charge controllers need to be water-resistant and usually come with an MC-4 connector which forms a water-tight seal when plugged together.
- The battery cable needs to be rated for the amount of power you plan to run through them. Therefore, it is good to oversize the cables and follow the manufacturer's recommendations when purchasing them.
- It is also advisable to install a fuse or breaker on the positive cable that leads from the positive battery terminal to the inverter. Doing this will prevent the inverter from trying to draw too much amperage from the batteries.

# Designing a Solar Power System

Designing a solar power system can be a very complex process, but it need not be. As long as you take the process step by step, you will be able to determine how your system will look with relative ease.

Start by answering a few questions:

## 1. WHAT ARE YOU GOING TO POWER?

The appliances that you are going to power with your solar power system is the primary driving factor in the design of your system. So, to begin, write a list of all the appliances you want to run from your solar power system.

**For Example:**
- Refrigerator
- Lights
- Charge laptop and phones
- Freezer
- Microwave

Once you have a list, make a table including the Watts the appliance uses on average. Include a column for the number of hours in a day that the device will be used.

**For Example:**

| APPLIANCE | WATTS | HOURS OF USE |
|---|---|---|
| Fridge | 100 | 24 |
| Lights | 60 | 5 |
| Laptop | 8 | 2 |
| Phone | 6 | 2 |
| Microwave | 1000 | .5 |
| Freezer | 50W | 24 |

Add a fourth column to multiply the wattage and hours for each appliance giving you the Wh. Add this column to determine the daily Wh for the appliances you want to run in a grid-down scenario.

**For Example:**

| APPLIANCE | WATTS | HOURS OF USE | WATT-HOURS |
|---|---|---|---|
| Fridge | 100 | 24 | 2400 |
| Lights | 60 | 5 | 300 |
| Laptop | 8 | 2 | 16 |
| Phone | 6 | 2 | 12 |
| Microwave | 1000 | .5 | 500 |
| Freezer | 50W | 24 | 1200 |
| TOTAL Wh | | | 4428 |

As you can see from the above table, this example gives us a daily Wh of 4428, which we could round up to be 4500Wh. So that means that your solar panels need to deliver a minimum of 4500Wh of power over a day to replace the energy you used in the battery bank. This does not consider the inefficiency of the inverter or that some days will produce less power than others. In reality, your solar panels will need to create an excess of power to charge your batteries sufficiently.

## 2. HOW MANY PANELS DO YOU NEED?

Before calculating how many panels you need to deliver that much power, you first need to determine how many hours of peak sunlight your panels are likely to receive. Fortunately, there are many online resources that you can use to find out how many hours of peak sunlight you can expect. One such resource is this:

unboundsolar.com/solar-information/sun-hours-us-map

Let us say, as an example, your area receives 5 hours of peak sunlight a day. That means, in five hours, your panels need to produce at least 4500 watts of electricity.

Let's assume that you are going to use 200W solar panels, and they are optimally placed. Then, all we need to do is multiply the panel's wattage by the hours of peak sunlight. So, if your location gets 5 hours of peak sunlight a day, we can determine how much power each panel will provide during a day.

**For Example:**

**200W** Panel x **5** Hours Peak Sunlight = **1000W** of daily power.

Our example appliance's daily power consumption would require at least five 200W solar panels! This chapter will centre around building a system to power only a small refrigerator for 24 hours a day instead of a list of appliances. This will provide a basic and clear picture of the steps involved and give you, the reader, the foundation to build your system.

If we select an average household fridge, we can expect average power consumption of 100W to 400W depending on the size, how often the doors are opened, how much thermal mass it is cooling, etc. In this example, I will use the low end of the wattage scale to demonstrate what a system that achieves the bare minimum would look like.

Once we do the math, we can determine what the average daily Wh for our fridge is.

**100W** x **24** hours = **2400Wh** a day

In this example, we only need three 200W panels to replenish the power that our refrigerator uses with 600W of power to spare, as long as we get five hours of peak sunlight each day. The extra capacity will come in handy for days where clouds obscure the Sun or that you need some extra energy to charge devices.

### 3. HOW BIG OF A BATTERY BANK DO YOU NEED?

Now that you know how to size your solar panels, we need to figure out how big a battery bank we need to run our fridge. One question we need to ask first off is:

### 4. HOW MANY DAYS DO WE WANT THE BATTERY TO PROVIDE POWER WITHOUT CHARGING?

There may be cases where your solar panels are not producing enough current to charge the battery bank. We need to account for this when designing our system. While it is a good idea to have a battery bank that will power your appliance for a week without needing a charge, this will result in a large and expensive battery bank. Being prepared for an extra day without the ability to charge the bank is a good start.

We know that our fridge will use 2400Wh a day, and if we want two days of autonomy, we will have a total power requirement of 4800Wh. These figures are AC power though, what we need is to know how much DC power we need.

### 5. HOW DO WE FIGURE OUT HOW MUCH DC POWER WE NEED TO PROVIDE THE REQUIRED AC POWER?

Next, we need to know what our inverter inefficiency is. When an inverter converts DC to AC power, some of that power is lost in the process. We need to account for this when calculating the power the battery needs to provide the inverter. For example, if your inverter is 90% efficient, you need to add 10% to your AC watt-hours to find the DC watt-hours.

**Example:**
10% of 4800Wh is 480Wh, so we need to add these together for our required DC input power to the inverter.

**4800 + 480 = 5280Wh** of DC power

### 6. HOW DO WE CONVERT WH INTO AH TO PICK THE RIGHT BATTERIES?

Now that we have arrived at a figure for the amount of power our battery bank needs to deliver, we must figure out how big that battery bank needs to be. Since batteries are measured in Amp-hours (Ah), not Watt-hours (Wh), we need to do some math to convert these values.

The formula for converting Wh to Ah is either:

**Wh=Ah*V**  or  **Ah=Wh/V**

If our system is going to be a 12V system, we can plug the values into the equations like this:

**Ah=5280Wh/12V**

This gives us **440Ah** as our battery size for two days of autonomy from needing to be recharged.

If you are like me and have alternate plans for charging batteries without the Sun and want the battery bank to be only enough to power the fridge for 24 hours a day with the batteries recharging every day, then the battery bank size would be **220Ah**.

The longer you want the batteries to power your appliance without recharging, the larger the system's capacity. So in this example, the battery bank capacities in relation to days with no recharging would look like this.

| | |
|---|---|
| Zero days - **220Ah** | Four days - **1100Ah** |
| One day - **440Ah** | Five days - **1320Ah** |
| Two days - **660Ah** | Six days - **1540Ah** |
| Three days - **880Ah** | Seven days - **1760Ah** |

As you can see, a battery bank that will sustain your fridge for a week of no sun would be very large and expensive.

### 7. HOW MANY BATTERIES TO BUY?

Now that we have the number of Ah required to power a fridge 24/7, we need to buy and install batteries for the battery bank. On the less expensive side are the SLA batteries, which are larger and heavier than lithium batteries. However, SLA batteries can not be discharged below 50%, which means that the total capacity of the battery bank needs to be double the required Ah to account for this.

On the other hand, lithium batteries can be discharged much deeper, so the total capacity of the battery bank can be closer to the required Ah of the system.

In this example project, I selected deep-cycle AGM batteries, which are 100Ah each. The six batteries of my battery bank, when connected in parallel, give me a voltage of 12V and 600Ah of total capacity or 300Ah of usable capacity.

The number and capacities of batteries you buy will be largely determined by the availability of the batteries and the space you have available to store them.

**8. HOW DO I WIRE THE BATTERIES TOGETHER?**

There are two ways that batteries are wired together, and each of these methods gives a different result.

**Series** – Wiring a battery bank in series means that the first battery has its negative terminal connected to the positive terminal of the next battery and the positive terminal connected to the negative terminal of the next battery. This is repeated throughout the battery bank. Doing this increases the overall voltage of the bank while keeping the capacity in Ah the same.

**Parallel** – Wiring a battery bank in parallel means that all the positive terminals are connected, and the negative terminals are connected. What this does is increase the overall capacity of the battery bank while keeping the voltage the same.

## Building the Battery Bank

The battery bank is the most expensive part of your solar power system. Therefore, it is important to store the batteries in an area where they are kept safe from damage and do not pose a safety hazard to others in your home. One way to secure a battery bank is to build a shelf or box for them.

In my case, I wanted to build a rolling battery box that could also hold the charge controller and inverter. It would be good to roll the batteries from one location to another without removing all the batteries, only to set them up again in another area.

### Tools Required

- Saw
- Drill with bits and drivers
- Tape measure and square
- Vice for crimping lugs or the proper crimping tool

### Materials

- Batteries – I used Sealed Lead Acid Batteries similar to these that are available on Amazon for $ 274.99 USD each
www.amazon.com/dp/B00YB26RYG

- Battery Cable – What I used was similar to this available on Amazon for $ 152.97 USD and includes cable lugs
www.amazon.com/Welding-Battery-Flexible-Terminal-Connectors/dp/B01MD1YL1I

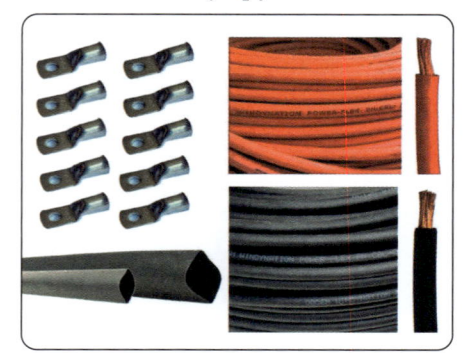

- 2 x 4 Lumber – Available at Home Depot for $ 8.37 USD each
www.homedepot.com/p/2-in-x-4-in-x-8-ft-Premium-Kiln-Dried-Whitewood-Framing-Stud-Lumber-96022/315592380

- Casters – These are available from Amazon for $22.99USD for a set of four
www.amazon.com/Casters-Locking-Polyurethane-Castors-HARDWARE/dp/B08HS381FH

- Charge Controller – This is the one I used which is $ 69.99 USD on Amazon
www.amazon.com/Controller-Discharge-Regulator-Protection-Anti-Fall/dp/B083KN9H22/

- Inverter – I used this one which is $ 189.99 USD on Amazon
www.amazon.com/Inverter-2000Watt-120Volt-Control-Display/dp/B07R511SR8

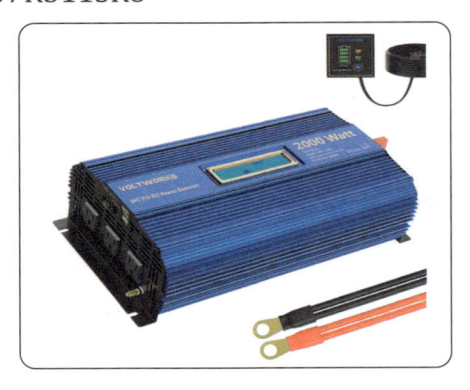

## Construction of the Battery Bank

1. Begin by measuring your batteries and figuring out what configuration you want the batteries to be. I laid the batteries out in a 2 x 3 configuration with a little space between each battery. Suppose you have a significant amount of batteries; you may not want to construct the rolling unit that I am. Instead, build a basic shelf and do not store the batteries on bare concrete.
2. Once I had my overall size, I cut material to make a basic frame for the bottom of my battery bank.
3. Once cut, I screwed all the pieces together, making the base of my battery bank.
4. I flipped the frame over and screwed the casters in place.
5. I loaded all the batteries onto the frame.
6. Once all the batteries were in their final orientation, I measured the distances between the terminals of the batteries to determine the cut size for my battery cables.
7. I cut the appropriate number and lengths of cables to connect the terminals in a parallel configuration.
8. I then crimped the lugs to each end of the cables.
9. Once the cables were put together, I wired the battery bank in parallel. I made sure to connect the positive terminals first then the negative terminals.
10. Once the battery bank is wired, I measured the overall height for a shelf to mount the inverter and charge controller.
11. I then measured my inverter so I could cut lumber to build the shelf to mount it.
12. I cut lumber to make four uprights that would hold up my shelf. I also cut two cross members to complete this shelf. I then attached these pieces to the battery bank.
13. I mounted both the inverter and the charge controller to the shelf.
14. Finally, I wired the batteries to the charge controller and inverter. I first connected the positive cable from the positive terminal on the charge controller to the first positive battery terminal. Then, I also wired the positive cable from the inverter to the same positive battery terminal.
15. I connected the negative cable from the inverter to the negative terminal on the same battery.
16. I connected the negative cable from the charge controller to the negative terminal on the last battery in the battery bank. This allows for more even charging of the battery bank than if I connected the positive and negative cables to the same battery in the system.

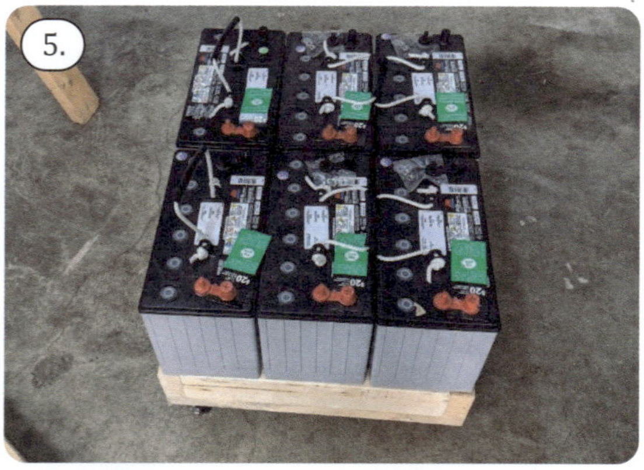
5.

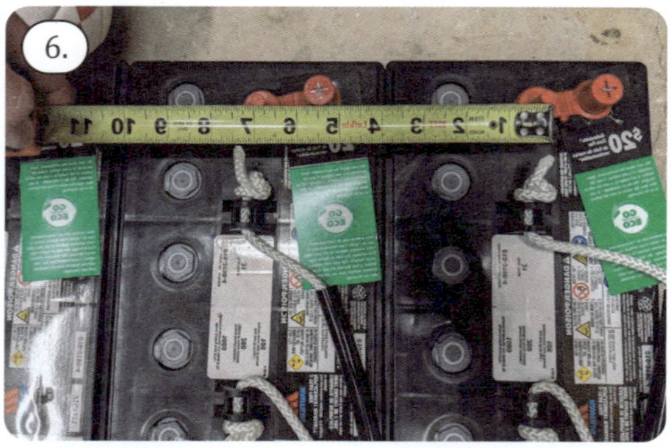
6.

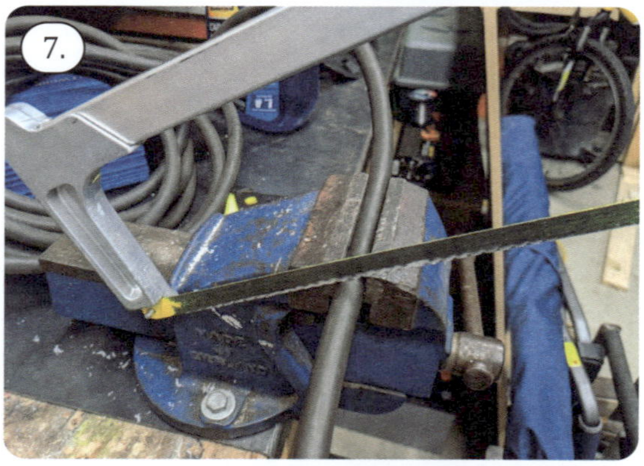
7.

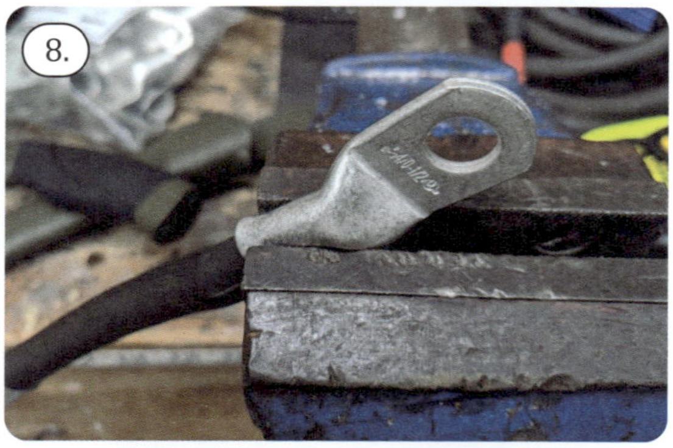
8.

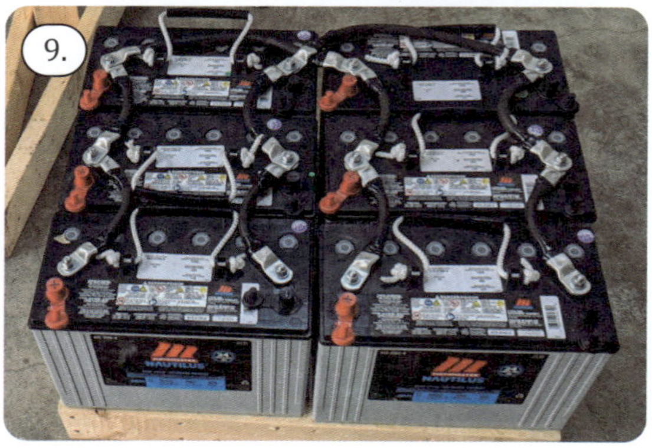
9.

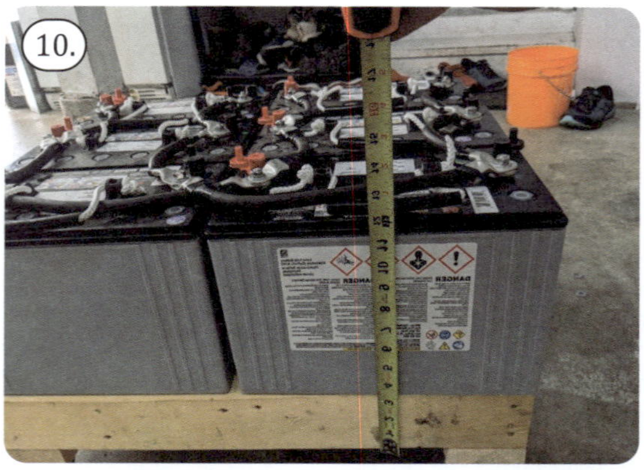
10.

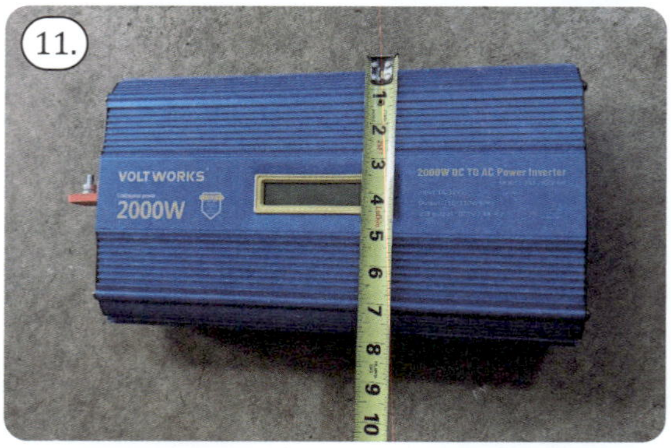

11.

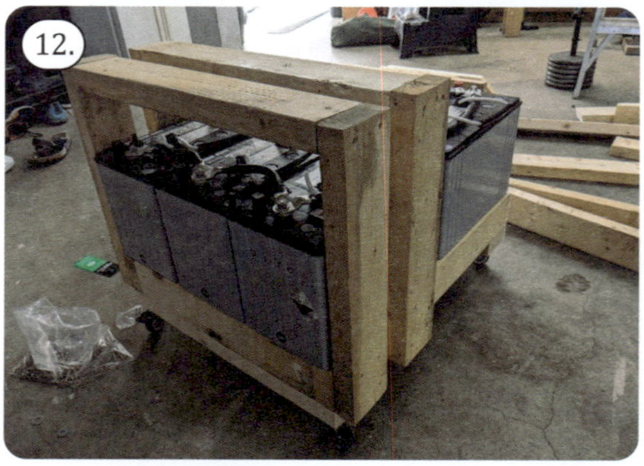
12.

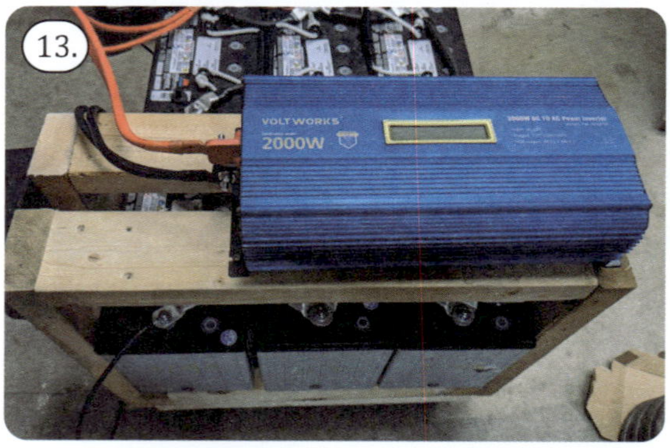

13.

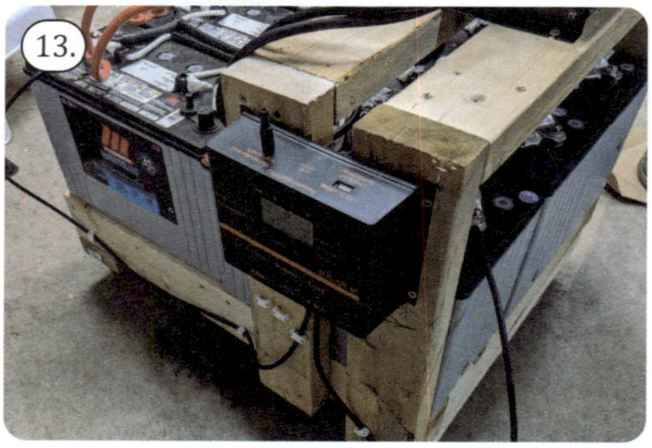
13.

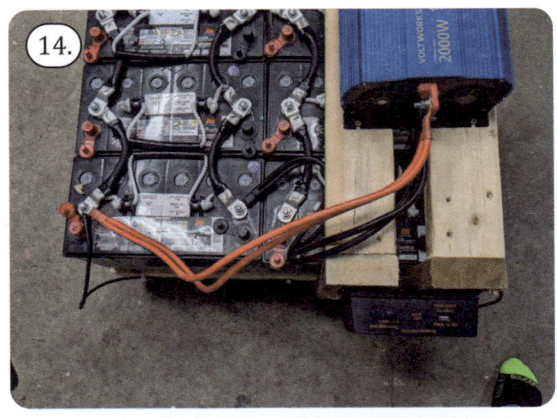

## Considerations

There are several considerations when putting a battery bank together.

- First is the type of batteries in the system. Flooded lead-acid batteries need to be stored upright and have off-gassing and maintenance concerns, while AGM batteries can be stored in any position and don't produce dangerous gases. Lithium batteries, on the other hand, are considered to be very safe and stable. Always check the manufacturer's instructions and safety guidelines before building your battery bank.
- Always connect the positive cable first and always disconnect the negative cable first.
- Keep the inverter and charge controller close to the battery bank to cut down on the power loss that will result from long runs of wire.
- Store the battery bank in an area with no flammable materials in case of sparks igniting any combustible gases.

## Installation and Wiring of the Solar Panels

There are a lot of methods and places that a solar panel can be mounted. The problem is that there are so many different roofing materials and styles that it is impossible to demonstrate how to mount the panels to a roof adequately. That being said, the positioning, wiring, and considerations are universal and will be described in detail here.

## Deployment of Solar Panels

There are a couple of ways that we can deploy solar panels. First, we can permanently mount them to our roofs to catch the most sunlight over a day. There are also motorized mounts that solar panels can be mounted on, which track the Sun's course through the sky. Unfortunately, these mounts are very expensive and probably out of reach financially for most people.

Permanently mounting a solar panel is a great option because it allows for a constant power flow to the charge controller. The only downside of this setup is that if you only intend to use the power system for emergencies, it may not be practical to have permanent panels on your roof, risking damage.

Solar panels can also be deployed when needed and stored inside when not required. This gives you the flexibility to deploy either full-sized solar panels or smaller folding solar panels. It also gives you the ability to alter the angle and position of the panels to make the best use of the available sunlight.

## Ideal Solar Panel Placement

Try to place solar panels to expose them to a maximum amount of direct sunlight to deliver the highest power levels to your battery bank. Unfortunately, since most of us could not dream of affording solar panels that track the Sun through the sky, we will have to do the best with what we have. In the Northern Hemisphere, solar panels should face True South, and the opposite is true for the Southern Hemisphere. This is because the Earth's tilt places the Sun to the South in the Northern Hemisphere and vice versa. Placing the panels in this way is the best way to maximize their exposure to the Sun's rays.

To best catch the Sun's energy, it is recommended to tilt the solar panels as well. As a rule of thumb, the tilt angle will equal the latitude where the panels are situated. So, for example, if you live at 50 degrees latitude, you should tilt your panels so they are at 50 degrees.

## Realistic Solar Panel Placement

Most of us will place solar panels on the roof of our homes or have panels that we can deploy rapidly in an emergency. However, as far as mounting panels to the roof goes, you are limited by which direction your roof faces and the pitch.

There are options for tilting roof-mounted panels

to achieve the ideal angle, but if you may not have areas of your roof that face the appropriate direction. You can either place panels on the ground or position roof panels exposing them to whatever sunlight you can. Less than ideal conditions may result in adding many more solar panels to your array to make up for the inefficiencies.

## Wiring Solar Panels

How you wire your solar panels has a lot to do with what charge controller you have. MPPT charge controllers are designed with panels wired in series, while PWM charge controllers pair with panels connected in parallel.

Wiring our panels in series is similar to what happens when we wire batteries in series. The voltage increases, but the current capacity stays the same. In comparison, wiring our panels in parallel keep the voltage the same but increases the current capacity.

When we wire panels in series, the whole system will fail if something happens to one panel. So, for example, if one panel were under some shade, it would drag the rest of the system down with it. Panels wired in parallel do not suffer this fate. Instead, if one panel fails, the current will bypass the failed panel.

## Mounting Panels on the Roof

Do not attempt to fabricate brackets or mounts for your solar panels. Instead, purchase installation brackets designed for the style and type of roofing material that you have.

Some examples of mounting systems are:
- Here is an example of a bracket that can adjust to achieve the proper tilt and costs $ 39.99 USD:
www.amazon.com/Adjustable-Brackets-support-Surface-off-grid/dp/B00IYWBOLA/

- These are very simple brackets that cost $ 11.39 USD but don't allow for tilting:
www.amazon.com/Renogy-Solar-Mounting-Bracket-Supporting/dp/B00BR3KFKE/

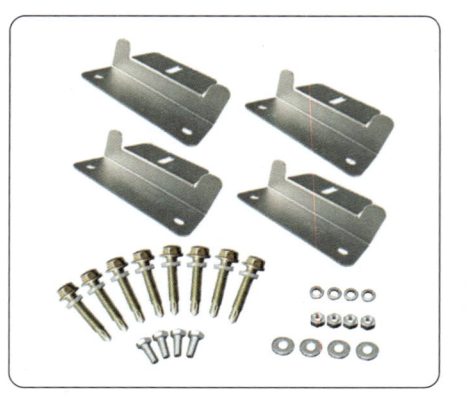

Always exercise caution and keep safety in mind when installing panels on your home's roof. If there is any doubt about your ability to complete the task effectively, it is best to hire professionals to do it for you.

## DIY Ground Mounting Option

It may be the best option to install your panels on ground level, in which case you will need to build some stands to hold the panels at the appropriate angle. These are very easy to construct and only require some easily obtained lumber and screws.

**MATERIALS**
- 200W Solar Panels – I used these which are sold on Amazon for $ 184.99 USD a pair
www.amazon.com/WEIZE-Watt-Monocrystalline-Solar-Panel/dp/B08721CBST/

- Heavy gauge wire with MC-4 Connectors – What I used was similar to these, which are

available on Amazon for $ 144.99 USD
www.amazon.com/WindyNation-Gauge-Black-Extension-Connector/dp/B01D7VBT2G/

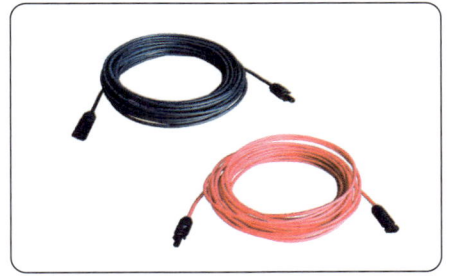

- MC-4 'Y' Cables – Like these that are sold on Amazon for $ 8.49 USD
www.amazon.com/PowMr-Branch-Connectors-Parallel-Connection/dp/B0822QMRCW/

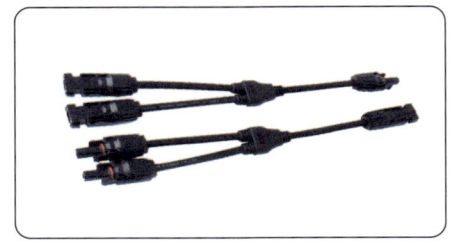

- 2 x 4 lumber - Available at Home Depot for $ 8.37 USD each
www.homedepot.com/p/2-in-x-4-in-x-8-ft-Premium-Kiln-Dried-Whitewood-Framing-Stud-Lumber-96022/315592380

**INSTRUCTIONS**
1. Measure the length and width of your solar panel.
2. Cut lumber to build the frame on which the panel will rest. Make sure this frame will go at least halfway up the panel. Assemble these pieces by screwing them together.
3. Lean the frame against a wall and use an angle finder to position it for the appropriate amount of tilt.
4. Lay a 2x4 on the floor alongside your frame. Butt the end of the 2x4 to the wall and scribe a line where the frame and this 2x4 intersect. Cut along this line and use this piece as a template for all the bottom side supports.
5. Cut lumber to build the frame on which the panel will rest. Make sure this frame will go at least halfway up the panel. Assemble these pieces by screwing them together.
6. Lean the frame against a wall and use an angle finder to position it for the appropriate amount of tilt.
7. Cut and install a cross-member to add additional support.
8. Install the solar panel.

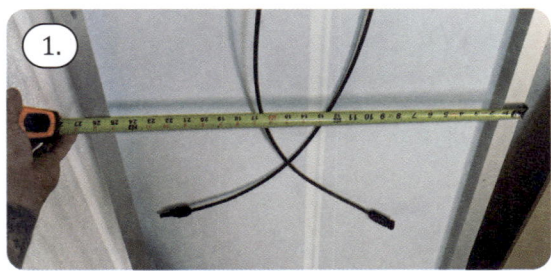

## Wiring the Panels in Parallel

In my case, I want to connect my panels in parallel because the charge controller that I selected is PWM and not MPPT.

When connecting wires to panels and panels to charge controllers, **ALWAYS COVER THE PANELS**, so they do not generate any current when making the connections.

1. Start by identifying which connector on the solar panel is negative and which is positive.
2. Connect the positive leads by using a 'Y' connector or a coupler.
3. Connect the negative leads in the same way.
4. Next, take a length of extension cable with a male connector on one end and a female connector on the other end that is twice the distance from your solar panel to the charge controller. We need the length to be twice the size required because what we want to do is cut this cable in half to get one positive and one negative cable.
5. Find the halfway point.
6. Cut and strip the cable.
7. Mark the positive and negative ends, then connect to the charge controller.
8. Connect the positive end to the positive side of the panels, then connect the negative end to the negative side of the panels.

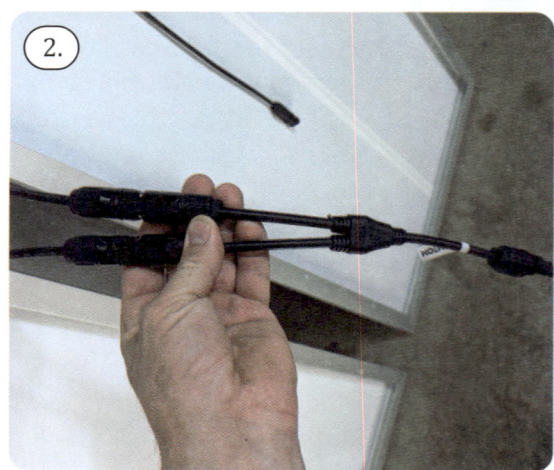

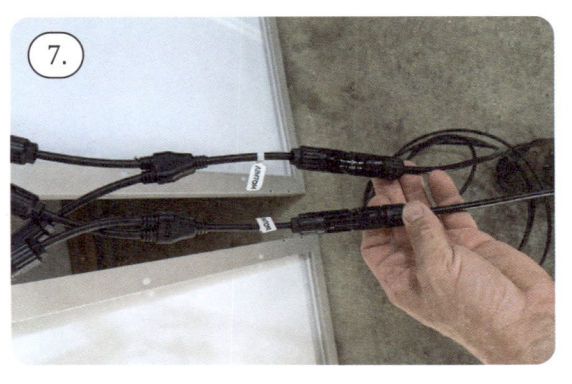

## Wiring the Panels in Series

There are cases where we want to have solar panels wired in series rather than parallel. To connect multiple panels in series, start by covering the panels to avoid electrical shock.

1. Identify the positive and negative ends.
2. Starting with the first panel, connect the negative power cable to the positive on the next panel.
3. Repeat this process with each panel.
4. At one end of your row of panels will be a positive connector, and the other end will be a negative connector. As with connecting panels in parallel, cut an extension cable in half to get two lines that are the lengths that you need to reach from the panels to the battery bank.
5. Connect the extension cables to the charge controller.
6. Connect the positive end of the cable from the charge controller to the positive side of the panels.
7. Connect the negative cable to the negative end of the panels.

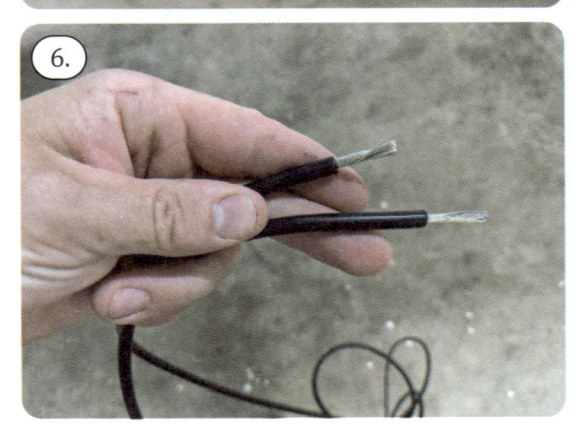

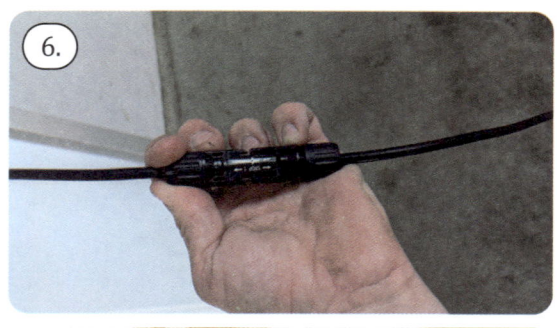

## Effective Use of Ground-Based Solar Panels

The system that I have described thus far is designed with the specific intent to maximize the amount of sunlight that the panels are exposed to. The idea is that we can place panels to catch the morning Sun then re-position periodically throughout the day to keep the panels under direct sunlight. Doing this also allows you to monitor the effectiveness of your placement by keeping an eye on how much power the panels are producing.

## Deploying a Portable Folding Panel

It is good to have one or two portable folding solar panels available to get some additional capacity. Deploying these panels takes minutes and requires no special builds or tools.

### MATERIALS

- Folding solar panel – I used this one which is sold on Amazon for $281.49USD
www.amazon.com/XINPUGUANG-Portable-Foldable-Generator-Controller/dp/B07XGKT22B/

- Extension cable with MC-4 connectors – Like this one available on Amazon for $ 144.99 USD
www.amazon.com/WindyNation-Gauge-Black-Extension-Connector/dp/B01D7VBT2G/

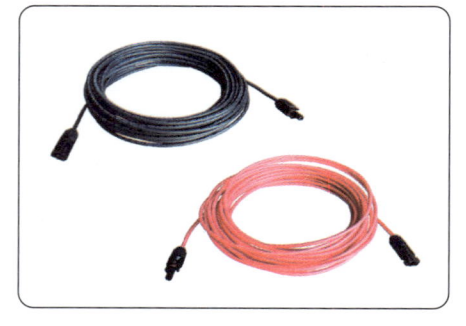

### INSTRUCTIONS

1. Cut an extension cable in half the same as you would for the larger panels.
2. Mark which end is positive and which end is negative, then connect to the charge controller.
3. Connect the folding panel to the cables, always connecting the positive end first then the negative end. (You can use two uncut extension cables to connect the portable panel to your deployed main panels. This, however, may reduce the versatility of the folding panel.)
4. Unfold the panel so that it is exposed to the maximum levels of sunlight.
5. Check the charge controller to monitor the amps coming off your solar panels to tweak their placement to pull the maximum power out of the Sun's rays.

# Connecting the Solar Power System to the Power Grid

In some areas, you can connect your solar power system to the power grid, which allows you to sell the excess power that you generate back to the power company. Exercising this option requires that you have permanently installed panels and that they, and the battery bank, are connected to your home's electrical panel.

Connecting a solar power system to the grid and your home's electrical system is outside the scope of an individual to DIY. There will be codes and regulations to follow, and you should only do so by using a qualified and licenced electrician and obtaining the proper permits.

# Putting Your Solar System to Use

In this example, we will be powering a refrigerator, but the steps involved will be the same regardless of the appliances you are powering.

1. Check that the battery has sufficient capacity to provide power.
2. Turn on the inverter.
3. Plug an extension cord into the inverter.
4. Plug the fridge or other appliance into the extension cord.
5. Confirm that the fridge is indeed operating correctly.

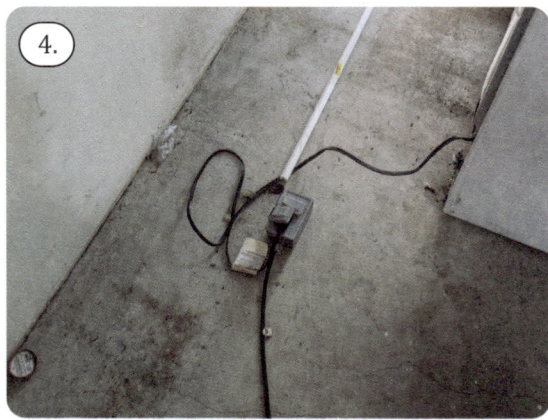

PROJECTS RELATED TO ELECTRICITY

# How To Make Your Own Wind Turbine

**COMPLEX DIFFICULTY**

Buying a small off-grid wind turbine system for your home can be expensive, for what seems like a simple machine. But if you're handy with tools, have some building materials lying around, or have parts salvaged from old machines, and you're looking forward to getting creative in your garage or backyard, you can try your hand at building your electricity-generating wind turbine - one that could charge your batteries at a fraction of what you'd pay for a store-bought wind turbine.

Before you embark on making a wind turbine, you need to make sure that there is plenty of wind blowing where you're living. Gusts of wind aren't enough to generate electricity from any wind turbine; so if you have sustained wind, small wind turbines can generate substantial and sustainable electricity.

## Materials Needed

For the build, you'll require some simple materials that you can easily get from local home improvement stores, online marketplaces, or you may even have them lying around. Here is the shortlist of things that you'll need to get started:

- A generator
- PVC piping
- Plywood
- Bearings
- Nuts and Bolts
- A drill
- A saw
- Electrical tape
- White Paint

## Building Your Wind Turbine

### STEP 1:

A good generator is the most essential component of the wind turbine. Always look for a low RPM per volt permanent magnet DC motor- it produces high voltage, enough to charge batteries, even for low rotational speeds of the turbine. Ametek DC motors, hub motors of electric bikes and Segways, treadmill motors, and fan motors of car engines are the best motors that can be used as DIY wind turbine generators. 12/24V permanent magnet generators can also be used. Never use a car alternator as a wind turbine generator because it requires immense speed to produce any electricity and isn't practical.

Here is a useful list of DC motors and generators, with costs, that can be used as a generator for wind turbines:

| Motor/ Generator Name | Cost | Where to look for/buy? |
|---|---|---|
| Ametek 30V DC Motor | $70-$150 | Amazon, EBay |
| Ametek 50V DC Motor | $99-$200 | Amazon, EBay |
| Treadmill motor | $91-$200 | Amazon, EBay, fitness stores |
| 12V DC radiator motor | $50 | Automobile stores |
| Electric bike hub motor | $150 | Amazon, EBay |
| DC generators | $40-$150 | Amazon, EBay, Home stores |

You can use any of the above motors or generators in your wind turbine, with the correct sizing of the wind turbine blades. This build used a 24V permanent magnet DC generator, which could generate 100W at its peak. I gave it a test by connecting the generator to a drill and attaching the wires to a dummy load, which showed 100W on the meter. With the correct sizing of the blades to spin the generators, these motors can generate usable electricity.

*Figure 1: Generator, 24V, Ametek, and common DC Generator*

**STEP 2:**
Once you have a generator, the next step is to make the blades. PVC piping offers a cheap and easy method to make blades for your wind turbine. You can use large 4", 6", 8" or larger PVC sections to make the blades. The table below provides the length of the blades corresponding to the power output of the generator.

| Power | Length of blade |
|---|---|
| 50W | 12" |
| 75W | 15" |
| 100W | 17" |
| 125W | 19" |
| 150W | 21" |
| 200W | 24" |

You'll know the capacity of your generator, so select the length of the PVC pipe accordingly. Chart out the length on a large piece of paper and draw a template. The side length can be slightly less than the diameter of the pipe section chosen and gradually tapered to the end. This forms the template of your blade, which you'll be using to cut out the individual blades.

*Figure 2: Drawing of the template*

Paste the template on the pipe and cut the pipe using a saw or PVC cutter following the template. You should have three blades cut out.

*Figure 3: Cutting the template using a saw*

*Figure 4: blades cut out*

**STEP 3:**
The next step is to make the tail boom out of a single PVC pipe to attach the generator, tail fin, and the yaw shaft. Take a section of smaller PVC piping, around 2-3" having a length that's equal to 1.2 times the length of the blade which you have selected, based on the above table.

Use the saw to cut out a section of the PVC pipe to place the generator, and similarly cut a slit on the rear end of the pipe for the tail fin.

*Figure 5: L shape cut out from tail boom for generator; Slit on the tail boom for tail fin*

Use the same size section of PVC piping for the yaw shaft. File out the tip of the pipe to the profile of the tail boom as shown in the bottom figure. Drill some holes on both the pipes and use a large bolt with bearing to attach the tail boom to the yaw shaft, such that the tail boom rotates freely.

*Figure 6: Attaching Yaw shaft to tail boom*

**STEP 4:**
Place the generator on the forward cut-out section of the PVC piping and fasten it tightly. You can use large hose clamps or nuts and bolts to tightly fasten the generator to the tail boom. Rigid fastening of the generator to the tail boom is essential for the turbine to operate smoothly. Use plenty of tape to cover up the generator.

*Figure 7: Generator Fastening*

**STEP 5:**
Use a piece of plywood, glass fiber, or any flat material to make the tail fin. You can be as creative as you want and choose any shape for the tail fin. The only rule of thumb you need to follow for the tail fin is that its area should be around 10% of the turbine blade area. Use a saw to cut out your desired tail.

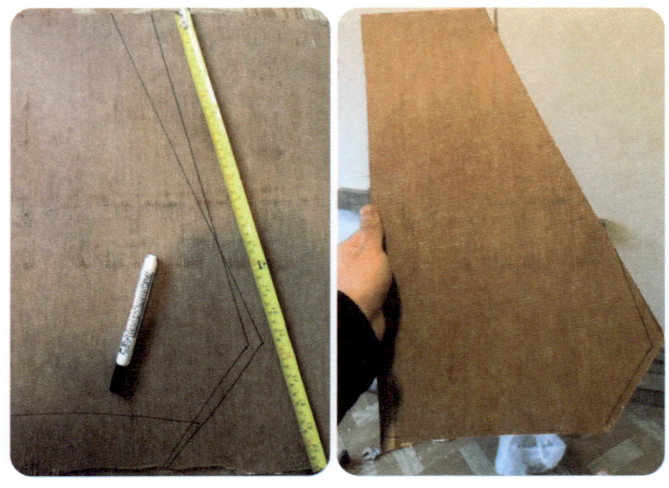

*Figure 8: Tail fin cut out*

The tail fin should be placed on the rear end of the tail boom. You can make a slit to place the tail fin on the boom. Use nuts and bolts on drilled holes to tightly fasten it.

*Figure 9: Slit for tail fin*

**STEP 6:**
The final step is to attach the blades to the generator. Usually, generators have a hub attached, which can be drilled to attach the blades. Otherwise, you can use a shaft coupling to attach the blades to the generator shaft. The angles between the blades should be roughly 120⁰ while attaching them to the generator.

*Figure 10: Blade attachment to generator*

Finally, paint the whole thing with a protective white coat of paint, then place the entire wind turbine on a tower with a bearing attachment, so that it can rotate freely to orient itself to the direction of the wind.

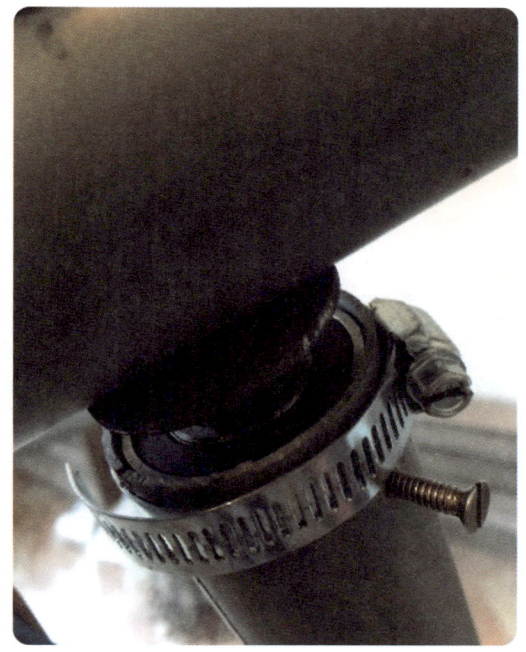

*Figure 11: Yaw Axis attachment for rotation*

The only thing keeping you from generating electricity from wind then is to erect it in a windy place. Once the turbine starts spinning, all you need to do is to connect the wires to a wind power system controller to charge your batteries. Any alternative energy store or online marketplace will have the controllers.

Once connected to a battery, it can generate substantial electricity. Of course, the electricity generated by your DIY wind turbine is nowhere near enough to power your entire home, but it's enough to charge your phone, laptop, or light up a room. Coupled with additional wind turbines and solar panels, you're well on your way to off-grid living.

*Figure 12: Wind Turbine*

PROJECTS RELATED TO ELECTRICITY

# How To Protect Your House Using An EMP Shield

**MEDIUM DIFFICULTY**     **30 MINUTES**

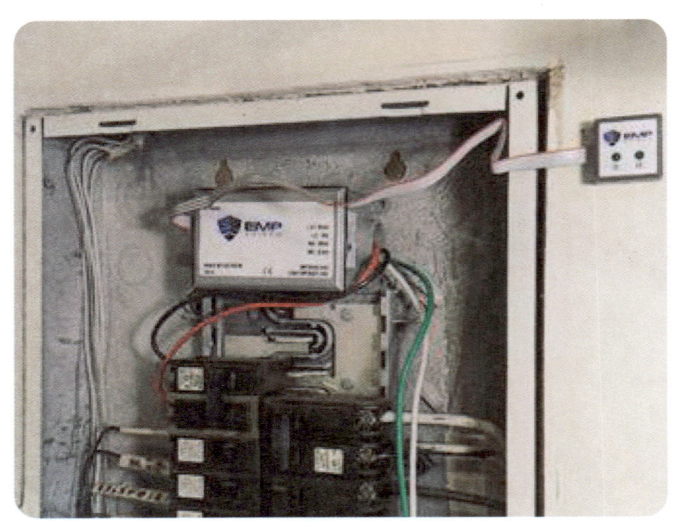

A power surge is a dangerous and damaging event, whether that power surge comes from a lightning strike or a powerful CME (coronal mass ejection) that hits the earth right on target. Either way, the electronics in your home and your ability to utilize power in general could be disintegrated in an instant.

The EMP Shield protects your home from these kinds of power surges and thus protects all of your electronics.

In 1989 a massive geo storm, brought on by the sun, blacked out half of Canada for an entire day! This stuff happens and we have not been hit by the largest of its kind, yet. The consensus is that a large enough geo storm would shut the lights out for good!

This is where a prep like the EMP Shield comes in to play. Even if your entire power grid experiences blackout, if your home systems and generator are protected then you will still have power. That is the value of installing this incredibly simple device.

## How it Works

The EMP Shield is designed and military tested to protect your home and appliances from the massive surge of power that can come from an EMP, solar flare, or even direct lightning strike. These pulses of electrons surge into your home through the grid or outside the grid and overwhelm your systems.

Once the surge fries your electronics there is really no going back. The EMP Shield acts in one billionth of a second to recognize that surge and disperse that surge so it does not overwhelm your home.

An EMP, solar flare, or direct lightning strike can affect the power grid for the short term or the long term. Either way, if you are protected, you will be able to feed power into your home and have the systems within the home operate (i.e., lights, stove, cooking, heating and so on).

If you can generate power through some kind of gas generator or solar system, then you will be able to power your home.

## How to Install an EMP Shield

The installation of the EMP Shield can be done by electricians. If you are uncomfortable working with electrical systems in any way, than you should get a professional to handle this.

If you can use a pair of wire cutters, a voltage pen, and a screwdriver than you will be able to install your own EMP Shield and there is a rewarding feeling that goes into installing and owning the processes that help sustain you and your family.

### Tools Needed

- Screwdriver Flat Head
- Screwdriver Philips Head
- Wire Cutters
- Voltage Pen

### Instructions

1. Begin the process by prepping the EMP Shield. Remove it from the box and inspect the unit to assure it is complete.
2. Next, we are going to locate the breaker box.
3. Using your screwdriver, remove the face place that covers your breaker box. There are six large screws around the face plate of your box. When you remove these the face plate will come off.
4. Next you are going to turn off the 2 x 20 amp

breakers that you are going to install the EMP Shield to.

5. Look for a smooth and clean location inside of your breaker box to affix the main box of the EMP Shield. Press the double sided tape into that location and assure a snug fit.
6. Based on the chosen location, you may want to trim the wires to assure you aren't left with excess slack wires getting in the way. Trim and strip the wires so the installation is efficient.
7. Locate the bus bar that runs the length of the breaker box because here you will be installing the EMP Shield.
8. Insert your green wire into a space in the bus bar and tighten the screw down to keep the wire in place.
9. Next, do the same with your white or neutral wire. Install it into the bus bar and then screw down on the wire to keep it in place.
10. DOUBLE CHECK the 20 amp breakers are in the off position. Use your voltage pen to assure there is no electricity going to that breaker.
11. Then insert the black wire into the top 20 amp breaker and tighten the screw to keep it in place.
12. Next, install the red wire in the bottom 20 amp breaker and tighten the screw to keep it in place.
13. You can now place the LED module somewhere outside the breaker box, on your wall, where you can easily see it. Press the double sided tape down firm to assure it stays affixed to the wall.
14. Check the installation by turning on the 20 amp breakers. The LED module should light up green to let you know that the EMP Shield is now working.
15. Place the breaker box cover over the new installation and screw it back in place.
16. As long as the LED Module stays lit your EMP Shield is working, and your home is protected.

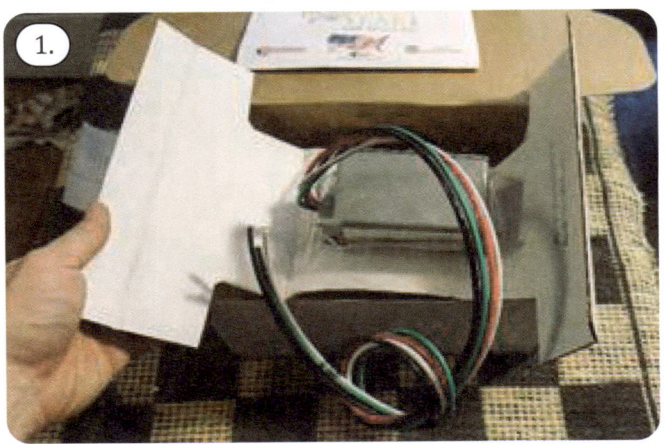

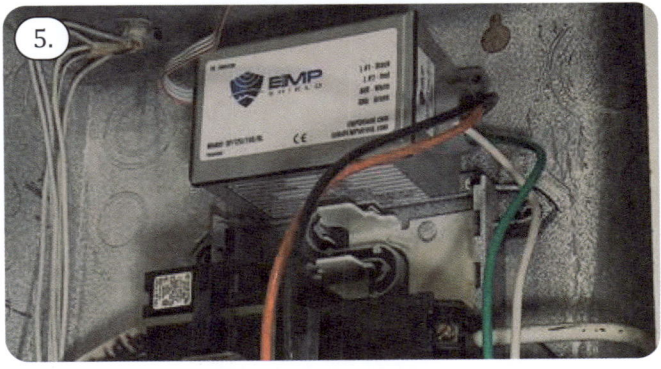

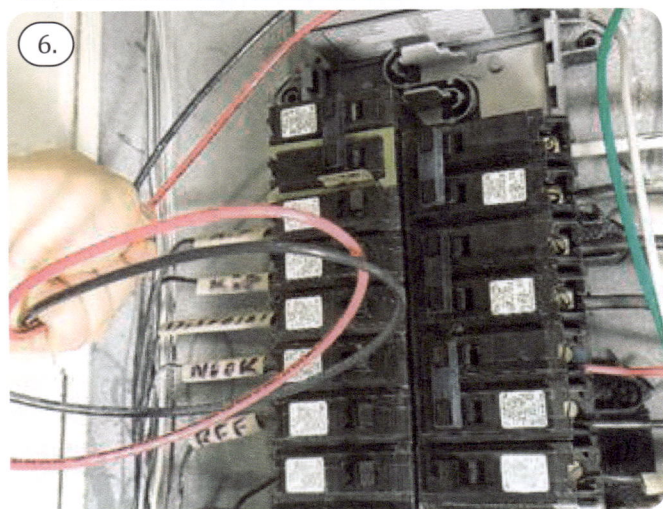

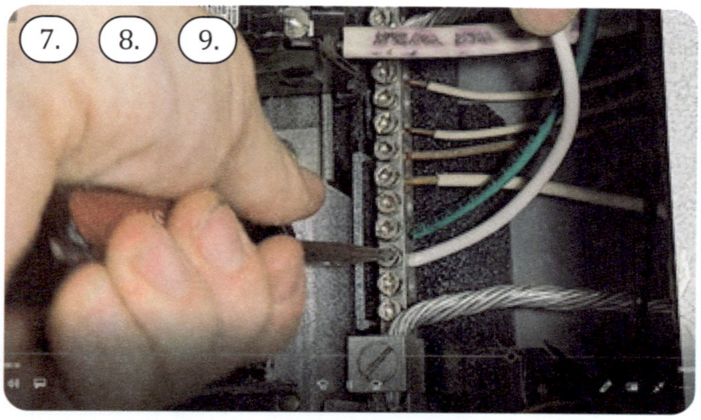
7.
8.
9.

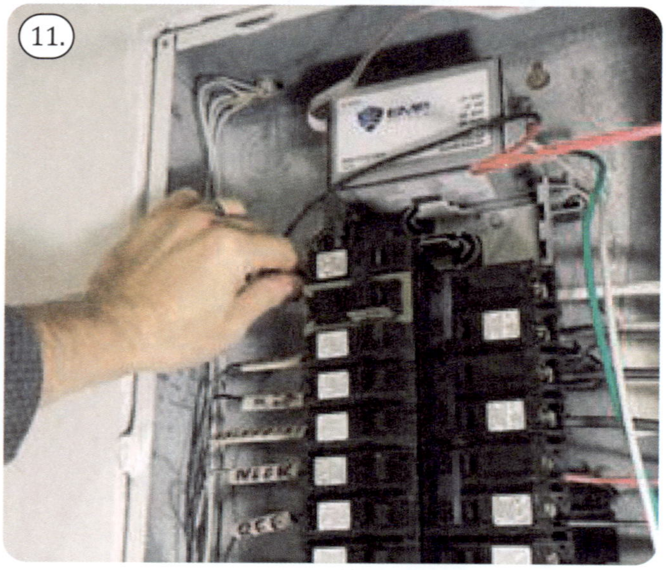
11.

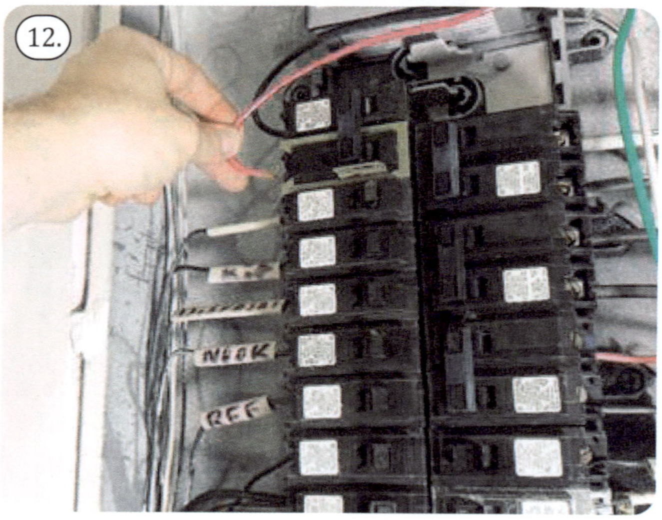
12.

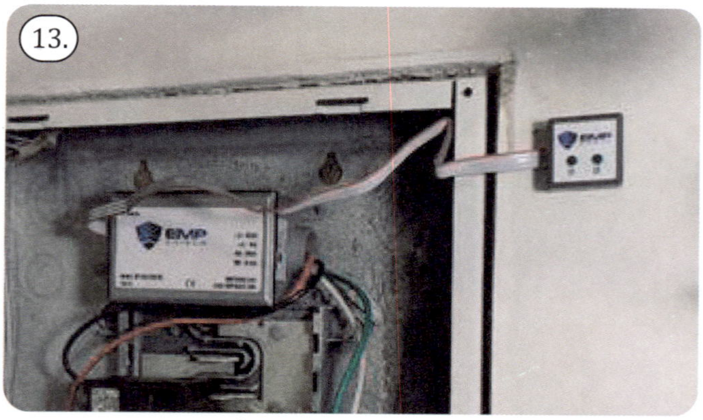
13.

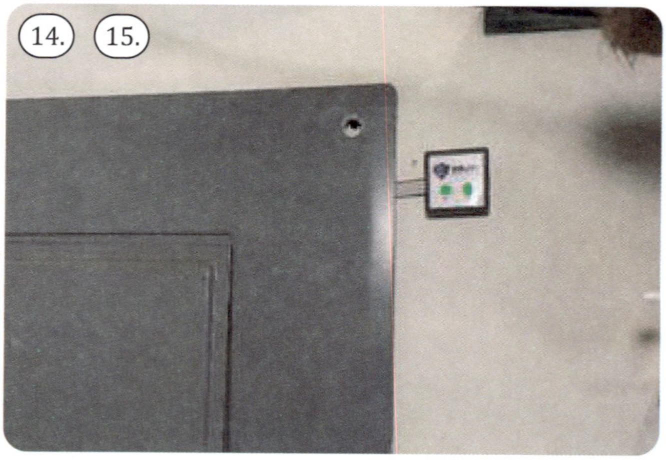
14.
15.

PROJECTS RELATED TO ELECTRICITY

# How To Turn A Car CB Radio Into A Powerful Transmitter

| MATERIAL COST | $ 235.00 | COMPLEX | DIFFICULTY | 2 HOURS |

Citizens Band radio, commonly referred to as CB radio, is a band of frequencies designated for anyone without an amateur radio license and callsign. Most commonly, CB radios are found in vehicles and used for communication on the road. Before cell phones and the introduction of affordable VHF radios, truckers and off-road enthusiasts would almost exclusively use CB radio to keep in touch while out on the road and in the bush.

## How Powerful Are CB Radios?

The Federal Communications Commission (FCC) regulates the maximum power that radios can use to transmit. In the case of CB radios, they have determined that their maximum power should be 4 watts. When operating on Single Sideband (SSB), the maximum allowed power increases to 12 watts. A mobile CB radio properly installed can have a transmission range between 2 and 15 miles.

The range of your mobile CB radio depends on a lot of different factors. The quality of installation, quality of coax cable, length of the antenna, and antenna placement all play a vital role in the power and range of your radio.

## The Best Way to Increase the Reach of Your CB Radio

While it would seem to make the best sense to install a linear amplifier to your CB radio system, there are two issues with this strategy. First, installing an amplifier is illegal, and then second is that it only increases the output power while not addressing the fundamental problems that limit radio propagation.

Even though CB radio is in the High-Frequency band (HF), and its radio waves can bounce off the ionosphere and propagate over long distances, local communications are still generally operating on a line of sight.

Radio waves can be interrupted and even blocked by all manners of obstacles. Even the foliage of trees can disrupt radio communications. The trick is to elevate your antenna above any obstacles in the area, and the best way to do this is to take that CB radio out of your vehicle and build a CB base station with a well constructed and matched antenna in your home. Having an excellent antenna matched perfectly will not help if you place that antenna in a poor location. Your goal should always be to elevate the antenna of any radio station above the level of any obstacles that would disrupt the path of your radio waves.

## Building a CB Base Station Ground Plane Antenna

For this build, we are going to construct a ground plane antenna. This antenna has a vertical radiating element and a ground plane formed by four wires connected to the coaxial cable's ground and angled below the antenna's bottom at a 45-degree angle. This is a simple and basic antenna that should take no more than an hour to construct.

## Tools Needed

You will need:
- Soldering Iron and solder
- Tape measure
- Hand Saw
- Linesman pliers
- Cordless drill and drill bits
- PVC primer and cement
- Sharp knife
- Glue
- Side cutters and wire stripper

## Materials Needed

You will need:

- A 10-foot length of ¾" Sch 40 PVC Pipe – Available at Home Depot for $2.95USD
  www.homedepot.com/p/Charlotte-Pipe-3-4-in-x-10-ft-PVC-Schedule-40-Plain-End-Pipe-PVC-04007-0600/100348472

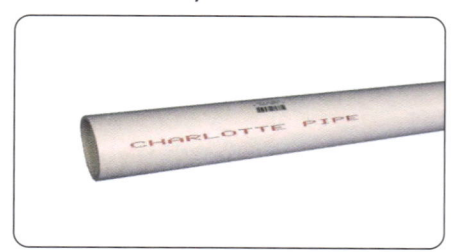

- A 10-foot length of 1" Sch 40 PVC Pipe - Available at Home Depot for $4.37USD
  www.homedepot.com/p/JM-EAGLE-1-in-x-10-ft-PVC-Schedule-40-Plain-End-Pipe-531194/202280936

- 20 feet of 14/2 Electrical wire (with ground wire) - Available at Home Depot for $13.13 USD
  www.homedepot.com/p/Southwire-25-ft-14-2-Solid-Romex-SIMpull-CU-NM-B-W-G-Wire-28827421/202316376

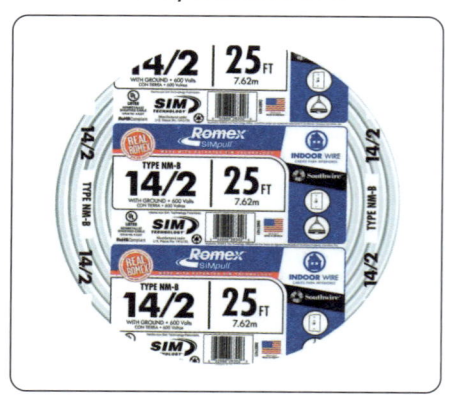

- 1 - so-239 UHF Female Connector - Available on Amazon.com for $6.79USD for a two-pack
  www.amazon.com/BOOBRIE-Chassis-Coaxial-Connector-Adapter/dp/B07DC1JYZL/

- 2 - ¾" PVC End Caps - Available at Home Depot for $0.61USD ea
  www.homedepot.com/p/Charlotte-Pipe-3-4-in-PVC-Schedule-40-Socket-Cap-PVC021160800HD/203811671?MERCH=REC-_-searchViewed-_-NA-_-203811671-_-N&

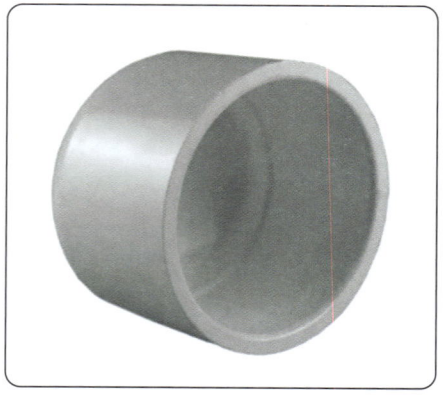

- 1 - ¾" PVC Tee - Available at Home Depot for $0.89USD
  www.homedepot.com/p/Charlotte-Pipe-3-4-in-Schedule-40-S-x-S-x-S-Tee-PVC024000800HD/203812197

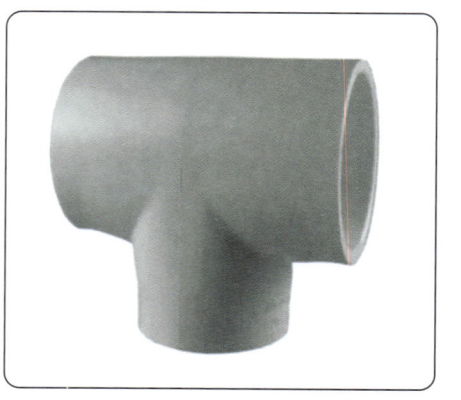

- 1 - 1" to ¾" Reducer – Available at Home Depot for $0.89USD
  www.homedepot.com/p/DURA-1-in-x-3-4-in-Schedule-40-PVC-Reducer-Bushing-C438-131/100346335

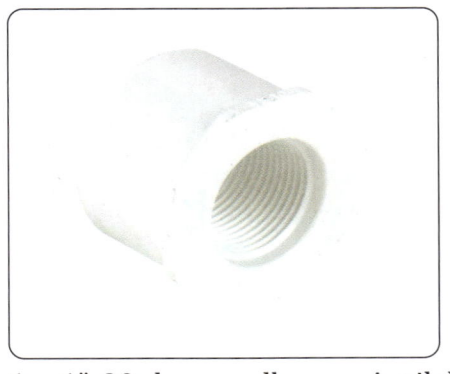

- 1 - 1" 90-degree elbow – Available at Home Depot for $1.20USD

www.homedepot.com/p/DURA-1-in-Schedule-40-PVC-90-Degree-Elbow-C406-010/100346841?MERCH=REC-_-searchViewed-_-NA-_-100346841-_-N&

- Para Cord – Available on Amazon.com for $ 10.89 USD

www.amazon.com/BENGKU-Survival-Mil-SPEC-Parachute-MIl-C-5040-H/dp/B07226B3FJ/

## Building the Antenna

The antenna we are going to construct can be mounted in a wide variety of ways, but for this chapter, I set this antenna up in my front yard rather than attaching it to my roof. I would suggest doing the same while building and testing your antenna before committing to mounting it to your home.

I used regular 14 guage electrical wire for this build. Still, this antenna's vertical and ground plane elements can be replaced with copper or aluminum rods or tubes to make the antenna stiffer. As long as the material is conductive, it should work. Use this build as a guide and make any substitutions or additions that you see fit.

1. First, cut two sections of 14/2 electrical wire at 104" each. Then strip the entire length's outer insulation, which will give you six individual 104" segments of 14 gauge wire.
2. Strip a couple of inches of insulation off one end of each of the white and black wires.
3. The SO-239 connector is going to be glued into one of the ¾" PVC end caps. Before that can happen, you need to drill an appropriately sized hole for the connector to fit in. Measure the end of the connector that you will end up soldering the radiating element. In this case, I measured it at a little over half an inch.
4. Drill a hole into the end of a ¾" PVC end cap to fit the SO-239 connector.
5. Next, solder the bare copper length of wire into the end of the SO-239 connector. This wire is going to be the antenna.
6. Run the wire through the hole in the PVC end cap.
7. Attach the remaining four wires to the screw holes on the SO-239 connector. Use the ends that you have stripped to attach to the connector. In this case, I made a loop on the end of the wire, running it through the screw holes. I then secured them further with some electrical tape. Glue the connector to the end cap at this point.
8. Next, cut two pieces of ¾" PVC to about 4 inches in length.
9. Attach these pieces to the ¾" PVC Tee as shown, then connect the 1" 90-degree elbow and the 1" to ¾" reducer as shown. You can glue these together now or do it after the antenna is tested and ready to be mounted.
10. Run the antenna wire through the open end of the 4-inch section of the PVC pipe attached to the PVC tee. Run this wire along its length until you reach the PVC endcap with the SO-239 connector and ground plane radials. Secure this end cap on the pipe.
11. Cut an eight-foot section of ¾" PVC pipe to house the antenna wire.
12. Cut a 2-foot section of paracord and drill a hole in the other ¾" PVC endcap large enough for the paracord to slide through.
13. Tie the paracord to the end of your antenna wire.
14. Run this wire through the eight-foot section of PVC pipe and secure the pipe to the ¾" tee. At

this time, attach a length of 1" PVC pipe to the 1" 90-degree elbow. This pipe is how you will be mounting it to your home, and the length will be determined by the placement and method of mounting. For this chapter's purposes, I left the pipe at around 8 feet in length to erect the antenna in my front yard for testing.

15. On the antenna's top end, run the paracord through the hole you drilled in the end cap and secure the end cap to the antenna.
16. Pull the paracord taut and tie a knot to secure it and the antenna wire in place.
17. Mount the antenna and extend the ground plane radials at an approximate 45 degree downward slope. I attached lengths of paracord to extend the radials out at an approximate 45-degree angle. You can also attach any non-conductive material to the ground plane wires to stiffen them and eliminate the need for paracord guylines.
18. Connect the coaxial cable to the antenna and run the cable to your CB base station.

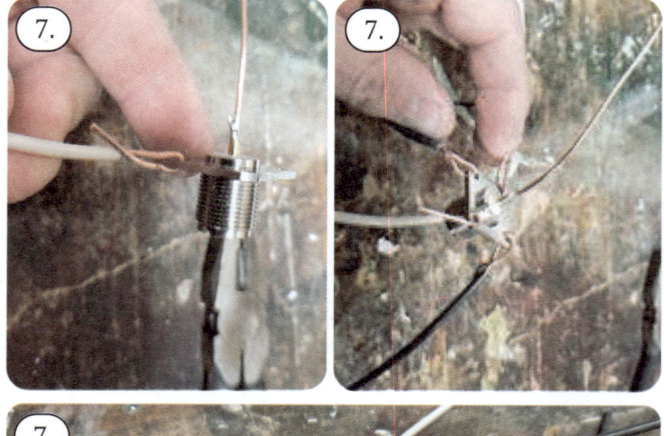

8.

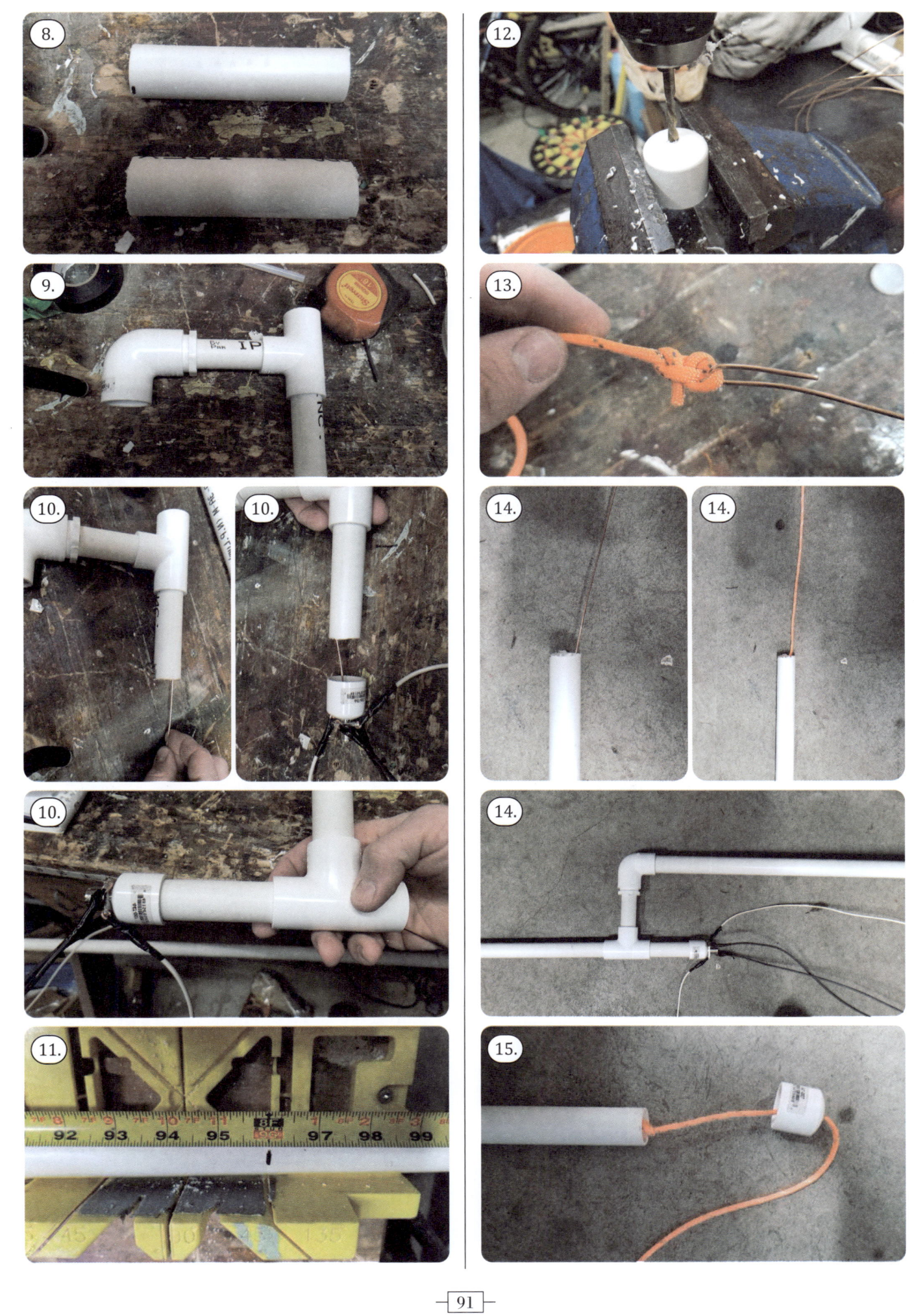

9.

10. 10.

10.

11.

12.

13.

14. 14.

14.

15.

## How to Establish Your CB Base Station

To build a CB radio base station, the first thing you need to do is figure out exactly where you will be mounting your antenna. The location of your antenna should be as high up on your home as practical. From there, determine the best spot to set up your CB radio as a base station. The largest determining factor is probably the transmission line route from the radio to the antenna. The goal should be to keep the run as short as possible because the longer the cable, the greater the signal loss on the way to the antenna.

Once you have determined where you will place the antenna and the transmitter, you need to set up your CB base station. To do this, you are going to need a few materials.

- ◆ A CB Radio – For this build, I used a Uniden Pro 510xl 40 channel CB radio that can be purchased on amazon.com for $ 40.56 USD as of this chapter's writing.
us.amazon.com/Uniden-PRO510XL-40-Channel-Display-Address/dp/B08HZRTSV1

- ◆ A Power Supply - I used a Pyramid PSV300 power supply that can be purchased on Amazon.com for $ 70.54 USD.
www.amazon.com/Universal-Compact-Bench-Power-Supply/dp/B000NPT4TK/

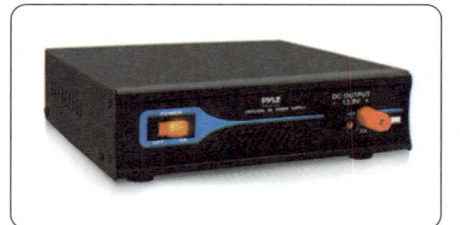

- ◆ Coax Cable – I used 50 feet of RG-58/U, but you may want to purchase a higher quality cable to reduce the feed line loss. A 50-foot length of RG-58 is available on Amazon.com for $ 17.77 USD.
www.amazon.com/PL-259-Antenna-Coaxial-Connectors-Extension/dp/B078V56SMV/

- ◆ Nano VNA - This is an inexpensive antenna analyzer sold on Amazon.com for $54.99 USD.

92

www.amazon.com/AURSINC-Analyzer-Measuring-Parameters-Standing/dp/B07T6LXNTV/

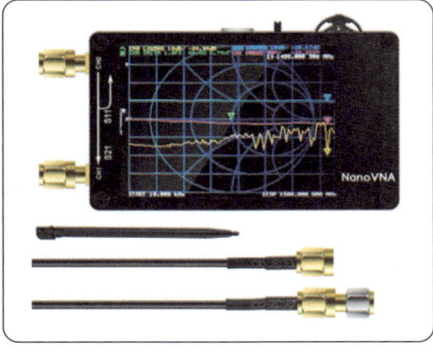

◆ SMA Male to SO-239 jumper - You'll need this to connect your Nano VNA to the antenna; it is available on Amazon for $ 10.50 USD.
www.amazon.com/Handheld-Cable-Coaxial-connects-Antennas/dp/B00MFRMLIA/

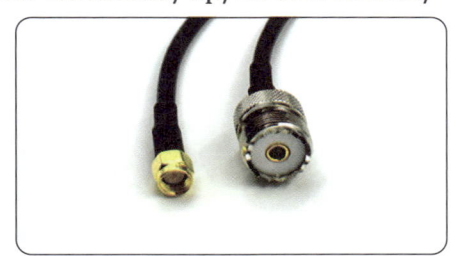

## Putting it All Together

1. Mount the antenna and run the coax transmission line to where you will install your CB base station.
2. Connect the power supply to the nearest wall outlet.
3. Assemble the CB radio but do not connect to the power supply. This will likely involve simply attaching the handheld microphone.
4. Ensure that both the power supply and the CB radio are turned off and connect the CB radio to the power supply.

## Tuning the Antenna

Before we transmit on our new CB base station, we need to determine the SWR of the antenna. SWR stands for standing wave ratio, and to put it as simply as possible, it is a way of measuring how much energy is being reflected back to the transmitter. In a perfect system, the SWR would be 1:1, but we do not live in an ideal world. Our goal on any antenna is to have an SWR that is less than 1.5. While you can connect an SWR meter between the CB radio and the antenna, I have chosen to use an inexpensive antenna analyzer instead. The reason I have done this is that the NanoVNA does not require the CB radio to transmit to determine the SWR of the antenna. I also like to use a NanoVNA because it has an extensive range of frequencies and many other functions besides checking SWR.

1. To check the antenna's SWR, I calibrated the Nano VNA for a frequency range of 26Mhz to 28Mhz. Since there are different versions and models of these antenna analyzers, you need to determine your individual model's calibration procedure.
2. Connect the antenna to the jumper, then connect the jumper to the NanoVNA.
3. Set the frequency to 27.4Mhz (CB channel 40's frequency) and check the SWR reading. In this case, the SWR reading was 1.44 at 27.4Mhz, which acceptable.
4. Then, check the lower end of the CB frequencies by dialling the Nano VNA to 26.96Mhz (CB channel one's frequency). In this case, I got an SWR reading of 1.26, which is ok.
5. If the SWR is higher on channel 40 than channel one, then the antenna can be shortened. The opposite is true if the SWR is higher on channel one than channel 40. Remember that an SWR of 1.5 or less is what we are aiming for. While I could adjust my antenna, in this case, since both readings are below 1.5, I decided to leave it be.

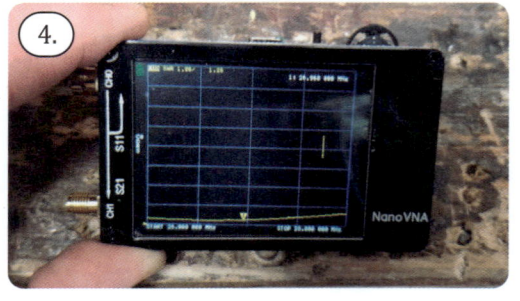

Once you are happy with how your antenna is tuned, connect it to the CB radio and do some test transmissions. If you are satisfied with its performance, go ahead and glue all the PVC connections and seal any areas where water can get in. Then mount the antenna as high as possible and enjoy your new CB base station.

While it may seem counter-intuitive to remove a perfectly good radio from your truck or car and instead install it in your home, this is the best way to maximize your rig's transmitting potential. Even though it is possible to bounce radio waves from a CB radio off the ionosphere and communicate with stations very far away, CB radios, like most radios, still operate the best when they have a clear line of sight. The simple act of building and raising an antenna will do wonders for the power of your transmitter.

# How To Use A Ham Radio In A Blackout

The world has become so interconnected that it is hard to believe that we could ever lose our ability to communicate with each other instantly. The major weakness of all our communication methods is the power grid that they rely on to function. Remove electricity and our overly complex communication systems break down.

Even though our communication networks have backup systems that will keep them operational in an emergency, such as a blackout, these systems can become unstable. We should all have alternate means of communication that are independent of systems that are government or corporate-controlled.

**Ham radio** is that alternate means of communication. While we are all familiar with the broadcast radio stations that we rock out to on our daily commute, there is far more to this medium than most of us know. The radio spectrum is a range of the electromagnetic spectrum that falls between 30Hz to 300GHz, and within this spectrum, there are several frequency bands designated for the use of radio amateurs.

One of the primary purposes of amateur (or ham) radio is to assist with communications in an emergency or disaster, so becoming an amateur radio operator is an important step that all preppers and survivalists should be taking. To legally access these bands and use them, one must become a licenced radio amateur and be issued a callsign.

## Get Licensed

In the United States of America, the Federal Communication Commission (FCC) licences amateur radio operators. They designate three classes of radio amateur, Technician, General, and Extra. The differences between these classes are primarily related to the bands they allow one to legally access.

The FCC website has more information on the amateur radio service in the United States.
www.fcc.gov/wireless/bureau-divisions/mobility-division/amateur-radio-service

For basic emergency preparedness, a Technician class licence is more than sufficient as it allows you access to all the VHF and UHF bands, which will be the most useful for localized communications.

## Get Equipped

The radios that you will buy largely depend on what level of emergency communication you will require. With ham radio, you can communicate with someone across the street or an ocean. It depends on the frequency bands that you are using and the power that your radio will put out through the antenna.

VHF and UHF radios are the usual starting point

for those beginning their journey into amateur radio because they are inexpensive and allow for widespread communication through local repeaters. They also do not require large antennas or power output like HF radios do. With a simple five-watt VHF handheld radio, one can do quite a bit in the ham radio arena.

Those who are brand new to amateur radio often purchase a cheap handheld radio, such as the dreaded Baofeng. With radios like these, you get what you pay for, and the low cost comes with poor build quality and less durability than their more expensive counterparts.

They perform well enough to transmit and receive effectively and are a decent option for a first radio or backup radios.

Spending more on a brand name radio will give you a radio with higher build quality levels and often more features. Suppose your local area has a lot of digital repeaters. In that case, it is a good idea to look at purchasing a digital radio that covers the most popular modes that your local repeaters support.

## Mobile Radio

Along with handheld radios, most amateur radio operators also purchase a mobile unit for their vehicles. These radios have the advantage of increased power and the ability to be used as a base station. A mobile radio used as a base station offers the advantage of better antenna placement since you can mount an antenna high on the roof of your home.

## CB/FRS/GRMS

While amateur radios are powerful and useful to have, most people around you will not have amateur radio licences. Thus, it is also good practice to have a few FRS/GRMS radios on hand and a CB radio. Since these radios do not require a licence (aside from GRMS, which you can obtain without a callsign or test), this will allow you to establish and maintain communications with people in your neighbourhood, since the range on these radios is only a few miles at best.

## Receivers

After a blackout or disaster, you will probably want to receive more information than you want to transmit. For this reason, investing in a scanner and shortwave radio receiver is a great way to gather information. Scanners can scan through more frequencies at a more rapid rate than your radio can, and shortwave receivers allow you to listen to radio broadcasts from outside your local area.

Another option is an SDR or software-defined radio. These devices are usually USB dongles that plug into the USB port on your computer and have a connection to attach an antenna. The dongle receives the radio signals, and the software in the computer translates them into audio. You can also create a Raspberry Pi based system that will run an SDR and give you the ability to receive an extensive array of radio frequencies while being powered by a rechargeable battery bank. If you can recharge batteries either through solar, inverter, or generator, then this is an option to investigate.

# Preparing for Emergency

The first rule of having radios for emergencies is to keep the batteries charged. You are also going to want a bare minimum of one extra battery per radio. There are aftermarket battery adapters that allow you to use standard AA or AAA batteries to power your radio in some cases.

If you are serious about using amateur radio after a power failure, you need to have a method of charging your batteries. A generator or power inverter is a good investment for your communications' security, but what you should be aware of is exactly how long it takes to charge the batteries of your ham radio equipment. Knowing this will help you plan when and for how long you will be firing up the generator.

Using a mobile radio as a base station is advantageous because you can use it in your home, and when the lights go out, you can power it from your vehicle while making use of a superior base station antenna.

Key Your Mic!

One of the best things that you can do to prepare for a blackout or other emergency is to check into the local nets that take place on your local repeaters. Talking to other hams ensures that your callsign gets out on the airwaves and logged into the individual net's records. You will have a better chance of being listened to after a disaster, blackout, or other emergencies if other ham radio operators have gotten to know you.

Talking on ham radio before an emergency teaches you how nets work and the various methods and procedures on the local radio airways. Along with talking on the radio nets, you should consider joining a local amateur radio club or an emergency amateur radio group in your area.

Amateur radio is a network of likeminded individuals who often will have a preparedness mindset. The most important prep you can make to secure your comms is to use this network and take advantage of all the knowledge that ham radio operators are always willing to share with a new ham.

# Frequencies

When you program your radios, the first thing you need to do is figure out what frequencies you will need to have in a blackout event. Even though your radio will not transmit outside amateur radio bands, it will likely receive frequencies outside of the amateur bands. Take advantage of this and program as many emergency frequencies as you can into your radio. Generally, you should look up and consider programing the following frequencies into your radio.

| Channel No | Priority CH | Receive Frequency | Transmit Frequency | Offset Frequency | Offset Direction | AUTO MODE | Operating Mode | AMS | DIG/ANALOG | Name | Tone Mode | CTCSS Frequency | C |
|---|---|---|---|---|---|---|---|---|---|---|---|---|---|
| 203 | ☐ | 145.45000 | 144.85000 | 0.60000 | -RPT | ☐ | FM | OFF | ANALOG | VCH01 | TONE | 100.0 Hz | 023 |
| 204 | ☐ | 145.17000 | 144.57000 | 0.60000 | -RPT | ☐ | FM | OFF | ANALOG | VCH02 | OFF | 88.5 Hz | 023 |
| 205 | ☐ | 145.27000 | 144.67000 | 0.60000 | -RPT | ☐ | FM | OFF | ANALOG | VCH03 | TONE | 100.0 Hz | 023 |
| 206 | ☐ | 146.58000 | 146.58000 | 0.00000 | OFF | ☐ | FM | OFF | ANALOG | VCH04 | OFF | 88.5 Hz | 023 |
| 207 | ☐ | 146.46000 | 146.46000 | 0.00000 | OFF | ☐ | FM | OFF | ANALOG | VCH05 | TONE | 100.0 Hz | 023 |
| 208 | ☐ | 147.42000 | 147.42000 | 0.00000 | OFF | ☐ | FM | OFF | ANALOG | VCH06 | TONE | 123.0 Hz | 023 |
| 209 | ☐ | 147.45000 | 147.45000 | 0.00000 | OFF | ☐ | FM | OFF | ANALOG | VCH07 | TONE | 100.0 Hz | 023 |
| 210 | ☐ | 146.52000 | 146.52000 | 0.00000 | OFF | ☐ | FM | OFF | ANALOG | VCH08 | OFF | 88.5 Hz | 023 |
| 211 | ☐ | 147.26000 | 147.86000 | 0.60000 | +RPT | ☐ | FM | OFF | ANALOG | VCH09 | OFF | 88.5 Hz | 023 |
| 212 | ☐ | 145.35000 | 144.75000 | 0.60000 | -RPT | ☐ | FM | OFF | ANALOG | VCH10 | TONE | 127.3 Hz | 023 |
| 213 | ☐ | 145.45000 | 145.45000 | 0.00000 | OFF | ☐ | FM | OFF | ANALOG | VCH11 | TONE | 100.0 Hz | 023 |
| 214 | ☐ | 145.17000 | 145.17000 | 0.00000 | OFF | ☐ | FM | OFF | ANALOG | VCH12 | OFF | 88.5 Hz | 023 |
| 215 | ☐ | 148.65500 | 148.65500 | 0.00000 | OFF | ☐ | FM | OFF | ANALOG | PEPCD1 | OFF | 88.5 Hz | 023 |
| 216 | ☐ | 148.68500 | 148.68500 | 0.00000 | OFF | ☐ | FM | OFF | ANALOG | EP1 | OFF | 88.5 Hz | 023 |
| 217 | ☐ | 143.82000 | 148.75000 | 0.00000 | -/+ | ☐ | FM | OFF | ANALOG | SARREP | OFF | 88.5 Hz | 023 |
| 218 | ☐ | 149.08000 | 149.08000 | 0.00000 | OFF | ☐ | FM | OFF | ANALOG | SAR | OFF | 88.5 Hz | 023 |
| 219 | ☐ | 149.49500 | 149.49500 | 0.00000 | OFF | ☐ | FM | OFF | ANALOG | SAR1 | OFF | 88.5 Hz | 023 |
| 220 | ☐ | 149.52500 | 149.52500 | 0.00000 | OFF | ☐ | FM | OFF | ANALOG | SAR2 | OFF | 88.5 Hz | 023 |
| 221 | ☐ | 166.89000 | 166.89000 | 0.00000 | OFF | ☐ | FM | OFF | ANALOG | SARBC | OFF | 88.5 Hz | 023 |
| 222 | ☐ | 169.11000 | 169.11000 | 0.00000 | OFF | ☐ | FM | OFF | ANALOG | NSRTAC | TONE | 146.2 Hz | 023 |
| 223 | ☐ | 162.66000 | 167.11500 | 0.00000 | -/+ | ☐ | FM | OFF | ANALOG | COQSAR | OFF | 88.5 Hz | 023 |
| 224 | ☐ | 162.10500 | 168.25500 | 0.00000 | -/+ | ☐ | FM | OFF | ANALOG | CFVSAR | OFF | 88.5 Hz | 023 |
| 225 | ☐ | 149.41000 | 149.41000 | 0.00000 | OFF | ☐ | FM | OFF | ANALOG | RMSAR | OFF | 88.5 Hz | 023 |
| 226 | ☐ | 163.29000 | 163.29000 | 0.00000 | OFF | ☐ | FM | OFF | ANALOG | NSSAR1 | TONE | 100.0 Hz | 023 |
| 227 | ☐ | 165.55500 | 165.55500 | 0.00000 | OFF | ☐ | FM | OFF | ANALOG | NSSAR2 | TONE | 141.3 Hz | 023 |
| 228 | ☐ | 162.18000 | 162.18000 | 0.00000 | OFF | ☐ | FM | OFF | ANALOG | NSSAR3 | TONE | 173.8 Hz | 023 |

| Loc | Frequency | Name | Tone Mode | Tone | ToneSql | Duplex | Offset | Mode | Power | Skip |
|---|---|---|---|---|---|---|---|---|---|---|
| 2 | 147.000000 | VA7OAC | Tone | 250.3 | | - | 0.600000 | FM | High | |
| 3 | 146.800000 | VE7RMR | Tone | 156.7 | | - | 0.600000 | FM | High | |
| 4 | 147.360000 | VE7RSC | Tone | 103.5 | | + | 0.600000 | FM | High | |
| 5 | 145.450000 | VECTOR | Tone | 100.0 | | - | 0.600000 | FM | High | |
| 6 | 146.610000 | VE7RVA | Tone | 110.9 | | - | 0.600000 | FM | High | |
| 7 | 147.280000 | VE7ASM | Tone | 110.9 | | + | 0.600000 | FM | High | |
| 8 | 145.310000 | VE7MFS | Tone | 127.3 | | - | 0.600000 | FM | High | |
| 9 | 147.260000 | VE7RNS | (None) | | | + | 0.600000 | FM | High | |
| 10 | 146.900000 | VE7RWR | Tone | 91.5 | | - | 0.600000 | FM | High | |
| 11 | 146.940000 | VE7RPT | Tone | 136.5 | | - | 0.600000 | FM | High | |
| 12 | 145.040000 | VE7PKV | (None) | | | + | 0.600000 | FM | High | |
| 13 | 145.110000 | VA7RSH | (None) | | | + | 0.600000 | FM | High | |
| 14 | 145.270000 | VE7RSH | Tone | 100.0 | | + | 0.600000 | FM | High | |
| 15 | 145.070000 | VE7LAN | (None) | | | + | 0.600000 | FM | High | |
| 16 | 145.350000 | VE7RBY | Tone | 127.3 | | - | 0.600000 | FM | High | |
| 17 | 0.000000 | | (None) | | (None) | | | FM | | |
| 18 | 0.000000 | | (None) | | (None) | | | FM | | |
| 19 | 0.000000 | | (None) | | (None) | | | FM | | |
| 20 | 146.460000 | BC4X4 | (None) | | (None) | | | FM | High | |
| 21 | 146.415000 | CH 1 | (None) | | (None) | | | FM | High | |
| 22 | 146.430000 | CH 2 | (None) | | (None) | | | FM | High | |
| 23 | 146.445000 | CH 3 | (None) | | (None) | | | FM | High | |
| 24 | 146.460000 | CH 4 | (None) | | (None) | | | FM | High | |
| 25 | 146.475000 | CH 5 | (None) | | (None) | | | FM | High | |

- Local Repeaters
- Commonly Used Simplex Frequencies
- FRS/GRMS/CB/Commercial Frequencies
- SAR Frequencies
- Local Fire/Police/Ambulance
- Local Emergency Services
- Local Electric/Gas Company
- Marine VHF (If you live near bodies of water)
- Airports and Aircraft Frequencies
- NOAA Weather
- Local Prepper Group Frequencies

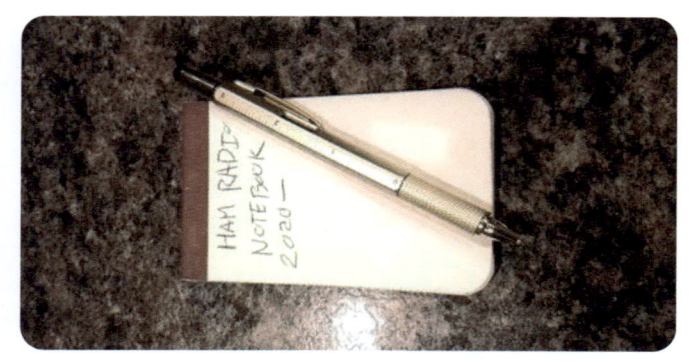

I like to have a notebook designated as my ham radio notebook, in which I write down some of the more common frequencies and some general, amateur radio notes. You can also find printable frequencies lists online, and when you program your radio, it is a good idea to print out the frequencies you have inputted into your radios.

## Use During a Blackout

When the lights go out, the first thing you need to remember is to stay off the local repeaters unless necessary. If there is a widespread power failure, then all these repeater sites will be on backup power, like a battery or generator. These backup power sources are finite. The repeaters' frivolous use will prevent legitimate emergency traffic from getting through and deplete the backup power more rapidly.

If you do not need to make contacts on the emergency radio nets, use a scanner or SDR to monitor the frequency and save your radio battery for when you must transmit. If you want to contact people in your family or group with amateur radio, designate pre-set times, frequencies, and procedures to make contact. Doing this will prevent any unnecessary drain of your precious battery resources.

## Declaring an Emergency

If you need immediate help and there is a direct threat to life, dial in the repeater or frequency, which is monitored for emergency traffic in your area. The correct method to call out for help is to call "Mayday, Mayday, Mayday" at the beginning and end of your transmission. One critical consideration is to take a moment to plan out precisely what you will say to accurately disseminate the information required to render whatever aid you need.

If you need to bring attention to a non-life-threatening emergency, call out "Break. Emergency" and your message.

## Check-in on Your Neighbours!

When you get an amateur radio licence, you take on the responsibility to help in emergency times. Walk around to your neighbours, ask them how they are doing, and if they require any assistance. You can then use the radio nets to relay any critical information to the authorities and offer your service as a liaison between your neighbourhood and the emergency management infrastructure.

I have thrown a lot of information at you to absorb in one chapter. To summarize, the essential takeaways should be:

- Get licensed.
- Have a plan for powering your radios.
- Keep the airways clear for real emergencies.
- Talk on the radio nets before a blackout or other emergency.
- Make use of the network of ham radio operators to learn as much as you can.
- Look after your neighbours.

Amateur radio is a fun hobby, but it can also be a critical lifeline in an emergency, so get licenced, learn everything you can, and stay prepared for when the lights go out.

PROJECTS YOU CAN MAKE TO KEEP INTRUDERS OFF YOUR PROPERTY

# Backyard Lights With Sensors That Turn On Automatically When Someone Walks On Your Property

**MATERIAL COST** $ 62.00    **EASY** DIFFICULTY    **40 MINUTES**

One of the most important security devices that you can install around your property is lighting. Illuminating the perimeter removes the veil of darkness that criminals use to conceal their actions. While military compounds can afford to illuminate their perimeter 24/7, most of us are not able or willing to have lights on all night. Instead, motion-activated lights provide us with safety and security without the need to have them turned on all day and night.

We can easily run down to the local Home Depot or point and click to buy a motion-activated light from Amazon, but building our own motion lights can, in many ways, be the better option.

The main reason to DIY our motion-activated lights is to allow for more flexibility in placement and operation. If you purchase commercially manufactured lights, the light's design limits you to how and where you will install them. When we construct our lights, we can position the lights, sensors, and power supply in areas that best suit our needs.

For example, you can position the sensor in a separate location from the lights allowing you to customize the trigger area to the illuminated area.

Building your motion lights also allows for further customizations, such as running the unit from a battery charged via solar panels.

## How These Motion Activated Lights Work

The lighting unit we are about to construct runs on 12 volts DC and uses a Passive Infrared Sensor (PIR) as a switch to activate the light when someone walks through the sensor's trigger zone. A PIR sensor registers the change in the temperature of a warm human body moving through the trigger zone, which closes the electrical circuit, supplying voltage to the light.

Using 12 volt DC power is beneficial because a lot of off-grid power is 12 volt DC run from batteries that are charged via solar, wind, hydro, etc.

### THE PIR SENSOR

Many PIR sensors are available online designed to be very easy to wire, even for those with limited knowledge in electronics. The one I selected for this build was inexpensive and easy to wire and mount.

The only downside that I could see was that I could not find any information about how water resistant this and other sensors like it are. If you plan to install these sensors where they will be exposed to harsh conditions, consider building or buying a housing to contain them.

### THE LIGHTS

Since this build uses 12DCV to operate, I chose to use lights designed for mounting to vehicles. These lights come with mounting brackets that allow for a wide range of mounting options. Since these lights were designed for off-road use, I was confident that I could install them outside without any fear of the elements damaging the lights.

## Building the Motion Activated Lights

### Materials

- For the wire, you can use any wire appropriate for hooking up 12 volts. In my case, my local hardware store only had 18 gauge thermostat wire, but you can find some decent hookup wire on Amazon for $22.98USD.
www.amazon.com/Silicone-Electrical-Conductor-Parallel-Flexible/dp/B07K9R9LBV/

- ◆ LEDMO Power Supply 12V available on Amazon for $11.99USD
www.amazon.com/ALITOVE-Adapter-Converter-100-240V-5-5x2-1mm/dp/B01GEA8PQA/

- ◆ Willpower 2PCS 18W 6inch LED Lights are available on Amazon.com for $16.99USD
www.amazon.com/Nilight-Driving-Lights-driving-Warranty/dp/B07217HPV5/

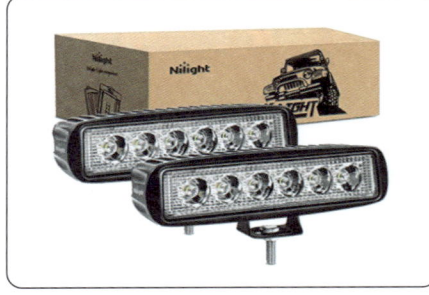

- ◆ RGBZONE DC12V 24V PIR sensor availlble on Amazon.com for $10.48USD
www.amazon.com/RGBZONE-Sensor-Function-Cotroller-Flexible/dp/B01E3NFOIW/

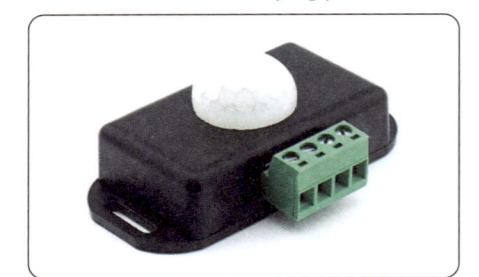

- ◆ Nails or screws.

## Instructions

Putting this unit together should take less than an hour. If your situation requires some special wiring or complex installation, then your project will take longer to complete. Before we get to the unit's actual building, we need to do a bench test to ensure our setup will operate correctly.

## Bench Test

1. Gather all the wiring components, lights, power supply and the PIR sensor.
2. Using the type and length of wire that you will be installing, connect the wire to the light. You can use any method that you are comfortable with. Make sure the connection is secure.
3. Secure the connection with black electrical tape.
4. Connect the opposing end of this wire to the output of your PIR sensor. Be mindful of the polarity.
5. Connect the power supply to the PIR sensor. Make sure you know which terminals are positive and negative.
6. Double-check all your connections and the polarity. Then position the PIR sensor to face away from you for testing or stand very still during the test.
7. Connect the power supply to power.
8. The light should turn on then turn off after a minute or so.
9. Test that the PIR sensor works by moving in front of it and confirming that the light turns on.

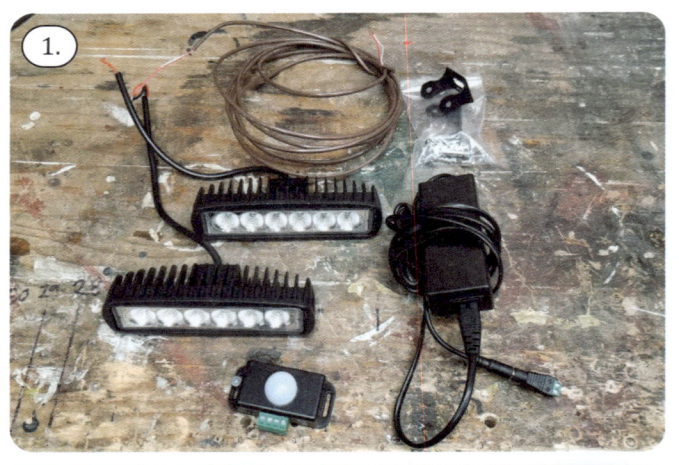

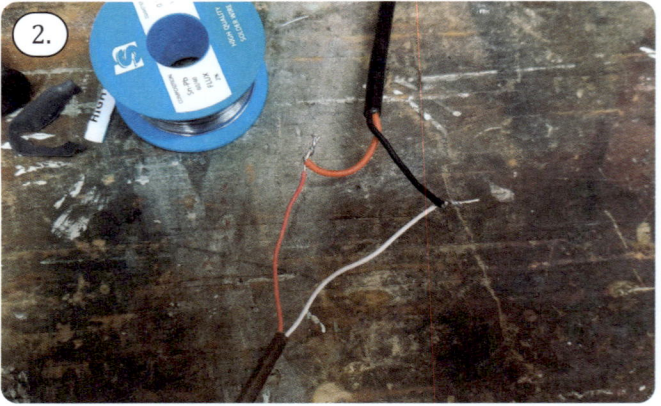

When we mount this unit, it is best to find a location that protects the sensor from the elements. The sensor that I have linked above provides no information as to its robustness, so I chose to mount the sensor so that it is protected from rain and the sun.

## Placement

1. Determine the trigger zone that you want to have the sensor cover. Then mount the sensor so that it covers that zone effectively.
2. Next, run the wiring and mount the light or lights that you will use.
3. Make your runs of wire from the power supply to the PIR sensor.
4. Confirm that the wiring is correct.
5. Supply power to the circuit but do not stand in the trigger zone while doing so.
6. Wait a minute or so for the light to turn off before walking into the trigger zone to test the circuit.

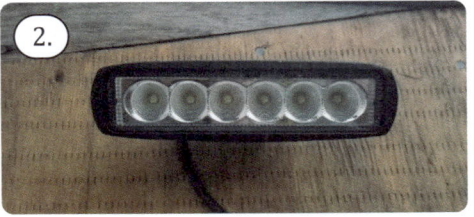

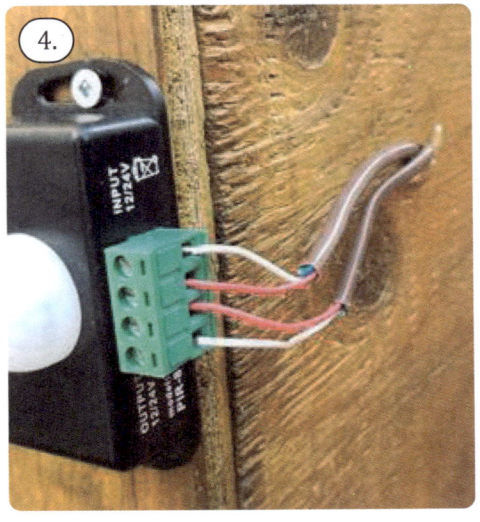

Variants
- Wiring a buzzer and the light can alert people inside the building that the sensor was triggered. This can be good if the light is in an area not immediately visible to those inside the building.
- You can also forgo the lights completely in favour of a siren or other alarm. Only use this if you are ok with responding to many false alarms or if you can adjust the sensitivity to minimize false activations.

The DIY backyard motion light may seem like an overly complicated build that solves problems that do not actually exist. The truth is that having the knowledge, skills and materials to construct one of these lights can and will lead to patching up holes in your perimeter security.

PROJECTS YOU CAN MAKE TO KEEP INTRUDERS OFF YOUR PROPERTY

# Backyard Traps Against Property Intruders

MATERIAL COST $ 25.00    EASY DIFFICULTY    30 MINUTES

For anyone who's had intruders enter their property or home, they know how violating an experience it can be. Preventing someone from entering your home starts at your property line.

It can involve setting traps as deterrents, as well as alerting you that people are entering your property.

In most jurisdictions, setting booby traps on your property to catch intruders is illegal. You will be both criminally and financially liable. It is vital to understand all rules, laws, regulations, etc., that affect what you can and cannot do in defence of your property.

Take a walk around your property and inspect all the various entry points. Look at gates, fences and open areas where someone might gain access.

One of the most out of sight areas around our homes is the backyard because most homes have them fenced in. Tall fences are great when your neighbour does nude yoga but are not so great when a prowler wants some privacy as they prepare to jump your fence.

Another issue with tall fences is that we cannot see who's approaching or concealed on the other side. Once an intruder jumps the fence, they are on your property.

The fences around your home are where you want to start thinking about placing traps. Defending the perimeter is the way you can deter or slow down intruders before you are surprised inside of your home.

## DIY Razor Wire

To scale a fence, you have to place your hands on top of that fence. Most of us don't want coils of razor or barbed wire running around our property, mainly because it's unsightly. Secondly, it may give people the impression that there's something inside worth protecting. Instead, we're going to want to use some more subtle ways to prevent people from climbing over.

This is where we can create our low-cost version of razor wire.

## Tools Needed

- Drill and bit drivers

## Materials

- Razor utility blades – These are available at Home Depot for $9.97USD for a pack of 100 www.homedepot.com/p/Husky-Heavy-Duty-Utility-Blades-Dispenser-100-Pack-HKHT19057/205037418

- Screws – You can use whatever you have on hand, but all you need are some #8 size 1-inch long wood screws which can be bought at Home Depot for $5.28USD for a pack of 100 www.homedepot.com/p/Everbilt-8-x-1-in-Zinc-Plated-Phillips-Flat-Head-Wood-Screw-100-Pack-801822/204275495

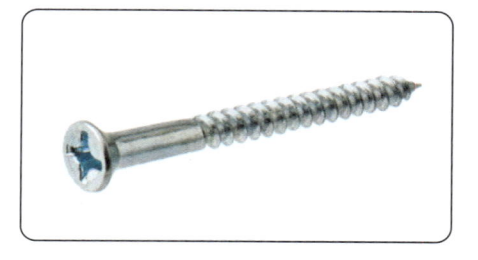

For $ 20.53 USD, you can install 100 razors on the fences around your backyard, giving you a lot of coverage and options.

## Instructions

Installation of these razor blades is straightforward and will take only a minute per blade to set up. It is not practical to place these along an entire fence line as it would take lots of blades, so you have to choose areas that you suspect someone is most likely to jump over your fence.

1. Place a razor blade against the fence on the top plate. Orient the blade so that about a quarter of an inch is sticking above the top plate.
2. Drive the screws into the top plate of the fence adjacent to the razor blade's angled edges.
3. This method is also very easily disarmed because the razor can be pulled up and away from the screws when you do not want it in use.
4. Space the razor blades out an inch or so from each other.

## Variations

- Instead of screws, you can use nails with a wide head on them. Roofing nails work pretty well for holding the razor in place.
- You can also glue broken glass to the top of your fence to deliver a similar effect.

## Spike Traps

Spike traps can come in all sorts of shapes and sizes. A garden hose with nails put through it, or boards with nails sticking out, or even strips of metal with nails or spikes tack welded to it. These can be very effective if someone is to step on them is the nails will go straight through their boots, rendering that foot virtually useless.

It's worth noting again that booby-trapping a home with traps like this is probably illegal, and you should only undertake these measures in the most extreme circumstances

## Tools

- Hammer
- Saw to cut wood

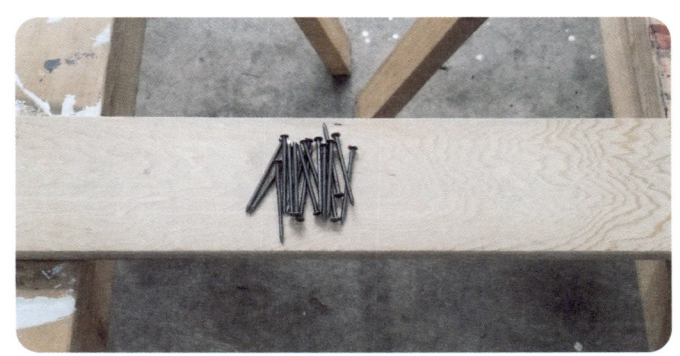

## Materials

- Nails – You can purchase a pound of common nails from Home Depot for $3.98USD
www.homedepot.com/p/Grip-Rite-10-1-4-x-2-1-2-in-8-Penny-Bright-Steel-Smooth-Shank-Common-Nails-1-lb-Pack-8C1/202308488

- Wood - Any plywood or boards will do as long as you can hammer several nails through them.

## Construction

1. Layout where the nails will go on the board, keeping them spaced a few inches apart. There is no need to crowd the board; the goal is to ensure that a few nails will impale any foot landing on the spike strip.

2. Hammer nails through the board.
3. Place the finished trap in areas that you suspect intruders would move through.

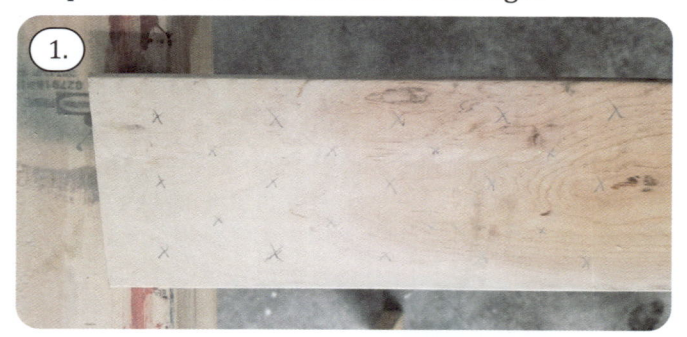

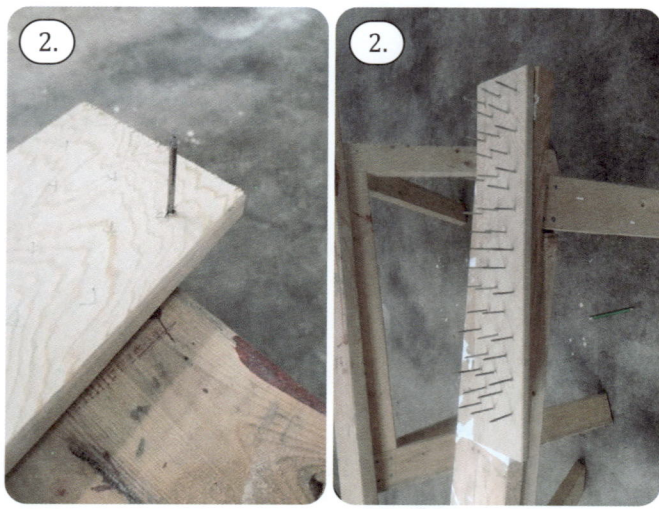

Place these traps in locations that someone may run through, hide behind, or jump over the fence. Placing a spike strip in front of any windows is also a good option. Be sure that you are very aware of the exact locations of these traps.

You can also turn these into a version of a punji stick trap by concealing them in the bottom of a pit and camouflaging the top. When someone steps on the top of the hole and their foot crashes through the camouflaging, the added momentum will drive the nails further into the intruder's foot.

## Placement

## Lights and Cameras

While not technically a trap, these are too often overlooked security preps for the backyard. Someone trying to gain entry into your property will do everything in their power to do so under cover of darkness or by lurking through the shadows. Being suddenly lit up is going to cause a lot of would-be intruders to run away.

Any lights used for security should be either motion-activated or active from dusk to dawn. A security camera should also cover each light so you can investigate why the light-activated without leaving the security of your home.

Always follow the manufactures directions when installing cameras and lights. When you are thinking about installing motion lights and cameras, you need to ask yourself some questions.

- Is there power available?
- Where would the light and camera cover?
- Will there be any blind spots?
- Which lights or cameras best suit my needs?

## Lights

When it comes to lights, basic motion-activated lights are easily obtained off Amazon or your local hardware store in some cases for as little as $ 20 USD.

A couple of examples from Amazon.com are as follows:

- For a $24.99USD option that is solar-powered
www.amazon.com/Beams-Solar-Wedge-Security-Outdoor/dp/B07W3QLRH4/

- For a light hardwired to your home for $ 36.99 USD
www.amazon.com/LEPOWER-Security-Waterproof-Detected-Entryways/dp/B07XK5Z8GD/

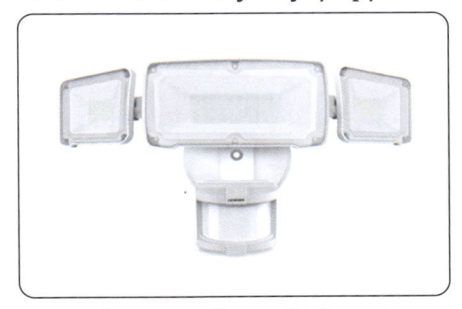

You can also purchase lights that turn on when the sun sets and turn off when the sun rises again. I use one of these lights to eliminate dark areas along my home's side towards my back gate.

- The light I use is available at Home Depot for $ 52.99 USD
www.homedepot.com/p/Lithonia-Lighting-Contractor-Select-OVFL-Series-20-Watt-White-Dusk-to-Dawn-Integrated-LED-Outdoor-2-Head-Flood-Light-OVFL-LED-2RH-40K-120-PE-WH-M-4/300577049

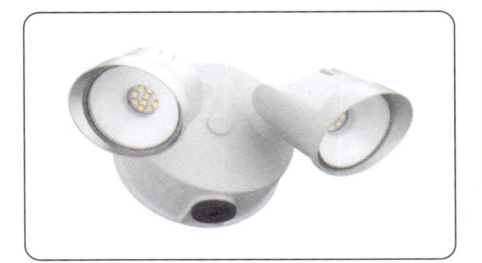

## Cameras

There are many options as far as cameras go, and the style and model that you choose will largely depend on your home and your individual needs. No matter which camera system you choose, there should be camera coverage over every door and gate. Use cameras in conjunction with lights as well. I like to have a camera that covers the motion detection zones of my motion lights.

I have had good experiences with the Wyze cameras, but they need to be protected from the elements with aftermarket housings when mounting outside.

◆ A three-pack of aftermarket weatherproof housings are $8.99USD from Amazon.com
www.amazon.com/Gresur-Adjustable-Weather-Protective-Housing/dp/B08D6S1ZCG/

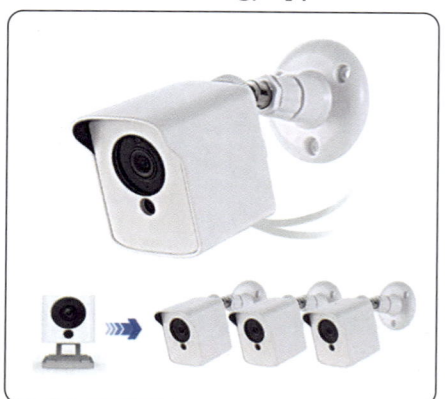

◆ Two V2 Wyze cameras cost $50.71USD from Amazon.com
www.amazon.com/Wyze-Indoor-Wireless-Camera-Vision/dp/B07G2YR23M/

◆ I found that I needed some extension power cables, which Amazon.com has for $12.99USD for a pack of two
www.amazon.com/Extension-Compatible-Wyze-Cam-NestCam-Charging/dp/B07QPHKNN6/

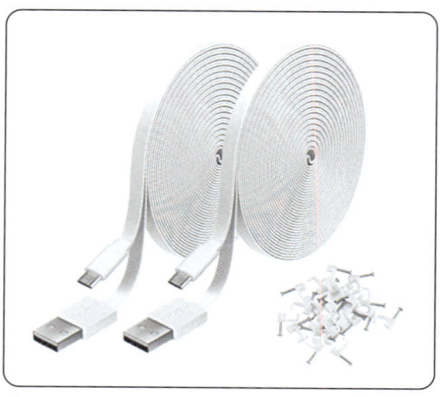

For $72.69USD, you can install two of these cameras around your home, covering the trigger areas of any motion lights that you have installed. To install a camera or two should take about an hour or so, depending on where you are planning on mounting them and how you will need to run the power supply cables.

Always be mindful of the law when installing traps on your property. Lights and cameras are the methods of catching intruders in the act that will keep you safe and secure inside your home. There is always the possibility that DIY razorwire and spike traps will cause intruders to double down on their efforts to break into your home rather than retreat, so be mindful of that as well.

PROJECTS YOU CAN MAKE TO KEEP INTRUDERS OFF YOUR PROPERTY

# How To Build A Trip Wire Alarm

**MATERIAL COST** $ 16.00   **EASY** DIFFICULTY   20 MINUTES

Early warning is one of the best defensive measures that you can deploy around your home and property. Tripwires are a fantastic way to have a passive network of devices around your property that require very little maintenance and attention. Building a tripwire alarm is cost-effective and very straightforward to do. You may have all the required components lying around the garage.

I have devised three separate tripwire alarms, one that is silent and used at a distance, one that is loud and good for up close and another that is primitive but still effective.

Placing tripwire alarms around your property can be defined as booby traps and, therefore, illegal in your area. You must understand all the laws and regulations in your area before placing any traps or devices around your property.

## What to Use as a Tripwire

In the following pictures, I have used orange paracord as a visual aid to show where the tripwire was in relation to the triggers. Do not use orange paracord as a tripwire. Do not use paracord at all for tripwires. Some examples of more appropriate trip wire material are:

- Military tripwire that Amazon sells for $ 13.40 USD.
www.amazon.com/USGI-Snare-Vietnam-Emergency-Survival/dp/B006GWTJIU/

- Kevlar tripwire is available on Amazon for $ 9.31 USD.
www.amazon.com/5ive-Star-Gear-Kevlar-Green/dp/B01ESTS8GG/

- #9 bank line, which you can find on Amazon for $ 9.95 USD.
www.amazon.com/SGT-KNOTS-Tarred-Twine-Bank/dp/B00F1YJ9B6/

- Braided fishing line (80lbs test), which Ebay sells for $ 26.53 USD.
www.ebay.com/p/672341991

Any of these options are great for setting good tripwires that should be virtually invisible to any intruders.

## Clothes Pin Silent Alarm

This tripwire alarm has the benefit of being silent and, if deployed correctly, can also go unnoticed by the intruder. Since this alarm is silent, it relies on someone to be on guard looking out towards where the tripwire is set to see the light that this type of tripwire alarm uses to signal that an intruder has entered the property.

### Tools

- Soldering iron
- Wire cutters
- Wire Stripers

## Materials

- Wooden clothespins are found on Amazon for $ 5.99 USD for a package of 50.
www.amazon.com/JABINCO-Pack-Wooden-Clothespins-About/dp/B0852TXHZG/

- Metal Tape is on Amazon for $7.88USD a roll.
www.amazon.com/Nashua-Multi-Purpose-Length-Width-Aluminum/dp/B002EX855S/

- Cheap LED Flashlight I found some on Amazon for $9.98USD for a four-pack.
www.amazon.com/BYB-Aluminum-Flashlight-Batteries-Backpacking/dp/B00V639BX2/

- 9-volt batteries are on Amazon for $ 11.99 USD for eight of them.
www.amazon.com/AmazonBasics-Everyday-Alkaline-Batteries-8-Pack/dp/B00MH4QM1S/

- 9-volt battery connectors I found some on Amazon for $5.99USD for an eight pack.
www.amazon.com/Battery-Connector-I-Type-Plastic-Housing/dp/B07TRKYZCH/

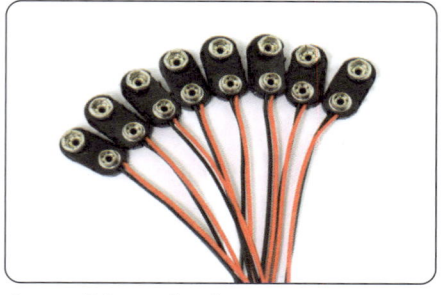

- A small length of copper wire you can find standard hookup wire on Amazon for $7.99USD.
www.amazon.com/Wire%EF%BC%8C66ft-Electrical-conductor-wire%EF%BC%8CTinned-temperatures/dp/B07SCJ69H4/

## Instructions

1. Disassemble the flashlight and remove the LED light bulb assembly.
2. Determine which points on the circuit board are negative and positive by experimenting with touching the 9-volt battery connector's connected leads until the light illuminates.
3. Wrap the jaws of the clothes peg with metal tape.
4. Tape the negative end of the nine-volt connector to the outside of one of the jaws of the clothespin.
5. Tape the loose wire to the outside of the other jaw.
6. Solder the positive end of the battery connector to the PCB board of the LED light, then solder the free end of the loose wire to the appropriate spot on the PCB board.
7. Tape or glue the battery to the bottom of the clothespin.
8. Tape or glue the light to the top of the clothespin.
9. Make a non-conductive trigger that you can attach the tripwire to. In this case, I wrapped cardboard in electrical tape and added a loop of wire.

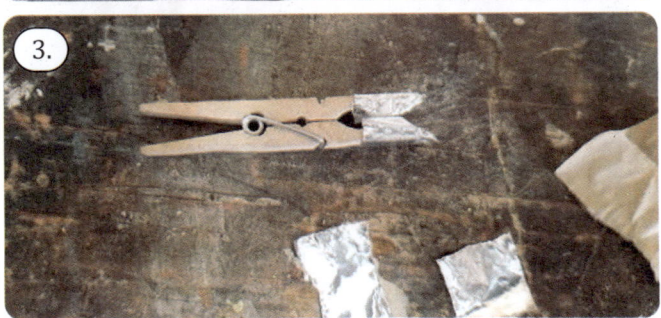

## Placing the Clothes Pin Tripwire Alarm

To place this alarm, find an appropriate spot to place the trigger so that the light will be facing whoever is on guard duty. A device like this is well suited for a treeline in front of an observation post (OP), especially if you can devise a way to shield the light in such a way that it is only visible to the OP.

## Sound Grenade Trip Wire Alarm

Sound grenades are personal alarms that people can use to deliver a 120db siren when they are activated. The intent is that the loud noise will deter a further attack and alert people around the victim that there is a crime taking place. We are going to employ this device to alert us to an intruder.

### Tools
- Drill and bits
- Hammer

### Materials
- Sound grenades are on Amazon for $9.99USD. www.amazon.com/iMaxAlarm-SOS-Alert-Personal-Alarm/dp/B07B42MGKS
- Steel Strapping found on Amazon for $6.06USD. www.amazon.com/Sioux-Chief-524-1022PK2-10-Feet-22-Gauge/dp/B00745VXN2/

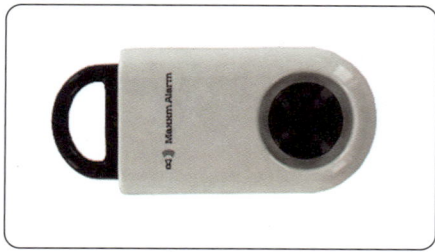

### Instructions
1. Test the key on the sound grenade to determine how much effort it will take to remove. You may have to modify the sound grenade key to slip out far easier.
2. Find a location that you wish to deploy this device close enough to your home that you will hear the siren.
3. Attach the sound grenade to one end of the span that you wish to cross with the tripwire.
4. Attach the tripwire to the key.
5. You may have to install a guide to have the wire pull the key straight out of the sound grenade.
6. Anchor the static end of the tripwire.

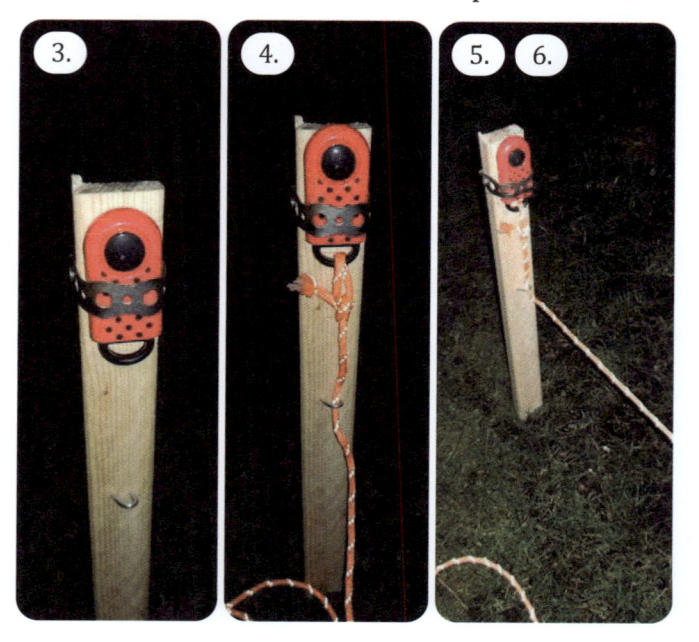

### Notes
- These devices, once activated, will not shut off until we replace the key or the device runs out of batteries.
- Test the device by activating it and leaving it in the area you want to deploy it. Then go inside your home to check where you will be able to hear the alarm.

## Cans and String Trip Wire Alarm

Sometimes one of the best systems is the ones that are virtually free to build and deploy. With some old soda cans, rocks, and cordage, you can set up many of these primitive tripwire alarms. The problem with these devices is that they are nowhere near as loud as the previous two, but they can be a great deterrent for those who move through your property.

The soda can tripwire alarm consists of a couple of cans with a handful of rocks or nuts and bolts and a length of cordage to act as the tripwire. What happens is that when someone's leg gets caught on the cordage, the two cans fall, causing quite the racket.

## Materials

- Aluminum cans are probably in your recycle bin already.
- Rocks, bolts, or nuts or anything else that will make a lot of noise.

## Instructions

1. Fill two or three aluminum soda cans with a handful of rocks or nuts and bolts.
2. Tie the cordage to each can's pull tab. This tripwire does not need to be tight. It simply needs to be high enough off the ground to make noise when the cans drop.
3. You may need to use a guide to make sure that the cans are pulled along with the tripwire as the intruder's foot drags it.
4. Secure the static end of the tripwire to a stationary object.

It needs noting again that booby-trapping your property is illegal in most if not all jurisdictions. You must know and understand what you are legally permitted to do and make your decisions based on your situation. These devices give an early warning to an intruder on your property, giving you the ability to mount a suitable defence but can cause injury if someone falls after tripping over the tripwire.

PROJECTS ON FOOD

# Bean And Rice Survival Soup

EASY DIFFICULTY

Soup is always a winner in our house especially on a cold day. There is nothing easier than grabbing a can from your pantry and heating it up on your stove. Unfortunately, canned soup these days, especially the fancy stuff, can cost you an arm and a leg and if you look at the list of ingredients often contains more sugar, salt, and preservatives than is healthy. Although we all love it, one can of Campbell's chicken noodle soup contains 800 mgs. of salt; that is almost 40% of your daily intake in one can! Fortunately, homemade soup is easy, cheap, and healthy, and can last just as long as the store-bought canned stuff.

One of my favorites, cheapest and healthiest, homemade soups to make is what I call **Beans and Rice Survival Soup**. Beans are for the protein, rice provides the slow burning carb energy, and all the other stuff gives you the vitamins and minerals your body needs to keep healthy. You can tweak the recipe to suit your tastes. Just keep in mind that the goal is to have a combo of ingredients that provides you with a "one pot wonder" healthy meal.

Pricewise my recipe works out to be less than a dollar per 12-ounce serving and unless you tweak it massively, by adding some fancy spices or exotic legumes, yours probably will too. All of the ingredients for this soup are easily available at any grocery store. Just go to the dried goods section.

Now, the key to a long-lasting Beans and Rice Survival Soup is that you do not use water. That is right, no water. Until of course you are ready to cook it. Instead, simply assemble your ingredients into your jar and store them, just like a packet of ramen noodles. Everything is in their own little baggy ready to be combined whenever you want.

## Here's What You Need

Make sure you have:
- A container (preferably a glass jar or something else that is rat/mouse proof)
- Zip lock/sealable bags
- A pot (for cooking)
- A spoon

## Ingredients:

- ⅔ cup dried beans
- 1 ½ cup rice
- 1 cup dried lentils (any color)
- 1 cup barley
- ½ cup dried split green peas
- ½ cup dried chickpeas
- 6 Tbsp. beef buillon (Make sure to check the directions on your buillon stock, some is stronger than others. This recipe is for roughly 6 quarts of soup, so measure accordingly.)
- 2 Tbsp. dried garlic powder
- 2 Tbsp. mixed herb
- 1 Tbsp. cumin
- 2 tsp. black pepper
- 2 tsp. salt
- 2 Tbsp. dried onion powder
- 2 tsp. chilli powder

## Putting Together the Beans and Rice Survival Soup

This recipe is big enough to be split between two quart-sized mason jars.
1. In one bowl combine all of your dried legumes, the beans, split peas, lentils, chick peas, and the barley. Mix well.
2. Pour half into one jar and half into the other.
3. Take you rice and put ¾ of a cup in one sealable bag and ¾ in another. Seal them up and put them on top of your legumes. The reason that the legumes and rice need to be separat-

ed is that when you prepare your soup the legumes are going to take a lot longer to cook than the rice, so you will add it separately.
4. Take all your spices and mix them in a bowl. Then portion out half into one small sealable bag and one into another. Place them on top of your rice bag in the glass jar and then cap it. That's it! Your soup is ready to be stored for literally years!

Now when you want to cook it up this is how.
1. Pour three quarts of water into your pot and put it on your stove at high heat. Add your bean mix first.
2. Once your water is boiling again, add your seasoning mix and stir until your bouillon is dissolved. Cover your pot.
3. Your legumes should be almost soft enough to eat after an hour and a half to two hours.
4. Finally, add your rice. Cook until the rice is ready to eat.

Enjoy your hearty and delicious soup! Pair it with some nice crusty bread or enjoy it on its own!

# Canning Amish Poor Man's Steak

**MEDIUM DIFFICULTY**

While canning vegetables and sauces at home is a fairly common activity, most people don't realize that canning meat is just as easy, safe, and delicious; if you take the right steps. If you don't believe me, then just ask the Amish; they have been off-grid for literally hundreds of years and are one of the healthiest people in the US.

Here I am going to share with you one of their recipes for canned meat, that is simple and delicious: Amish Poor Man's Steak. As with all recipes, you can tweak this one any number of ways but the key to this steak lasting a long time in your pantry is the canning method at the end.

Simply put, Amish Poor Man's Steak is seasoned ground beef patties smothered in gravy. Pair a couple of these patties with some home-canned green beans and carrots and some instant mash potatoes and you have a proper meal.

Unlike others, I will not be relying on store-bought soup and gravy packets to season my food. So here is what you are going to need. For this recipe I am going to use 2.5 pounds of ground beef. All the ingredients listed below can easily be found at your neighborhood grocery store. If they don't have dried mushrooms, they can easily be found at any Asian food market.

## Ingredients Needed

For the steak:
- 2.5 pounds of lean ground beef
- 2 stalks of celery
- 1 carrot
- 1 large onion
- ½ cup bread crumbs
- 2 eggs
- ½ tsp. black pepper
- 1 tsp. salt
- 1 tsp. dried herbs mix
- ½ cup milk

For the gravy:
- Beef buillion
- 3 Tbsp. flour
- 3 Tbsp. butter
- ½ tsp. pepper
- ½ tsp. salt
- 1 cup dried mushrooms
- 1 tsp. dried herbs mix
- 4 diced garlic cloves or 2 tsp. dried garlic powder
- 2 cups milk

## The Recipe

**PREPARING THE STEAK**

1. Dice up all your vegetables as seen below. The dice should be fairly fine, not blender fine, but close to it.
2. Put all those vegetables in a bowl/container big enough to hold them and all the remaining ingredients.
3. Add in your salt, pepper, eggs, dried herbs mix, breadcrumbs, and milk. Stir together.
4. Next, add your ground beef. I like to mix it with my hands. Mix until all the ingredients are evenly integrated.
5. Take the lid of your canning jar as a mold and start making "steak" patties.
6. Place them on an oven tray, preheat your oven to 375 degrees Fahrenheit and cook them for 40 minutes.

## PREPARING THE GRAVY

1. Rehydrate and dice finely your mushrooms.
2. Peel and fine chop your garlic.
3. Add mushrooms and garlic and cook until garlic and mushrooms brown slightly.
4. Make your roux by melting butter and add about 2 tablespoons of flour and stir vigorously until they are mixed.
5. Pour in milk and continue stirring until gravy just begins to boil and thicken.
6. Lower the heat and season with salt, pepper, and dried herbs.

## CANNING YOUR AMISH POOR MAN'S STEAK

Now that you have your steaks and gravy, it's time to can them. Begin by stacking your steaks inside your mason jar all the way to the top. Then pour in your gravy, again all the way to the top. Firmly cap your jar.

Sterilize your jars of delicious canned Amish Steak. To do this, you need to grab a pot big enough to hold your mason jar. Fill it with water and get that water up to a nice rolling boil. Then gently place your mason jar into the water making sure it is completely submerged.

Once the water gets back to a rolling boil, leave your jar to sterilize in the water for at least 3 hours.

Unlike fruits or some vegetables, which usually only require 10 or so minutes in the boiling water bath, here we are dealing with meat, so the longer the better.

At the end, remove your jar and let it cool. As it cools the "button" on the top of the jar should compress down. This is your signal that the contents inside are sealed and that your canning was a success.

If it doesn't, the sterilization process didn't work so either you have to start over, or you can eat those steaks over the next couple of weeks, as long as you keep them refrigerated.

Some people may think that when dealing with meat, you always need to pressure can it. However, the Amish do water bath canning when it comes to meat and doing it safely for hundreds of years. I follow in their footsteps, particularly for this recipe, but this does not mean I encourage you to do the same. Do the research and decide for yourself. Either way, Amish Steak is undeniably delicious. Give it a try!

# How To Dry Meat And Turn It Into Powder

**MEDIUM DIFFICULTY**

If you are a fan of beef jerky, and really who isn't, then you must try Jerky powder. You may have seen it before at the gas station without really knowing what it was. It is usually in little cannisters the same size as tobacco chew. And though you might have assumed it was some strange-flavored version of tobacco, don't worry, there is no tobacco in jerky powder. It's just pulverized beef jerky.

You can have it just as it is. Grab a pinch full and put it under your lip and enjoy as a burst of beef jerky goodness melts away in your mouth. It is also great as an additive to all sorts of food. Use it wherever you might throw in beef stock or bacon bits. It gives smoky richness to stews, it's fantastic mixed into mashed potatoes, and even into your macaroni cheese.

And like just about everything else, the homemade stuff is much tastier than the store-bought kind. You can tweak your recipe a thousand different ways, depending on the cut of meat you use and the sauce you marinade it in. The only consideration you must take into account when making beef jerky powder, as opposed to regular beef jerky, is that in order for you to get a powder-like consistency, the meat should be on the leaner side and the marinade should contain a minimal amount of sugar or sugar-like ingredients. This is because in order to blend up your jerky it needs to be dry. Fat, which is greasy, and sugars, which are sticky, are going to make getting your jerky dry enough difficult.

With that in mind, below is my favorite recipe for Jerky powder. If you have ever made jerky before, then you already know half of what you need to make powder. Whether you use your oven or a dehydrator is up to you, but I am a bit of a minimalist so here I am going to use a regular oven.

First, I will go over the marinade, then the oven drying method, then how to cut it up and shred it into a powder. Now when I say powder, I do not mean we are going to make jerky flour, but rather something more the consistency of sawdust. That might not sound delicious, but trust me, don't knock it untill you've tried it.

## Preparing the Marinade

Generally, I am a fan of all kinds of marinades from your sticky honey soy sauce types to your more dry and peppery varieties, but again keeping in mind that this jerky is going to become powder, the marinade I am going to use here is closer to the dry and peppery spectrum.

This recipe is for about 2 pounds of beef. If you are making your jerky with more or less, adjust the recipe accordingly. All the ingredients for it can be easily found at any neighborhood grocery store.

## Ingredients:

- 2 pounds lean beef cut (I use the top side, you can also use silver side, or if you want to be fancy, flank steak)
- ⅓ cup soy sauce
- 1 Tbsp. liquid smoke
- 1 Tbsp. garlic powder
- 1 tsp. onion powder
- 1 tsp. black pepper
- 1 tsp. allspice
- 1 tsp. chili powder (or flakes)
- 1 tsp. apple cider vinegar

## Preparing the Meat

1. First, cut your jerky into thin long strips. The thinner the better.
2. Mix all the marinade ingredients together in the zip lock bag.

3. Put the cut-up beef into the zip lock bag. I find putting the bag marinade into an ice cream container helps to stabilize everything.
4. Mix well and put into the refrigerator overnight or at least for 12 hours. I find it best to put the bag into a container in the refrigerator on the off chance that if the bag bursts open, you don't have a mess. Also, it is best to turn the bag over a couple times so that the beef inside is evenly marinaded in the sauce.

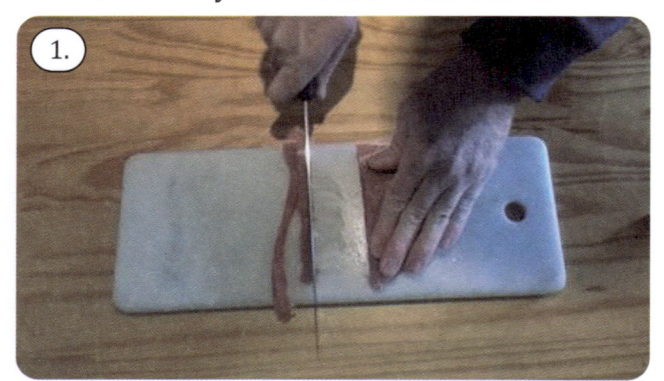

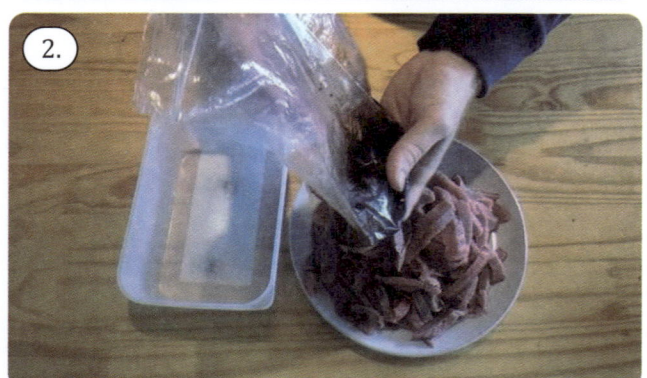

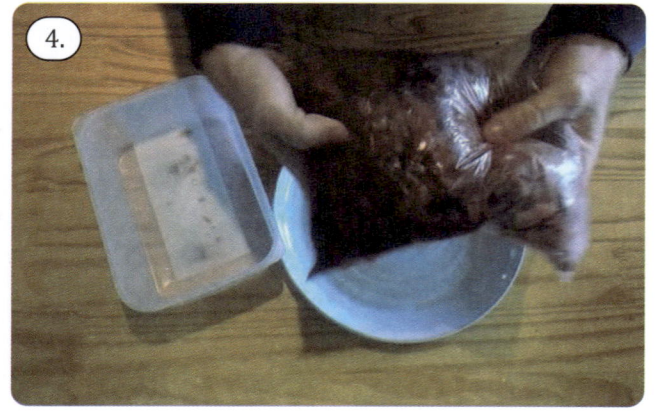

## Drying Your Jerky

1. Take an oven tray and cover it with foil.
2. Place the oven rack on top of it and lay out your beef strips onto the rack. You can space them close together. The beef shrinks.
3. Set your oven to about 320 degrees and place your tray with beef into the oven.
4. Leave the oven door cracked open using a spoon.
5. Now it's time to wait. Your Jerky should be ready in about 2 hours, but it all depends on how thin you cut the meat.
6. When your jerky is dry to the touch, almost crispy, take it out and let it cool.

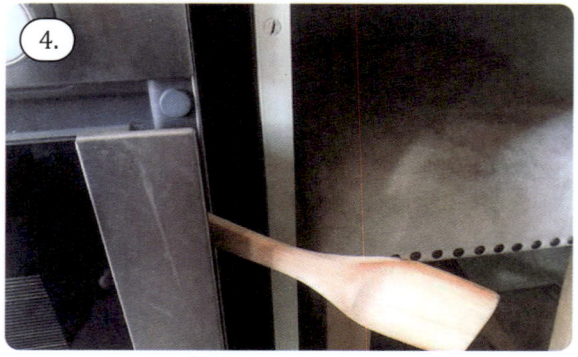

## Making the Powder

1. Once your jerky is cool and dry, dice it up roughly with a knife.
2. If it feels soft while you are cutting it, you can place it back in the oven for another 20 minutes at the same 320 degrees.
3. If it cuts easily, then you can throw it straight into a food processor or blender and pulse it to your desired consistency. I like mine to still be a bit chunky, again sawdust consistency, not powdery.

If you want your Jerky to be closer to a powder consistency, maybe to use in a smooth gravy, all you need to do is blend it more. If you still aren't getting the consistency you want, try cooking your jerky longer. But be careful there is a fine line between delicious tasting jerky and burnt strips of meat. I find that the consistency this recipe produces is perfect from most applications, even gravy.

If you keep it in an airtight container, your Jerky powder should last you a good six months without refrigeration and longer with it. Enjoy!

PROJECTS ON FOOD

# How To Make 2400 Calorie Emergency Ration Bars Designed To Feed You For A Full Day

EASY DIFFICULTY    30 MINUTES

Across the table from a government worker I was discussing the importance of emergency food. The discussion was centered on freeze dried meals and canned foods.

We were discussing the feasibility of both in a serious disaster situation. We were not talking about the novelty power outage where we all have fun bringing out all the emergency preparedness tools and toys.

Rather the situation where we are helping neighbors, fighting oncoming floods or trapped by the fallout of a life-threatening disaster.

It was in that moment he stressed the importance of convenience in a disaster. His example was cereal and shelf stable milk.

He described it as follows, "It takes no time at all to put together and will sustain your family members without complaint." I would be lying if I said this didn't change my point of view on disaster foods. 'Could *it be so simple*?' I thought to myself. More importantly, I began to realize how necessary this convenience could be.

Of course, there is a food that presents the ultimate in convenience and perhaps the best choice in a situation like this is the high calorie emergency ration bars.

These bars are often built in a **2400-calorie pack that is designed to feed you for a full day**. The rations are often broken into 4 squares of 600 calories each.

These rations are not only used by preppers and survivalists, but backpackers and hunters utilize them as well. This is a testament to their efficiency as a calorie provider. Of course, the elk hunter wants a delicious back strap for dinner but these rations are a nice second option.

Below I will outline the process of creating your own. If you follow the steps, you will have your own answer in a disaster scenario, or something to take on your next hike.

## Materials and Ingredients Needed

As far as tools go, you will need:
- 12-inch-deep baking pan
- 1 wooden spoon
- 1 small saucepot.

As far as ingredients go, you will need:
- 3 Tablespoons Olive oil
- 2 Cups Maple syrup
- 4 Tablespoons Raw Honey
- 2 Tablespoons Peanut butter
- 1 Cup Frosted Flakes
- 3 Cups Oatmeal
- 1 Cup Protein powder
- 1 Cup Almonds
- 1 Cup Raisins.

## Making Your Own Ration Bars

1. Begin by combining your honey, olive oil, and maple syrup in a sauce pot. Heat this mix over a medium heat and stir it frequently until it begins to simmer.

2. Add your two tablespoons of peanut butter to the mix in the pan. Stir the peanut butter until it melts into the syrup mix. Be careful! this syrup mix will be very hot and if it gets on your skin it's nearly napalm!

3. Take the remaining dry ingredients and add them to a large bowl or two large bowls. You don't want these bowls to be filled more than halfway, as you will be doing a lot of mixing in these bowls. If they are too full with just the dry you will have a terrible time mixing in your liquid in the next step.

4. Once you have thoroughly mixed up your dry ingredients, take the hot syrup peanut butter mixture and add it into your dry ingredients. While it's still hot, mix to coat your dry ingredients thoroughly. Make sure it's thoroughly mixed and all ingredients have a nice sheen to them.
5. Preheat your oven to 375 degrees. Dump your mix into a baking pan. This pan should be at least 2 inches deep. Be sure to press and pack this mix down tight. This will allow for tight squares to be cut from this mix.
6. Bake in the 375-degree oven for 20 minutes until the edges begin to brown.
7. Allow the mix to cool and cut into 2×2 squares. Each square will be roughly 600 calories. Packing together 4 of these squares will equal 2400 calories and be enough calories to push through a long hunting trip or life-threatening disaster situation.
8. You can even portion them in little muffin pans, if you want to get fancy. I like the little pucks to be honest.

PROJECTS ON FOOD

# How To Make Dandelion Bread

EASY DIFFICULTY

Dandelion is one of the more recognizable plants in the world. Often considered a weed to the urban gardeners, dandelion is a very nutritious plant with many medicinal benefits. Every part of the plant is edible, from the roots to the flowers.

Dandelion is a rich source of vitamins, minerals, and antioxidants. The raw greens contain high amounts of Vitamins A, C, and K while also being a source of calcium, potassium, iron, and manganese. They also have some vitamin E and small amounts of some B vitamins. Dandelion root is a source of inulin, a type of fibre that helps support healthy gut bacteria. The root is a great non-caffeinated substitute for tea or coffee.

Dandelions are generally considered safe to eat, but the risk will never be zero as with any foraged food. There is the possibility of allergic reactions in people who are allergic to plants such as ragweed, and people with sensitive skin may develop contact dermatitis.

If you choose to consume Dandelion, do so in very small amounts at first, and if you react unfavourably to it, do not consume it again. You can also do the universal edibility test to determine how you will respond to this plant.

When harvesting dandelions, only do so from areas you know have not been sprayed with pesticides or other chemicals. Your yard is probably the best area to harvest. Since we only need the flowers, you can pluck the flower head off the stem. You are going to want enough to get about a cup of petals per loaf of bread.

Dandelion bread is very easy to make and requires only six store-bought ingredients. Baking a loaf of Dandelion bread is also a good activity to get kids active in the kitchen.

## Ingredients

The ingredients can be found at most grocery stores, and the Dandelion flowers can be harvested from any area free of pesticide use.
- ◆ One cup of clean, fresh Dandelions
- ◆ 2 cups of flour. Flour is $3.26USD for a 5-pound bag at Walmart

www.walmart.com/ip/King-Arthur-Flour-Unbleached-All-Purpose-Flour-5-lb-Bag/10535106

- ◆ 2 tsp of baking powder. A container of Baking powder is $1.82USD at Walmart

www.walmart.com/ip/Rumford-Double-Acting-Non-GMO-Baking-Powder-8-1-oz/252551170

- ◆ 1 egg. A dozen eggs are $4.35USD at Walmart

www.walmart.com/ip/Great-Value-Large-White-Eggs-72-Oz-36-Ct/142616435

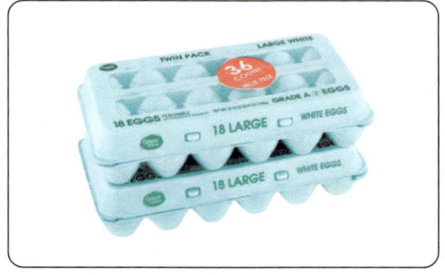

- 1 1/4 cup of milk. A gallon of is available from Walmart for $3.45USD

www.walmart.com/ip/Great-Value-2-Reduced-Fat-Milk-128-Fl-Oz/10450115

- 3 tbsp vegetable oil. Vegetable oil is $2.00USD at Walmart for a 48 fl oz container

www.walmart.com/ip/Great-Value-Vegetable-Oil-48-fl-oz/10451002

- 1/3 cup honey. A twelve oz jar of honey is $ 4.18 USD at Walmart

www.walmart.com/ip/Busy-Bee-U-S-A-Honey-12-oz/10292906

## The Step by Step Recipe

1. Preheat oven to 400 degrees Fahrenheit and line a loaf pan with parchment paper.
2. Using a sharp knife, cut the petals off the heads of the Dandelions that you've harvested.
3. If you wish, you can keep the petals whole or chop them as fine or as coarse as you want to.
4. Mix the flour, baking powder, and Dandelions in a large bowl along with a pinch of salt.
5. In another bowl, whisk together the oil, egg, milk, and honey.
6. Pour the milk mixture over the dry mixture and stir until incorporated. Do not over-mix.
7. Pour the mixture into the loaf pan and bake for 15 minutes, then reduce the temperature to 350 degrees Fahrenheit and bake another 20 minutes until a toothpick inserted in the middle comes out clean.
8. Remove from oven and allow to cool slightly before slicing.

Dandelion bread can be stored for up to five days in an airtight container, but it can also be frozen for longer-term storage.

## Taste Test

Dandelion bread has a taste that was slightly sweet and was not overpowering with Dandelion flavour. I would say that this bread would be good with some butter or honey alongside morning coffee or tea. The absence of processed sugars in this bread is very apparent, but the honey makes up for it quite nicely. I think Dandelion bread is a great way to add Dandelions to your regular diet. Making a loaf or two of Dandelion bread is a great way to introduce this plant into your diet. Baking it into a loaf of bread will help introduce the plant to picky eaters and give your family the possible health benefits of the plant, while being very delicious.

PROJECTS ON FOOD

# How To Make Hardtack (Emergency Survival Bread)

**EASY DIFFICULTY**

There's an old adage that says, "Man cannot live by bread alone." (I Googled it, and it turns out it's from a Bible verse.) So, when I stop to think about what foods I would want to have available in an emergency, of course, bread rose to the top of the list.

But if you know anything about bread—baking it, eating it, storing it - then you know it's prone to going bad quite quickly. And that's due to several factors, starting with yeast. But butter, oil, and milk can also be the culprits that cause your favorite loaf or rolls to mold over and rot. Any bit of moisture—the moisture that gives it loft, makes it airy, and that makes it a perfect vessel for sandwiches, cheese, and so much more—is at the root of why you cannot preserve bread for the long term. That and a lack of acid.

I figured, though, that there has to be some way to add bread to my emergency pantry.

Of course, you can freeze bread. And if you're committed to fresh bread for the long term, that's likely your best option. But if your electricity is out, then you're out of luck. That bread will eventually mold and go bad.

Then I thought, maybe I can make bread in a can. And I'll just say, while I found a couple of recipes online that explained how to do this (apparently giving gifts of canned breads, especially fruit breads, as holiday gifts was a thing a couple of years ago), I also found literally dozens of articles that said: **"No. Absolutely positively do not can bread or eat canned bread."** (Boston brown bread seems to be an exception, most likely because it's made in giant manufacturing facilities with who knows what preservatives. It is tasty, though, so it's a viable option).

The bottom line is that canned breads are not safe to eat. Trapping moisture and oxygen in a glass jar, it turns out, delivers an environment that is perfect for breeding microorganisms that can be not only harmful but that have the potential to kill you. Botulism is a prime candidate for scary things that can grow in your canned bread.

According to Richard Andrew, a food safety and nutrition educator with Penn State Extension, "There are no reliable or safe recipes for baking and sealing breads and cakes in canning jars, and storing them at room temperature for extended lengths of time." I don't know about you, but for me, botulism isn't worth the risk.

I did, however, find one viable option, and it's been around for centuries. Have you ever heard of hardtack? Hardtack is also known as survival bread, and with this food item, the term bread is used ... loosely.

Hardtack was used on ships as they crossed the Atlantic or navigated to and from exotic lands hundreds of years ago. It was also popular with pioneers and settlers as it can, when properly stored, last for years.

It's also ridiculously easy and inexpensive to make. Just be sure to temper your expectations, because hardtack is probably like no other bread you've ever eaten. It's not soft, fluffy, or flakey. It bears no resemblance even to the driest, most crisp cracker you've ever eaten.

Hardtack is, in a word, hard, and in another word, bland. It's so hard that to eat it, it must be soaked or submerged in some form of liquid for at least 5 to 10 minutes. Without soaking it in water, milk, soup, stew, brine, coffee, tea, or some other liquid, hardtack is virtually inedible. It was created specifically to be a long-lasting survival food that would not spoil.

In addition to being long-lasting, hardtack may also thicken the liquids to which it is added, making them more filling and satisfying, which is always a good thing in a survival situation. So let's get cooking, shall we?

## What You Will Need

To make hardtack bread, you will need the following items:

- measuring cups and spoons
- mixing bowl
- fork or wooden spoon
- baking tray or cookie sheet
- rolling pin
- knife

- skewer or chopstick
- optional: biscuit cutter or jar lid

You will also need the following ingredients:
- 2 cups of all-purpose flour
- ¾ cup of water
- 1 ½ teaspoons salt
- optional: dried herbs or seasonings

With these ingredients in these proportions, you can expect to make 10 to 12 "biscuits" or "crackers." When I made the recipe, I ended up with about 14 total pieces of hardtack.

As you can tell from the ingredients list, it's very easy to double or even triple this recipe, if you want to make a lot all at once.

## The Step by Step Recipe

### STEP 1
Preheat the oven to $375°F$. Combine the flour and salt in a mixing bowl. You want to make sure the salt is well dispersed through the flour before the water is added.

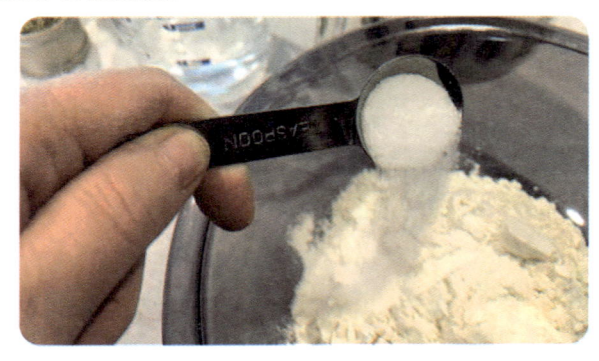

### STEP 2
Add the water.

### STEP 3
Mix thoroughly with a fork or wooden spoon.

The dough should be well incorporated and relatively dry but not sticky.

If your dough is too sticky to work with, add additional flour, one tablespoon at a time. (I did not have to add any extra flour.)

### STEP 4
Turn the dough out and work it into a ball with your hands.

(My dough was crumbly, so I had to work loose flour from the bottom of the bowl into the dough ball.)

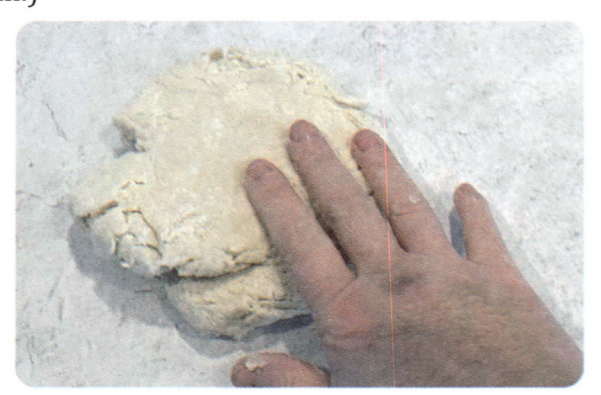

If necessary, you can add a little flour to your work surface to prevent the dough from sticking.

### STEP 5
Roll the dough out with a rolling pin to a thickness of about ½ inch.

### STEP 6
Cut the dough into 3-inch squares with a knife or into rounds with a biscuit cutter. (I used a canning jar lid to make rounds because my biscuit cutter is now a tool for use only in my art studio.)

### STEP 7
Poke several holes into each piece of hardtack using a fork, skewer, or chopstick.

You should poke the holes all the way through the dough. This step prevents the hardtack from puffing up when it bakes.

### STEP 8
This next part isn't required, but I was feeling fancy when I was testing this recipe, and if you want to add something to your hardtack to give it a little bit of flavor, feel free to do so.

Remember, you do not want to introduce any moisture to your recipe. With that in mind, I sprinkled the tops of my "biscuits" with a mix of dried Italian herbs (from last summer's herb garden).

### STEP 9
Rollout any remaining dough, and again, cut out squares or rounds. This time I cut the dough into squares, poked holes into each with a skewer, and added a dried "Everything Bagel" seasoning for a little (very little) excitement.

### STEP 10
Place the remaining pieces of hardtack dough onto your baking sheet.

#### STEP 11
Place your baking sheet in a preheated 375° oven and bake for 30 minutes.

#### STEP 12
After 30 minutes, remove the hardtack from the oven (both the oven and the hardtack will be extremely hot. Use oven mitts to keep from burning yourself. Using a spatula, flip all the hardtack and return the pan to the oven for another 30 minutes.

#### STEP 13
Remove your finished hardtack from the oven! Here are a few photos of the finished bread:

#### STEP 14
To ensure my hardtack will last for as long as I need it to (as well as to protect it from rodents), I'll vacuum seal it and store it in my pantry.
Don't forget to soak your hardtack before eating it!

PROJECTS ON FOOD

# How To Make Lard

**MEDIUM DIFFICULTY**

Before industrial oil producers started pumping out barrels of vaguely defined vegetable oil for mass consumption, one of the most common types of oil used around the world for cooking was lard. Unlike many of the newer mass-produced oils, lard has no trans-fats and, just like olive oil, is rich in oleic acid which has a range of health benefits. Best of all, it tastes amazing and can be used in a variety of cooking applications from frying, to baking, and even to preserve meat with little or no refrigeration.

Lard also has a long shelf life of around six months, or longer if kept sufficiently cold, and if you are a fan of nose-to-tail ethical meat eating, it gives you the perfect way to use up all those fatty off cuts that you might be tempted to just throw down the garbage disposal. But what exactly is lard and how can it be made?

Lard is rendered pig fat. Just pig, nothing else. Rendered cow and sheep fat are different and are called tallow. Usually, the pig fat used to make lard is from the back of the pig or from what is called the "leaf", which is a layer of fat that surrounds the pig's kidneys and lion. Leaf fat lard is considered "high grade" stuff because it spreads easily and is said to have a "clean" taste but really fat from anywhere on a pig will make a perfectly delicious and serviceable lard.

Now what is this rendering process? Generically, rendering is when you heat up a substance in order to separate it into different parts. When you are rendering pig fat to make lard you are separating the oil, lard, from what is variously called the "cracklin".

After the rendering process is finished, these leftover crunchy bits make a great snack. You can chow on them as they are, sprinkle them with a variety of spices, or grind them up and add them to all sorts of other good eats.

The liquid that separates from the cracklin is lard. In its liquid form lard is a pale-yellow oil but as it cools it solidifies and turns a beautiful white. Making your own lard is easy and cheap and, depending on how much you make, can set you up for weeks or even months of delicious meals.

There are two ways to render pig fat to make lard: the "wet" method and the "dry" method. The dry method is the simpler of the two and the one I that I will demonstrate below. Lard made from either method is fine for most purposes. The main difference is that the dry method produces a lard with a lower "smoke point", meaning that it is not ideal when cooking at very high temperatures. The downside of the wet method is that you don't get the tasty by-product of cracklin.

## What You Will Need

- pig fat
- a pot
- a stove (gas, or electric, or even wood burning)
- a glass jar (mason jars are best because you can seal them nicely, but any glass jar will do)
- a strainer
- some paper towels
- a spoon to stir

Because making your own lard has not (yet) gone viral, pig fat is not usually sold alongside the pork chops at your neighborhood grocery store or butcher shop.

But don't worry; it is still easy enough to find. Because most groceries still butcher at least some of the meat they sell on site, simply asking the butcher behind the counter if they have any fat "in the back" will usually produce the goods. Online you can find it for a huge variety of prices. so it pays to look around.

## The Step by Step Process

Once you've got your fat, the next step is to cut it into roughly one-inch chunks.

Then place your pot on your heat and poor just enough water into the pot to barely cover the bottom of it.

Once your pot it hot, the water should be just bubbling. Throw in your cut up pork fat and reduce your heat to something approximating "medium." Now comes the waiting. You will be leaving this pork fat to render down for approximately 2 hours, depending on how much fat you are using. But don't just leave it. Check back in on it every 15 minutes or so to make sure the fat isn't sticking to bottom of the pot.
After 30 minutes it should look something like this:

After an hour, the oil should be noticeably separating from the cracklin and both should be darkening up nicely into a cool amber color.

After the first hour, keep checking your pot until your crackling starts to turn noticeably browner; this signals that the majority of the lard has separated from it and it is now beginning to fry itself. Once this happens, turn off your heat and sieve out your cracklin and lay it out on a few paper towels to dry.

While the lard is still in liquid form, pour it into your glass jar and seal it. As it cools down to room temperature it will solidify and turn white.
You can then store it in the fridge, where it will last for up to a year or at room temperature where it should be fine for about six months. I like to do a little bit of both, keeping some on my counter and leaving the rest in the fridge.

Now that you have your lard, the uses for it are almost endless. You can spread it on bread just as you would butter, mix it with herbs, use it to fry up some chicken fried steak, or to make flaky pie crusts.

PROJECTS ON FOOD

# How To Make Pemmican

**MEDIUM DIFFICULTY**

One of the biggest challenges in a survival scenario is coming up with protein and fats to consume. Your body needs protein and fat to stay functional for other survival tasks. If you do not prep in advance, this means lots of hunting, fishing, and trapping.

That being said, you can preserve your meat as you get it. This would give you a stockpile of protein and fats for whenever you need it. Obviously, freezing meats is the preferred method for preservation. So, what happens when you have no electricity? Meat left out at room temperature can be spoiled in a matter of hours. If you bring home more meat than you can eat in about two meals, the rest of it will be wasted. However, making that meat into pemmican can preserve it for future consumption. Pemmican is a portable and preserved mixture of dried meat, rendered fat, and other ingredients that can be left out at room temperature for months, if not longer. Native Americans created pemmican to give them a food source that is both preserved and portable. Scouts, hunting parties, and nomadic tribes all had to travel dozens if not hundreds of miles at a time. Pemmican was the ideal food source to throw in their packs for the long journey.

## Meat Preparation

Before you can make pemmican, you will need some dried and shredded meat. Ideally, you want to use a meat with a low-fat content such as venison, rabbit, or lean beef.

First, you will need to either grind your meat or cut it into thin strips against the grain. Cut off any fat you see before moving forward. If you cut the meat into strips, they need to be ¼ inch thick or less. If you partially freeze your meat first, it will cut and grind better. An electric deli meat slicer can work great for thin slices.

Next, you need to put a rack on a baking sheet and spread out the meat on the rack. With ground meat, I like to pound it flat and partially freeze it so it stays together.

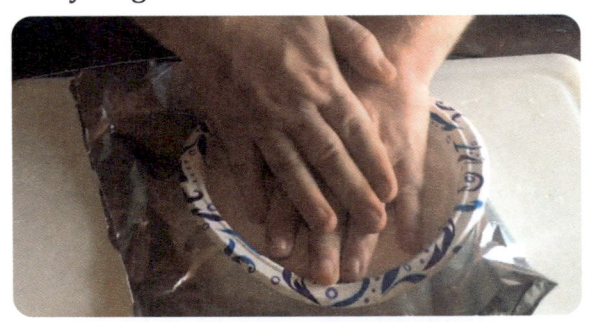

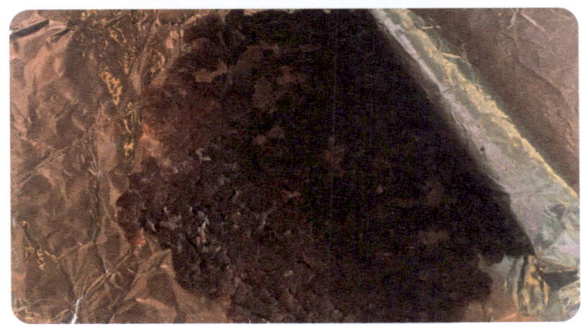

Set your oven to 175°F and let it dry for at least eight hours. Add salt and pepper to your meat to help draw out moisture.

You can flip the meat every few hours, so it dries more evenly. When finished, it should be completely dry and hard as a rock.

If you do not have access to an oven, you can accomplish the same thing over a fire. You will need to build a rack up high enough from the fire that it dries but does not cook. In an open space like that, you may need to dry it for a full day or even longer. You have basically made jerky at this point. Next, you need to grind up your jerky in a coffee grinder or food processor. You can also buy jerky and grind it up if you prefer. There are even little tins of ground up jerky that you can find from time to time. You now have your shredded and dried meat to combine with other ingredients.

## Let's Make Pemmican

You can add all kinds of dry ingredients to pemmican to add flavor and nutritional value. However, there are two primary ingredients that are always needed. This is your dried and shredded meat and some rendered fat. I like to use lard and just melt it down to a liquid. You can also use chicken fat or beef fat if you prefer. It just needs to be a fat that is fairly solid at room temperature.

Anything that you add beyond these two primary ingredients will shorten the shelf life. However, if you want to try some different flavors you can add nuts, dried fruit, oats, honey, or anything else that will not spoil. You want to combine your meat and fat at a two to one ratio. If you have eight ounces of meat, you need about four ounces of fat.

Put all of the meat in a bowl and add the liquid fat a little at a time as you mix it together. You want enough fat that it will hold together if you make a ball, but you do not want it to appear watery. Then add any other ingredients you want. You may want to grind them up to a finer consistency, so the pemmican cakes do not fall apart.

Get a muffin tin and place a sheet of plastic wrap over one of the cups. Put two good spoonfulls of your pemmican mixture into the cup and press it down flat with a spoon or the bottom of a small cup.

Then wrap up your pemmican cake and throw it in the refrigerator or set it in a cool, dry place. As the fat cools, the pemmican cake will harden so it holds together.

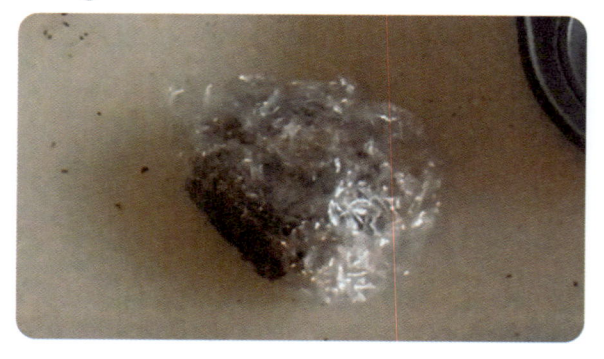

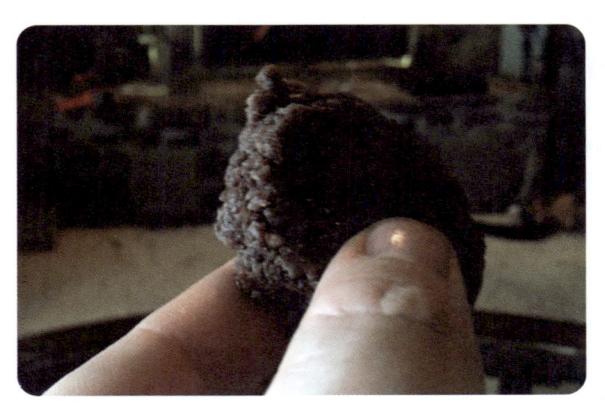

## Cost and Nutritional Value

Here is the breakdown on cost, nutritional value, and where you can buy these ingredients:

◆ Lean Ground Beef 93/7 mix
Cost - $4.87/lb.
Calories-680 Protein-92g Fat-32g Carbs-0g
crowdedline.com/product/all-natural-93-lean-7-fat-lean-ground-beef-roll-1-lb/

◆ Lard
Cost - $3.44 for ½ lb. or $6.88/lb.
Calories-8400 Protein-0g Fat-228g Carbs-0g
www.amazon.com/Morrell-Snow-Cap-Lard-Pack/dp/B00XLYOM4W/ref=sr_1_7?d-child=1&keywords=Lard&qid=1613679318&sr=8-7

So here are your totals for 1.5 lbs. of pemmican:
**Total Cost: $8.31 Total Calories: 9080 Total Protein: 92g Total Fat: 260g Total Carbs: 0g**

Now you would just need to add in the cost and nutritional values for any other ingredients you decide to add. As you can see, the figures on calories, fat, and protein for every dollar that you spend are incredible.

For just $8.31 you can easily feed yourself for a week or longer on pemmican.

Pemmican is one of those unique foods that can last for a long time without refrigeration. I suggest you take the time to practice making pemmican, so you are ready if SHTF. However, I also suggest that you make some in advance and set it aside with all of your other preserved foods. This will make you even more prepared if you ever need those fats and proteins for a long journey.

PROJECTS ON FOOD

# How To Preserve Eggs

EASY  DIFFICULTY

Eggs, one of the most versatile and commonly eaten foods in the world, are a fantastic source of vitamins, minerals, and animal protein. And they come in their own packaging which makes them great for long term storage and off the grid living. If stored in a cool place, fresh eggs that have not been cleaned, bleached, or otherwise processed can last on their own for a good month. That is because eggs fresh from the hen come naturally coated in what is called a "bloom." This bloom seals the eggshell, which despite appearances is actually porous, preventing bacteria from infecting the egg. Refrigeration of course also retards bacterial growth.

There are many other ways to store eggs for at least a year without refrigeration. Here I am going to discuss three of them and show you step by step how they are done. All of them work on the principal that with a little help the eggshell is perfectly capable of keeping its precious contents safe for human consumption. The goal is to strengthen the eggshell's natural bloom, or to add another layer of protection to keep those nasty bacteria at bay.

## Preserving Eggs with Mineral Oil

You can find Mineral Oil online or in physical stores. Here are two suggestions on where to get it from:

◆ Amazon
www.amazon.com/Mineral-Earthborn-Elements-Cutting-Utensils/dp/B07H466M71/ref=sr_1_13?dchild=1&keywords=mineral+oil&qid=1620385761&sr=8-13

◆ Walgreens
www.walgreens.com/store/c/walgreens-mineral-oil/ID=prod6154213-product

The first and most straightforward way to do this is with food grade mineral oil. Mineral oil, as opposed to vegetable or animal oil, is a by-product of the refinement of petroleum. It is used for a variety of purposes from cosmetics, medicinally (it will clear you out!), and even as a wood preservative. Accordingly, it is easy to find and quite cheap. Any pharmacy will have it and of course you can find it easily enough online. Depending on how much you buy, it will set you back around $7 dollars. Just make sure it is food or medicinal grade. As an added bonus, a little of it goes a long way. Just a tablespoon of the stuff is enough to coat about a dozen eggs. All you need to do is take a paper towel, or any piece of clean cloth, dip it in the oil, and rub the outside of each egg thoroughly. These oiled eggs, if kept in a coolish place will easily last 9 months. In fact, any oil, even lard or butter, can be used in the same manner with a similar effect. The benefit of mineral oil is that because of its purity it won't go rancid like lard or butter eventually will.

**How to Do It:**
First pour your mineral oil into a small bowl.

Grab your eggs and paper towel/cloth.

And start rubbing!

Place the coated eggs back in their crate and into a cool place.

## "Waterglassing" Your Eggs with Pickling Lime

You can find Pickling Lime online or in physical stores. Here are two suggestions on where to get it from:

◆ Amazon
www.amazon.com/Mrs-Wages-Pickling-1-Pound-Resealable/dp/B0084LZU1Q

◆ Walmart
www.walmart.com/ip/Pickling-Lime-16-oz-Zin-524974/891358416

Waterglassing your eggs involves submerging them in a bath of water that has been mixed either with sodium silicate or calcium hydroxide, more commonly known as "pickling" or "slacked" lime. Just as with the mineral oil, the idea is that this water bath will bolster the eggshell's own bacteria fighting capabilities. The term "waterglass" comes from the fact that silicate is also one of the building blocks of glass. Lime, however, is easier to find and cheaper, so I will be demonstrating with it. Pickling lime can be found online or even usually at any nearby big box grocery store for around $10 dollars, depending on how much you buy.

The ratio of pickling lime to water is 1 ounce lime to 1 quart water. If you use tap water, make sure to boil it as it probably has fluoride in it, which will inhibit the preservative properties of the lime. Take any pot/bucket that is big enough to hold all your eggs; I'm using a roughly one gallon one for 30 eggs which is plenty. Pour in your water and lime and stir until it is all dissolved. Then simply place your eggs in the solution arranging them so they are fully submerged. And that is it, put them in a cool place and your eggs will easily last you a year or more.

**How to Do it:**
Get a pot, eggs, water, and your lime.

Pour the lime into the bucket and stir until it is dissolved.

Place your eggs into the water solution, making sure that they are all submerged.

Place the bucket of eggs in a cool place.

## Preserving Eggs with Isinglass

You can find Pickling Lime online or in physical stores. Here are two suggestions on where to get it from:

◆ Amazon
www.amazon.com/Mrs-Wages-Pickling-1-Pound-Resealable/dp/B0084LZU1Q

◆ Sound Homebrew Supply
www.soundhomebrew.com/isinglass-45-ml/

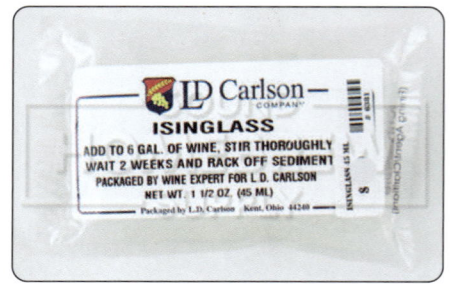

If you want to stay away from any mineral-based preservatives, then there is this final option. Isinglass is a powder that is derived from the swim bladders of fish. It is commonly used in the wine and beer industries as a clarifier because it binds itself to suspended particles and then sinks to the bottom of whatever liquid it is put into. During WWII, however, the British found that isinglass could also be used as an egg preservative. The concept is the same as that of water glassing, but instead of lime we use isinglass, which forms into a gelatin-like substance when mixed in the right proportion with water. This gelatin provides an extra layer of protection by blocking up the tiny holes in an egg's shell.

Isinglass is fairly easy to find online or at your local homebrew supplier. And as with the pickling lime, a little bit goes a long way. The ratio of isinglass to water will vary depending on the type of isinglass you get. Sometimes it comes as a clear "paper" as seen below and sometimes as a powder. Generally, the ratio is something like 1 part isinglass to 10 parts water. The goal is for the isinglass to dissolve into the water completely so that upon cooling it solidifies into a gelatin.

### How to Do it:

First, heat up enough water to fully submerge the eggs you want to preserve and pour in your isinglass.

Stir until it starts to thicken.

Arrange your eggs in a clean container.

Pour in your isinglass water until the eggs are fully submerged.

Wait for it to cool to the point that the gelatin has set.

That is all there is too it!
Eggs preserved in all three of these ways should also last you at least a year.

PROJECTS ON FOOD

# Meal In A Bag: Hamburger Gravy And Mashed Potatoes

EASY DIFFICULTY

Whether you have been on a military tour or just on a tour hiking around your nearby national park for a few days, you have probably had an MRE bag meal. Now, certainly some are better than others. Many of the ones that you buy from outdoors outfitters are pretty fancy and promise a lot. But if you are like me, most of them have been disappointing.

When it comes to MREs, I have found that the ones that keep it simple tend to come out the best; so with that in mind here is a recipe that I have made for a homemade Meal in a Bag that I think comes out very tasty: good old hamburger gravy with instant mashed potatoes. While I usually try to steer clear from overly processed powders, both for health reasons and because they never taste as good as the real thing, this recipe is going to use a fair bit of pre-made ingredients. Most of them can be found easily at your nearby grocery store.

This recipe has two parts: the gravy and the mash. You will be storing the ingredients for each part separately because they don't store well together. While long term storage is usually accomplished with canning, using glass jars, here I am going to stay true to the MRE-style of using mylar bags. Mylar bags are made of food-grade plastic and aluminum foil and once sealed can keep out bad bacteria and lock in freshness. Usually when you buy them, they also come with oxygen absorbers that you put into the bag before sealing it up. These little guys are important. If you don't add them, then bacteria can grow inside the bag even after it is sealed.

## What You Will Need

- Mylar bag (You can find them easily online www.amazon.com/6-5x4-Black-Mylar-Storage-Dried/dp/B08N5P58GC and at your neighborhood Home Depot) www.homedepot.com/p/Harvest-Right-Mylar-Starter-Kit-with-50-Mylar-Bags-50-Oxygen-Absorbers-and-12-in-Impulse-Sealer-MYLARKIT/305561948 
- Iron or hair straightener (This is for sealing the mylar bag.)
- ¼ cup freeze-dried hamburger meat (This one can be a little tricky to find but again you can get it online. If you don't want to order online, you could try to make your own.)
- 1 cup Instant Mash Potato powder
- 1 tsp. Beef Stock cube or powder
- 1 Tbsp. full fat milk powder
- ½ tsp. mushroom powder
- 1 Tbsp. flour
- 1 tsp. garlic flakes
- 1 tsp. onion powder
- ½ tsp. mixed herb
- ½ tsp. black pepper

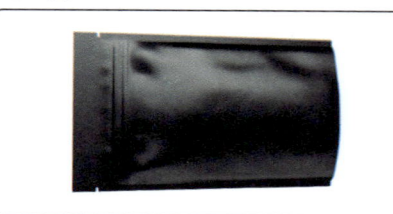

## The Step by Step Recipe

1. Simply place your freeze-dried ground beef into the mylar bag.
2. Mix all the other ingredients together and put in a separate plastic bag.
3. Close that bag up carefully to get as much air out of it as you can and place it into the mylar bag.
4. Seal up the mylar bag.

It really is that simple.

Now, when it comes to cooking time you can either use the bag itself as the container to cook everything in, or as I prefer, use a pot over the stove or campfire. All you need to add is 1-1 ½ cups hot water.

1. Remove your plastic bag of mash potato mix and rehydrate your ground beef either in the bag or in pot. Close/cover it up and wait 10 minutes for the ground beef to rehydrate.
2. Then pour your potato mix and stir until your mash fluffs up.
3. Enjoy!

PROJECTS ON TRAPS YOU CAN MAKE FOR ANIMALS AND BIRDS

# Automatic Traps For Animals

**MATERIAL COST** $ 45.00   **MEDIUM** DIFFICULTY   30 MINUTES

Hunting is hard. Trapping is not much easier but can work for you while you are doing other things. There is also the advantage of placing a large volume of traps, which increases the odds of success. Trapping has a steep learning curve, but as long as you pay attention and learn from failure, setting traps can be a very effective means of procuring protein.

One can easily construct many traps either in the wild or at home with readily available materials. The following are traps that I always keep in my arsenal of protein procurement if I need to use them.

Most jurisdictions have licencing requirements for the trapping of animals. In most areas, using these techniques outside of an actual survival situation will be considered illegal. Always read and understand all rules, regulations, licencing, and laws you are subject to.

## DIY Wire Snare

The snare is one of the most basic trapping methods and can be very useful when constructed and deployed correctly. While it is possible to use brass snare wire or picture wire, a snare built with a more sturdy material will hopefully prevent animals from destroying the snare and escaping.

I have found that building these snares usually takes less than ten minutes per snare, and if set up in an assembly line, the time to make these snares will be much less.

## Materials

- 1/16" Aircraft cable – You can purchase this at Home Depot for $12.97USD for 50 feet
www.homedepot.com/p/Everbilt-1-16-in-x-50-ft-Galvanized-Steel-Uncoated-Wire-Rope-811072/300018981

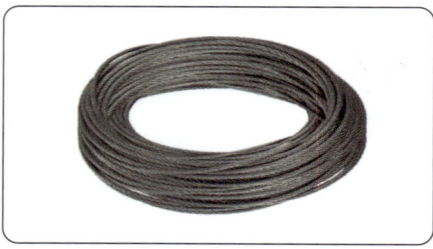

- 1/16" Aluminum Ferrules – Available at Home Depot for $3.46USD for a pack of ten
www.homedepot.com/p/Everbilt-1-16-in-Aluminum-Ferrules-10-Pack-42574/205887624

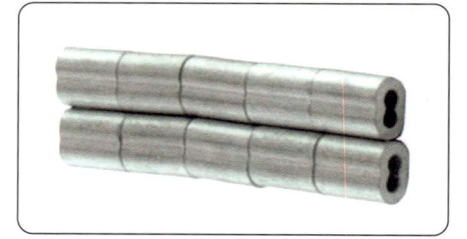

- ½" Flat Washers – Available at Home Depot for $5.94USD per pack of 25
www.homedepot.com/p/1-2-in-Zinc-Plated-Flat-Washer-25-Pack-802334/204276390

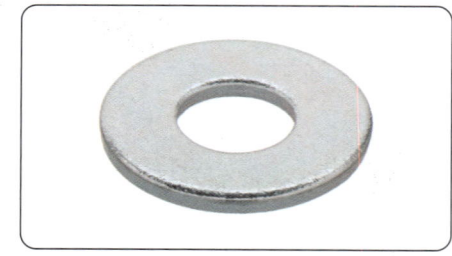

- 10-24 Nuts - Available at Home Depot for $ 6.96 USD for a pack of 25
www.homedepot.com/p/Hillman-Stainless-Machine-Screw-Hex-Nut-10-24-958/204794767

- Swivel – Available at Home Depot for $ 5.98 USD each
www.homedepot.com/p/Everbilt-0-25-in-Galvanized-Eye-and-Eye-Swivel-44094/205874115

## Tools

- Drill and drill bits
- Bench Vise
- Hammer
- Good quality side cutters

## Constructing the Snare

Constructing these snares is a straight forward process, and each snare will take around ten minutes to construct.

1. Start by cutting a 36-inch section of cable for each snare you want to create. From a 50 foot roll of wire, you can get 16 individual snares.
2. On one end of the wire, slip one of the 10-24 nuts and compress it onto the wire by either squeezing in a vice or smashing with a hammer.
3. Secure the washer in the vise.
4. Drill two holes in the washer directly across from each other large enough for the wire to slide through easily. I used a 3/32" drill bit.
5. Using the bench vise bend the washer in half at a 90-degree angle.
6. Run the other end of the wire through one hole of the washer, as shown in the photo above.
7. Run the wire through the other hole as shown.
8. Slip a ferrule onto the open end of the wire.
9. Slide the swivel onto the end of the wire.
10. Create a loop that secures the swivel to the end of the snare.
11. Crimp the ferrule using a crimping tool or side cutters.

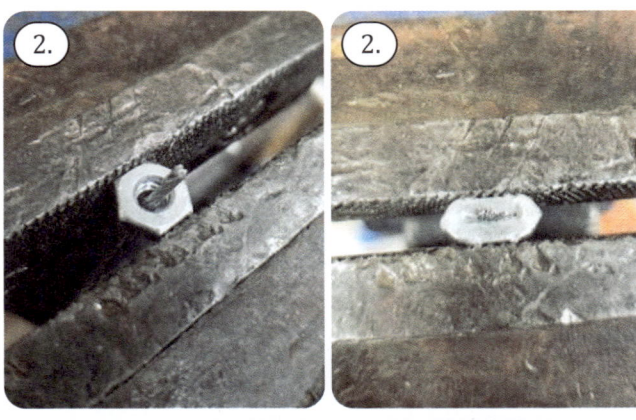

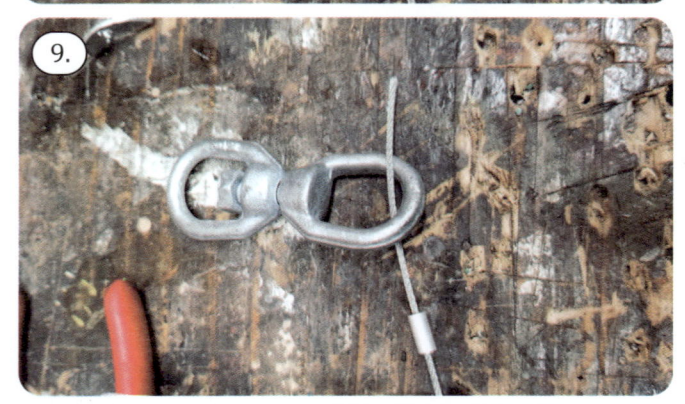

## Placing the Snare

1. Find an area where your target species of animals are likely to move through. Anchor the snare to a stake or tree by securing the swivel with bailing wire.
2. Place the snare, propping it up with sticks to keep the loop open.

## Twitch Up Snare

This trap uses a trigger system that is adaptable to other methods of trapping and killing game. The advantages of using a twitch-up snare are that having the snare lifted after the trap is triggered eliminates the need for a locking device and also elevates your dinner in the air, hopefully out of reach of any scavengers.

### Tools

- Saw
- Knife

## Materials

The good news is that you should be able to source everything you need from nature, but it will be far easier and quicker to use store-bought cordage like paracord.

- Paracord – Paracord is available on Amazon.com for $10.98USD

www.amazon.com/BENGKU-Survival-Mil-SPEC-Parachute-MIl-C-5040-H/dp/B07226B3FJ/

## Constructing the Trap

A twitch-up snare can either have a sapling or branch as the trap's engine or a suspended weight that drops when the trap is triggered. Either method will work, so choose the one that suits the area that you are trapping.

## Construction of a Twitch Up Snare

1. Locate an area that has evidence of animal movement through it.
2. Cut two branches that are about 1 inch in diameter at between 12 and 18 inches long. Sharpen one end of these branches to a point.
3. Cut three slightly thinner branches (between ½ inch and ¾ inch in diameter) at around 10 inches long and another at 4 or 5 inches long.
4. Lash one of the 10-inch braches to both the braches that you have sharpened as a crossbar.
5. Drive the sharpened branches into the ground parallel to the expected travel direction.
6. Take the 4-inch branch and carve a groove into the center of it large enough to accommodate the paracord.
7. Cut a length of paracord long enough to run from the trigger area to the sapling or counterweight you are using for this trap.
8. Tie a loop at the end of the paracord. Run the other end of the cord through this loop, creating a noose.
9. Attach the 4-inch branch to the paracord using the groove that you've carved. I like to use a clove hitch for this.
10. Tie the tag end of the paracord to either a sapling or counterweight.
11. Assemble the trigger mechanism by placing the 4-inch branch behind the crossbar. Then place the other 10-inch branch on the opposite side that the crossbar is mounted.
12. Use the four-inch branch to hold the lower 10-inch branch in place, as shown in the photo above. As long as there is tension on the line pulling up, the branches will hold themselves in place. Lay a stick on the bottom cross branch and position the snare over top of it.
13. At this point, when the lower branch has pressure applied down onto it, the branch slips down, allowing the noose and paracord to spring upwards.
14. Experiment with different setups using this trigger system to find one that works the best for you and the area you live in.

## Placement of a Twitch Up Snare

These traps work well along travel corridors. Find a spot that you see evidence of animals moving through and place the trap along their route. If you bait the trap so that the noose drapes over the trigger stick, the loop will tighten around the animal's neck when the animal tries to take the bait. Alternatively, the noose will tighten around the animal's foot, hopefully elevating them into the air. Trapping is a far more efficient means of protein procurement than hunting, but it requires some knowledge and skill. Trapping is not as simple as setting snares; it requires knowledge of the local animals and their behaviour so that you can determine the most likely locations for trap sets. Take the time to learn, and get out in the bush to observe animals, do some tracking, and become familiar with their habitat because the time you will need to depend on your trapping skills to feed your family is too late to start learning.

# Automatic Traps For Backyard Pests

| MATERIAL COST  $ 3.78 | EASY DIFFICULTY | 15 MINUTES |

Several kinds of pests may infest your backyard, possibly doing more damage than merely ruining the backyard cookout. Mice and rats carry disease, wasps, and hornets can be deadly to those who are allergic, and mosquitoes can transmit several diseases. The good news is that you probably have everything you need lying around the garage and shed to build traps to rid your outdoor space of these irritants.

## Bucket Trap for Rats And Mice

Everyone is familiar with the classic snap traps for mice and rats. Having dealt with a rat-infested backyard myself, I have found that these traps are more dangerous to my fingers than the rats. Sometimes what we need is to present the rodents with something they've never seen before.

A bucket trap works by luring the rodent to the top of a ramp, where they find a rotating peanut butter coated can of death. The plan is to have them reach for the can, which rotates under their weight, and they fall into the bucket of water. Once they fall in, the vermin swim around in circles until they get tired, drown, and die.

### PREVENTION

An ounce of prevention is worth a pound of cure; this is very true for rats and mice. The simple act of preventing them from entering and wanting to stay in your backyard is far more effective than any trap you can build or buy. The very first thing you should do when noticing you have a rodent infestation in your backyard is to identify and remove all food sources that they are consuming. The rat infestation in my backyard was solved not by the continued onslaught of traps and pellets from my air rifle or drowning in a bucket trap but by relocating a bird feeder. I positioned it so that they had to expose themselves for much longer to eat, and they decided to no longer take that risk and found a different yard in which to live.

In some cases, rats and mice may be transiting through your yard. There could be no food for them to eat, and all they're doing is using your property as a highway to get from point A to point B. In these cases, try to plug up any holes they're getting in through and using bleach around their entry and exit points to help keep them at bay.

## Tools

- Drill and Drill Bits
- Saw
- Pliers

## Materials

- Five Gallon Bucket – Home Depot carries these for $3.78USD www.homedepot.com/p/The-Home-Depot-5-Gal-Homer-Bucket-05GLHD2/100087613

- Coat Hanger – Needs to be a wire coat hanger
- Soda Can – Any empty soda can will do
- Small wood screws
- Strips of wood – These will act as the ramps that the rodents will travel up to their deaths, and you can use anything you happen to have lying around that will do the job

## Construction

1. Remove the pull tab and drill two opposing holes into a soda can. Make these holes large enough for the coat hanger wire to slip through easily. The holes must be on centre so that the can rotates freely.
2. Drill two opposing holes of the same size in the rim of the bucket.
3. Cut the longest length to straight wire that you can out of the coat hanger.
4. Slip the wire through one hole in the bucket. Then through both holes in the can and through to the other side of the bucket. The can should be in the center of the bucket opening.
5. Bend the ends of the wire at ninety-degree angles to prevent the wire from falling out.
6. Fill the bucket about half of the way full of water. Then smear an even layer of peanut butter over the surface of the can.
7. Place the bucket in an area that has vermin activity and install ramps.
8. Check the bucket every morning and carefully dispose of the carcasses.

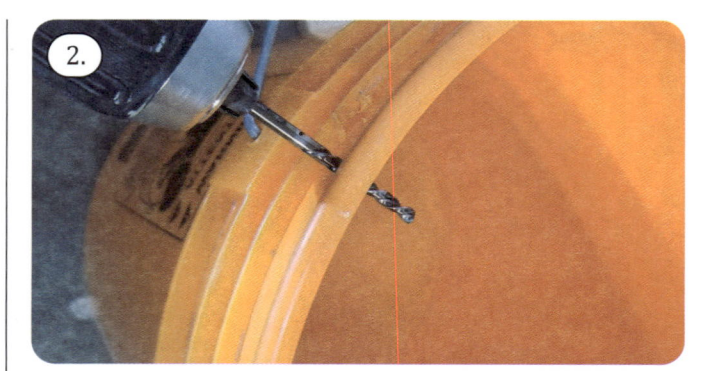

**7.**

### Placement

Look for areas that you see mouse or rat activity. These could be areas that you see droppings, holes where the little buggers come out of, known areas that they would like to hide such as woodpiles, or around potential food sources. When placing a trap, make sure that you've done everything in your power to make sure the rodents can easily access the ramps.

## Wasp\Hornet Trap and Mosquito Trap

Wasps and hornets are annoying, but if they sting someone who is allergic to their stings, these pests can become deadly. On the other hand, Mosquitos are dangerous as well; they can carry diseases such as Zika and West Nile Virus.

While these pests are essential for the ecosystem, they are not always welcome in our backyards.

### PREVENTION

Wasp and hornets are out looking for food, and most of our back gardens have a lot for them to eat. It is important to clean up and dispose of dropped and rotting fruits or vegetables. We also need to keep vigilant in inspecting our properties for wasp and hornet nests, annihilating them with extreme prejudice when we find them.

The best way to prevent mosquitos is to eliminate all instances of standing water on your property. This is where these little buggers breed, and removal of all standing water is the first step to reducing mosquitos in your backyard.

Building and placing several traps for these pests is straightforward and probably virtually free because the materials for this build are right now in your recycle bin and around your kitchen. Each trap took me less than five minutes to build, and I had all the materials on hand in my home.

### Tools
- Knife or scissors

### Materials

- Any plastic soda or water bottle – The size only limits the volume of wasps and hornets you can trap and kill. You can use a couple of large bottle traps or a larger number of smaller traps spread out around your property. A two-litre bottle is ideal, but I used a one-litre bottle for this demonstration.
- Duct Tape – Used to keep the two pieces of the bottle trap secure.
- Bait – Soda, sugar water, or fruit juice in the summer and fall, lunch meat or hamburger in the spring and early summer for wasps and hornets. Use a mix of sugar water and yeast for mosquitos.

### Construction

1. Cut the bottle around a third of the way down the neck.
2. Invert the portion of the bottle you cut into the bottom of the bottle.
3. Secure in place with duct tape.
4. Bait the trap, placing to lure the wasps and hornets away from where people may be eating or congregating.

**1.**

- All you have to do is mix in a few spoonfuls of sugar into enough water to fill the bottom of the trap below where the bottleneck is. Once the sugar dissolves, add a splash of vinegar to keep the bees away. Then pour the bait into the trap.

Mosquitoes are looking for carbon dioxide, which is why they're attracted to you. Our exhaling of carbon-dioxide causes them to fly in our direction because they know that aminals produce CO2 and have blood to suck. To bait a mosquito trap, we want to try to emulate this production of carbon dioxide, and the best way to do that is to use sugar and yeast. These two ingredients will react to create carbon dioxide gas and be irresistible to mosquitos.

## Bait for Wasps/Hornets

Wasps and Hornets have evolving tastes throughout the changing seasons. In the spring and early summer, wasps and hornets like to beef up with some protein. In these cases, bait your trap with a bit of rotting meat; however, as the summer continues and we get into early fall, they're looking for sugary goodness, so you'll bait your trap with sugar water.

- To make this bait, all you need to do is dissolve a few spoonfuls of brown sugar into some warm water.

- Stir until dissolved.

- Sprinkle in a teaspoon or so of yeast. Stir until dissolved and use to bait the trap.

# Fruit Fly Trap

Fruit flies often are found inside the house, and this trap can be very useful in your kitchen or out on the back deck. These incests are not dangerous but are very irritating during your backyard barbeque.

Creating this fruit fly trap is very simple and is one that I often use when we get a couple of fruit flies that have found their way inside the house and when we are eating outside and find that too many fruit flies are buzzing around.

## Materials

- A bowl or dish – The size is not too important. I like to use a small dish that is not too obtrusive.
- Pure Apple Cider Vinegar – If you do not have any on hand, any local grocery store will carry this.
- Dish soap – Regular everyday dish soap is all you need. The purpose of this is to break down the surface tension of apple cider vinegar, so the fruit flies drown more easily.
- Saran wrap – Any piece of clear saran wrap will do.

## Construction

1. Pour some apple cider vinegar into the bowl.
2. Add a couple of drops of dish soap.
3. Mix.
4. Place saran wrap over the top.
5. Poke holes in the Saran wrap with a pencil or cut slits with a knife. The goal is that the fruit flies can fly in but not get out.

## Placement

Place the trap in areas where you see fruit flies, or place the trap in areas you want to lure the fruit flies to. You don't want to attract fruit flies into an area that you're eating outdoors, and it is better to draw them away from where people will be annoyed by them.

As you can see, it's straightforward to construct multiple traps to help rid yourself of backyard pests. None of these traps contain toxic chemicals, are overly complicated or time-consuming to create, and none of them involve overly expensive materials. As with anything, use your imagination to create variations on these traps and baits to suit your needs and environment.

PROJECTS ON TRAPS YOU CAN MAKE FOR ANIMALS AND BIRDS

# Automatic Traps For Fish

**MATERIAL COST** 💵 31.00    **MEDIUM** 🕛 **DIFFICULTY**    **1 HOUR** ⏰

Human beings have been fishing for at least 40,000 years, and for a good reason. Fish are a fantastic protein and fatty acid source while generally requiring a low-calorie expenditure to gather. In the twenty-first century, most of us head out onto the water with a rod in hand. Still, those of us who do fish recreationally understand that the odds are not in our favour.

When our lives depend on what we can catch, gather, and hunt, betting on our skills with a spinning or fly rod is not a good wager. Instead, we need to stack the deck in our favour by using techniques that do the fishing for us, while we are focusing on other survival aspects.

While we all want to try out new techniques, what I will detail here may not be legal in your area. Before trying any new fishing method, read and understand the rules and regulations for your area. You alone are responsible for the actions you take while out on the water.

## Gill Net

A gill net catches fish in three ways. Fish either become wedged in the net, their gills become caught in the net's lines, or the net tangles around the fish. This type of net is called a gill net because when a fish makes it partially through the net's openings, when they try and back out, the net's lines become caught in the fish's gills, trapping them.

A gill net can also be tailored to the size of the fish that you are looking to catch. By adjusting the openings' size, you control the size of fish that will become caught in the net. Larger openings mean that smaller fish will swim through while larger fish will become caught.

## Making a Gill Net

Constructing your gill net can seem overly complicated and time-consuming. Still, it is not tricky in reality, and once you get a good rhythm going, the process does not take as much time as one would think. The 30" by 30" net I made, as an example, took about one hour for me to construct.

## Materials

Constructing a gill net requires a few simple and easily obtained materials:

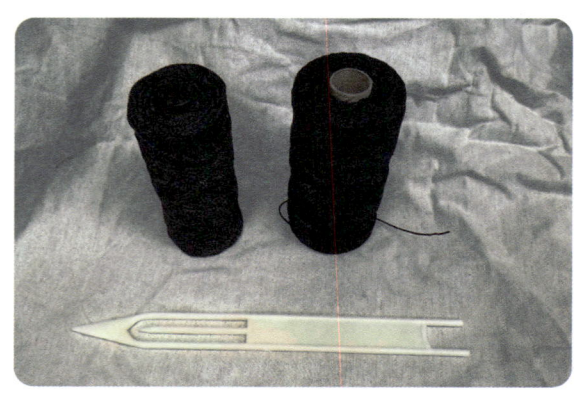

◆ **Net Needle** – You can easily make your net needle, but I chose to purchase some off Amazon.com for $ 7.99 USD.

www.amazon.com/Plastic-Fishing-Equipment-Netting-Shuttles-Size/dp/B0197MUEB6/

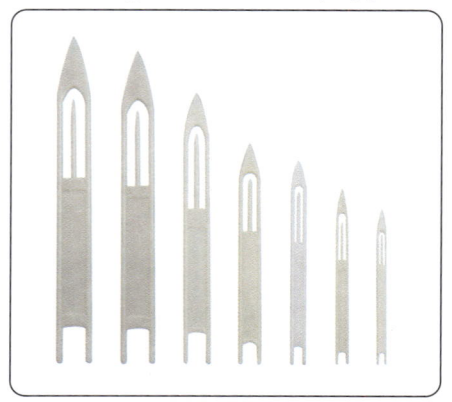

◆ **Cordage** – I used some tarred nylon twine (commonly known as bank line). I used the #36 bank line for the mainline, and for the actual net, I used the #18 bank line. If you wish, you can use a fishing line to make a gill net, but you'll need to make sure that it is strong enough. You can purchase some bank line rolls from Amazon.com for $22.95USD ea for either the #18 size or #36.

www.amazon.com/SGT-KNOTS-Tarred-Twine-Bank/dp/B00EVX5Y8A/

- **Mesh Gauge** – This is how you will create uniform-sized openings in your gill net. A mesh gauge can be any material that you have on hand. Wood and plastic are good options. Keep in mind that the mesh gauge width will be approximately half the mesh's finished size. For example, if you want a three-inch opening, you'll want to use a one-and-a-half-inch mesh gauge.

You can construct several gill nets of various sizes for a little more than a $50.00USD investment. You can also unravel the #36 bank line's strands to give yourself even more cordage to make more nets. Your only limitation on the size and number of gill nets you can make is the volume of cordage you have at your disposal.

## Instructions for Making a Gill Net

1. String a length of your #36 bank line at about chest height. The size depends on how large you want your net to be. Leave enough excess to be able to anchor the net on either side. It is better to have too much line than not enough.

## Loading the Needle

2. Load your net needle with the #18 bank line. Start by tying a clove hitch on the tip in the open centre of the net needle.
3. Wrap the bank line down and around the notch at the bottom of the needle.
4. Flip the needle over, bringing the line up to the tip, looping around it, and back down.
5. Flip the needle over again, repeating the process until the desired length of cordage is loaded on the needle.

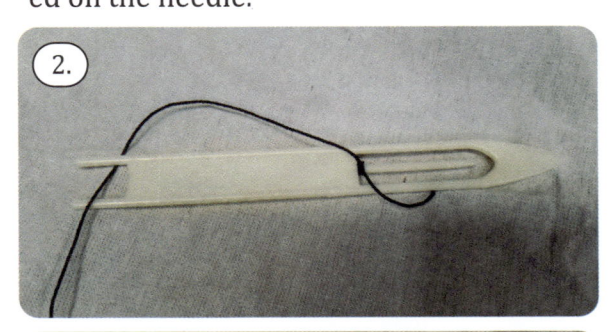

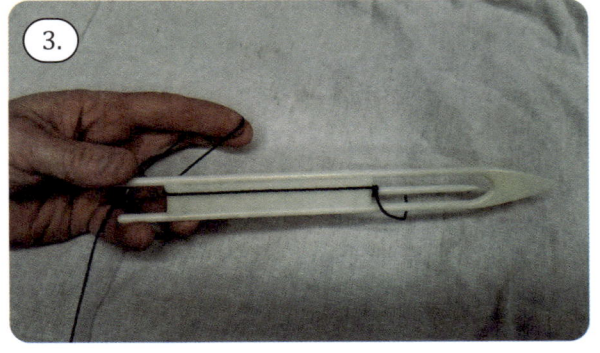

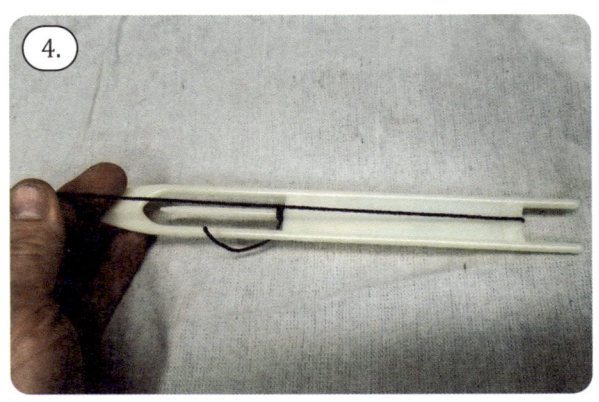

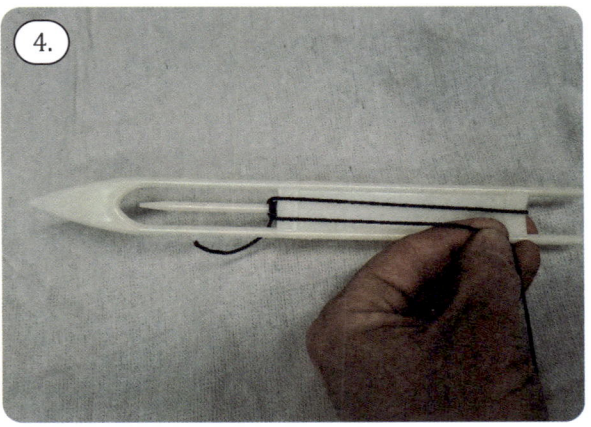

## Weaving the Net

1. Tie off the loose end of the line from your net needle to the head line with a clove hitch.
2. Bring the mesh gauge up to the head line and running the thinner bank line behind, up, and across the mesh gauge.
3. Using the net needle run the line over and behind the head line. Bring the needle and line back through the loop you've created and pull snug keeping the line wrapped around the mesh gauge.
4. Repeat the last step but instead of the line being wrapped around the mesh gauge, tie it to the head line. This finishes the clove hitch that forms your first loop.
5. Repeat this procedure until you have the desired number of loops.
6. To start the next row, hold the mesh gauge below the last loop.
7. Run the net needle and line under the mesh gauge and up through the loop.
8. Pull this line down and hold it taut with a finger or thumb.
9. Run the net needle around the loop that you brought the net needle up through.
10. Bring the needle up through the loop you have made and pull tight, moving your thumb out of the way as the knot tightens.
11. Repeat this procedure for the rest of the row.
12. To make the next row repeat this procedure

back the other way.

13. Continue following these steps until the net is at the length that you want. To terminate the net, simply cut the line at the last knot. You can add a hitch or two to fully secure it or leave a tag end to fasten a weight to the net.

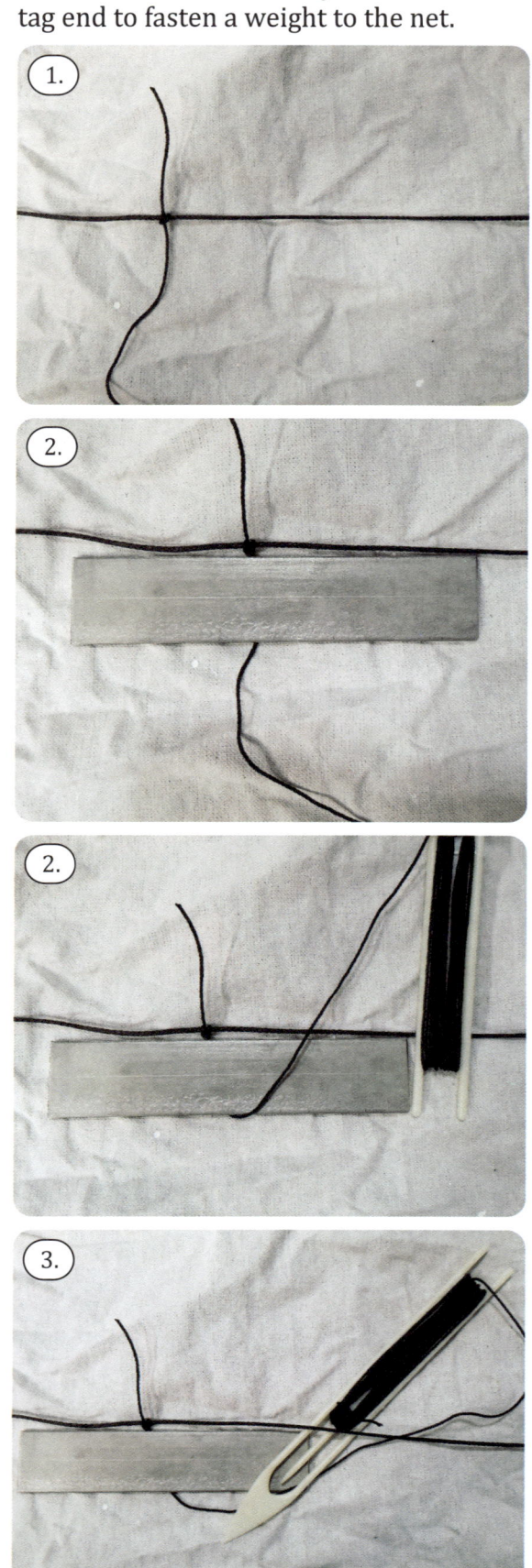

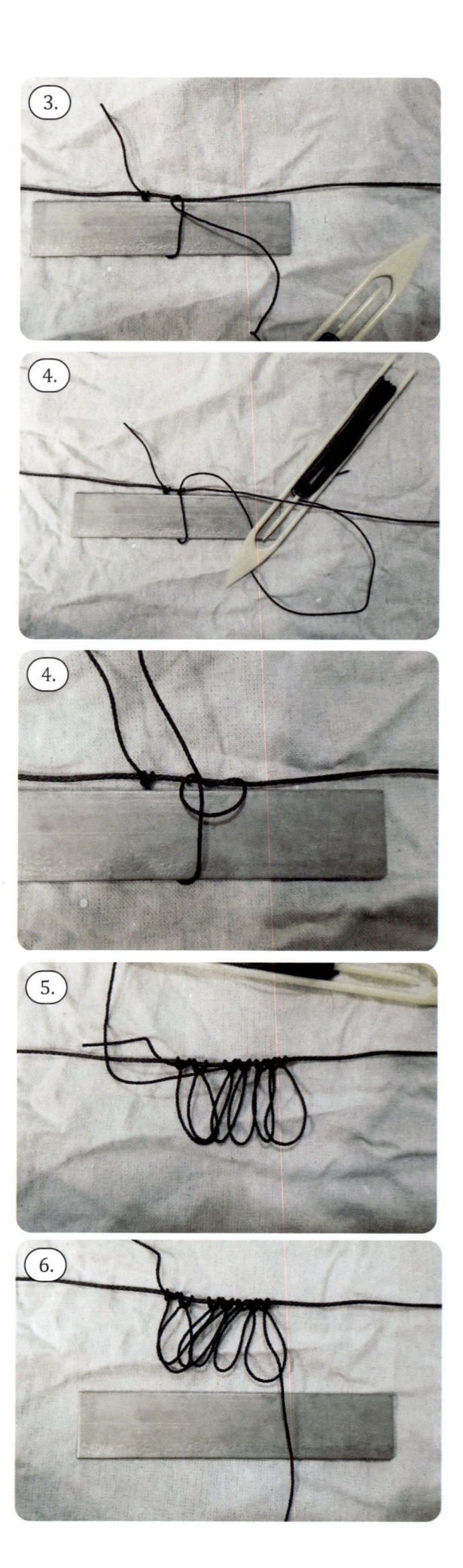

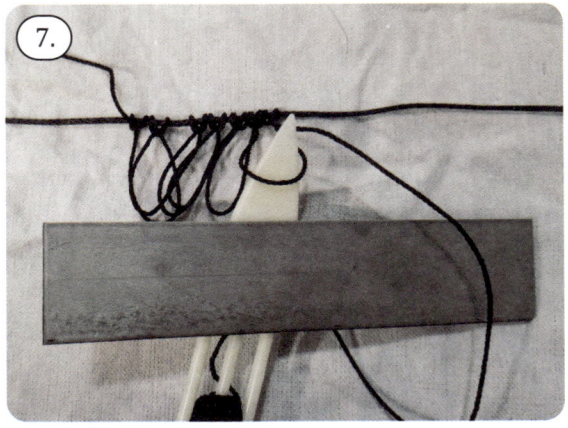

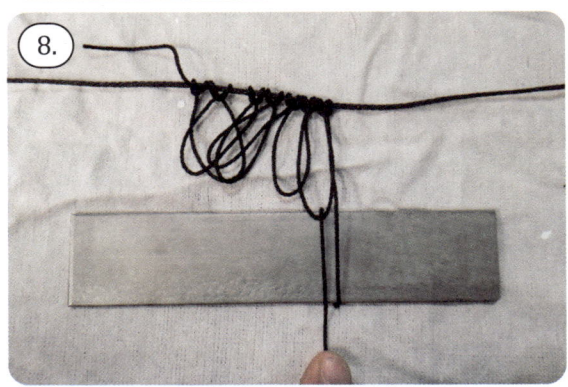

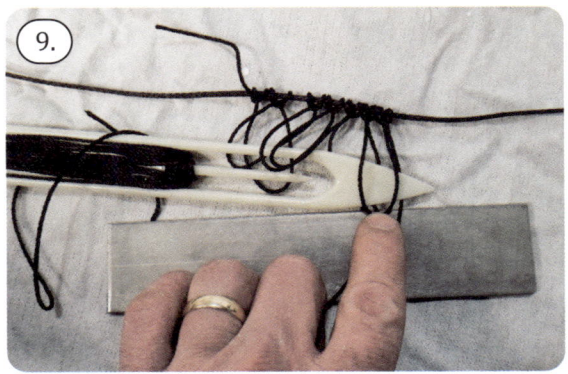

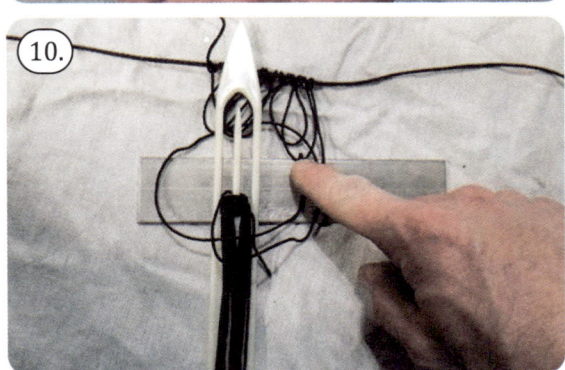

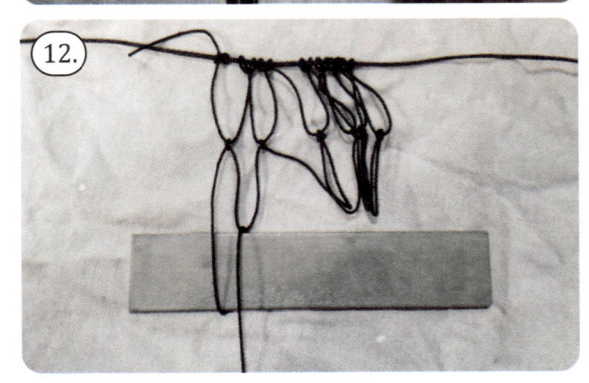

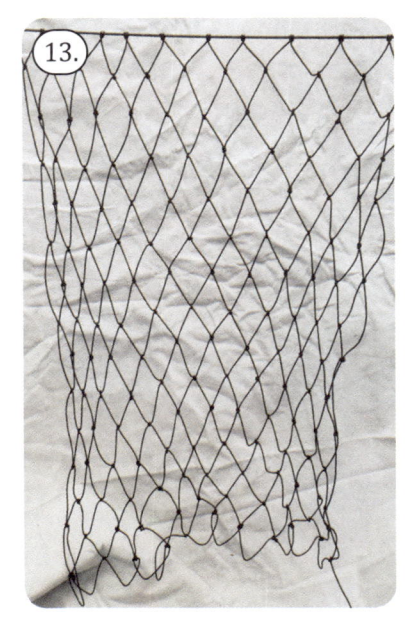

## Deploying the Gill Net

Locate an area that would likely have fish swimming through it. You can secure the headline to a stick or log that you can use to extend the net over water, weighing the bottom of the net down with rocks or other weights. Suppose you have ready access to each side of the waterway. In that case, you can use the head line to suspend the net in the precise position that you want it deployed using weights to keep the net opened as wide as possible.

## Trot Line

A trotline is one of the simplest passive fishing methods you can deploy aside from the gill net. A line with hooks suspended beneath it, the trotline does the fishing for you. The best part is that all you need is some #36 bank line and as many hooks and lengths of line that you wish to add.

## Materials

- **#36 Bank line** – Amazon.com has one pound rolls for $ 22.95 USD.
www.amazon.com/SGT-KNOTS-Tarred-Twine-Bank/dp/B00EVX5Y8A/

- **Fishing Line** – This is available on Amazon.com for $ 11.38 USD for a spool of 25-pound test.
www.amazon.com/Berkley-Trilene-Casting-Monofilament-Service/dp/B0091HDOII/?th=1

- **Fishing Hooks** – Amazon.com has collections of different sized hooks that allow you to pick the most appropriate hook for the size and species of fish you are hoping to catch for $ 12.99 USD.
www.amazon.com/Tailored-Tackle-Freshwater-Assortment-Baitholder/dp/B07C68PXG2/

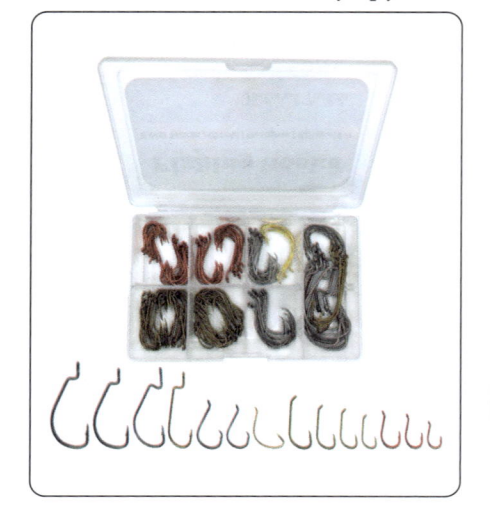

- **Swivels** – You can find these on Amazon.com in a kit that has a variety of sizes for $9.99USD.
www.amazon.com/Siasky-Connector-Stainless-Accessories-31lb-104lb/dp/B07SM4DTVL/

These items will give you the ability to deploy as many trotlines as a one-pound roll of bank line will allow.

## Making a Trotline

Placing a line in the water with more than one hook is illegal in the area that I live, so that I won't be demonstrating the deployment of a trotline across a waterway through pictures or video. The actual deployment of a trotline depends on the waterway that you are running the line across and the fish species you are pursuing. Gaining local knowledge of fishing in your area is the best way to be successful using this technique.

1. Prepare your main line by tying swivels into it using either half hitches or alpine butterfly loops.
   Keep the swivels at least four feet apart to prevent tangles. If you are planning on running long drop lines, make the spacing greater.
2. Cut and attach hooks and bait your drop lines. You can leave a loop in one end to make attaching the drop lines to the mainline easier.
3. Attach one end of the line to an anchor point.
4. Deploy the line across the waterway by using a boat or wading, attaching the dropline to your swivels as you go.
5. Secure the other end of the mainline to an anchor point on the opposing shore. I like to use a clove hitch for this. Tie a marker on the line where your trotlines cross the shore so they do not pose a tripping hazard.
6. When checking and rebaiting your trotline, don't be afraid to adjust the depths of the hooks. If it is not catching fish or if your bait is left untouched, change your setup.

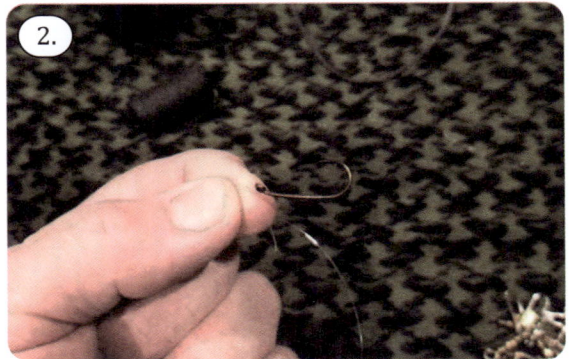

Fishing is a fantastic way to gather protein in a survival situation. Using these methods allows you to deploy several traps and cover large areas of water. This is far superior to procuring individual fish using a rod and reel and allows for better allocation of your time resources.

PROJECTS ON TRAPS YOU CAN MAKE FOR ANIMALS AND BIRDS

# Automatic Trap-System For Birds

**MATERIAL COST** $ 49.00  **EASY** DIFFICULTY  **20 MINUTES**

In an off-grid survival situation procuring food will be challenging. One of the most difficult aspects of obtaining protein is that there may be days where you will have good luck in hunting and trapping, but there will be more days where the wild game will be too elusive. However, an old saying goes, 'live meat never spoils,' and this trap will capture birds without harming them, providing you with live protein.

The advantage of this is that you can save the live birds for times when other protein sources are scarce and, in the process, grow them into larger, healthier birds.

## How This Automatic Trap for Birds Works

This trap uses a simple mechanism to slowly lower birds into a cage, after which a counterweight resets the trap for the next bird. The cage is large enough to hold several large birds, and the top should be made from a solid material so the birds can walk around the roof of the cage with ease. The mechanism by which the birds find their way into the trap is a five-gallon bucket attached to a simple lever and counterweight.

The bucket has cutouts for the bird to step into and is suspended by a rope connected to the lever counterweight mechanism. The bucket is suspended above a hole in the roof large enough for the bucket to drop into.

The bird steps into the bucket and the bucket lowers into the cage. When the bird steps out of the bucket once in the cage, the counterweight returns the bucket to its starting position, trapping the bird in the cage.

To entice the birds into the trap, one could use birdseed, nut butter, grains, or other favourite foods of your chosen prey.

## Building the Automatic Bird Trap

The construction of the automatic bird trap is a straightforward process requiring materials that you could easily purchase from a hardware store or scavenge in a grid-down scenario.

## Tools Required

- Saw
- Hammer
- Sharp knife
- Drill with drivers and bits
- Tape measure and square

## Materials

- 2 x 2 x 8' lumber which you can find at Home Depot for $3.48USD.
www.homedepot.com/p/2-in-x-2-in-x-8-ft-Furring-Strip-Board-Lumber-75800593/304600525

- Chicken wire which is sold at Home Depot for $14.62USD for a 24" x 25-foot roll.
www.homedepot.com/p/PEAK-25-ft-L-x-24-in-H-Galvanized-Steel-Hexagonal-Wire-Netting-with-1-in-x-1-in-Mesh-Size-Garden-Fence-3353/315112258

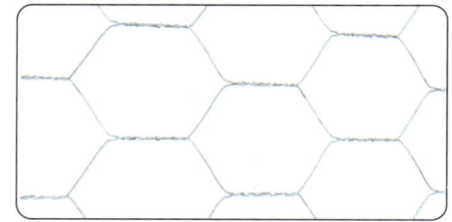

- Five-gallon buckets which are available at Home Depot for $ 4.98 USD.
www.homedepot.com/p/The-Home-Depot-5-Gal-Homer-Bucket-05GLHD2/100087613

- Five-gallon bucket lid which is also available at Home Depot for $ 2.48 USD.
www.homedepot.com/p/The-Home-Depot-5-gal-Orange-Leakproof-Bucket-Lid-with-Gas-

ket-5GLD-ORANGE-LID-for-5GL-HOMER-PAIL/202264044

- A length of rope which I found at Home Depot for $ 5.51 USD for 100 feet.
www.homedepot.com/p/CORDA-1-4-in-x-100-ft-Hollow-Braid-Poly-Rope-PB7703/305347534

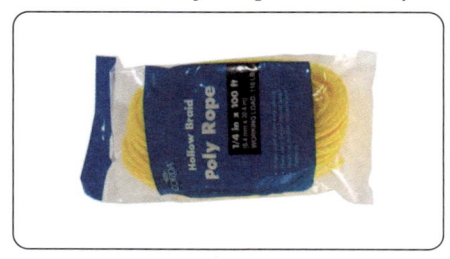

- #8 x 2" Screws which you can find at Home Depot for $ 11.98 USD for a box of 161.
www.homedepot.com/p/SPAX-8-x-2-in-Philips-Square-Drive-Flat-Head-Full-Thread-Yellow-Zinc-Coated-Multi-Material-Screw-161-per-Box-4101020400506/202041005

- Fence staples like these I found at Home Depot for $ 5.98 USD per box.
www.homedepot.com/p/Grip-Rite-3-4-in-Hot-Dip-Galvanized-Staples-1-lb-Pack-34HG-PNS1/100148501

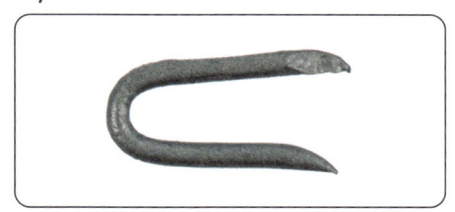

- Water bottle to use as a counterweight.

## Instructions

1. Either buy or build a suitably sized cage. The cage's dimensions will be determined by the number of birds you want to catch and the space you have to house the cage. If you are building the enclosure, create a simple frame using the 2x2's after which you will sheet the bottom with plywood and the top with either plywood or another material like foam board. The advantage of using foam board is that it is easier to cut.
2. Wrap the sides of the cage with the chicken wire securing in place with the fencing staples.
3. Cut large openings in the sides of the bucket large enough for a bird to walk through and into the bucket. Secure the lid to the top of the bucket.
4. Use the bucket to layout and cut a hole in the top of the cage. Make sure that the opening is large enough to allow the bucket to pass through it without interference.
5. Construct a simple lever with some 2x2s. Do this by drilling a hole at the end of a 2x2 which you will secure to the corner of the cage. The height of the 2x2 should be high enough that the bucket can be comfortably suspended slightly above the top of the cage.
6. You will secure another 2x2 to the one you just drilled and mounted. One end should be directly over the hole. Mark the point where the two boards intersect and match drill a hole the same size as the first one you drilled.
7. Drill holes at either end of this 2x2 to secure a rope for the counterweight and bucket.
8. Attach a rope to the end over the hole and to the handle of the bucket. Make sure that the bucket will hang into the hole without touching the sides.
9. Attach the counterweight to the other side of the lever. Adjust the weight of the counterweight until it easily lifts an empty bucket from the floor of the cage to above the cage.
10. Place something underneath the counterweight to stop lifting the bucket to a point slightly below the top of the cage.
11. Place bait around and inside the bucket.

## Using the Automatic Bird Trap

Birds will not be easily fooled. They will require some time to become comfortable with the situation, but when they do, the trap will be very effective at trapping them alive and unharmed. As the bird steps into the bucket, the bucket will lower into the cage with the bird inside. As long as the bird stays inside the bucket, the counterweight will not return the bucket to the start position.

As the bird steps out of the bucket and into the cage, the counterweight will raise the bucket to the start position leaving the bird trapped in the cage.

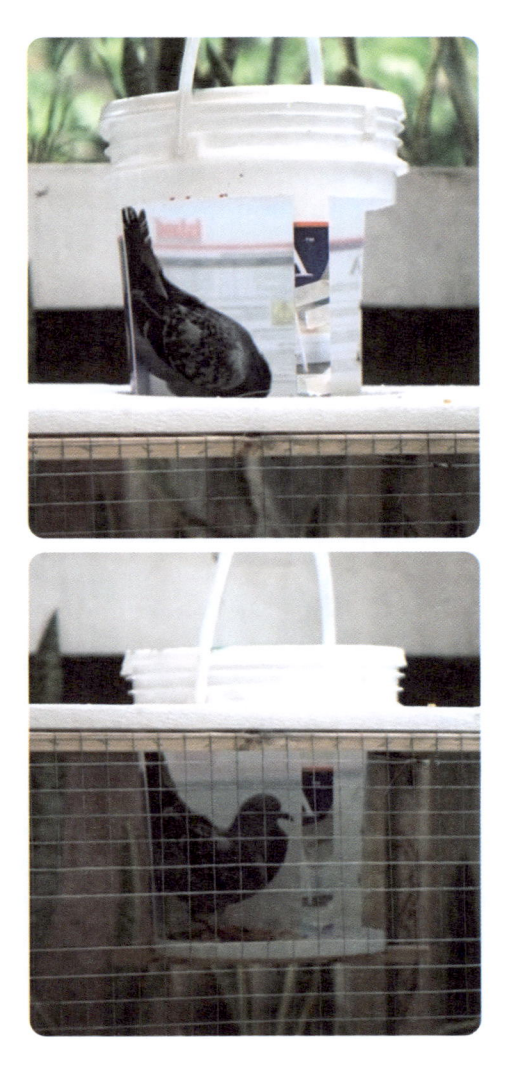

## Variations

The automatic bird trap can also have a few variations that are worth noting.

- Installing a door in the side of the cage will make removing the birds a lot easier.
- If you have a coop which you will be housing these wild birds to fatten up for use as food in the future, you can build and install this trap adjacent to this coop to trap and introduce more birds without actually handling them.
- If you leave some birds inside the cage, they may attract others to the trap.

There is an excellent probability that you may have most of the materials around your home or in the surrounding area to construct this trap. Therefore, the automatic bid trap is a fantastic trap to keep the plans in mind for the possibility you find yourself and your family desperate for food.

OTHER PROJECTS TO DO IN YOUR BACKYARD

# DIY Air Conditioner

**MATERIAL COST** $53.00　　**DIFFICULTY** EASY　　50 MINUTES

Beating the heat is difficult when the grid is fully functional, but when the grid is down, a sweltering summer's day will make staying cool is much more challenging. Fortunately, with a few items that you may have around the home, you can build a functional DIY air conditioning unit powered through either 12 volt DC power or standard household 120-volt electricity. The advantage of making a 12-volt option is that it is appropriate for off-grid applications in which battery banks are being used.

**How Does this DIY Air Conditioner Work?**
There are several different styles of DIY air conditioners, most of which follow the same process of pushing air across an ice-cold surface. What this does is cool the air before it exits the air conditioner through some kind of outlet. The design that I am going to detail here is no exception as it uses a cooler to hold ice and a fan to push the air across the ice and out the outlet as cool air.

## How Effective Is the DIY Air Conditioner?

Truth be told, this style of an air conditioner is not going to cool an entire home effectively, but it will be suitable for small areas where you can sit and allow the cool air to blow directly at you. Unfortunately, this is also a design that is not easily scaled up to cool more extensive areas. However, this style of air conditioning unit would work quite well in confined spaces such as vehicles, small rooms, or tents.

The critical factors regarding the air conditioner's effectiveness are the size and power of the fan and the quantity and cooling potential of the ice. With this also is the availability of ice. Acquiring ice in a grid-down situation is going to be challenging and will require working freezers. However, if you are in a position where you have a surplus of electrical power, then a DIY air conditioner is an option that you could look into.

### Advantages of Building a DIY Air Conditioner

- Commercially available air conditioning units require significant amounts of power, and while your homemade version is not going to be as efficient, it will draw far less energy. So in a grid-down situation where you need to stay cool, one of these units can help bring the temperature down in a small room.
- The design of this DIY air conditioner is so simple that all you need to do is replace melted ice with freshly frozen ice.

### Disadvantages of the DIY Air Conditioner

While this style of air conditioner is effective at blowing cool air, it has a few drawbacks.

- The first is that you need to destroy a cooler to build it effectively. Thus, a project like this is best suited for a cooler you are no longer using or have replaced with a newer, better model. An alternative is to use inexpensive Styrofoam coolers instead.
- The second disadvantage is that cutting an inlet and outlet into the cooler compromises the cooler's ability to insulate, which in turn will cause the ice inside to melt more rapidly than if the cooler was intact.
- This design of a DIY air conditioner requires the use of electricity. While you can operate it using a 12-volt fan that you can hook up to battery power, the most likely scenario is that you will use a fan that plugs into 120-volt power. This would require either a generator or a battery bank and inverter. If you decide to use one of these air conditioners in a grid-down situation, you will need to consider the amount of power that it will draw.

- The final disadvantage is that this design requires ice, which can be challenging to acquire in a grid-down scenario. Also, the rate at which the ice will melt will probably be faster than the rate at which you can make more ice.

## Building the DIY Air Conditioner

The construction of the DIY air conditioner is a straightforward process that requires minimal skills and tools to accomplish. There are also several variations that one can develop to create similar air cooling units using readily available materials.

## Tools Required

- Saw
- Tape Measure
- Silicone caulking

## Materials

- A cooler similar to this one that I fold on Amazon for $ 44.99 USD.
www.amazon.com/Coleman-Performance-Cooler-48-Quart-Blue/dp/B0000DH4LT/

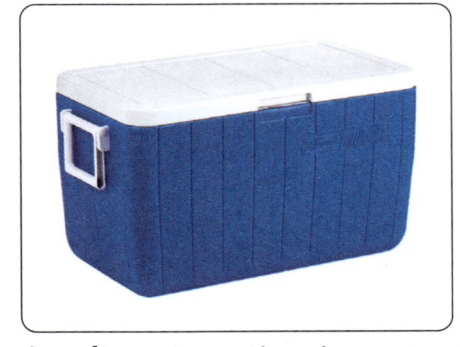

- An alternate option is a styrofoam cooler which can be found at Amazon for $ 25.99 USD.
www.amazon.com/Unknown-Styrofoam-Cooler-Box/dp/B07NDWQFH2

- A fan which can be either 120 volts which I found on Amazon for $ 13.99 USD
www.amazon.com/Comfort-Zone-Desk-Fan-Whisper/dp/B001MEK8Q4/

or a 12-volt fan which is available on Amazon for $ 19.98 USD.
www.amazon.com/ELUTO-Oscillating-Adjustable-Portable-Cigarette/dp/B086TVGYR4/

- 3 inch 90 degrees adjustable elbow, which I found at Home Depot for $ 4.98 USD each.
www.homedepot.com/p/Master-Flow-3-in-90-Deg-Round-Adjustable-Elbow-B90E3/100112500

- Silicone caulking, which can be found at Home Depot for $ 2.82 USD. www.homedepot.com/p/DAP-Alex-Plus-10-1-oz-White-Acrylic-Latex-Caulk-Plus-Silicone-18103/100097524

## Instructions

Building the DIY air conditioner is a fairly straightforward process that requires minimal skills and tools to construct effectively. The coolers I used for this build are Styrofoam, but the directions and methods are the same regardless of the cooler you choose to build your air conditioner from.

1. This design uses two 90 degree adjustable elbows to allow cold air to be blown up from the bottom of the cooler, through the elbows and out into the room you will be cooling.
2. Use one of the elbows to lay out where the hole in the side of the cooler will be. You want this elbow to be high enough not to be submerged if the bottom of the cooler fills with water. It also needs to be high enough to allow for good airflow.
3. Cut a hole in the side of the cooler. You want the hole to be not much bigger than the diameter of the elbows. The tighter the fit, the more retention of the insulation ability of the cooler will be.
4. Install the two elbows so that one is pointing down into the cooler, and the other is oriented in the direction that you want to blow the cool air.
5. Seal the joint with caulking.
6. Disassemble the fan you choose to use, removing anything that is not necessary for the fan to operate correctly and safely. This will probably only entail removing the stand.
7. Use the fan to lay out where you would like the hole in the lid. Position it opposite where the outlet is.
8. Cut the hole into the lid. Try to keep the fit as tight as possible.
9. Mount the fan to the lid through whatever means are appropriate.
10. Place frozen bottles or ice into the cooler.
11. Replace the lid tightly.
12. Turn on the fan.

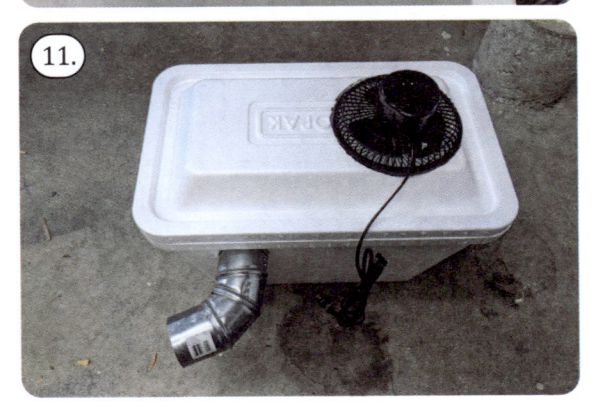

## Testing the DIY Air Conditioner

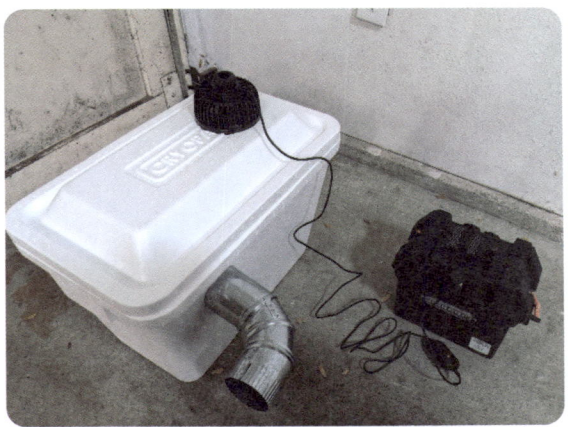

I built two versions of this air conditioner, one using a 12-volt fan and the other using a 120-volt fan. The basic design of these units was identical, the only difference being the type of fan that is powering the unit.

Both air conditioners blew air through the unit and expelled cold air from the outlet, but the one that used a 120-volt current had weaker airflow than the 12-volt fan. Additionally, I found that airflow could be increased or decreased with tilting and rotating the two 3 inch elbows.

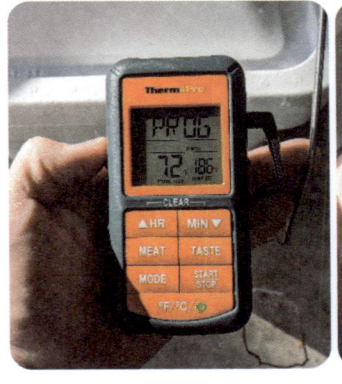

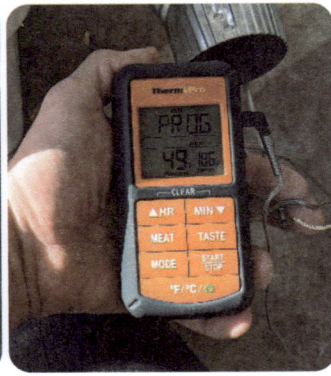

With an ambient air temperature of around 70 degrees Farhenhight, the outlet of each of the DIY air conditioners that I built got as low as 49 degrees with an average temperature of 53 degrees. There is little doubt that the DIY air conditioner is nowhere near as effective as any commercially bought unit. Still, it does blow cold air and eventually would reduce the temperature in a room by a few degrees, hopefully making it a little more habitable.

## Variations and Improvements

For a DIY air conditioner to operate effectively, the air inside the cooler must stay as cold as possible. Therefore, the flow of air through the cooler needs to be fast enough to push enough cold air into the space you're trying to cool but slow enough to allow the hot air to cool as it passes through the unit. There are several variations and improvements that one could experiment with.

- Instead of using a fan at the top of the cooler, use an inline booster fan at the outlet. This will act to pull the air through the unit rather than push the hot air down into the unit.
- Fill the airspace in the top portion of the cooler with insulation or foam to improve the insulating properties of the cooler.
- Seal the joints where the fan and the outlet are with expanding foam
- If you have access to very cold water, you can use a copper coil inside the cooler to run cold water through instead of using ice. This will be slightly less effective than ice, but if you can cycle the water through the cooler, you can avoid the need to create ice repeatedly.
- Instead of using ice cubes, freeze plastic bottles or gallon milk jugs with water. Remember to leave room for the ice to expand as it freezes.

This is by no means an exhaustive list of variations; through some experimentation, you will no doubt be able to tweak and perfect your DIY air conditioner.

The DIY air conditioner is not going to be as efficient as commercially available portable air conditioning units and will never replace central air. That being said, in a grid-down situation where you need to cool small spaces during sweltering days, putting together one of these units is quick, easy, and uses readily available materials. Of course, these units are not ones you would have for daily use, but the ease of construction makes this a good option when central air or portable air conditioners are not viable options.

OTHER PROJECTS TO DO IN YOUR BACKYARD

# DIY Charcoal Briquettes To Have In Case Of Emergency

EASY DIFFICULTY

There are a number of reasons why you may want to have a steady supply of charcoal briquettes at hand. For example, are you looking for a way post-collapse to keep moisture from playing havoc with your guns? Why not make your own charcoal dehumidifier?

All you have to do is place a few charcoal briquettes in a metal coffee can, punch some holes in it, and then place it in your gun cabinet. Replace it every few months and you'll have helped to nip moisture in the bud.

Perhaps you're wanting an easy means of keeping charcoal handy for future DIY water filters. Perhaps you just want to cook your venison so that it tastes the way it should.

Whatever your reasons are, access to charcoal may not even be a possibility post-collapse. Here is how to make your own DIY charcoal briquettes.

## Here Is What You Need

There are actually a number of different ways out there that will help you to make your own charcoal, but many of them call for ingredients that you likely won't have readily available post-disaster.

DIY charcoal briquettes need to be as simple as possible and that means with as few ingredients as possible:
- Charcoal dust
- Water
- Cornstarch (or newspapers).

Provided you have access to those three ingredients, you can make your own charcoal briquettes.

## Here Is the Process

**Step 1**: Gather the black charcoal from a recent fire.

Make yourself a big campfire and burn down a lot of wood until it's nothing more than black charcoal. That's exactly what you want.

Once the fire has died and the coals are cooled, gather up as much of that black charcoal as you can.

I avoid the white ash. Getting water on the white ash will make lye, and you don't want to get chemical burns on your hands.

**Step 2**: Ground your charcoal up into a small powder.

It doesn't matter if you put it in a bag and hit it with a hammer, use a mortar and pestle, or smash it between a couple of rocks. Somehow, you just have to get that charcoal ground up into a fine black dust.

Do that with all of the charcoal that you've gathered, and then set it aside in some form of container.

I used a 5-gallon bucket and a big log from a pine tree I'd just cut down. You'll feel like you're churning butter going about things this way, but it gets the job done.

**Step 3**: Using a stove, campfire, or some other source of heat, mix up your cornstarch and your water into a thick porridge-like paste.

Your best bet here is to heat up the water while slowly pouring the corn starch in and mixing until you get the right amount.

This is going to serve as your binding agent for the briquettes – holding all of the charcoal dust together into a nice, uniform shape.

While I don't have a set recipe for how much cornstarch you're going to need, I will say this: you'll need a lot.

It ended up taking me an entire container's worth to get to where I felt I was getting close to porridge-y.

If you want something a bit more scientific, here are some actual recipes for making your own charcoal:

- 10 kg of charcoal dust and 0.3 kg of cassava starch
- 4 kg sawdust, 40 kg charcoal dust, 2.5 kg starch, 1 kg calcium carbonate
- 10 kg charcoal dust, 5 kg sawdust, 1 kg cassava starch, 0.5 kg limestone
- 10 kg charcoal dust, 5 kg sawdust, 1 kg mashed newsprint.

In a survival situation though, you're not going to have access to all of the various ingredients. Use what you have to make what you can.

Survival is often about ingenuity with limited resources.

**Step 4**: Mix in as much charcoal dust as possible.

Stir in as much as you can here. The more you can get in there, the better. Ideally, quality charcoal briquettes are in the neighborhood of 90% charcoal.

**Optional Step – Mix in Newspaper Shavings**

This isn't required, but I did it to assist with the lighting process.

Newspaper can act as an accelerant within charcoal, helping to ensure your charcoal lights quicker.

Seeing that paper is common in homemade cement style mixtures, I figured it would help the briquettes to bind well too.

I tore up two full sheets of newspaper into little pieces. If you have access to a paper shredder, or the ability to really get those newspaper pieces tiny, I would recommend taking full advantage of such.

Doing so would increase the surface area of the newspaper, helping to give you a quicker lighting process.

**Step 5**: Pour the sooty, gooey mess into egg cartons.

These are a great at-the-ready uniform means of shaping all of your charcoal briquettes. Once you've filled up as many of these as you can, set them to the side and let them dry.

At the end of this drying period, your charcoal should be ready to use.

It took 3 days of drying in the Southern sun for my charcoal to get to the consistency I wanted it to be.

On Day 2 I speed things up by sticking it in a solar dehydrator that had just burnt some tomato slices to little black rings.

### How It Worked

Like most of my attempts at lighting charcoal, I needed a bit of help to get these guys lit.

While I've typically used lighter fluid in past grilling attempts, I figured that may not be available if you're in a survival situation.

So, I used my favorite means of fire assistance: Vaseline-soaked cotton balls. I lit three of those, threw them in my hobo stove full of homemade charcoal, and ended up with a little fire.

Using a little Lodge cast-iron skillet, I then proceeded to fry one of my chicken's eggs.

While the charcoal did burn down completely to white/brown ash, I do think this particular batch would have been better served via adding more accelerant to the mix.

There's no doubt in my mind that the black ash component was 90$^+$% of the total mixture as desired.

More newspaper is what should have been added, however. That would have enabled a much better burn.

Black ash in and of itself doesn't end up drawing enough oxygen to burn really hot. Accelerant is what makes that happen.

Should I have had a significant amount of sawdust, or more finely shredded newspaper accessible, this would have resulted in an even more potent batch.

That being said, the charcoal of this batch worked just fine, it just needed a bit more oomph.

Making your own charcoal is quite a bit of work, but it is doable.

By the time you pound ashes into dust, heat up your starch mixture, stir a big vat of glop, add accelerant, pour the goo into molds, and let everything dry, you've expended quite a bit of effort.

However, if for whatever reason it's charcoal you need in a survival situation, there is a way to do it.

Hopefully, you'll have found the above informative and a good addition to your mental toolbox of DIY survival skills.

OTHER PROJECTS TO DO IN YOUR BACKYARD

# DIY Dollar Store First Aid Kit

EASY DIFFICULTY

While everyone hopes that they'll never need to break out a first aid kit, an event will inevitably arise that requires you to break out the bandages and maybe a whole lot more.

Everybody, with no exception, needs to have a well-equipped first aid kit on hand.

While there are plenty of fairly comprehensive first aid kits available for purchase, really good quality kits with plenty of supplies can get expensive.

There are kits out there that will cost you upwards of a couple hundred bucks.

If a store-bought kit isn't in your budget, you might consider a DIY option.

However, if you go shopping at the average drug store or even big box stores for all of the items that you'll need in your kit, it's a guarantee that you'll spend as much or more than you would if you just purchased a ready-made kit.

The other issue with store-bought kits is that they don't necessarily contain items that are specific for the needs of your household.

Of course, general first-aid supplies come fairly standard, but what about addressing your family's specific medical needs? Store-bought kits frequently don't have a lot of space for additions, either.

The solution to both of the above issues? A kit curated by you for your family, put together with items from your nearest dollar store.

Here, the closest 'everything for a dollar' retailer was the brand new Dollar Tree store that just opened up this week.

Though we had a Dollar Tree store in the next town over before this one, the new store had a much better selection of medications and supplies, plus a great selection of containers both to keep the kit organized and to act as a storage case.

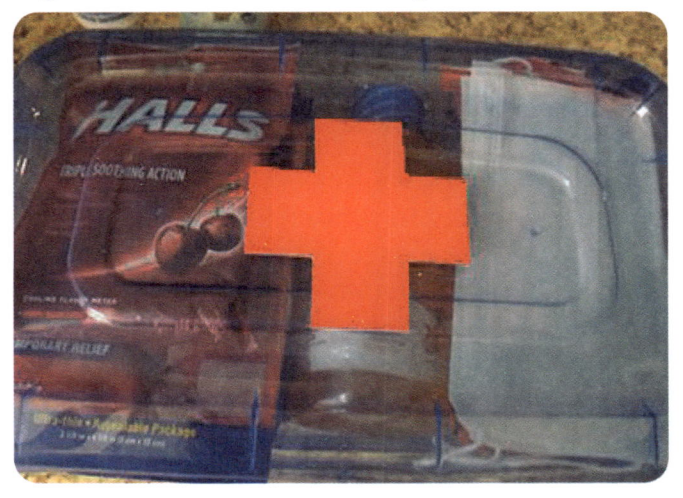

Let's go over some basic supplies that you'll need to get your dollar store first aid kit started.

Later, we'll go through a few additions you might consider making, based on common medical conditions or issues.

## Basic First Aid Kit Supplies

Here is a detailed list of the supplies you may need to add to your First Aid Kit.

- **Gauze pads** – Ideally both large and small, so you can deal with whatever size injury comes your way;
- **Gauze roll** – For injuries that need to be wrapped;
- **Adhesive bandages** – Pick up several different sizes and be cautious of the type of materials used in construction if there are any allergies or sensitivities to latex or other adhesives;
- **Triple antibiotic ointment** – Put on bandages to help prevent infection and reduce scarring;
- **Medical tape** – For taping down gauze;
- **Gentle tape** – This 'tape' lacks the usual adhesives and only sticks to itself. It's great for applying pressure to wounds or overuse injuries,

like tennis elbow or carpal tunnel;
- **Thermometer** – A digital thermometer is an easy way to check body temperature;
- **Hot and cold packs** – I found great old-fashioned cold/hot water bottles that can be reused, and they seem to be pretty decent quality. There are also instant heat and cool packs in my kit;
- **Antibacterial wipes and hand sanitizer** – Make sure hands are germ free before you begin first aid on yourself or someone else;
- **Nitrile gloves** – Maintain basic precautions when it comes to other people's body fluids to prevent the spread of bloodborne pathogens;
- **Face masks** – Reduce the risk of contracting or passing on airborne pathogens;
- **Elastic bandage** – These are a great multi-purpose, reusable item that has many uses, from splinting to supporting pulled muscles, to acting as a pressure bandage for wounds. Consider grabbing a couple, particularly if you have lingering joint injuries in your household;
- **Scissors** – For cutting tape or bandages;
- **Witch hazel** – Gentle antiseptic that soothes skin; great for rashes or bug bites, cleansing small wounds, and general skin care;
- **Peroxide** – For serious infection prevention and care, plus wound debridement;
- **Alcohol prep pads** – For quick disinfection of skin or wounds (but only use on open skin in a pinch, these will really sting!); may also be used to disinfect hard surfaces;
- **Eye drops** – For rinsing eyes and reducing eye irritation, plus providing relief for dry eyes;
- **Cough drops** – For coughs, colds, and sore throats;
- **Tissues** – Nothing is more miserable when you've got a cold than no tissues, plus these are great for basic clean-up in a pinch;
- **Tweezers** – For removing splinters or other foreign objects;
- **Garbage bags** – To clean up messes effectively and reduce the potential for the spreading of infection;
- **Electrolyte replacement drink** – This is especially helpful in the summer, or if you've got a house full of sensitive tummies;
- **Plastic boxes** – These will be used to hold your kit and the various components of the kit as well. An organized first aid kit is an effective first aid kit in an emergency situation.

## Individualized Items and Why You'd Need Them

- **Medications** – What you need will really depend on your family's unique situation, your climate, etc., but you ought to consider acetaminophen, an NSAID, allergy medicine, cold medicine, anti-itch topical medication, and stomach relief like antacids or Pepto;
- **Candy or glucose tabs** – If you have a diabetic in your household;
- **Essential oils** – If you have any go-to EOs that you use for your family, consider storing small amounts in your first aid kit, as well as some carrier oil;
- **Sunscreen and aloe** – If you live in an area where overexposure is common;
- **Epi-Pen or Benadryl** – For severe allergies. Find out how to get free EpiPens;
- **Moleskin** – For feet prone to blisters;
- **Magnifying glass** – For those with poor eye sight; You can't treat an injury you can't see clearly!

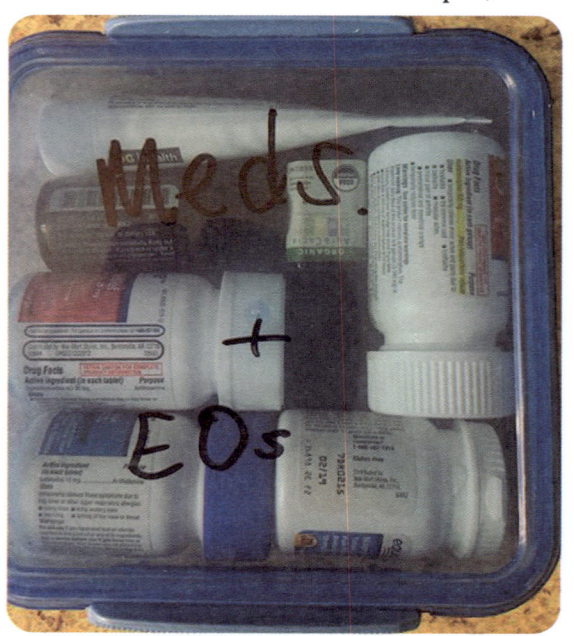

◆ **Penlight** – For carrying out first aid treatment in low light;

# Putting Your Kit Together

First, create an inventory list to tape to the underside of the lid of your first aid kit box and be sure you date the list and mark off anything that's used up (or replace it immediately).

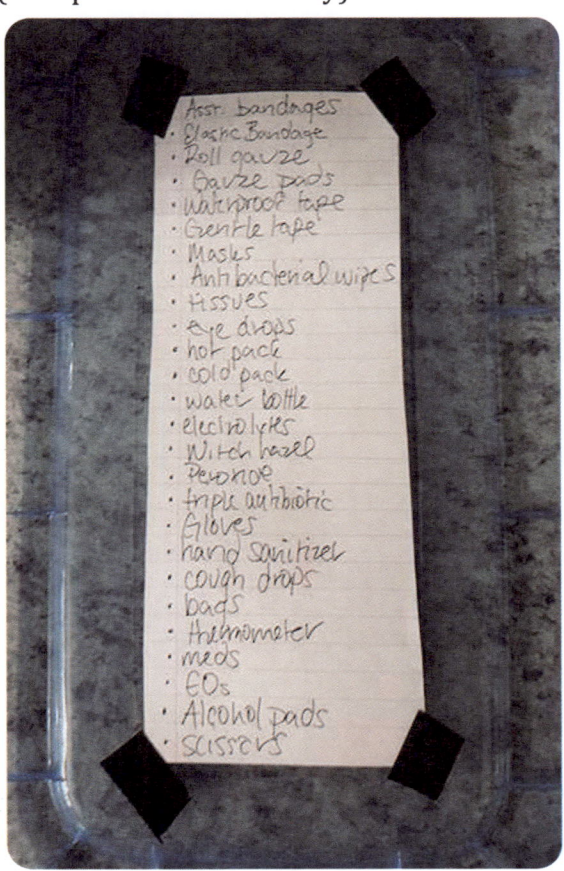

By utilizing discount stores like the Dollar Tree, you can create a well-stocked first aid kit for very little cash, leaving your family well-prepared and your bank account relatively unscathed.

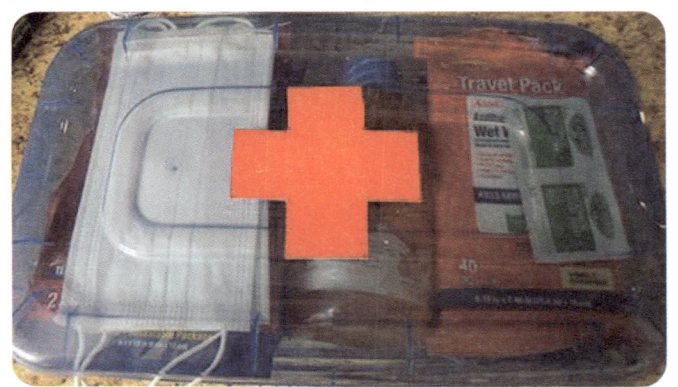

You can stick a large red cross symbol on the top of the lid to indicate universally that it's a first aid kit. Use a smaller lidded container for bandages, one for gauze, and one for medications to keep these items from getting wet in case of leaks.

Create simple labels for each container. You can even use a permanent marker like I did, rather than more formal labels.

OTHER PROJECTS TO DO IN YOUR BACKYARD

# DIY Rocket Stove

**MATERIAL COST** $ 20.00  **EASY** DIFFICULTY  **10 MINUTES**

Fire is one of the most helpful tools that you can have for survival. It can keep you warm, provide light, cook food, and purify water. The smoke can fend off predators, keep insects away, and kill bacteria. The ashes can be used for toothpaste, to soothe an upset stomach, and to camouflage your skin for hunting.

However, fire also provides its own unique set of challenges. If the fire is not contained, it can damage property and can be life threatening. If the smoke is not channeled away, it can fill up a room and make it impossible to breathe. Fire is also finnicky. It requires a steady flow of oxygen and a constant supply of fuel. It can be tough to deal with all of these variables.

Prior to furnaces and central heating, fireplaces and wood stoves were the ideal option for this purpose. They contain the fire for safety purposes, channel smoke up and away from the home, and supply a steady flow of oxygen to the fire. They also allow you to continually add firewood to keep the fire going. Both of these systems are just complex versions of a rocket stove.

## What Is a Rocket Stove?

A rocket stove is any structure that draws in oxygen from a channel at the base and controls smoke with a vertical chimney. They are typically L shaped and can be made with any fire-resistant material such as bricks, cinder blocks, steel pipes, or even mud and rocks. You can build huge rocket stoves designed for years of cooking and heating, or you can build a portable one out of a coffee can and a soup can.

For the purposes of this project, I built a rocket stove with standard red bricks. I wanted to have one large enough that it could be used for several years, but small enough that I could break it down and move it if needed.

Please be aware that any material used that is not fire treated could have moisture inside. As the fire heats up this material, the moisture will vaporize and will start to make the bricks pop and crack. This is not a danger to the fire or the structure, but you should probably take a few steps back when it happens. Small shards of brick can sometimes go flying. After about 10 minutes, this should stop.

## Materials Needed

I happened to have some standard red bricks lying around for this build. If you need to buy bricks, they are usually less than $1 per brick. It took about 50 bricks to build this rocket stove which works out to about $20 in materials. Below is a link for bricks similar to what I used. I also included a link for fire bricks that will not pop when they get hot.

www.lowes.com/pd/Pacific-Clay-Common-Full-Red-Clay-Standard-Brick/4514218

www.lowes.com/pd/Unbranded-Fire-Brick-Full-Size-2-5-in-x-4-5-in-x-9-in/5000270269

## Instructions

1. Lay out the foundation of your rocket stove. As you can see, I used two bricks side by side for my air channel at the bottom. Then I laid out a larger base for the chimney.
2. Close off your air channel at the top. Lay bricks across your foundation so that the air channel is covered at the top.
3. Build up your chimney. Start stacking bricks up for the walls of your chimney. I built mine up until it was about three feet tall. The opening at the top was about one foot by one foot. Don't worry about any small gaps between bricks. The air will still flow properly.
4. Load up the tinder and kindling. Just like building any fire, you will be lighting a tinder bundle and dropping it down to the bottom of the chimney. You will then be sticking lots of kindling sticks down the chimney to fuel the fire.

In this example, the snow had just melted and all of the kindling was soaking wet. Because of the controlled air flow, it dried out and lit up quickly.

5. Add fuel logs. If you are just wanting to boil water, cook something quickly, or shake off the cold, you will not need logs. If you want to keep it going for several hours, drop a couple small logs down into the burning kindling.

The rocket stove not only contains the fire, controls the smoke, and provides air flow, but the bricks or any material that you use will absorb heat from the fire. Even after the fire goes out, the stove will continue to radiate heat for hours. This is great to conserve firewood when you are sleeping.

There are few builds as simple as a rocket stove that make such a difference. Working with a rocket stove is easily two to three times easier than trying to build a teepee fire on the ground. It takes a little planning and a little time to put it together, but it is definitely worth the effort.

If you get a chance, try building a small one in the back yard. If you have practice putting together a rocket stove now, it will make the process that much easier in the future. Plus, it's so much more interesting than a fire pit.

OTHER PROJECTS TO DO IN YOUR BACKYARD

# DIY Smokehouse In A Barrel

EASY DIFFICULTY

Building your own smokehouse is the same as making barbecue – all you have to do is turn modest, everyday ingredients into something incredibly satisfying.

Smokers are made in lots of different ways, but in this chapter I'll be sharing two with you.

The first one is easier to make and will need very little of your precious time to complete. However, you need a specific location for it and extra space for digging.

The second one is more refined and "better looking". It is made with higher attention to detail. This model is great for any small backyard spaces, it doesn't require digging and you can move it around.

Let's dive into how I built these smokehouses.

## 1. Building Your Basic Smokehouse

As far as tools and materials go, you will need:
- An Empty Barrel;
- Steel Mesh;
- Iron rods;
- Iron hooks;
- Iron sheet;
- Grinder;
- Shovel;
- Firewood.

This will be very easy to build, if you follow these eight simple steps.

### Step 1. Choose Your Location

Because you are going to dig a hole, it is best you locate your smokehouse in your backyard. Find that perfect spot and dig a knee-deep hole.

### Step 2. Carve Out the Bottom Part of Your Barrel

The second step I took was to take the barrel and carve out the bottom part with a grinder. This will allow heat and smoke through, when smoking the meat.

### Step 3. Put the Firewood into the Hole

Organize the firewood appropriately in the hole. Make sure you also throw in some flammable content, like paper and small twigs to simplify starting your fire, which will be the next step you take.

### Step 4. Cover the Hole with Steel Mesh

I got some steel mesh and covered the hole as well. Ensure that your structure and the top part of the hole is strong enough to handle the weight of the barrel.

### Step 5. Place the Barrel on Top of the Hole

Place the barrel over the top of the hole, where the steel mesh ends, so that you can channel the heat and smoke straight to your meat. Then when it is into position, cover the base with some dirt, so all of the smoke will enter the barrel.

Also, I placed a small mesh at the bottom of the barrel, if the meat will somehow fall from its place, it will not fall on dirt and fire.

### Step 6. Place the Iron Rods on the Barrel

The next step I took was to take the three iron rods and placed them on top of the barrel.

These rods will be used to hang the meat that you will be smoking.

174

#### Step 7. Hang the Meat

It's now time to hang the meat. Take the iron hooks, hook the meat on them, and hang them on the iron rods.

#### Step 8. The Meat Will Be Ready

Depending on whether you are smoking your meat to eat it or to preserve it, the time for it to be ready will vary. This also depends on the type and size of your meat.

One big advantage of this basic smokehouse is that smoke goes slowly to your meat (through the hole), which allows you to leave it alone, and do whatever you want whilst it gets ready.

This basic DIY smoker is really easy to make, plus you don't need to invest a lot of time into it.

## 2. Building a Custom DIY Smokehouse

The second type of smokehouse that we will be getting into is a bit different. This one is more customized and needs more time to build.

As far as tools and materials go, you will need:
- An empty barrel;
- 5 iron rods;
- Small hinges;
- 4 small screws;
- Electric drill;
- Grinder;
- Spray or Paint;
- Firewood.

If you are looking to impress your friends when they come over for a visit, then this second custom DIY smokehouse will do the job. It is portable, fancy, but most importantly, it gets the job done. Follow me as I share how I created my own.

#### Step 1. Make an Opening on the Lower Third of Your Barrel

The first thing I did was to make a rectangular opening on the lower third of the barrel using a grinder. This should be big enough to fit your wood.

I then took the square metal plate that I carved out and put it back in along with two small hinges, making a door. This door will be used to put in, or reduce the firewood.

### Step 2. Paint the Barrel

It's now time to spray paint the outer part of the barrel with any color that you like. Place the barrel on an elevated plane and start painting.

### Step 3. Leave the Barrel to Dry

We are now done creating and designing our smokehouse – place it in a sunny area so that the paint can dry up quicker.

### Step 4. Drill and Pluck in the Iron Rods

The next step is to drill 5 holes on the upper third of the barrel, then pluck in the five iron rods.

### Step 5. Start Smoking

Open the door of your barrel and put in some firewood and start the fire.

Make sure you hang the meat only after the fire stops blazing ,so that it doesn't get burned. Enjoy!

DIY smoking has been around since the beginning of time. This is mainly because of the nostalgic memories it creates after eating those deliciously prepared meals.

If you don't have a smokehouse yet, what are you waiting for? Follow the above instructions and make your own!

# DIY Stove Made From Used Tire Rims

**MEDIUM DIFFICULTY**     **1 HOUR**

I had two used tire rims and I decided to make a stove. They have enough holes for the fire to breathe well and I could easily create an opening to fuel the fire. The easiest thing to do was to put the two rims on top of each other. This gave me enough height and space inside to fuel it.

## Materials Needed

I first gathered everything I'd need:
- 2 tire rims
- A drill
- A grindstone bit for the drill
- A wire grinder bit for the drill
- A grinder
- A welder
- A piece of cloth
- A welder's mask
- Acetone
- Protective gloves
- Heat-resistant spray paint (optional).

## Building the Stove

### Step One: Cutting it to Shape

I first grabbed the two rims and put them on top of each other. With the help of a crayon, I drew out the size that I wanted the door to be. After I got that, I took the two rims apart and started cutting the door out with my grinder.

To make sure it didn't cut my hands, I went over the edges with the drill. I put on my stone grinder bit and made it smoother.

### Step Two: Taking off the Top Layer of the Tire Rims

When I was done, I grabbed my drill and placed the wire grinder bit onto it. This will remove the paint on top and let me paint it with black heat-resistant spray paint.

### Step Three: Welding the Two Tire Rims Together

After I had removed the top layer, I got my welder and my welder's mask ready.

Make sure to always use the mask when welding and never look at it without protection while it's happening. Be careful how you use it, and always wear gloves.

**Step Four: Painting**

I had three cooking trays that I didn't really use, so I thought they would be perfect as a stand for the stove. The two longer ones will hold it up, while the square one will be used to take out the ashes after use. I covered them all with black heat-resistant spray paint. I did the same with the stove itself.

**Step Five: Trying It Out**

I prepared some wood and fired it up. I used pine wood to light it. Pine wood is full of resin, so it burns quicker and better than other wood. This was perfect to make a fire in seconds.

I stuffed it as full as I could with wood. I only needed to use one piece of paper, most likely because of the resin in the wood.

It was able to push the flames out at the top, which I hadn't thought of.

I tried out different things that I could use on top of it. For example, I could cook some steak on this cooking disk. Or make some soup in this pot. Or cook a chicken in this cast iron cooker.

This tire rim stove was an easy and practical build that most likely will be used a lot around my house. One of the best features of it is that you can simply put it inside the car and take it anywhere you go.

OTHER PROJECTS TO DO IN YOUR BACKYARD

# EMP Proof Cloth: Easy EMP Protection For Your Car And Generator

EASY DIFFICULTY    10 MINUTES

I believe everyone should have a backup generator. I get to use mine once or twice a year when the power goes out. When Hurricane Irma came, we didn't have power for ten days. Our generator, which runs on both propane and gasoline, kept our food from spoiling and powered all our appliances.

Thank God we had that generator during that dark time!

But what if an EMP were to hit America?

I can't even imagine how vital a generator would be then. Many reports show us that the power grid would be functioning again in about five years.

The problem with an EMP is that it also fries the generators—even those that are not plugged in. Just the fact that they are lying around somewhere means that their electrical components will be completely fried, rendering them useless.

That's why if you want your generator to function after an EMP, you should keep it in a Faraday cage. Basically, a Faraday cage is a completely sealed metal cage. Everything that's inside the cage, but does not touch the metal of the cage, is relatively safe against an EMP.

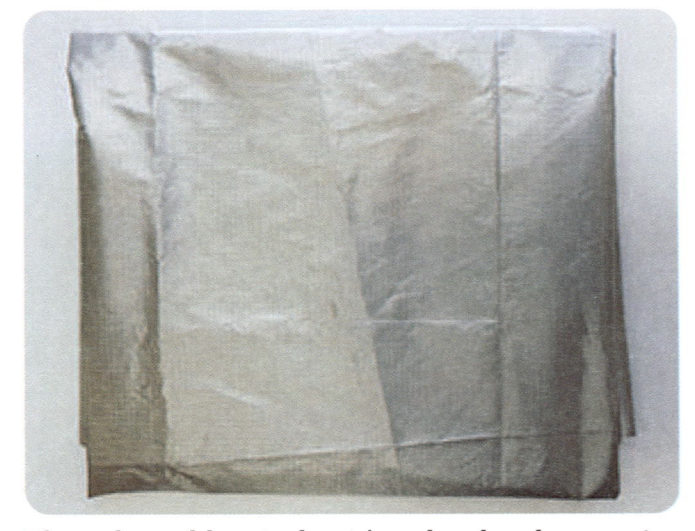

The only problem is that it's so hard and expensive to find a cage big enough to cover your generator.

But not long ago I discovered an EMP-proof cloth that basically blocks out all electromagnetic signals, working just like a Faraday cage.

Developed after years of extensive research by top U.S. scientists, it's an excellent way to protect a large stash of electronics or even bigger items, such as cars, generators, motorcycles, and so forth.

I had to test it myself to see how well it works. I used my generator, an old AM radio, and a cellphone as testing subjects. And I'm going to show you exactly how you can test it out yourself, just to be absolutely sure that it works.

I decided to get my generator out of the garage for this project. You're going to need two other devices if you want to test this out yourself: a cellphone and an old AM radio.

The reason why you need both might not be obvious, so I'll explain:

Your cellphone uses high frequencies, while the AM radio uses low frequencies. If both are blocked, then you are safe. If you haven't properly wrapped the generator, you'll know because you will be able to either make calls to your cellphone, hear the station on the radio, or both.

First, spread out as much cloth as necessary on a table. Make sure you have enough to wrap around the entire surface of the equipment you're trying to protect. Otherwise, you risk leaving exposed spots, and all your hard work will have gone to waste.

Don't worry though. You can try again. I also failed to wrap it properly the first time. This is why it's important to have your cellphone and AM radio ready.

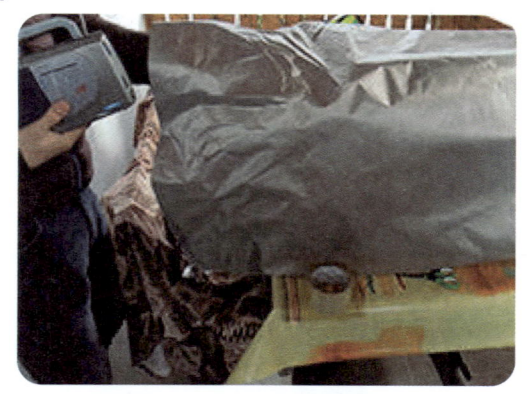

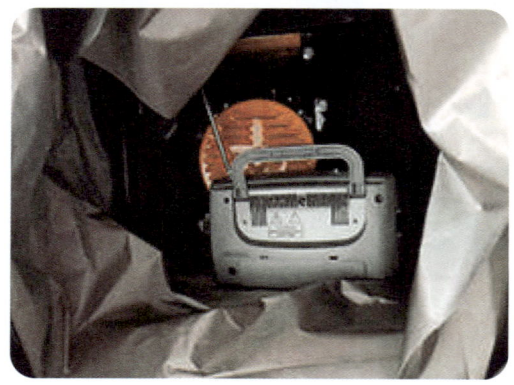

The cloth is made with powerful EMP shielding materials that will protect your generator from the effects of an EMP or CME.

Paper thin and practically weightless, the EMP cloth is made out of 23% copper + 27% nickel, and 50% polyester.

At 15 feet long by 3.5 feet wide, it's designed to fully cover any type of home generator, including diesel, solar, gasoline, propane, and virtually any other type of generator.

Similar to a Faraday cage, it provides 98% military-grade protection against electromagnetic waves.

You can find EMP-proof clothes online (Amazon, EBay, etc.).

Now that you've ensured your generator is well sealed, you can rest assured if an EMP hits.

**Laptop**

**Generator**

**Walkie-Talkie**

OTHER PROJECTS TO DO IN YOUR BACKYARD

# How To Build A Fuel Storage And How To Preserve It

EASY DIFFICULTY

Modern society is heavily dependant on fossil fuels and this dependency is very apparent when there is any disruption of supply. When an SHTF scenario occurs, or we see a prolonged grid-down situation, fuel supplies are going to evaporate rapidly. This makes fuel storage an important aspect of our preparations and is one that has some special considerations.

We need to think about a few safety considerations when storing fuel for the long term.

The fact that gasoline and diesel are flammable is the first and most important safety consideration when handling and storing fuel. Fuel stores should never be near any ignition source. When handling fuel, start by discharging any static electricity your body may have built up by touching a grounded metal object. Under no circumstances should you smoke or have any open flame near your fuel stores.

Never fill a jerry can that is inside of your vehicle or in the bed of your truck. There is a significant risk of static discharge that will ignite the fumes, causing bodily injury or even death. Always fill jerry cans by placing them on the ground.

Avoid getting gasoline or diesel on your skin or in your eyes. If you do get fuel in your eyes, immediately flush them with fresh water and seek medical aid.

The fumes that gasoline or diesel gives off are toxic and can cause death if inhaled over long periods. The area you are storing fuel needs proper ventilation to eliminate the build-up of fumes.

## Where to Store Gasoline and Diesel

Fuel needs to be stored at a minimum of 50 feet away from any possible ignition sources. Ideally, all fuel and other flammable materials should be stored in a shed or other outbuilding and never inside your home. If you need to store fuel inside your garage, position the containers as not to have them close to ignition sources so that fumes do not enter your home.

Don't place jerry cans on the bare ground instead of building a shelf or storage rack to keep them off the cold ground. At the least, place a sheet of plywood under the jerry cans that have to sit on the concrete.

Be aware of all regulations, fire codes, building codes, and safety guidelines when deciding where to store fuel and how much fuel to store. There may be rules and regulations restricting the amount of fuel a homeowner can legally store on their property and how large the containers used to store that fuel may be.

## Fuel Storage Containers

Any container that you will use to store fuel must be certified and approved to hold that fuel. Many jurisdictions restrict homeowners to using containers of a maximum of five gallons, so storing your fuel in jerry cans may be the only option available to you. Keeping your fuel stores in smaller containers also makes it easier to take the fuel with you during a bug out.

Along with the containers being certified, they must indicate which fuel is inside the containers. Many commercially available containers are colour-coded to make identification easier. Regardless of the colour, these containers need to have markings that indicate which fuel the container holds.

- Red – Gasoline
- Yellow – Diesel
- Blue – Kerosene
- Green – Oils

The regulations for fuel storage containers are updated from time to time, and it is important to be aware of any changes.

Under no circumstances should you attempt to fabricate your fuel storage container; always purchase certified and approved containers to store the fuel you plan to store.

## How Much Fuel to Store

Ultimately, the amount of fuel you will store will be determined by the regulations and codes in your area. Beyond that, you will need to take an inventory of all the equipment you plan to operate in a post SHTF or grid-down scenario.

For a short-term emergency, a few five-gallon jerry cans are probably going to be more than sufficient to fuel what you need. On the other hand, if there is a long-term emergency or a total grid-down situation, you will have to consider what you want to operate and how much fuel those pieces of equipment require.

Unless you can have a large fuel storage tank, operating a motor vehicle during a prolonged emergency is probably not practical. For the most part, our fuel stores focus on powering vital equipment such as generators.

For example, my fuel storage revolves around running a generator for a prolonged emergency situation such as a massive earthquake. I know that my generator will run for 10 hours on a full 3-gallon tank of gas at 50% load. I also know that I can run the generator for three hours a day and keep the food cold and the freezer frozen.

If I want to keep the generator running for two weeks, I have to do a little math to determine the amount of gas I need to store.

My generator will run for three days at three hours a day before refilling.

This means that every three days, I expend one tank or three gallons of gasoline.

To figure out the amount of fuel for 14 days, I divided 14 by 3 to figure out how many tanks of gas I needed to plan for. I got a result of 4.6666666, which I rounded up to 5 tanks of gasoline.

One tank of gas for my generator is 3 gallons, so that means all I have to do is multiple the 3 gallons per tank by the five tanks, which I'm planning on needing to get a result of fifteen gallons of gasoline.

Fifteen gallons of gasoline happens to be three 5-gallon jerry cans of gasoline.

I also have a five-gallon jerry can to fill the lawnmower and pressure washer, but I don't include this fuel as my fuel storage. Since this gas is untreated and I like to keep it fresh, it will be the first fuel into the generator gas tank, extending my generator run time.

## Preserving Gasoline and Diesel

Gasoline begins to break down rapidly after as little as 30 days. The short shelf life poses a problem for the long-term storage of gas.

Diesel fuel falls victim to moisture and algae

growth when stored for long periods. For the most part, diesel will last up to a year in storage, so if you rotate through your diesel stores regularly, treating this fuel with a fuel stabilizer is not required.

## Fuel Stabilizers

One of the best ways to extend the life expectancy of your fuel is to add a fuel stabilizer to each jerry can when filling. Fuel stabilizers are a mix of petroleum additives that help slow gasoline from absorbing moisture and breaking its molecular bonds. Diesel fuel stabilizers help inhibit water absorption and bacterial growth.

Adding fuel stabilizers to gasoline will extend its useful lifespan to at least a year. If you store the gas in a cool, dry place in a sealed approved container, this life span can be as many as two years. I have found that I can pour year and a half old stabilized gasoline into my truck's gas tank without any issues.

## Rotating Fuel Stores

One of the best ways to keep your fuel storage fresh is to rotate the fuel. In my case, I have three five-gallon jerry cans as long-term fuel storage. Each can is filled with stabilized gasoline and is for long-term fuel storage for my generator. I rotate the fuel stores every six months by pouring the can with the oldest gas into my truck's fuel tank. I refill that jerry with fresh gas, add the stabilizer and put it back into rotation.

Using this method, the oldest gas that I will have in my stores will be a year and a half old.

I used to keep the generator full of stabilized gasoline but stopped that practise because I found it inconvenient to siphon the fuel out of the tank when the gas reached the end of its reasonable life expectancy. If you choose to store gasoline or diesel in your equipment's fuel tank, be sure to stabilize the fuel and rotate it out appropriately.

## Building Your Long Term Fuel Storage

Once you have determined what types and quantities of fuel you will store, you'll need to find a suitable location that is cool and dry and out of direct sunlight.

## Materials

◆ Five-gallon jerry cans are available at Home Depot for $ 23.97 USD.
www.homedepot.com/p/Scepter-5-Gal-Smart-Control-Gas-Can-FR1G501/308163379

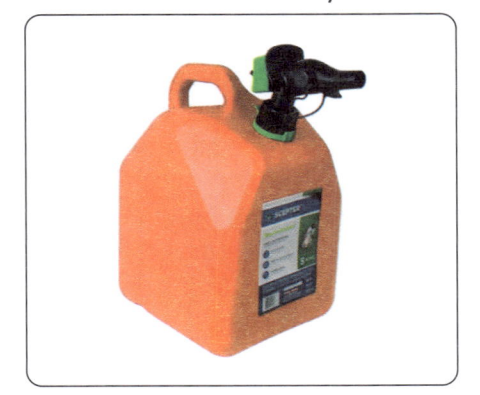

- Fuel stabilizer is sold at Home Depot for $ 8.98 USD a bottle.
www.homedepot.com/p/Sta-Bil-Storage-Fuel-Stabilizer-8-oz-Treats-20-Gallons-of-Fuel-22208/100123778

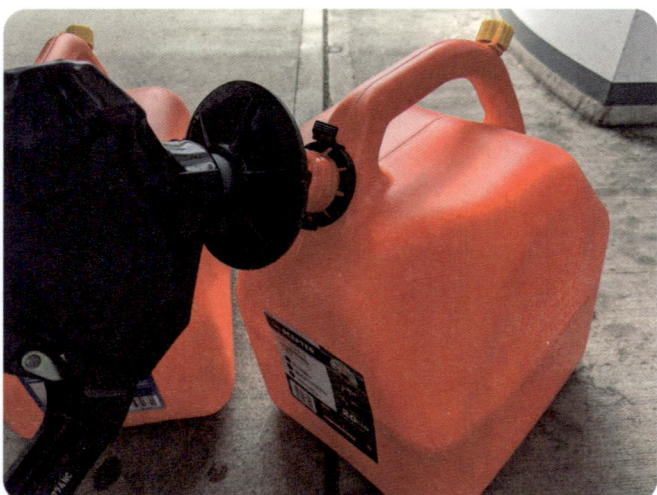

The fuel of your choice in my case at the time I wrote this fifteen gallons of gas cost me about $72.00. To outfit oneself with fuel storage of 15 gallons, such as what I have personally, costs $152.89 and takes less than an hour to set up.

If you are starting your fuel storage for the first time, fill all of your jerry cans and add the appropriate amount of fuel stabilizer.

Set a timeline for the rotation of the jerry cans. Since I am using three jerry cans, a six-month rotation interval makes the most sense. If you are storing more fuel, you will have to devise a different rotation schedule or rotate out more fuel to create a rotation that will result in your oldest fuel being not older than a year and a half.

Check on the condition of the fuel in the other cans when rotating. You can pour a small amount of fuel into a glass jar and examine it for signs of going sour.

Have a system in mind for the rotation of the jerrycans, considering that you may not remember the plan you came up with. I like to keep things very simple by placing a piece of duct tape on each jerry with the month and year due to be rotated out. Think about how you will transport fuel in a bug-out scenario and purchase containers that will fit the gear you are bugging out with.

While, in most cases, it is good not to hold all of a certain prep in one location, your fuel stores should stay together to minimize the risks associated with gasoline and diesel.

If you rotate your fuel by filling your vehicle's gas tank with old stabilized gas, be aware of any loss of power, hard starting, rough idle, etc. This could be a sign that you may need to adjust your rotation interval to reduce the age of the oldest gas in your fuel stores or that the fuel stabilizer you are using is not effective.

Modern society runs on fossil fuels, and when the pumps run dry, you will be left with whatever stores of gasoline or diesel you have squirrelled away. There will come a time when the jerry cans are empty and the world around you is devoid of fuel, but with a little forethought and preparation, you can keep your gasoline and diesel equipment operating longer than those around you.

OTHER PROJECTS TO DO IN YOUR BACKYARD

# How To Build A Greenhouse

**MATERIAL COST** $ 314.82    **COMPLEX DIFFICULTY**    **6 HOURS**

If we want to grow our food, we find ourselves slaves to the seasons and limited as to when and how we can plant. The good news is that with a load of lumber and some glass or plastic, we can create an artificial environment that we control despite external conditions.

Greenhouses work by converting light energy from the sun into heat that we trap inside the greenhouse. Light from the sun enters through the glass or plastic of the greenhouse, heating plants and air inside the structure. Since the greenhouse is a closed environment, this heated air has no escape, providing a nice warm environment for plants to grow despite the temperature outside.

It can get very hot inside a greenhouse, so it is important to allow the hot air to escape through windows or a fan. On the flip side, if the environment outside is too cold, you may need to place a heater inside the greenhouse to maintain a temperature that your plants need to thrive.

### Placement of the Greenhouse

We rely on the sun to heat our greenhouse, so placing the structure in an area exposed to a large amount of direct sunlight is the most important consideration. The goal is to have as much surface area of the greenhouse exposed to the sun's rays for the longest period. Generally speaking, if you are in the Northern hemisphere, having the greenhouse maintain a southern exposure is ideal. Failing this, an eastern exposure is a decent alternative so that the greenhouse will catch the sun's morning rays.

### Material Options

The two main options for the frame of your greenhouse are wood and metal. Unless you have access to a welding machine and fabrication equipment, wood will probably be the best option for constructing a greenhouse. Wood is easier to work with, widely available, and the most affordable option.

The greenhouse floor can be wood, concrete, or bare earth and, in many ways, comes down to your preference and the materials you have available to you. Concrete takes time and skill to make, and a wood floor can increase the cost of your greenhouse.

A greenhouse needs a transparent covering to allow the sun's light into the structure while not letting the heat out. While glass and plastic are not great insulators, they are good for buildings like greenhouses because they let the light in, trapping some of the heat inside.

Glass is difficult to install and can be expensive, with plastic being a far more economical option. There is a distinct advantage to plastic in a grid-down situation as well. Plastic sheeting can be repaired using duct tape or tuck tape, while a pane of glass, once broken, is broken forever.

There are a lot of designs for greenhouses available online, many of them free of charge. The one I have designed and chosen for this build is a lean-to-style of greenhouse, which can be a free-standing structure or attached to the side of a building.

## Tools Required

- Saw
- Square
- Level
- Drill with drivers and bits

## Materials

- 2x4x8' lumber is sold at Home Depot for $ 6.98 USD each.

www.homedepot.com/p/2-in-x-4-in-x-96-in-Prime-Whitewood-Stud-058449/312528776

- #8 – 2 ½" screws are available at Home Depot for $ 9.50 USD per pound.
www.homedepot.com/p/SPAX-8-x-2-1-2-in-Philips-Square-Drive-Flat-Head-Full-Thread-Zinc-Coated-Multi-Material-Screw-1-lb-Box-4101010400606/202041007

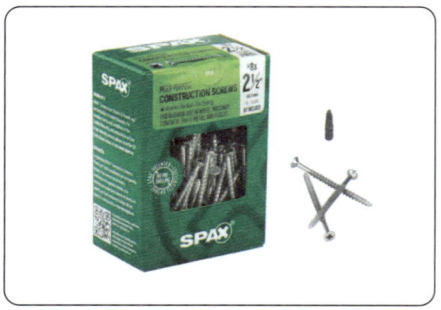

- Hinges can be found at Home Depot for $ 8.98 USD per package of three.
www.homedepot.com/p/Everbilt-3-1-2-in-Satin-Nickel-5-8-in-Radius-Security-Door-Hinges-Value-Pack-3-Pack-14874/202818703

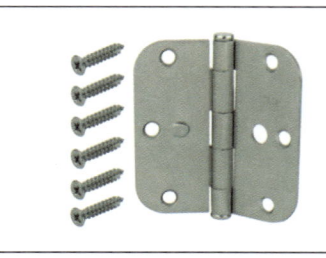

- The 6mil vapour barrier is available at Home Depot for $ 64.00 USD a roll.
www.homedepot.com/p/HDX-10-ft-x-100-ft-Clear-6-mil-Plastic-Sheeting-CFH-D0610C/204711636

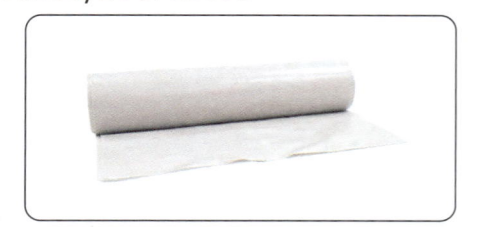

## Instructions

### Getting the Dimensions

1. Begin by determining the overall footprint that your greenhouse will occupy. Measure the length and width of the area and use these dimensions when modifying the design that I detail here. In my case, I wanted a greenhouse that would be a lean-to design that is eight feet long by six feet wide and around eight feet in height at the tallest point.

### Building the Sloped walls

1. Layout the uncut boards that will make up the greenhouse side where the doorway is. The picture above shows how I laid my boards out.
2. I chose to have a doorway that was 30 inches wide and 84 inches to the top plate of the door. I laid out the upright 2x4's that would make up the doorway marking the 84-inch mark on the centre 2x4. Across my three upright 2x4's I laid a 2x4 that would make up the top plate of this greenhouse wall.
3. Align the top plate with the 84-inch mark on the inner doorframe and the outside edge of the higher side of this wall.
4. Scribe where this top plate crosses the three uprights and cut these boards on this angle.
5. Cut all the 2x4's and assemble this wall.
6. Build the opposing wall directly on top of this one but omit the doorway.

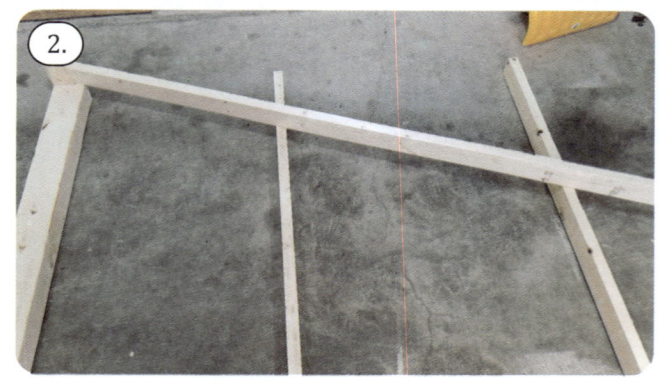

## Building the Straight Walls

1. Since I wanted a height of around eight feet, I made a wall by joining a top and bottom plate made from eight-foot 2x4's with vertical eight-foot 2x4's spaced 24 inches centre to centre.
2. The short wall was made the same way but using vertical 2x4's cut to 69 and a half inches. I measured the short end of the side walls to get this dimension.

## Putting it All Together

1. Lay the eight-foot wall on the ground.
2. Stand one side wall up, screwing it in place.
3. Do the same with the opposing wall bracing the walls if required.
4. Stand the eight-foot wall up, squaring up the walls afterwards.
5. Attach the short wall.

## Putting on the Roof

1. Cut three 2x4's that will become the rafters at the appropriate angle to fit between the two walls and flush with the top plates. To find this angle, place a 2x4 underneath the top plates as shown above, and scribe a cut line on both ends of the 2x4.
2. Secure the rafters in place.
3. Cut two 2x4's to fit in between the rafters. These will make the opening for the ventilation window. Once you have determined the window's location and size, screw these 2x4s in place to make that opening.

## Make the Door and Window

1. Measure both the door and window frame and cut 2x4's to build a door and window that will be at least a quarter of an inch smaller than the frames.
2. Screw these frames together and reinforce them to keep them square.
3. Attach vapour barrier to these frames with staples.

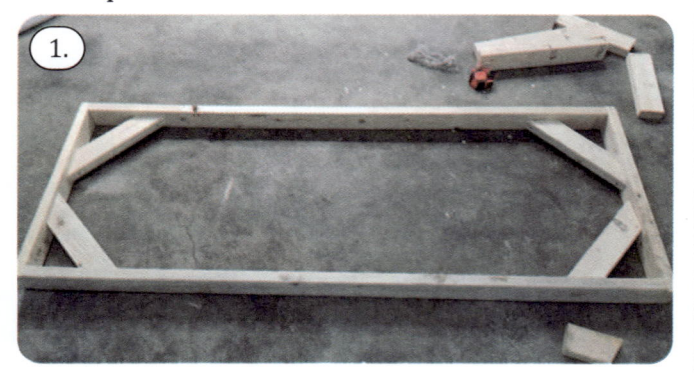

## Finishing the Greenhouse

1. Wrap the greenhouse in vapour barrier stapling as you go.
2. Cut an opening in the vapour barrier for the window and secure the vapour barrier with staples.
3. Wrap the roof in the vapour barrier and secure it with staples.
4. Install the door and widow.

## Things to Consider

There are a few things that you should consider now that you have a functional greenhouse.

◆ Install a thermometer/hygrometer so you can monitor and regulate the conditions in the greenhouse.
◆ Install some LED lights that are either low voltage or battery operated.
◆ Installing a fan will help you to control the conditions inside the greenhouse. You could use a switch that measures humidity to activate the fan when the inside of the greenhouse gets too humid for the plants you are cultivating.
◆ Keep a heater inside the greenhouse for use in the winter when the greenhouse has difficulty staying warm.

Food security is paramount in a grid-down situation and having a greenhouse is an important step to extending your growing season. The upfront cost of building a simple greenhouse will pay off dividends in fresh homegrown produce and herbs.

OTHER PROJECTS TO DO IN YOUR BACKYARD

# How To Build A Hinged Hoophouse For A Raised Bed

**MATERIAL COST** $ 115.00    **MEDIUM DIFFICULTY**    **1 HOUR**

A raised bed allows you to manage the soil and the conditions that affect your growing area. It is an important part of a successful garden. However, you cannot manage temperature in a raised bed garden.

There will come a time when the weather cools and your plants succumb to the frost. Unless you create a hoop house.

The typical hoop house is a pretty simple thing to construct. You can plunge a few lengths of rebar into the ground on either side of your garden. Then you just fold some PVC pipe over the bed to create the hoops and secure them on the rebar. Simply slide the rebar up inside the PVC (½ inch PVC is great for this).

Now, all that's left to do is simply cover this with a high mil plastic sheeting and clip it in place. That is a simple hoop house.

When it comes time to harvest, water, or manipulate what's under the plastic, you need to unclip it and remove the plastic. It gets to be a pain.

The good news is, there is a better way. You can build a hinged hoop house which basically turns your raised bed into a hoop house that you can open and close at will, without disturbing the plastic. The hinged hoop house is easy to build and offers many benefits:

- Extends growing season
- Protects plants against strong winds
- Increases early season growth
- Can protect from overexposure

## Tools

You will need the following:
- Table Saw
- Handsaw
- Electric Drill
- Razor Blade
- Small Drill Bit
- 1/16 Drill Bit

## Materials

The materials that you will need are:

- 4-48inch 2x4s $ 6.68 USD
- 4-56inch 2x4s $ 13.36 USD

www.lowes.com/pd/Severe-Weather-Common-2-in-x-4-in-x-8-ft-Actual-1-5-in-x-3-5-in-x-8-ft-2-Prime-Treated-Lumber/4756851

- 4-48inch pieces of flat trim $ 15.00 USD

www.lowes.com/pd/Pine-2-S4S-1-x-4-x-8-ft/1002622996

- 2 Inch Screws $ 10.00 USD

www.lowes.com/pd/Grip-Rite-PrimeGuard-Ten-7-x-2-in-Polymer-Deck-Screws-1-lb/3353692

- 1 ¼ Inch Screws $ 10.00 USD
  www.lowes.com/pd/Power-Pro-8-x-1-1-4-in-Ceramic-Deck-Screws-200-Count/1000363843

- 2 Sets of Hinges $ 7.00 USD
  www.lowes.com/pd/Gatehouse-3-1-2-in-Satin-Nickel-5-8-in-Radius-Mortise-Door-Hinge/4772467

- 1 Handle Fixture $ 7.00 USD
  www.lowes.com/pd/Gatehouse-Black-Gate-Pull/1000138521

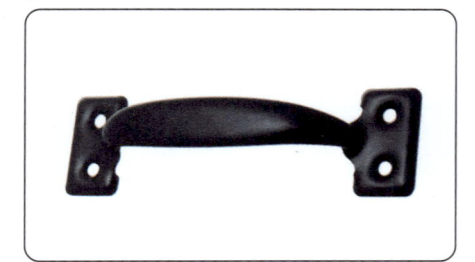

- 4-¾ Inch PVC Caps $ 4.00 USD
  www.lowes.com/pd/LASCO-3-4-in-x-3-4-in-dia-Cap-PVC-Fitting/1067811

- 2-1 to ¾ Inch T Fitting $ 5.00 USD
  www.lowes.com/pd/LASCO-1-in-x-1-in-x-1-in-x-3-4-in-dia-Tee-PVC-Fitting/3371562

- 3 Lengths of PVC Pipe $ 10.00 USD
  www.lowes.com/pd/Charlotte-Pipe-3-4-in-dia-x-10-ft-L-480-PSI-PVC-Pipe/3133085

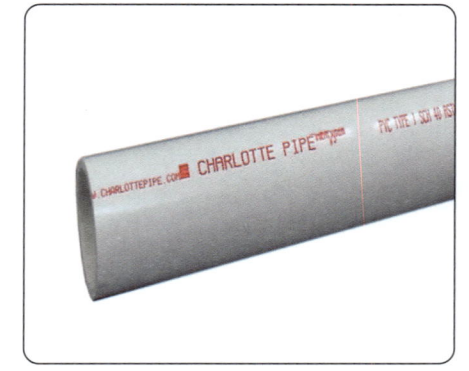

- 20 Mil Plastic $ 10.00 USD

## Process

1. Begin by laying out two of your 48 inch 2x4a and 2 of your 56 inch 2x4s over your raised bed to create a bench or frame for your hoop house to be built on. Drill these in with 1 ¼ inch screws.
2. Lay the rest of your 2x4s out on top of the ones you just affixed to the raised bed. This will be the frame of the hinged hoop house. Pre-drill the holes in the wood where the two pieces intersect and since 1-2 2 inch screws to keep the frame together.
3. Once your frame is secure, you will pre-drill your PVC caps and affix them to your 2x4s at each of the four corners. Use the 1 ¼ screws here. The 2-inch screws will literally screw through your frame and into the boards below. Then you will not be able to open the hinged hoop house!
4. Next you are going to attach the hardware using all of the screws included in the package. First place two hinges on the back side of the hinged hoop house. Make sure the front

of the hoop house is easy to access and you have enough room to open it with the hoops attached. Also add the handle.
5. Test the handle and hinges to make sure it opens.
6. Next, cut your PVC pipes the length needed to create your hoop. Slide the T fittings over the pipe and then slip the PVC pipe into each of your PVC caps that are drilled to the corners of your hoop house.
7. Secure your T fittings at the peak of your hoop with a 1 ¼ inch screw. Then cut a length of pipe long enough to fit into each of the fittings. This will fortify your plastic in the event of heavy rains or snow. Without a little fortification your plastic might tear or stretch under the pressure.
8. Now it's time to cover the hoops with your plastic. Give it a rough positioning and pull it tight in some areas before you begin using the trim to permanently drill it down.
9. Pull the plastic tight under the trim and then drill it down with three 1 ¼ inch screws in each piece of trim.
10. Once all the trim is secure and your sheeting is tight, your hoop house just needs to be trimmed up and then you have finished the build. You can use another piece of 2X4 to prop it open in the summer.

7.

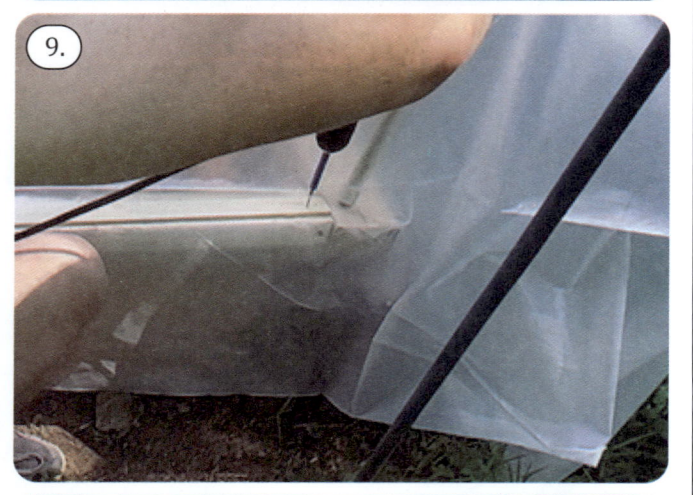

8.

9.

10.

Bring on the cool season! Your hinged hoop house is now complete, and you are ready to plant some cold weather crops when the cool seasons come. You will find that things like leafy hearty greens and brassicas do the best in your hinged hoop house over the winter.

You are going to love how easy this thing is to operate and how it can protect your garden from a number of issues. It will turn early season into an event and late season into a time to harvest rather than a time to plow the garden over and wait for spring.

OTHER PROJECTS TO DO IN YOUR BACKYARD

# How To Build A Raised Bed

MATERIAL COST $ 78.00     MEDIUM DIFFICULTY     3 HOURS

There are many ways to build a raised bed. Some methods are easy and some are complicated. The raised bed is a very important part of having success when you are gardening. It elevates your plants and also allows you the opportunity to modify the soil in any way you see fit.

Growing directly in the ground puts you at the mercy of flooding rains, poor soil conditions and diseases. When you grow in a raised bed you just have more control. They can also keep your plants from being trampled by family, kids and animals that run around the yard.

You can also easily add rebar and PVC pipe to your raised bed to create a simple hoop house that can be used to overwinter heartier crops and push them to grow faster in the spring.

Let's look at this simple build so you can start creating your own raised bed garden.

## Tools

You will need:
- Table Saw or Hand Saw
- Shovel
- Metal Rake

## Materials

Here is a list of the materials you will need:
- 8 Old Castle Planter Blocks or Round Planter Blocks $23.00 USD
- 4 - 2 x 6 x 8s $45.00 USD
- Compost & Manure $7.50 USD
- Topsoil $7.50 USD

## Process

1. Before you touch any materials, you are going to first define where your raised bed will be placed. This will require that you watch the sun and make some decisions about the area. You should get between 6-8 hours of direct sun in that area. You should also be able to add more raised beds to the area.
2. Using your table saw or hand saw cut all of your lumber directly in half to give you 8 identical pieces. They should all be 4ft long.
3. At this point you have all of the materials that you need to build your raised bed. Move the lumber and the planter blocks to the area where you plan on building the raised bed.
4. You will want to prep the area for your raised bed. Remove as many weeds as possible. Dig up the ground where you're raised bed will be built. Just turn the earth over but leave it in place. This will help aerate it.
Rake the loose dirt around so that the ground becomes level.It is important to turn the dirt over because the roots of your plants may dig below the soil you add to your raised bed.
5. Set your first two planter bricks about 4 feet apart. Then slide your first piece of lumber between the two bricks.
6. Next add two more bricks around the same distance from the first two to create the full perimeter of the first layer of your raised bed.
7. Top each one of your planters' bricks in the first layer with another brick. Each brick should have another one placed on top of it.
8. Repeat the process above by sliding the lumber into place so that it can create the second and final layer of your raised bed. At this point the building of the bed is complete.

At this point you are ready to plant in your raised bed. You can plant vegetables, herbs, flowers, or all of the above in this raised bed.

This is an exceedingly simple build. Moreover, it is a build that can be modified in any way you see fit. We have merely used 4ft by 4ft dimensions. However, your raised bed can be any size you like.

With these planter bricks you can even create a staircase style raised bed where you have a single layer followed by a double layer and then a triple layer.

This simple build is effective and easy to break down and move around. If you have extra lumber laying around, you can cut the costs down significantly.

## Filling Your Raised Bed

1. Start with a base layer of partially composted materials. You can pull this right out of your own compost pile.
2. Add a layer of compost and manure. Rake this around to cover up your partially composted materials.
3. Finally, fill the bed the rest of the way with topsoil. Then a light layer of mulch to finish.

OTHER PROJECTS TO DO IN YOUR BACKYARD

# How To Build A Small Storage Shed From Pallets

**COMPLEX DIFFICULTY**

The goal of simplifying my life led me to try and declutter the interior of my home and make space around the garden.

The first assignment I had for myself was to remove all the tools which were laying around in the house. Because I don't have a workshop or a barn, this meant that I had to build a small storage shed in my backyard, to store all these items. If perhaps you were looking to do the same, I have put down all the steps for you to follow.

There are also other possibilities to build a storage shed, however I found this one to be a very cheap, simple, and effective way to build it.

## Tools and Materials Needed

The tools you will need are pretty standard and easy to get:
- Hammer
- Tape measure
- 90-degree ruler
- Saw
- Pliers
- Level.

Since this shed will be made from wood pallets, the majority of needed materials come from there:
- 10 wood pallets for my shed;
- A pack of 3 and one of 4-inch screws;
- Wooden frames;
- Wooden rafters;
- Varnish or paint;
- Door knobs, if desired, in the end.

## Building the Small Storage Shed

### Step 1: Map out the structure of the back part of your shed

### Step 2: Start filling up the rectangular structure

Remove all screws from the pallets with a pliers and a hammer. Then fill the inner side of the rectangle with lumber.

Start filling up space in the rectangular structure, by placing one lumber over another. This is done so that water cannot enter inside when it is raining.

### Step 3: Elevate the back of your storage shed that you just finished

Upon finishing the back part of your storage shed, elevate it and see if it is properly aligned.

### Step 4: Create the frame of the front part of your shed

The back is now finished. We now move on to creating the frame of the front part of your shed. Start by connecting the bottom part of the back and front, followed by the top. Doing this, will result in your structure being able to stand on its own without any support.

Make sure it is equal in length with the back part.

### Step 5: Close the sides of the frame

Because the frame is set, it is now easy to fill the sides with lumber using the 3-inch screws.

### Step 6: Start creating the frame of the roofing

You are now done with the base structure of your backyard storage shed. You are going to have to start creating or mapping out the roof.

Having done that you will move on to connecting all the pieces of lumber. Remember the one-on-top-of-the-other rule we have been using to keep out the rain.

After finishing the first part of your roofing base, create an identical base to the one you created first.

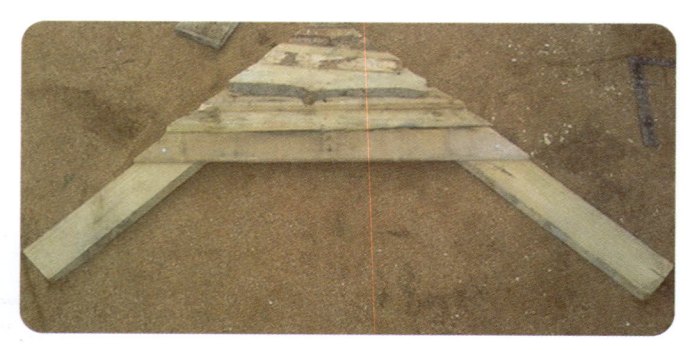

### Step 7: Place the two roofing frames on the top of your base shed

Having finished creating the two roofing frames you will have to place them on top of the base shed that you created earlier.

Now connect the two frames starting from the front to the back. Fill up the remaining space of the roof with lumber. Also insert some screws diagonally, where the roof touches the top of the frame.

### Step 8: Cover the remaining negative spaces

After finishing the roof, you will find that you are left with negative spaces left by the roof itself, and the base of your shed. You will have to cover them so that rainfall does not enter your shed. And also this will strengthen the connection between the roof and the shed walls.

### Step 9: Place your shed on top of rafters

This process will need for you to ask somebody for help. You need to lift the shed and put it on top of the wooden rafters.

Fill the bottom part of the shed with lumber so the floor will be finished.

Note: This step can be done before the building of the roof, whilst the materials and the rest of the structure are not yet heavy, or right at the beginning, you could build it straight on top of them. However, my brother helped me, I thought this way would be easier.

### Step 10: Map and create your doors and install them

Start by creating the frame of your first door and filling it up with lumber. Move on to the second door.

After that, you have to screw in your hinges and install the doors.

### Step 11: Construct Your Preferred Interior

I made my model divided in half: one part for the larger or longer objects, the other for shelves and space to hang smaller tools.

I filled up the mid area with lumber to complete the shelf in one half of the shed, starting from the bottom to the top.

Then went to the other side and hammered in some screws where I hang some of my larger tools. The advantage of screws is that you can easily take one out and insert it again in another spot, for a different tool; no mapping required.

### Step 12: Construct the outside floor

You have three rafters protruding from underneath your shed. Get some lumber and cover them so that your shed is complete. Your shed will have better foundation if those rafters are longer and the flooring is essential to keep the base dry when it's raining.

### Step 13: Finishing touches

Add two doorknobs. Since I don't need to lock this shed up, I don't need a sophisticated and safe mechanism.

Varnish or paint the shed, so it will not get damaged from the sun or rain.

After you have finished this DIY project, start using it by collecting the tools and place them in their specific designed places.

Depending on your personal budget and preferences, you can add roof tiles, windows if you make it bigger (in this case you need longer logs, not pallets), etc.

Keep in mind that this shed is not intended to have a nice design. I built it from some leftover pallets I had, in order to have my tools organized in one space.

Also, regarding the foundation, please note that this type of shed can be easily moved in any corner of your backyard if needed. So there isn't a solid and finished foundation on which you build the shed. Make sure the location of the shed will be safe and solid.

This shed was built for my personal use and it does its job perfectly!

OTHER PROJECTS TO DO IN YOUR BACKYARD

# How To Build A Smokehouse

**MATERIAL COST** $ 201.00    **COMPLEX DIFFICULTY**    **3 HOURS**

It is unclear exactly when the human race discovered that smoke can help preserve meat, but the process has been used to preserve foods for thousands of years. Throughout the globe, in rural areas, families would often have a smokehouse on the property. These days, when we speak about smoking meat, we usually refer to the process of slowly cooking meat through hot smoke.

However, when our goal is food preservation, we need to cold smoke our food which does not achieve temperatures high enough to cook the food but instead preserves the meat through curing and drying.

### What Is Cold Smoking?

Cold smoking occurs at temperatures below 85 degrees Fahrenheit, so the process does not cook the food. During this process, the food is held in the food safety danger zone of between 40 and 140 degrees Fahrenheit where microbial growth can become rapid. This means that we should only cold smoke meats that have been salted, cured, or fermented.

The curing process removes moisture from the meats, and the cold smoking further dries the meats, which provides a hostile environment for bacterial growth. After smoking the meat, it can last months without freezing.

## Building a Smokehouse

The construction of a smokehouse is as simple as building a smoke chamber and a firebox. Connecting the two will be a pipe through which the smoke will flow and cool. There are many designs for a smokehouse, and a quick Google search will deliver thousands of variations. Whether you copy my design verbatim or design your smokehouse, it must meet a few requirements.

First, it must hold the smoke inside the chamber without leaking too much smoke outside. One of the best ways to seal the chamber is to use wood that is 'tongue and grove' so that the boards nest together tightly, helping to provide a sealed chamber.

Second, the smoke chamber needs to be separated from the firebox so that the smoke is made to cool before reaching the smoke chamber.

Third, you will need some type of firebox in which the wood will burn and create smoke. In my case, I used a homemade wood stove for this smokehouse, but you can use anything that will allow you to smoulder woodchips and direct the smoke to the smokehouse. I would suggest using a wood stove because the chimney will be a diameter that will be easy enough to find ductwork for. If you need to purchase a firebox, consider options like these:

◆ This tent stove is $ 119.99 USD at Amazon.
www.amazon.com/GBU-Tent-Stove-Portable-Fireproof/dp/B08GJ73SHZ/

◆ Another outdoors wood stove for $ 214.99 USD on Amazon.
www.amazon.com/Guide-Gear-Large-Outdoor-Stove/dp/B08H8N99S5/

- Or this one for $ 189.99 USD at Amazon. www.amazon.com/US-Stove-CCS18-Outfitter-Portable/dp/B07JZD8JDH/

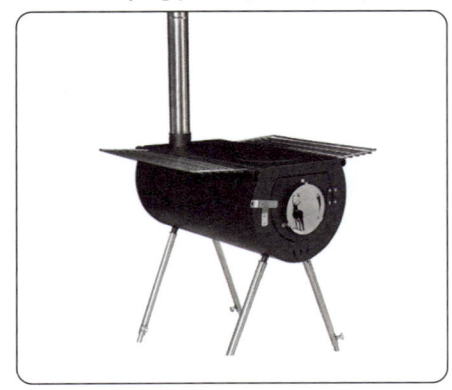

## Smokehouse Construction

### Tools Required

- Drill and bits and drivers
- Square and level
- Saw
- Tape measure

### Materials

- 2x2x8' lumber which Home Depot sells for $ 3.78 USD each. www.homedepot.com/p/2-in-x-2-in-x-8-ft-Furring-Strip-Board-Lumber-75800593/304600525

- Eight-foot long cedar fence boards which I found at Home Depot for $ 10.67 USD each. www.homedepot.com/p/Pattern-Stock-Gorman-Tongue-and-Groove-Board-Common-1-in-x-6-in-x-8-ft-Actual-0-688-in-x-5-37-in-x-96-in-168PTG/204787882

- #8 x 2 ½" Screws that are found at Home Depot for $ 9.50 USD per pound. www.homedepot.com/p/SPAX-8-x-2-1-2-in-Philips-Square-Drive-Flat-Head-Full-Thread-Zinc-Coated-Multi-Material-Screw-1-lb-Box-4101010400606/202041007

- #8 x 1 ½" Screws that are available at Home Depot for $ 9.50 USD per pound. www.homedepot.com/p/SPAX-8-x-1-1-2-in--Philips-Square-Drive-Flat-Head-Full-Thread-Yellow-Zinc-Coated-Multi-Material-Screw-197-Box-4101020400406/202041002

- 4" x 60" duct, which can be found at Home Depot for $ 10.42 USD. www.homedepot.com/p/Master-Flow-4-in-x-5-ft-Round-Metal-Duct-Pipe-CP4X-60/100196725?MERCH=REC-_-PLP_Browse-_-NA-_-100196725-_-N&

- 4" adjustable HVAC elbows are sold at Home Depot for $ 8.74 USD each. www.homedepot.com/p/Speedi-Products-4-in-26-Gauge-90-Degree-Round-Adjustable-Elbow-SM-26A90-04/206199025

◆ Metal tape is $ 4.98 USD at Home Depot.
www.homedepot.com/p/Nashua-Tape-1-89-in-x-30-yd-Dryer-Vent-Installation-Duct-Tape-1529836/207203955

◆ Hinges are available at Home Depot for $ 8.98 USD for a pack of three.
www.homedepot.com/p/Everbilt-3-1-2-in-Satin-Nickel-5-8-in-Radius-Security-Door-Hinges-Value-Pack-3-Pack-14874/202818703

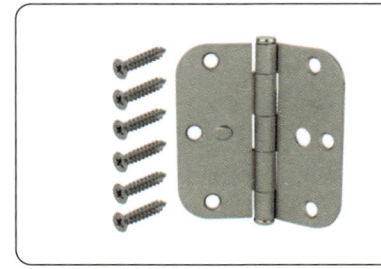

◆ Hasps are available at Home Depot for $ 3.98 USD.
www.homedepot.com/p/Everbilt-3-1-2-in-Zinc-Plated-Adjustable-Staple-Safety-Hasp-15122/202033919

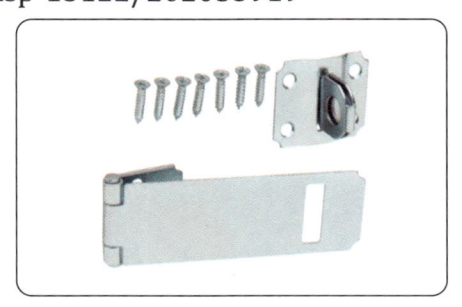

## Instructions

The smokehouse I describe here is a 2x2 lumber frame covered with tongue and groove cedar boards and fed by a 4-inch pipe that leads to the firebox.

### Finding the Dimensions

1. Determine the overall size of your smokehouse. I decided to build a smokehouse that would make good use of the lengths of cedar boards. In my case, the ones that my local Home Depot had in stock were six feet long, so I cut them into four 17 5/8" sections which will cover all four walls of my smokehouse.
2. To figure out the height, I assembled the cedar boards that would make up the walls of my smokehouse until I felt that I had a good height. I then measured these boards and found that the height would be 30 inches.
3. To find the dimensions of the 2x2 lumber frame, arrange the cedar boards as they will be when covering the exterior of the smokehouse.
4. Measure the inside dimensions of these boards and use them to construct the top and bottom frames for the smokehouse.

**Building the Smokehouse**
1. Start by building the frames for the top and bottom of your smokehouse.
2. Join these frames with four sections of 2x2 lumber cut so that you will have the correct overall height. In my case, I cut these at 27 inches which gave me an overall height of 30 inches.
3. Install cross members that will support racks for laying or hanging food to be smoked.
4. Cover three sides of the frame with the cedar boards leaving the side that will be the door open.

**The Roof**
1. To make this build as simple as possible, I chose to make a roof with a 45-degree slope and to form this, all I had to do was use a 24-inch square to determine the minimum dimension that the rafters of the roof will be. Place the square on the top frame like shown above to figure out how long your rafters need to be.
2. Decide how much you want your roof to overhang and cut four pieces of 2x2 to make the roof rafters. If you are making a large smokehouse, you'll need to add extra rafters for additional support. Screw the cut piece together to make the rafters.
3. Cut and install three 2x2's to join the rafter pieces together.
4. Set the roof on the smokehouse, taking a piece of 2x2 laying it on the smokehouse frame but behind the roof's rafter. Scribe the roof's angle on the board to determine how to cut it to fit inside the rafter and provide a surface to secure the roof to the frame.
5. Cut and install these pieces.

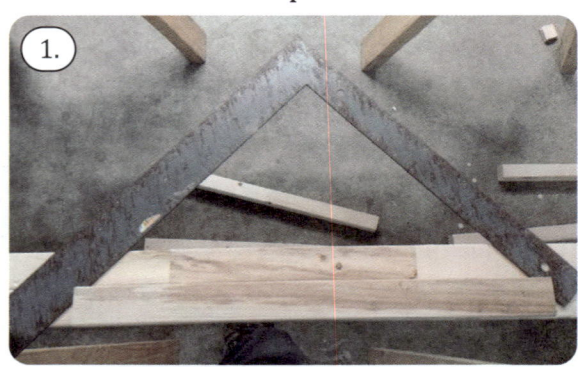

**Building the Door**
1. Measure the inside dimensions of the opening for the door. Subtract a quarter to a half an inch from these dimensions for clearance and cut four pieces of 2x2 to make a door frame to fit this space.
2. Lay the boards that will make up the front of the smokehouse on the opening and center the frame on these boards.
3. Lay out and cut the profile of the door's fame on these pieces.
4. Secure the boards to the door and the front of the smokehouse.
5. Attach hinges and a hasp.

**Completing the Smokehouse**
1. Seal the bottom of the smokehouse with plywood or cedar boards.
2. Finish sheeting the front and back of the smokehouse by placing boards on top of the existing boards and scribing the cut lines to make them fit the smokehouse profile.
3. Attach these boards.
4. Sheet the roof by laying boards and securing them from the peak to the end of the rafters.
5. Drill vent holes near the top of the smokehouse.
6. Cut a hole for the 4-inch adjustable elbow by laying it on the side of the smokehouse that you want the smoke to enter. To do this, I laid the elbow on the smokehouse's side and scribed a line around the elbow.
7. I then drilled a series of holes around this circle.
8. Then I used a saw to cut the rest of the circle out.
9. Install the elbow.
10. Place the smokehouse in the final position and run the length of 4-inch ductwork to the smokehouse from the firebox.

## Operating the Smokehouse

To operate the smokehouse, light a small fire in the firebox and fuel it with small chips or sawdust from your smoking wood. Keep this fire smouldering for the entire duration and monitor the internal temperature with a thermometer. You can either use a wireless thermometer or install a thermometer through the side of the smokehouse. There are many ways to light and use a firebox to provide the smoke for your smokehouse. There are also a wide variety of woods to choose from. The most important consideration is to have a small smouldering fire that will provide enough smoke to fill the smokehouse and enough wood to fuel the fire for 12 to 24 hours.

Smoking meat takes practise and commitment to get right and should never cut corners during the process. There is a lot of information regarding the curing and smoking of meat and other foods before you decide to attempt to cold smoke your food. Smoking meat is a great method of food preservation that only requires that you monitor the process while it does all the work for you.

OTHER PROJECTS TO DO IN YOUR BACKYARD

# How To Build A Solar Dehydrator

**MATERIAL COST** $ 160.00  **MEDIUM DIFFICULTY**  **3 HOURS**

Here is a simple, inexpensive, and easy to assemble project that will dry your fresh vegetables and other fresh produce.

The principle is simple. Air travels over solar heated plates and then through a chamber where the produce is placed on shelves made of expanded metal that allows the air to pass through.

The dehydrator consists of two chambers. The horizontal one heats up the air moving through it and the vertical chamber stores the produce and allows the warm air to rise and flow out through the top of the chamber.

The whole project is designed to make use of only one sheet of half inch plywood. So, all the sizes are determined by the size of the sheet.

The length of the horizontal warming section is half the length of the sheet and the vertical sections are all provided for by the rest of the sheet.

In this example we used Perspex that came from an old shower door, but any transparent material will be fine to use. Basically, all you want is for the transparent sheet to allow the sunlight through and channel the air up to the vertical chamber.

It is a good idea to have the dehydrator on wheels so that it can be moved around with ease. This is particularly important if you use ceramic tiles to warm the air.

## What Type of Produce Can Be Dried in the Dehydrator?

All types of deciduous fruit can be dried in the dehydrator although there is no reason why citrus could not also be dried in a similar fashion. I use the dehydrator to dry mushrooms and tomatoes primarily. The mushrooms are dried and then placed in a liquidiser which reduces them to a powder. They do a great job of enhancing the flavour of any mushroom dish.

## Tools

Some basic woodworking tools are required. The essential ones are:
- Saw (power saw will speed things up but a crosscut hand saw will also do)
- Drill (a cordless drill makes things easier and can also be used to drive screws at home)
- Square
- Measuring tape
- Appropriate drill bits (check to match the screws)
- Screwdriver.

And if you have a table saw, then things will be much easier, but you can get away with the essential list.

## Materials

Here is a list of the materials that will be required:
- One sheet of half inch plywood $ 25.00 USD.

www.lowes.com/pd/15-32-Category-SYP-Pine-RS/1003163962

◆ Sheet of clear Perspex or glass to suit $12.00 USD.
www.amazon.com/Acrylic-Plexiglass-Plastic-Perspex-Engraving/dp/B08XYLRQZR/?th=1

◆ Three wheels to make it move around $ 21.00 USD.
www.amazon.com/Oregon-72-107-Universal-Diamond-Plastic/dp/B0018TWDOI/

◆ Four pieces of open mesh for the shelves $ 29.00 USD.
www.amazon.com/DocaScreen-Standard-Window-Screen-Roll/dp/B079YY5SJZ/

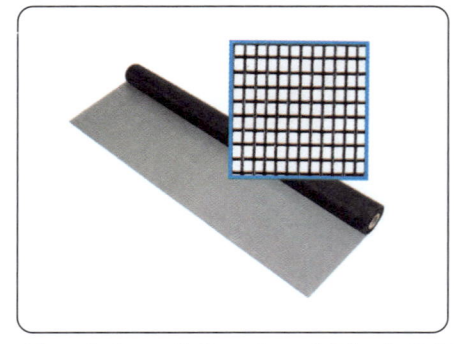

◆ Aluminium foil painted black $ 15.00USD (Ceramic tiles painted black will be an added advantage).

www.amazon.com/Ceramic-Alcohol-Painting-Decorating-Ceramics/dp/B07XRZ7HP6

◆ Two hinges for the door $ 12.00 USD.
www.amazon.com/Boao-Stainless-Folding-Furniture-Hardware/dp/B087CGCNJ4/?th=1

◆ Door clip to keep the door closed; A door handle if required ($6.00 USD).
www.amazon.com/Upgrade-Thickened-Stainless-Brushed-Sliding/dp/B0892H3KMH/

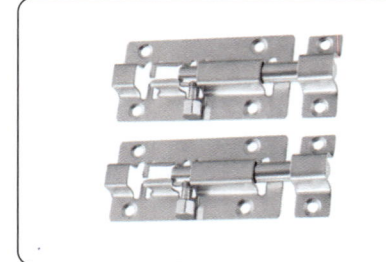

◆ Screws to assemble $ 4.00 USD.
www.lowes.com/pd/Power-Pro-One-6-x-1-in-Bronze-Epoxy-Flat-Exterior-Multi-Material-Screws-40-Count/1000310091

◆ Small bottle of glue $ 13.00 USD.
www.amazon.com/Gorilla-Clear-Glue-ounce-Bottle/dp/B07GQ1CT47/

◆ Double sided tape $ 13.00 USD.
www.amazon.com/EZlifego-Multipurpose-Removable-Transparent-Household/dp/B07VNSXY31/

◆ Black paint $ 5.00 USD.
www.lowes.com/pd/Krylon-FUSION-ALL-IN-ONE-Matte-Black-Spray-Paint-and-Primer-In-One-NET-WT-12-oz/1000460293

◆ Paint brush $ 5.00 USD.
www.lowes.com/pd/Project-Source-Polyester-Flat-3-in-Paint-Brush/50369832

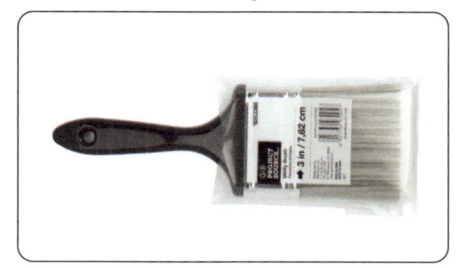

And if you are going to keep the dehydrator outside where it will be exposed to rain, then you will need some wood sealer or paint to preserve the wood.

## Building the Dehydrator

To make things simple we will be making two boxes: one for the heating section and one for the produce storage area.

### Building the Heating Box

To make the heating section you will need to cut the base and then the two sides. The two sides and the base should be equal to half the width of the full sheet of plywood.

As a guide, you want the sides to be around four inches wide. In total the base and the sides should take up about a quarter of the full sheet.

If you have access to a table saw, I would suggest you cut two slots on each side piece to accommodate the Perspex. It is easier to do this before you assemble the sides and base. If you don't have a table saw it isn't a problem, you can simply screw the Perspex to the top of the sides.

If you can cut the slots for the Perspex, you can slide it out as required.

The base and the two sides are joined together with screws and a little bit of glue. If you are going to screw the Perspex to the top of the sides, drill the holes for the screws but only fit four screws to secure the Perspex because it will have to be removed to fit the aluminium heating section.

Remember to use flat head screws and allow for a lose fit in the Perspex to avoid cracking the Perspex when you fit the screws.

Now is a good time to attach one of the wheels to the middle of one end of the box.

With the side's assembled it's time to lay a couple of sheets of heavy aluminium foil in the base of the heating box. I used a roll of heavy duty aluminium foil and stuck it down with double sided tape. I fitted the aluminium up the sides of the box and trimmed it at the slot.

When the aluminium was all in place the top layer was given two coats of blackboard paint.

I had some spare ceramic tiles just over twelve inch square which I also painted black and placed inside the heating box for a little extra heat generation.

If you have a couple of spare tiles, paint them black but only lay them in the box when you have placed the dehydrator in its final position, as they add a fair bit of weight.

When you have finished painting the aluminium, fit the Perspex back on top of the box.

And that is our heating box done.

## Building the Storage Box

Start with the base and now you need to work off the size of the heat box as the heat box is going to slide into the storage box.

Cut the base one and a quarter inches wider than the base of the heat box.

Drill holes in the base and screw the sides onto the base.

Check that the heat box will fit between the sides and the base of the storage box.

Cut the front piece of the storage box to allow for the air to pass from the heat box into the storage box.

Now you can fit the guides for the shelves and it would also be a good time to make the shelves. The shelves can be made from any material that allows a free flow of air. I used expanded metal but feel free to use whatever you see fit as long as the air can pass through it easily.

## The Last Few Steps

For the roof you, will need two pieces of plywood cut into wedges.

This is to ensure that the warm air can escape and in doing so a draft is created that draws more warm air up through the storage box.

I would suggest the wider side should be approximately three to four inches wide and tapering down to about one inch at the smaller end.

The easiest way to do this is to cut a rectangle with the longer sides the size of your storage box sides and the shorter sides about three to four inches. Now mark a diagonal and cut along the line. You will end up with two wedge shaped pieces for your roof sides.

Cut the roof section so that when you attach the sides to it, they will rest on the top of the storage box sides.

I fitted two small pieces of wood on either side of the storage box to keep the roof section in place. Now fit the two wheels to the base.

And finally, you will need to make a door. Using two hinges fit the door either opening to the left or right. Your preference.

I chose to fit the heat box to the storage box, but you can keep them separate and slide the heat box into the storage box when you want to use the dehydrator. This will save you storage space but if you would like to join the two boxes together this can be easily done by fitting a piece of plywood on either side of the storage bow and screwing it to the heat box as shown below.

## Drying Times

Place your dehydrator in a north to south position so that the heat box will be in the sun for the day. It is important to understand that the ambient humidity is going to influence the drying time.

Some items are anhydrous and will reabsorb moisture overnight, (mushrooms will do this) so it is important to remove them from the drier as evening approaches and place them in a sealed container for the night.

The mushrooms and tomatoes below were place in the drier in the morning and removed the same day in the evening.

The produce will reduce in size quite significantly as they dehydrate so the trays can be well stocked for drying.

OTHER PROJECTS TO DO IN YOUR BACKYARD

# How To Build A Solar Oven

MATERIAL COST  $ 36.00    EASY DIFFICULTY    30 MINUTES

Did you know that the sun hits our planet with enough energy in one hour to power our planet for a year? Yes! That's a fact. We are bombarded with free energy from the sun and we sparsely take advantage of it.

Maybe you have some solar panels on your home, or you aspire to get some. Of course, we are just scratching the surface when it comes to the power of the sun. For centuries we have been using the sun to dry meats and preserve other foods. With a little advanced technology, we can now cook food to completion using the sun!

### What Is a Solar Oven?

A solar oven is a container that is able to capture the sun's direct rays and hold the heat of the sun so that it can be used to cook food without fire or any other type of fuel. The sun is more than capable of cooking your food.

There are many companies that are selling these ovens for hundreds of dollars, if you are interested in putting out that kind of money. These are high quality ovens that will cook foods thoroughly without the use of fire or any other kind of fuel!

These ovens come in a variety of sizes, but they all use a similar technology. They are capturing the sun's rays and use the heat and energy to cook foods. We have employed the same technologies in this build but at a much lower expense.

## Building Your Own Solar Oven

I have made DIY solar ovens in the past and, to be honest, they have not performed as well as I would have liked. While many would agree that building a solar oven from a cardboard box is a bad idea, we are on a mission to turn this humble resource into a means of cooking food with only the power of the sun.

This build is going to include two new and affordable items that will turn any cardboard box into an effective solar oven.

The first are stick on mirrors to send a clear reflection of the sun towards the food. These are cheap and easy to apply to cardboard box flaps.

The second is the Fresnel lens. These are used to start fire and are the perfect tool for maximizing your solar energy for cooking while also holding in the heat.

## Tools

You will need a razor blade or a knife. That's it!

## Materials and Cost

◆ 2 Cardboard Boxes (one a little smaller than the other) $ 21.75/13.50 USD for 5, $ 4.35 / $ 2.70 USD each

www.amazon.com/dp/B088QF8PDY/ref=em-c_b_5_t

www.amazon.com/dp/B088QD3PH7/ref=em-c_b_5_t

◆ 2 Sheets of Black Construction Paper (or spray paint the box black inside) $ 6.10 USD for 50

www.amazon.com/Tru-Ray-103061-Construction-Paper-Black/dp/B00563PXHQ/

◆ 6 Mirror Stickers $ 22.99 USD for 4

www.amazon.com/SLDIYWOW-Acrylic-Sticker-Removable-Decoration/dp/B095C5S1D4/

- Fresnel Lenses $8.99 USD for 2
  www.amazon.com/Magpro-Acrylic-Magnifying-Magnifier-Eyesight/dp/B07MFYT4ZR/

- Scotch or Masking Tape about $ 3.00 USD for one
  www.amazon.com/Scotch-Magic-Tape-Inches-2-PACK/dp/B00RB1YAL6/

## Process

1. Begin by removing the flaps from the smaller box and then nest it inside the other.
2. Next place or glue the black construction paper into the bottom of the box.
3. Remove the covers and the glue paper from the mirrors and place them on your box flaps to cover as much area as possible.
4. At this point you are going to position your Fresnel lenses, so the textured side is facing upward. You have to be careful here because these lenses are so powerful that they might burn through your box!
5. With your lenses in position, you are now going to position your mirrors in a way that you can catch and reflect as much of the sun as possible back into the box. You will know when you have captured the sun correctly because you will see the light across the surface of the lens.
6. Using tape or sticks to hold these in place, begin to position the mirrors so that you get maximum sun from each mirror to shine on your oven. This might take a little time but, in the end, it will maximize the heating ability of your solar oven.
7. Add a thermometer to test that your oven is working. You will see the temperature rise dramatically in no time.
8. Now just choose something to cook and give it a try.

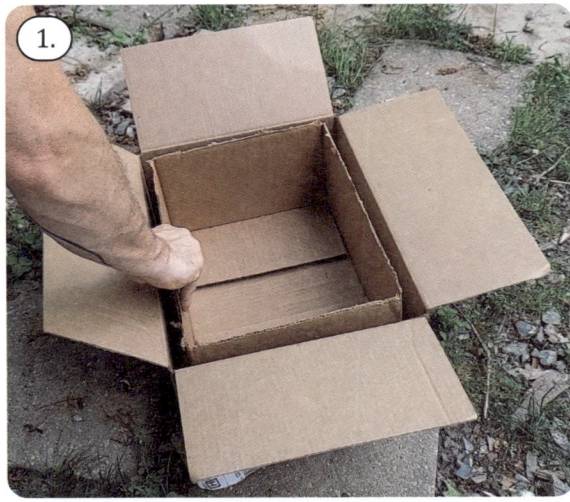

## 5 Great Foods to Cook in a Solar Oven

Here is a short list of foods that you can cook in our solar oven once it's ready:
- Baked Breads
- Quick Breads
- Baked Desserts
- Egg Frittatas
- Baked Pastas

Using the oven, we cooked a little bacon and egg frittata in a simple soup pot. The oven worked incredibly and cooked this dish up even on a windy day with some sparse cloud cover.

The mirrors were being moved around by the wind and the clouds took away the direct sunlight but in less than a couple of hours we had our frittata cooked and ready to eat without the use of any fuel other than the power of the sun.

# How To Build A Water Heater

**MATERIAL COST** $ 90.00  **DIFFICULTY** COMPLEX  **5 HOURS**

The majority of today's homes heat water with either electricity or natural gas. When we remove these from the equation, we discover the reality of how much energy it takes to heat water. Placing a pot of water over a fire is a good method for heating some water, and you should absolutely do so whenever possible, but there is an easier DIY alternative.

## How Does this Water Heater Work?

The off-grid water heater I detail here requires a wood-burning stove, and we are going to harness the heat energy that radiates off of it to warm up the water. All that is needed is to build a run of copper pipe along the sides of your wood stove through which cold water will enter, and hot water will exit.

Since copper is such an amazing conductor of electricity and heat, the pipe will become heated and transfer that heat to the water inside. What this creates is an 'on demand' hot water system.

Heating water inside a pipe creates pressure, and if that pressure has nowhere to go, there is a significant risk of the pipe or fittings bursting. Make absolutely sure that you understand the risks and have a plan for dealing with the inevitable buildup of pressure before undertaking this project.

One of the easiest ways to avoid excess pressure is to keep water moving through the pipes. Doing so will allow the heat to continuously heat cold water rather than superheating water that is not moving.

Installing a pressure relief valve is also a great way to keep the system from bursting due to excessive pressure.

What I suggest doing is to keep the runs of copper pipe removable as a complete unit. This gives you the ability to drop it in place and connect it to the water supply when you need hot water, and remove it when not in use.

## The Wood Stove

Building your wood stove is not difficult as long as you have access to a welding machine, angle grinder, and a supply of steel. I made a woodstove for this project out of an empty 20-pound propane tank that I had lying around. If you do not have access to a welding machine, you can purchase wood stoves online.

◆ This tent stove is $ 119.99 USD at Amazon.
www.amazon.com/GBU-Tent-Stove-Portable-Fireproof/dp/B08GJ73SHZ/

◆ Another outdoors wood stove for $ 214.99 USD on Amazon.
www.amazon.com/Guide-Gear-Large-Outdoor-Stove/dp/B08H8N99S5/

◆ Or this one for $ 189.99 USD at Amazon.
www.amazon.com/US-Stove-CCS18-Outfitter-Portable/dp/B07JZD8JDH/

## BUILDING A WOOD STOVE FROM A 20 POUND PROPANE TANK

Turning a propane tank into a wood stove is not difficult and requires only a few easily obtained materials to build. Unfortunately, there is no way to accomplish this build without using a welding machine, angle grinder, and an oxy/acetylene cutting torch or plasma cutter. These tools also require some skill to use, and many safety considerations need to be taken.

Welding and cutting of metal can be dangerous, and proper safety procedures must be followed to ensure your health and safety. Always wear the appropriate personal protective equipment and be aware of all the risks and hazards before attempting this build.

## Tools
- Welding machine
- Angle grinder with a cut off wheel
- Cutting torch or plasma cutter

## Materials
- Empty and clean 20-pound propane cylinder don't buy a new cylinder it will not be cost-effective, instead repurpose an old, expired cylinder.
- 1"x1"x1/8" mild steel angle, which you can purchase at Home Depot for $ 7.7 8USD per 36-inch length.
www.homedepot.com/p/Everbilt-36-in-x-1-in-x-1-8-in-Steel-Angle-801457/204225879

- 4" stove pipe I rolled my stovepipe from a sheet of 16 gauge mild steel. Several stores sell stove pipes in a variety of styles and sizes.
- Piano hinge is available at Home Depot for $ 17.78 USD for a 72-inch length.
www.homedepot.com/p/Everbilt-1-1-2-in-x-72-in-Bright-Nickel-Continuous-Hinge-16115/202034032

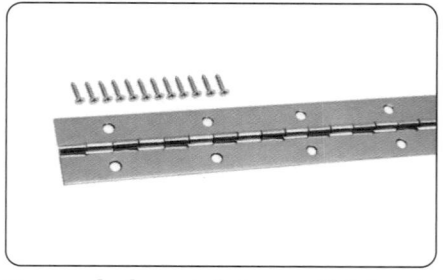

- Expanded metal is available at Home Depot for $ 22.98 USD a sheet.
www.homedepot.com/p/Everbilt-24-in-x-3-4-in-x-24-in-Plain-Expanded-Metal-Sheet-801427/204225784

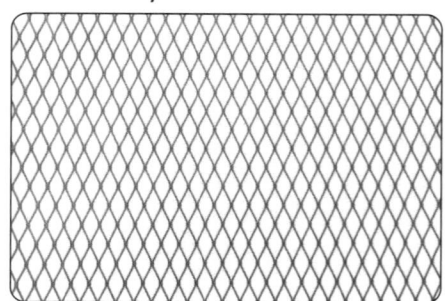

## Instructions

1. Empty the propane cylinder and thoroughly clean it inside and out. Be sure that all the liquid propane is removed before proceeding further.
2. Remove the rings at the top and bottom and remove all the paint from the tank's exterior.
3. Lay out and cut the opening for the door. Make the opening large enough to load wood into the stove comfortably.
4. Save the piece that you cut out to fabricate the door.
5. Secure this piece to the rest of the woodstove with a section of piano hinge. Add a handle at the same time.
6. Fabricate a base from the 1x1x1/8 angle. I chose to make it 12 inches square.
7. Cut four legs on a slight angle so that they will slope upwards to join with the cylinder.
8. Weld the base frame onto the stove body.
9. Cut a hole in the top to accommodate the four-inch stove pipe.
10. Slide the stovepipe into the hole and weld it in place.
11. Cut some expanded metal to the inside diameter of the wood stove and place it inside the stove.

1.

2.

3.

4.

5.

6.

6.

7.

8.

## Tools

You will need:
- Copper tubing cutter ◆ Sandpaper
- Soldering torch, solder, and flux
- Cordless Drill and bits

## Materials

### a) For A Side Mounted Heater

The materials you'll need are:
- ½" Copper Pipe available at Home Depot for $ 20.76 USD.
www.homedepot.com/p/Mueller-Streamline-1-2-in-x-10-ft-Copper-Type-L-Pipe-LH04010/100354232

- ½" Copper 90-degree elbows are $ 0.75 USD each.
www.homedepot.com/p/Everbilt-1-2-in-Copper-Pressure-90-Degree-Cup-x-Cup-Elbow-Fitting-C607HD12/204620176

- ½" to ¾" NPT copper fittings (select the ones that will work with your setup). Home Depot sells these for $ 8.61 USD.
www.homedepot.com/p/Everbilt-1-2-in-x-3-4-in-Copper-Pressure-Cup-x-FIP-Female-Adapter-

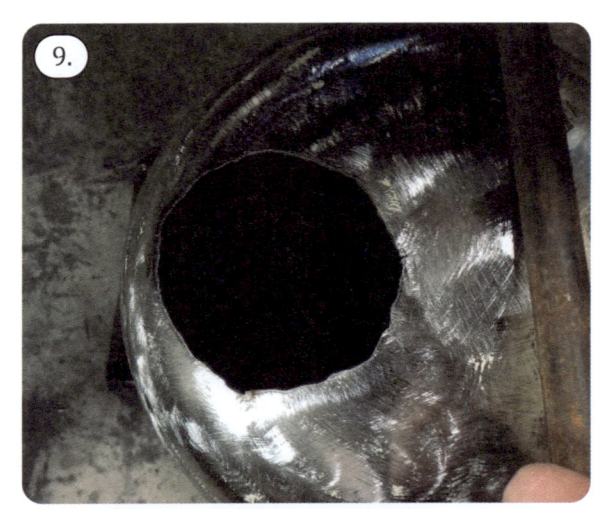

## The Heater

How you run the pipe will depend on your woodstove's shape, but the basic principles are the same. What we are trying to do is snake the pipe along the side of the woodstove to get as much pipe as possible exposed to the heat. We can do this in two ways. We can use pipe elbows to snake the pipe along the side of the stove, or we can use a coil of copper pipe and wrap it in a tight coil around the chimney of the woodstove.

The difference between these two methods is that there will be less heat from the chimney, and therefore the water will not be as hot. However, since using the woodstove sides create hotter water, the risk of too much pressure is ever-present and needs to be accounted for.

Fitting-C603HD1234/204620626

### b) For A Chimney Heater

The materials you'll need are:

- 3/8" x 10' copper pipe coil available at Home Depot for $ 19.98 USD per 10-foot coil.
www.homedepot.com/p/Everbilt-3-8-in-x-10-ft-Soft-Copper-Refrigeration-Coil-Tubing-3-8-R-10RE/203654362

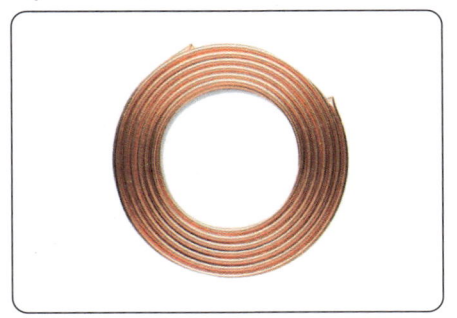

- 1/2" to 3/4" NPT fittings available at home depot for $ 8.61USD.
www.homedepot.com/p/Everbilt-1-2-in-x-3-4-in-Copper-Pressure-Cup-x-FIP-Female-Adapter-Fitting-C603HD1234/204620626

- 3/8" to ½" copper reducer sold at Home Depot for $1.98USD each.
www.homedepot.com/p/Everbilt-3-8-in-x-1-2-in-Copper-Pressure-Fitting-x-Cup-Reducer-C600HD21238/204620287

## Instructions

### a) Side Mounted Heater

1. Measure the height of the woodstove side that you want to place the heater on while figuring out how many vertical runs of pipe you will use.
2. Measure the height of the elbows and how far the pipe will fit inside of them. The difference between these dimensions multiplied by two is the length that will be subtracted from the heater's height to figure out the cut size.
3. Cut enough small lengths of pipe to join the 90-degree elbows together. At the same time, cut the straight sections.
4. Cut two six-inch lengths of pipe for the inlet and outlet.
5. Trial fit all the components together.
6. Solder the 90-degree elbows together to form the 180 degree turns in the pipe run.
7. Layout the heater on the stove to check the fit.
8. Solder the joints together. Don't forget to install the fittings on the inlet and outlet so you can connect the water supply.
9. Drill holes for bolts to hang the heater on the side of the stove.
10. Install bolts that are long enough to hang the heater on. In this case, I used 2 ½" ¼-20NC bolts. Thread a nut on until it reaches the smooth section of the bolt.
11. Insert the bolts into the holes and secure them on the inside of the stove with a nut.
12. If needed, use a piece of metal strapping to hold secure it only on one end so it can be easily lifted out of the way to remove or install the heater.

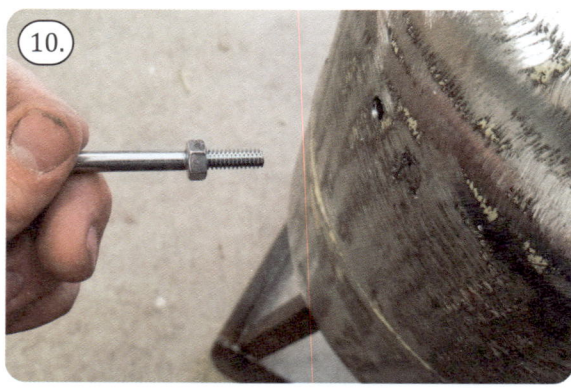

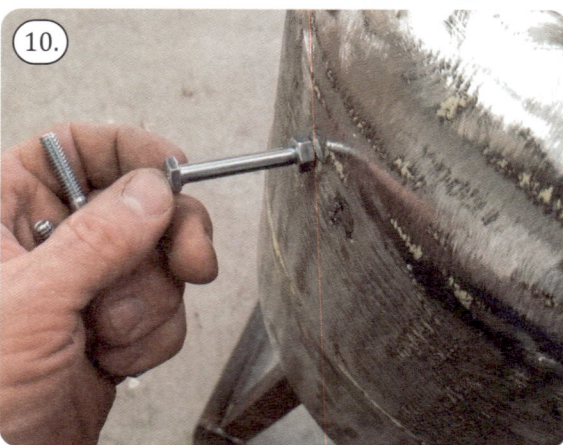

### b) Chimney Heater

1. Solder the ¾" NPT fittings on each end of the coil of copper pipe. You will probably have to use reducers to shink the pipe diameter from ¾" to 3/8".
2. Carefully wrap the copper pipe coil around your woodstove's chimney, leaving a length of straight pipe at the inlet and outlet. Use sand

or salt inside of the line to prevent kinking.
3. Add the spigot to one end and connect the other to your water supply.

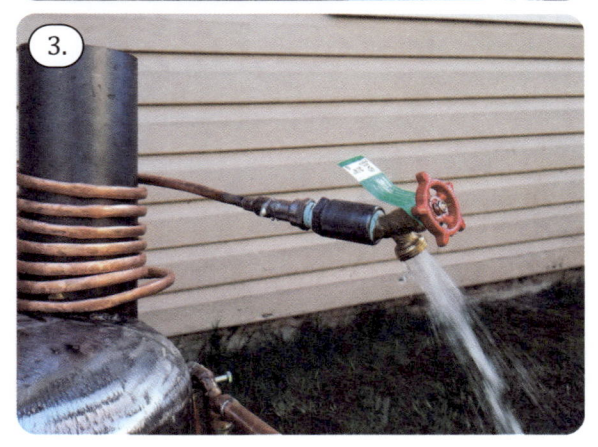

## Using the Water Heater

There are a few options when it comes to operating this water heater. The first is to use it as an on-demand type of system where you draw the coil's water as needed to get hot water. The problem is that there will be a buildup of pressure within the system, and you will need to have a pressure relief valve in the system. My preference is to keep the coils removable so that you can quickly and simply install the heater on the stove when needed and remove it when not in use.

Harnessing the heat that a wood-burning stove emits is a great use of this radiant energy to provide us with heated water. Being able to get hot water on demand is one of those comforts that will make a grid-down scenario a little bit more comfortable.

OTHER PROJECTS TO DO IN YOUR BACKYARD

# How To Build An Indoor Greenhouse

**MATERIAL COST** $411.56    **MEDIUM DIFFICULTY**    **2 HOURS**

In a grid-down scenario, we will not have the luxury of popping down to the local grocer to buy our vegetables and fresh herbs. If you are a person who likes to garden, you will be very aware that most areas have a definite growing season. The problem is that we still need to eat even when plants are not growing outside.

Since our homes are nicely climate-controlled, it makes sense to bring some plants inside to keep them growing during the cold and dark winter months. Inside our homes' walls, we can easily provide a warm, well-lit, and moist environment for the plants to grow in. This is where a small indoor greenhouse comes into play.

### Why Use an Indoor Greenhouse?

There are many reasons we would want to use a greenhouse indoors, but the primary reason is that we can exercise far greater control over the conditions when we move the plants inside our homes. Temperature, humidity, and moisture are a few of the variables that we can fine-tune to maximize our plant's growth potential. Since the plants are inside our homes, we can also check on their condition with greater frequency.

### Things to Consider

You will need to consider several factors before beginning construction:

- How much sunlight makes its way into the house. Walk around your home, examining all the areas around your windows to determine which areas have the greatest amount of direct sunlight. There are situations where there will be no good access to natural sunlight. In these cases, you will need to use grow lights in place of the sun.
- After you find a location with good sunlight or a space that you will provide artificial light, you need to determine the maximum size that the greenhouse can be.
- Once you have a location in mind and know what size of indoor greenhouse you can construct, you can determine which plants you can grow. It is important to choose vegetables and herbs that your family enjoys and will fit the space. It is beneficial to plant some herbs that provide medicinal benefits in an off-grid or a grid-down situation.
- It would be best if you also considered whether you want to grow vegetables and herbs all the way to harvest or grow seeds for transplant later in an outdoor garden. This will have a determining effect on the size of your greenhouse and the volume of plants that you can grow at a given time.

### Indoor Greenhouse Design

Once you have a plan for what plants you are going to grow, you'll need to acquire suitable containers for them, and the size of these containers will be what you use as a template for how you are going to plan and build your indoor greenhouse. Be it pots, planters, or trays; you need to make sure that they will easily fit with room to grow.

### What to Grow in an Indoor Greenhouse

Indoor greenhouses are often used to grow seeds into seedlings which are transplanted into gardens outside. You can also grow a wide variety of herbs, vegetables, and even fruits as long as you have the available space to devote to their cultivation. Please do your research before cutting any wood and plan for what you are going to grow and how you will grow it.

Be mindful of the individual needs of each plant, and design your greenhouse around these needs.

## Construction of the Indoor Greenhouse

The instructions that I am providing here are for the greenhouse that fit my needs and space. I used four 15" x 8" plastic planters as the containers for the dirt and plants. You will have to adjust your greenhouse size according to what containers you choose to house the plants.

# Determining the Size

Begin by laying out your planters in the orientation that works best inside of your greenhouse. Once you are satisfied with their position, measure the length and width, which will be the basis for which you dimension the shelf or selves that the planters will be sitting. Once you have the length and width, add an inch or so to each dimension to determine your greenhouse shelf cut sizes.

# Tools Required

You will need the following tools:
- Saw
- Square
- Carpenters pencil
- Drill with bits and drivers
- Exacto knife
- Staple gun
- Carpenters glue

# Materials

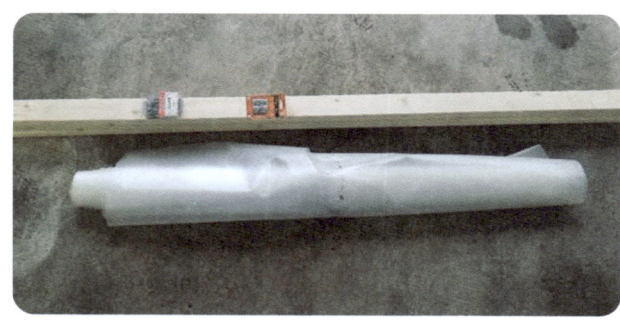

As far as materials go, you will need:
- 1" x3" x8' lumber available at Home Depot for $ 4.81 USD each. I used nine boards for my build.
  www.homedepot.com/p/1-in-x-3-in-x-8-ft-Spruce-Pine-Fir-Common-Board-307488/306896206

- 6 Mil vapour barrier available at Home Depot for $64.00USD per 100 ft roll. It may be possible to find lower prices if you select alternative plastic sheeting.
  www.homedepot.com/p/HDX-10-ft-x-100-ft-Clear-6-mil-Plastic-Sheeting-CFH-D0610C/204711636

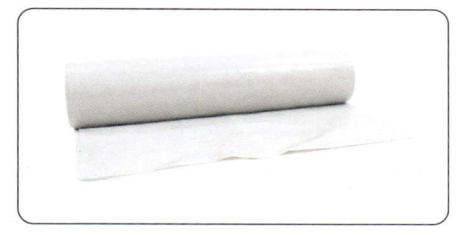

- #6 x 1 ½ inch wood screws are available at Home Depot for $ 6.25 USD for a pack of 100.
  www.homedepot.com/p/Everbilt-6-x-1-1-2-in-Phillips-Flat-Head-Zinc-Plated-Wood-Screw-100-Pack-801792/204275507

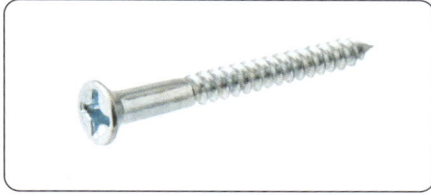

- #6 x 2-inch wood screws are available at Home Depot for $ 5.97 USD for a one-pound box.
  www.homedepot.com/p/Grip-Rite-6-x-2-in-Phillips-Bugle-Head-Coarse-Thread-Gold-Screws-1-lb-Pack-2GS1/100176505

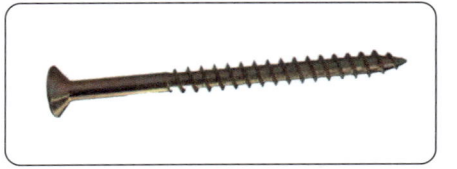

- Small hinges are available at Home Depot for $ 2.18 USD.
www.homedepot.com/p/Everbilt-1-in-Zinc-Plated-Non-Removable-Pin-Narrow-Utility-Hinges-2-Pack-15161/202034166

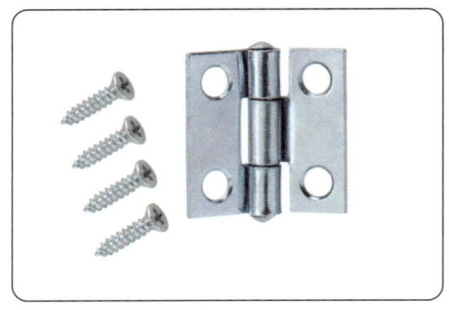

- Staples are found at Home Depot for $ 13.64 USD for a pack of 1000.
www.homedepot.com/p/Arrow-T50-1-2-in-Stainless-Steel-Staples-1-000-Pack-508SS1/203030843

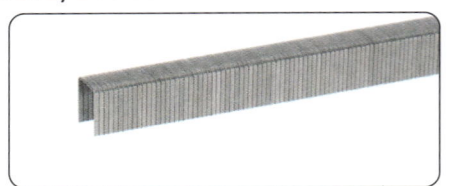

- Planters are available at Home Depot for $ 5.18 USD.
www.homedepot.com/p/15-in-x-7-99-in-Black-Bronze-Plastic-Window-Box-WB100F-BB/203621275

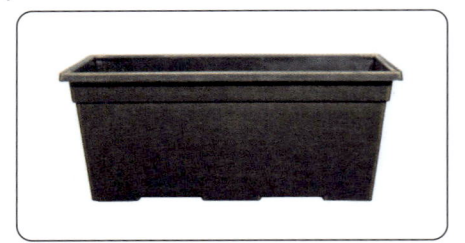

- Soil can be found at Home Depot for $8.97USD.
www.homedepot.com/p/Miracle-Gro-25-qt-Potting-Soil-Mix-72781431/206457033#product-overview

# Building the Indoor Greenhouse

## Building the Shelf

1. I started by cutting the material for the shelf. The inside dimensions were made to match what I determined them to be during the design phase. In my case, I cut five pieces at 33 inches and two pieces at 18 inches.
2. I test-fit the cut pieces before securing them with screws and glue. In this case, I chose to use three cross braces to support the planters.
3. I made sure to place the planters inside of the shelf to confirm that they will fit appropriately.
4. Once I was happy with how everything fit, I glued and screwed the shelf together.

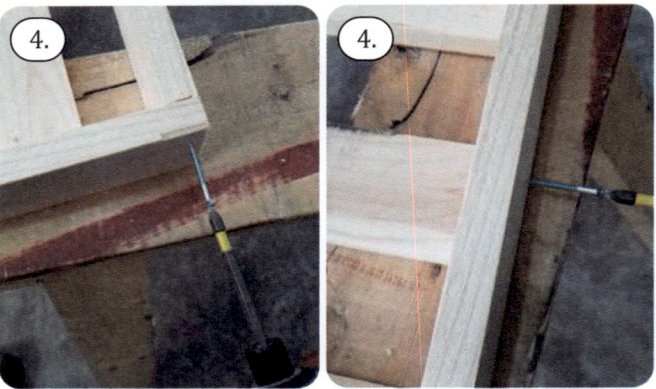

## Building the Sides

1. To achieve the height that I wanted, I cut two pieces of the 1x3 lumber in half to give me four 48" uprights.
2. Knowing that my shelf width is 18", I spaced my uprights so that they were parallel, square and 18" apart.
3. To determine the angle of the top for my green-

house, I laid a board across the two uprights until it was sitting at an angle that I found agreeable. I made sure to leave space where the cross member and the rear board meet to accommodate the greenhouse door.

4. I then marked the cross piece where it met with the uprights, which are now my cut lines for the upper cross members.
5. I cut the cross members and tested the fit. Given the boards' width, I had to drill holes approximately halfway through the uprights' width so the screws would have less material in which to drive through.
6. After drilling, I glued and screwed the upper cross-members in place.
7. I glued and screwed an 18" lower cross member about 3 inches from the side pieces' bottom.

## Putting it All Together

1. The two side panels are connected at the top rear by two boards that, in my case, measured 34 ¾" long. I glued and screwed them in place, forming an 'L' shape.
2. I installed the shelf at an appropriate height, glueing and screwing it in place. Always check the height before continuing and make adjustments as needed.
3. I attached more cross-bracing on the bottom and at the top front of the greenhouse.
4. With the greenhouse frame now complete, I placed the planters inside to check the fit.

## The Door

1. Constructing the door was very straightforward. I cut two boards at the top opening's full width and two more boards that will fit in between these longer boards once installed.
2. I had to drill holes to accommodate the screws again.
3. I made sure to test fit the pieces before glueing and screwing them together.

## Wrapping the Greenhouse

1. I cut a piece of vapour barrier long enough to wrap around the greenhouse, and then I loosely wrapped it around the greenhouse.
2. Starting at one corner, I folded a bit of the plastic over the top opening's edge and stapling it in position.
3. I then continued in this manner around the perimeter of the greenhouse. I had to cut and trim the plastic at the interior corners as I went around.
4. Once the perimeter was secured, I flipped the greenhouse upside down and cut the plastic at each corner so that each side of the greenhouse had a plastic section that could be folded and secured to the shelf's underside. I made sure each of these sections was long enough to cover the bottom of the shelf fully.
5. I folded the four plastic sections one at a time over onto the bottom of the shelf, securing and trimming as necessary.
6. I laid the door down on a section of plastic and folded, trimmed and stapled to get a snug fit of plastic around the outside surface of the door.
7. Then I secured the door in place with hinges.

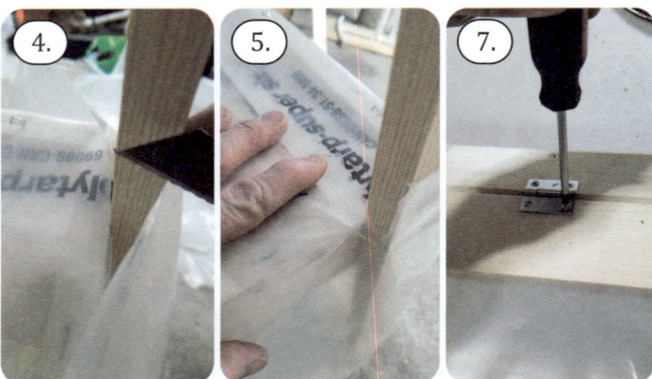

Place the greenhouse in position and place the dirt-filled planters inside. It is a good idea to include a thermometer with a hydrometer to monitor the greenhouse conditions. Plant and water whichever seeds you see fit.

Building an indoor greenhouse may seem like a daunting project to undertake, but it is not difficult. For a few hours of your time, you can provide your family with food during the cold winter months and give your plants a nursery in which to get the best start at life before moving to your garden.

OTHER PROJECTS TO DO IN YOUR BACKYARD

# How To Build An Off-Grid Shower

**MATERIAL COST** $ 183.00    **MEDIUM DIFFICULTY**    **2 HOURS**

When the grid goes down, our need to stay clean does not disappear along with the electricity; it simply becomes more complicated. Water is a precious resource at the best of times, but water's value increases exponentially in any off-grid situation. While we need to bathe still, we must do so in a much different way while preserving our water stores.

### A Few Considerations
- Setting up an off-grid shower is most likely going to take place out of doors. This means that all the water that runs out of the shower is going into the ground. It is critical that you only use biodegradable or natural soaps so that your showers do not contaminate the soil.
- The average shower uses 20 gallons of water; in off-grid scenarios, that equals 20 days of water for one person. Your off-grid showers have to use as little water as possible.
- The shower that I am detailing here uses a 5-gallon bucket to fill with water before showering manually. If you are willing to take cold showers allowing the bucket to fill with rainwater may be an option that you can consider.
- Drainage is going to be a huge consideration. You will want to be sure that all of the water drains away from anywhere you do not want it to be.
- Try to set the shower up in an area that offers the maximum level of privacy for the users.

This shower's construction is not overly complicated and requires materials that you can easily find at the local hardware store. There are many modifications and variations on the design and style that you can do to suit your own needs, some of which I will mention later.

## Tools
You will need:
- Drill with drill bits and drivers
- Saw
- Wrenches
- Two-foot square
- Staple gun
- Level

## Materials
As far as materials go, you will need:
- Nine 2x4x8' boards which are at Home Depot for $ 6.35 USD each.

www.homedepot.com/p/2-in-x-4-in-x-96-in-Prime-Whitewood-Stud-058449/312528776

- Four 1x4x8' boards that Home Depot sells for $ 6.43 USD.

www.homedepot.com/p/1-in-x-4-in-x-8-ft-Premium-Kiln-Dried-Square-Edge-Whitewood-Common-Board-914681/100023465

- #8 x 2" Screws found at Home Depot for $ 6.25 USD per pack of 50. You should pick up two packs of these.

www.homedepot.com/p/Everbilt-8-x-2-in-Phillips-Flat-Head-Zinc-Plated-Wood-Screw-50-Pack-801862/204275485

225

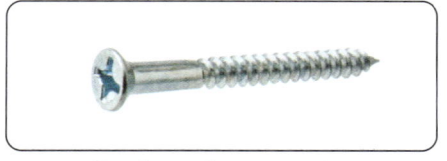

- One roll of 6 Mil Vapour barrier, which you can find at Home Depot for $ 64.00 USD per 100 ft roll.
www.homedepot.com/p/HDX-10-ft-x-100-ft-Clear-6-mil-Plastic-Sheeting-CFHD0610C/204711636

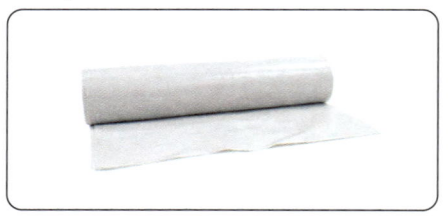

- 48" x ¾" wood dowels are at Home Depot for $ 3.62 USD each.
www.homedepot.com/p/3-4-in-x-48-in-Raw-Wood-Round-Dowel-HDDH3448/203360200

- A shower curtain can be found at Home Depot for as low as $ 6.80 USD.
www.homedepot.com/p/Bath-Bliss-PEVA-70-in-x-72-in-Blue-and-Green-Mandala-Design-Shower-Curtain-5388/304017680

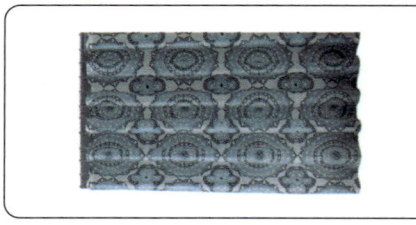

For the shower head and valve assembly, the following components are all that I could find at my local Home Depot, which is never very well stocked. Feel free to substitute components to make your setup more streamlined than mine.

- Showerheads are available at Home Depot for as low as $ 9.98 USD.
www.homedepot.com/p/Glacier-Bay-3-Spray-3-5-in-Single-Wall-Mount-Fixed-Adjustable-Shower-Head-in-Chrome-8462000HC/303528559

- Showerhead arms are $ 13.98 USD at Home Depot.
www.homedepot.com/p/Glacier-Bay-8-in-Shower-Arm-and-Flange-in-Brushed-Nickel-3075-505/204511156

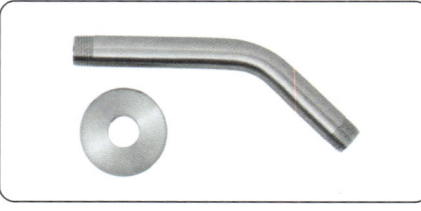

- PVC ball valve with ¾" FNPT fittings are $ 3.35 USD at Home Depot.
www.homedepot.com/p/Homewerks-Worldwide-3-4-in-PVC-Schedule-40-FIP-x-FIP-Ball-Valve-VBVP40B4B/202369937

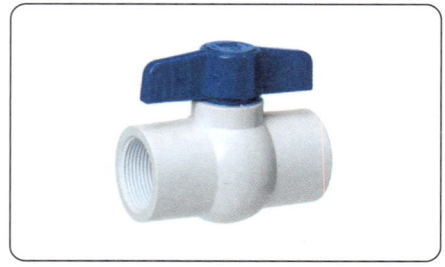

- ¾" MNPT to ½" FNPT Reducer is $ 0.98 USD at Home Depot.
www.homedepot.com/p/Charlotte-Pipe-3-4-in-x-1-2-in-PVC-Schedule-40-Reducer-Bushing-PVC-02112-1600HD/203850956

- ¾" NPT Couplings can be bought at Home Depot for $ 1.00 USD.
www.homedepot.com/p/Charlotte-Pipe-3-4-in-PVC-Schedule-40-FPT-x-FPT-Coupling-PVC021020800HD/203811424

- 3 - ¾" MNPT to ¾" Slip-on adapter purchased at Home Depot for $ 0.52 USD.
www.homedepot.com/p/DURA-3-4-in-Schedule-40-PVC-Male-Adapter-10-Pack-CP436-007/202101747

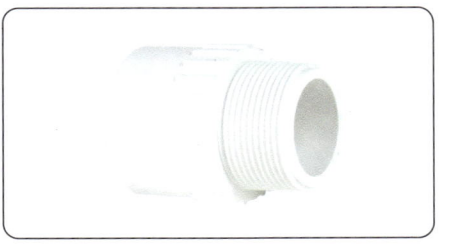

- ¾" Sch 40 PVC Pipe $ 1.60 USD at Home Depot for a 24" length.
www.homedepot.com/p/VPC-3-4-in-x-24-in-PVC-Sch-40-Pipe-22075/202300505

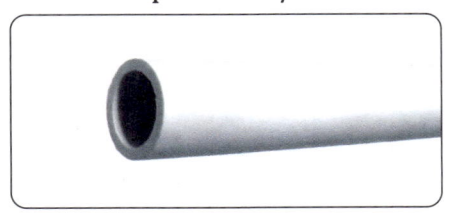

- 5 Gallon Buckets are $ 3.78 USD at Home Depot.
www.homedepot.com/p/The-Home-Depot-5-Gal-Homer-Bucket-05GLHD2/100087613

## Building the Shower Head Assembly

1. Begin by installing the showerhead onto the showerhead arm.
2. Cement a small section of ¾" PVC between two of the ¾" adapters.
3. Screw on the coupling, then the reducer bushing.
4. Attach the showerhead arm.
5. Attach the ball valve.
6. Drill a hole in the side of the bucket large enough for the threaded end of your last adapter to fit into. Do not drill this hole too close to the bottom. Make sure the fitting will fit into the hole cleanly.
7. Push the threaded end of the adapter through the hole from the inside, so it is sticking out.
8. Attach the rest of the assembly.
9. Test the unit for smooth operation and leaks before continuing.
10. You may need to silicone around the fittings through the bucket.

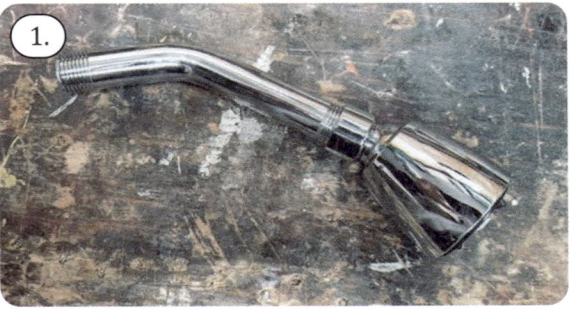

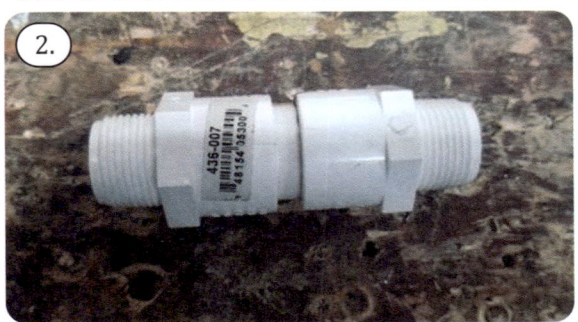

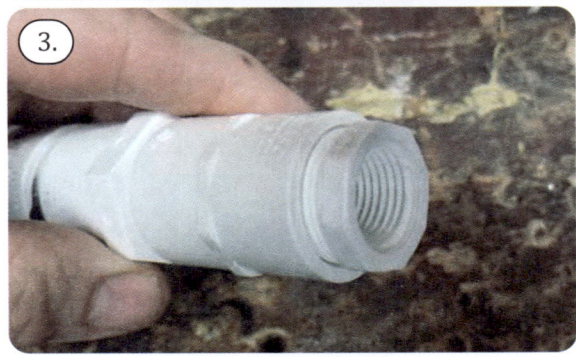

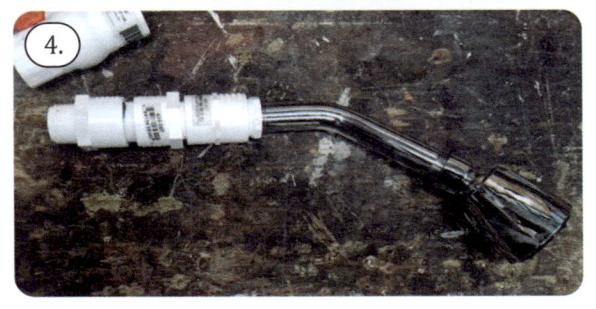

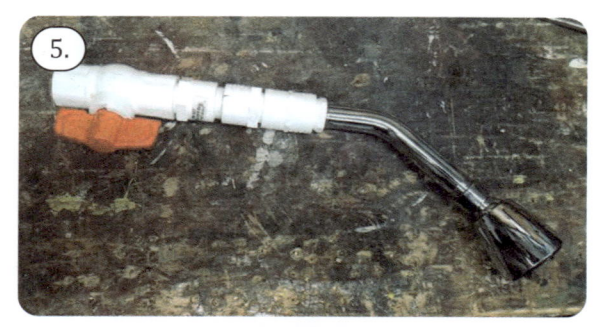

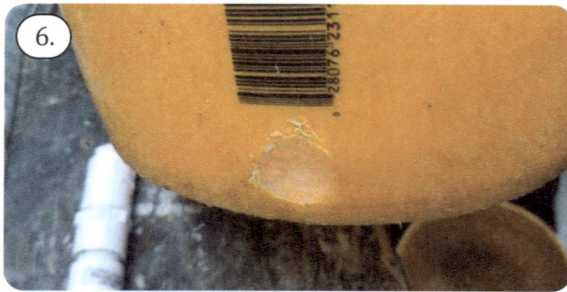

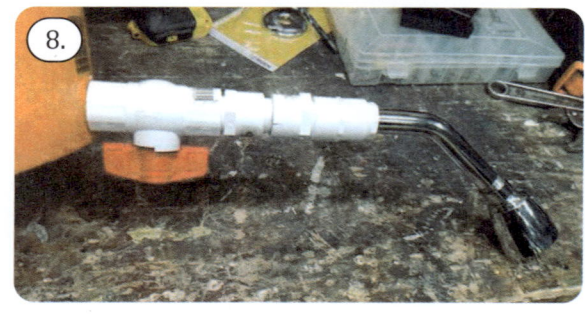

## Building the Shower

The off-grid shower I constructed used the following cut list I devised to make good use of the materials I purchased. For example, the 48" pieces are obtained by simply cutting an eight-foot 2x4 in half. You can adjust these dimensions to suit your needs.

**Lumber Cut List**

**2" x 4" x 8' Lumber**
- 4 pieces @ 84"
- 5 pieces @ 48"
- 3 pieces @ 45"
- 2 pieces @ 41"
- 2 pieces @ 6"

**1" x 4" x 8'**
- 8 pieces @ 48"

## Construction of the Base

1. Make a 48" square frame using two of the 48" pieces and two of the 45" pieces.
2. Place one more 45" piece into the middle of the frame as reinforcement.
3. Screw the frame together and confirm that it is square.
4. Layout the eight 48" 1x4's on the top of the frame, spacing them out evenly. No need to measure, space them evenly by eye.
5. Secure these to the frame with screws.
6. Sand the top surface of the 1x4's so that bare feet walking on it will not get splinters.

## Building the Frame

1. Find a suitable location to place your shower where it will provide the necessary privacy and drainage.
2. Level the base.
3. Attach the four 84" uprights checking for square and level as you go.
4. Join these uprights together with two of the 48" pieces and two of the 41" pieces. At the same time, think about how you want to orient the bucket and the opening of the shower.
5. Secure the last 48" piece six inches away from the inside edge where the bucket will sit.
6. Attach the two six-inch pieces between these supports for the bucket to sit. Space them about six inches apart.
7. Wrap the outside of the structure with the vapour barrier. You have the option to enclose the three sides of the frame fully or, as I did, leave space at the top and the bottom. Begin securing the vapour barrier, starting at the entrance stapling it in place as you go.
8. You can screw a shower curtain rod or dowel into the opening and hang a shower curtain if you wish.
9. Place the bucket on top of the platform.

## Using the Off-Grid Shower

1. Fill the bucket with warm water.
2. Open the valve and get your body wet.
3. Shut off the valve and use soap and shampoo to cleanse yourself.
4. Re-open the valve to rinse the soap and shampoo off your body.

## Variations

- I chose to use a vapour barrier because it was opaque enough for my liking. If you are more modest and want a covering that can not be seen through, you can sheet the outside of this in plywood. Using plywood will make this shower very dark, and you will need to add in some lighting.
- Instead of 1 x 4 slats, you could sheet the base with plywood as long as you provide adequate drainage in the way of a floor drain. This has the advantage of being able to direct the flow of water away from the shower area by using pipes.

There is no substitute for a shower with a proper amount of water pressure, but when the grid goes down, we will have to make due with what we can build ourselves. The bucket and showerhead assembly on their own are pretty useful for use while camping or in a hunting camp. It is beneficial to have the components for the off grid shower ready to go for when the grid fails us.

OTHER PROJECTS TO DO IN YOUR BACKYARD

# How To Build An Off-The-Grid Stone Grill Oven

**MATERIAL COST** $ 183.00    **MEDIUM DIFFICULTY**    **2 HOURS**

Building a brick oven can be a headache. In this chapter, I'm going to show you exactly what you need to consider before building it and what materials and tools you will need.

## Planning Oven Size

Plan your oven size before buying the materials. Obviously, the bigger the oven will be, the bigger the quantity of materials you will need. In my case, I built an oven that has a length of 47 inches, a width of 23 inches, and a height of 27 inches at front and about 39 inches at bottom.

The back of the oven and the sides are slightly higher than the front of it. The reason behind this is I need easy access to the grill while working on it, but I want the food on the grill to be protected in case of wind or other similar things.

Next, I'll discuss the materials I used to build this oven. If you want a bigger oven, make sure you adjust the number of bricks needed and the quantity of mortar.

## Materials Needed

You will need:
- 170 Bricks 9X4.5X2.5 inches $ 119.99 USD
www.lowes.com/pd/Oldcastle-Red-Cored-Brick/3433312

- Mortar (3 bags * 25 kg) $13.00 USD
www.lowes.com/pd/QUIKRETE-10-lb-Gray-Type-N-Mortar-Mix/3006119

- Strong metal sheet (2 pieces) - I used a sheet of 10 mm width I had at home. You will need a sheet that is at least the size of the final oven (length*width), if not a bit bigger
www.lowes.com/pd/Hillman-12-in-x-24-in-Steel-Solid/3054563

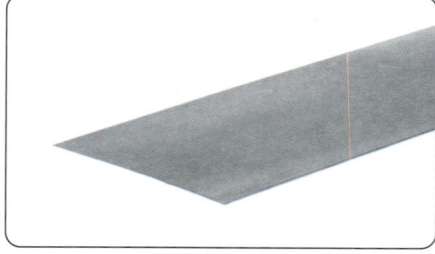

- 2 Cement Blocks for the Base $ 7.00 USD
www.lowes.com/pd/Square-Gray-Concrete-Patio-Stone-Common-16-in-x-16-in-Actual-16-in-x-16-in/3034746

- Stainless steel grill rack $ 24.00 USD
  www.lowes.com/pd/Heavy-Duty-BBQ-Parts-Stainless-Steel-Briquette-Grate/3808187

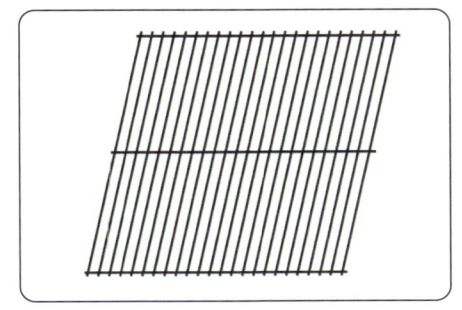

- Cloth

## Tools Needed

As far as tools go, you will need:
- Angle grinder (needed to cut the bricks and the metal sheet)
- Electric drill with a mortar mixing paddle (optional - it helps preparing the mortar)
- A trowel
- A bucket

## The Building Process

In my case, I used two cement blocks as a base. That will give it more stability and will make it last longer. If you don't have any cement blocks, you can use some cement to build a base. Let it dry for 1-2 days before moving forward with the construction.

## Step 1: Prepare the Mortar

In order to do this, you will need to mix your mortar with some water in a bucket. Don't prepare all the mortar as you start. This will cause the mortar to dry. Instead, do half a bucket or a bucket at a time.

Read the instructions of the mortar you bought and make sure you follow the instructions carefully. Most of the time, you will only need to add about ⅓ water of the quantity of mortar and mix it using the electric drill.

When you're done, it should be consistent but a bit liquid and flexible.

## Step 2: Start Building the Base of the Oven

Basically, what we need to do is to fix the bottom row of bricks. Using the trowel, take some mortar and put it on the bottom of the brick. Then, carefully fix the first brick on the base. Once that is done, make sure you add some mortar on the margin of the brick that will get in contact with the brick near it, so they stick to each other.

The grill consists of two sides: the left side, where the grill will be placed, and the right side, where I built a small kitchen countertop that is extremely useful. Based on the size of the stainless-steel grill you bought, make sure one of the sides is slightly bigger - approx. 0.8 inches. In my case, I had to make the left side a bit bigger than the right side, to make sure the stainless-steel grill would fit later on.

Be careful and try to put the same quantity of mortar between the bricks, this will make the oven look consistent and beautiful.

When you're done, you should have something like this:

## Step 3: Keep Adding Bricks Over the Base Until We Reach the Fire Base Level

We want the base of the fire spot to be about 8-12 inches under the grill. That is the best distance for cooking both vegetables and meat. In my case, because I wanted the height of the front of the oven to be about 27 inches (11-bricks rows), I added the base of the fire spot after 7 rows of bricks.

## Step 4: Place the Metal Sheet as the Base for the Fire Spot

Once we reach the fire base level, we need to place the metal sheet over it. This will be the base of the fire. If you want, you can also drill some holes in a few places so the ashes can fall down.
Once you place the metal sheet over the bricks, make sure you center it and you have about 0.4 inches over each side of the bricks
Once we reach the fire base level, we need to place the metal sheet over it. This will be the base of the fire. If you want, you can also drill some holes in a few places so the ashes can fall down.
Once you place the metal sheet over the bricks, make sure you center it and you have about 0.4 inches over each side of the bricks.

## Step 5: Cut the Corners of the Bricks and Place Them Over the Metal Sheet

This is something I didn't do and I regretted later on. I thought that the metal sheet was thin enough to be able to build over it, but that made things a bit complicated.
What you need to do is cut a few bricks as seen in the image below:

Then, it's much easier to build over the metal sheet:

## Step 6: Add a Few Extra Rows of Bricks Before Placing the Stainless-Steel Grill

We are now building the distance between the fire spot and the grill. I added 3 rows of bricks before placing the grill. That means the distance between the fire and the stainless-steel grill is roughly 8 inches.

## Step 7: Cut the Corners of the Bricks and Place the Grill in the Channel

We'll need to cut the corners of the bricks like we did at step 5, when we placed the metal sheet over the bricks. The only difference is we want to be able to remove the stainless steel to be able to wash it properly.

Cut the corners like in the image below:

When fixing the bricks with mortar, make sure the mortar doesn't get over the stainless-steel grill. If that happens, remove the extra mortar because what we want to achieve is to have a channel where the stainless-steel grill can get in and out very easily.

## Step 8: Adding the Metal Sheet as the Base of the Kitchen Countertop

For this step, we'll need to do exactly what we did at step 4. However, in this case, I decided to add bricks over the metal sheet to get a more stable base for the kitchen countertop. You can see how I did it in the image below:

## Step 9: Add Mortar Over the Bricks Covering the Metal Sheet

I added mortar to fill the gaps between the bricks and to get a nice flat kitchen countertop, like in the image below:

Additionally, what you could do is place a floor tile or a marble slab over the mortar to get an easy to clean kitchen countertop. I didn't do this, and I just used mortar as the base for the countertop, but I think this will be one of the next upgrades.

## Step 10: Add a Few More Brick Rows on Sides and Bottom of the Oven

This is not compulsory, but I decided to do it because I think it looks better and it will also protect whatever food you're grilling in case of wind.
It should look something like this:

## Step 11: Clean the Extra Mortar While it Is Still Not Too Dry

Using water and a cloth, clean the extra mortar that got on the bricks while building. This will improve the aspect of the oven.

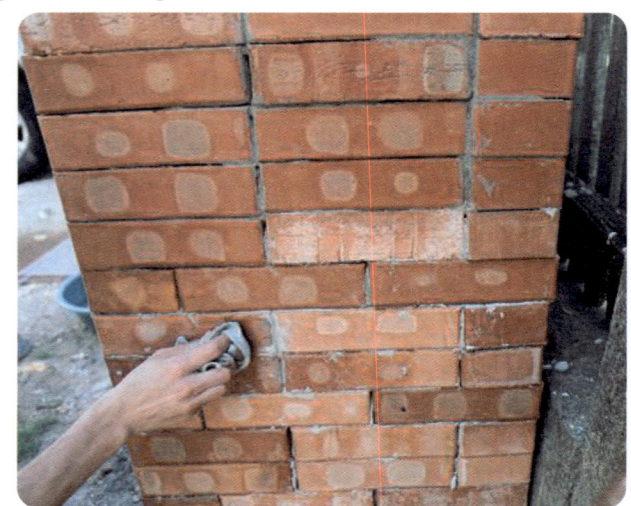

OTHER PROJECTS TO DO IN YOUR BACKYARD

# How To Build An Off-The-Grid Washing Machine

**MATERIAL COST** $ 12.00    **EASY DIFFICULTY**    **10 MINUTES**

When the grid goes down, our need to wash our clothing does not disappear with the electricity. The issue is that we are so used to pressing a button and having a machine do all the work for us. Hand washing of clothing takes a significant amount of time that can be better spent on other tasks. With a little ingenuity and some materials you may have to lay around the home, you can construct off-grid washing machines.

We need to take a few considerations when washing clothing in an off-grid scenario that would not normally cross our minds.

Water is such a precious resource during any off-grid situation that using any of it for cleaning clothing seems wasteful. The truth is that using potable water to wash clothing is, in fact, wasteful. This is why you should only use non-potable water for cleaning tasks. Rainwater or creek and lake water are good options since these sources would require filtering or boiling to render them safe to drink.

Without a city sewer system to whisk our dirty water away, we need to seriously think about how we will dispose of the dirty soapy water. Wherever you decide to direct the wastewater, it needs to be away from freshwater sources you use for drinking water, that animals use for drinking water, or that contain fish or other aquatic lifeforms.

The soap that you use to clean your clothing needs to be as environmentally friendly as possible. You can purchase many non-toxic detergents, or you can make your soaps with widely available recipes.

### Washing Machine Options

Clothes washing options in a world before electricity was often a basin full of soapy water where you would soak and scrub your clothing, after which they would be rinsed and hung to dry. An old-school washing board and a clothes ringer are also really good options for off-grid clothes washing. The problems with these methods are that they still take too much time out of your busy day. The two options that I will detail here are off-grid washing machines that offer a mechanical advantage and are self-contained units. With either of these machines, you can walk away from the chore of washing clothes to 'let them soak' without any worries.

### DIY Off-Grid Washing Machines

These two washing machines differ in their complexity but are fairly simple to build. The first only requires a plunger and a bucket but is limited in how much clothing it can wash, while the second is more complex and requires a larger drum and a bicycle to build.

## The Plunger Washing Machine

If you have a Home Depot bucket and lid along with a household plunger, you have a simple off-grid washing machine.

## Tools

As far as tools go, you will only need drill and bits.

## Materials

Here's a list of the materials you'll need:

◆ Plunger, which you can find at Home Depot for $ 5.29 USD.

www.homedepot.com/p/Genuine-Joe-23-in-L-x-5-75-in-Dia-Yellow-Value-Plus-Plunger-GJO85130/206592801

- 5-gallon Bucket which Home Depot sells for $ 3.78 USD.
  www.homedepot.com/p/The-Home-Depot-5-Gal-Homer-Bucket-05GLHD2/100087613

- Lid for a 5-gallon bucket which is sold at Home Depot for $ 2.28 USD.
  www.homedepot.com/p/The-Home-Depot-5-gal-Orange-Leakproof-Bucket-Lid-with-Gasket-5GLD-ORANGE-LID-for-5GL-HOMER-PAIL/202264044

## Instructions

1. Cut a hole in the middle of the lid large enough for the plunger's handle to fit.
2. Slid the lid over the plunger handle.
3. Fill the bucket no more than halfway with clothes and pour in water and some detergent.
4. Put the lid/plunger assembly onto the bucket.

## How to Operate the Plunger Washing Machine

The operation of the plunger washing machine is very simple. With the clothes, water, and detergent in the bucket and the lid firmly secured, move the plunger up and down in a plunging motion. Do this for a few minutes, then leave the bucket alone to soak for a while. Repeat the plunging action and let it soak again. Repeat this process depending on how soiled your clothing is. Drain the water, then fill with clean water and repeat the plunging process replacing the water as you go until the clothes are rinsed to your liking. Finally, wring out the clothing and hang them to dry.

## Bicycle-Powered Washing Machine

If you have an old bicycle lying around along with a little lumber, a drum, and a few miscellaneous bits and pieces, you can make a washing machine that you can power by pedalling.

### Tools

You will need:
- Saw
- Tape Measure
- Drill with bits and drivers

### Materials

As far as materials go, you will need:
- A drum such as an old 55-gallon drum. Purchasing one of these new is not cost-effective; instead, try and repurpose something you already have or find a source to buy a drum used.
- Three pieces of 2 x 4 x 8' lumber which is sold at Home Depot for $ 7.98 USD each.

www.homedepot.com/p/2-in-x-4-in-x-8-ft-Premium-Kiln-Dried-Whitewood-Framing-Stud-Lumber-96022/315592380

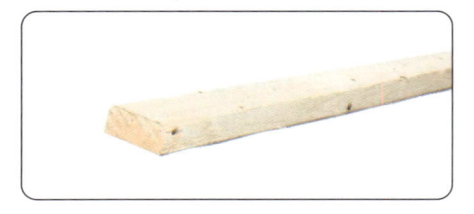

- ¾" wood dowels are found at Home Depot for $ 3.80 USD.
  www.homedepot.com/p/6412U-3-4-in-x-3-4-in-x-48-in-Pine-Round-Dowel-10001806/203334066

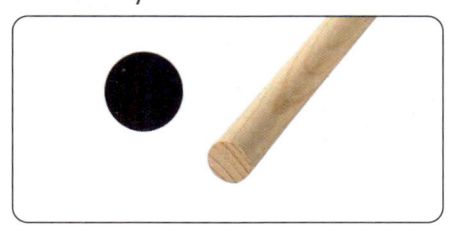

- ¾" PVC Pipe which is $ 3.56 USD at Home Depot.
  www.homedepot.com/p/Charlotte-Pipe-3-4-in-x-10-ft-PVC-Schedule-40-Plain-End-Pipe-PVC-04007-0600/100348472

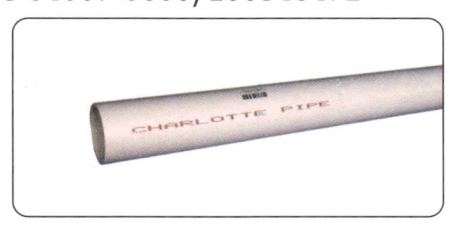

- Hinges can be found at Home Depot for $ 3.18 USD for a package of two.
  www.homedepot.com/p/Everbilt-2-1-2-in-Zinc-Plated-Non-Removable-Pin-Narrow-Utility-Hinges-2-Pack-15165/202033979

- A Hasp can be bought at Home Depot for $ 3.98 USD.
  www.homedepot.com/p/Everbilt-3-1-2-in-Zinc-Plated-Adjustable-Staple-Safety-Hasp-15122/202033919

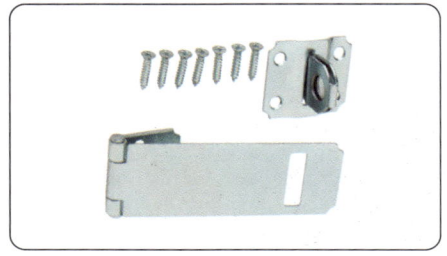

- #8 x ½" Machine Screws can be found at Home Depot for $ 1.18 USD per package of eight.
  www.homedepot.com/p/8-32-x-1-2-in-Combo-Round-Head-Zinc-Plated-Machine-Screw-8-Pack-803091/204274611

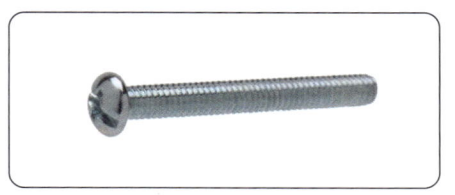

- #8-32 nuts are $ 9.34 USD for a box of 30.
  www.homedepot.com/p/Hillman-Stainless-Machine-Screw-Hex-Nut-8-32-957/204794772

- Old bicycle inner tube.
- Bicycle.

## Instructions

1. Measure your drum to determine the dimensions for the off-grid washing machine frame.
2. Layout some uncut 2x4's to mock up how the ends of your stands will look. Make adjustments to achieve a height from the ground to where your axle will sit that is at least equal to the diameter of the drum.
3. Cut some 2x4 lumber for the ends of the frame, making sure to mitre the ends so that they will sit flat on the ground.
4. Screw these parts together to make two end frames.
5. Measure the height of the drum and figure out how long you want your PVC pipe to be. Then cut cross bracing for your frame so that the PVC pipe will fit in between the end frames.
6. Cut the cross bracing and screw it into place. Check that the dowel will sit in the cross of each end frame.
7. Drill holes in the centre of either end of the drum large enough that the PVC pipe fits tightly.
8. Layout and cut out the opening for loading in the clothes.
9. Cut four pieces of Bicycle tire inner tube to line the edge of this opening.
10. Cut the inner tubes along the length to open them up.
11. Either glue or secure with machine screws these inner tubes to the drum opening edges so that at least half an inch of rubber will stick out from the edges of the opening.
12. Attach hinges and hasp to the door and the drum.
13. Slide the dowel into the PVC and mount it onto

the frame.

14. To make the off-grid washing machine bicycle operated, mount a bike so that the rear wheel is resting on the drum. In my case, I used an old children's bicycle where I secured the front forks and allowed the rear tire to rest on the drum under its weight. You will have to devise your methods to suit the shape, size, and type of bicycle you have available.

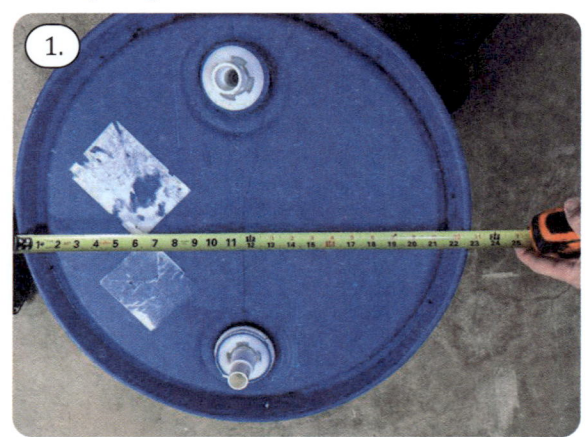

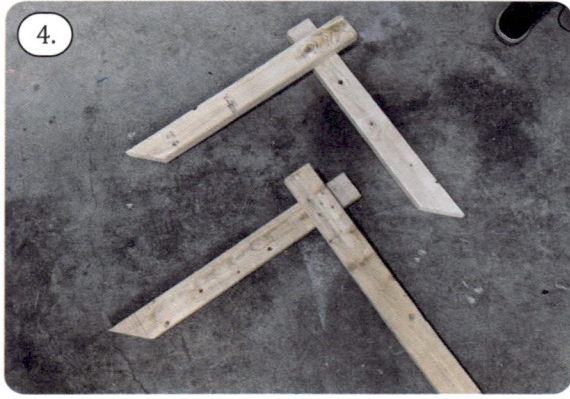

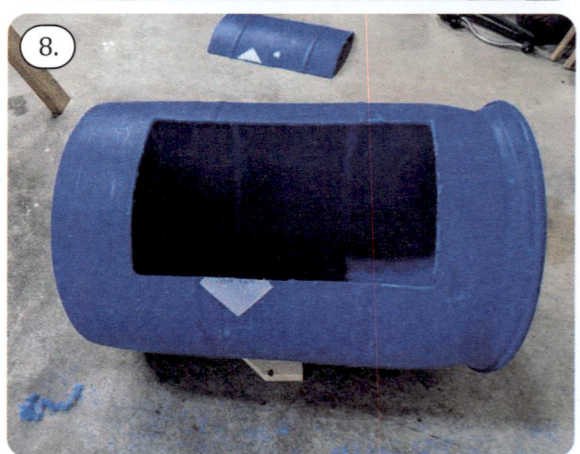

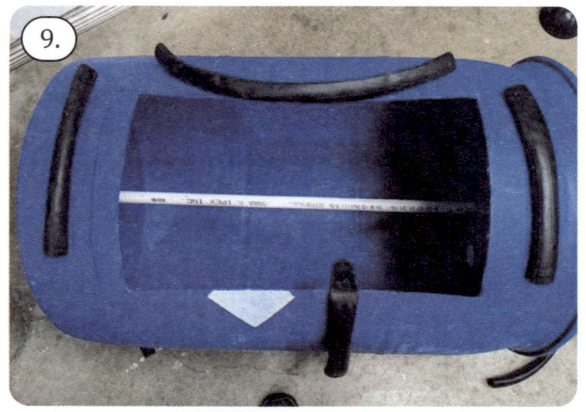

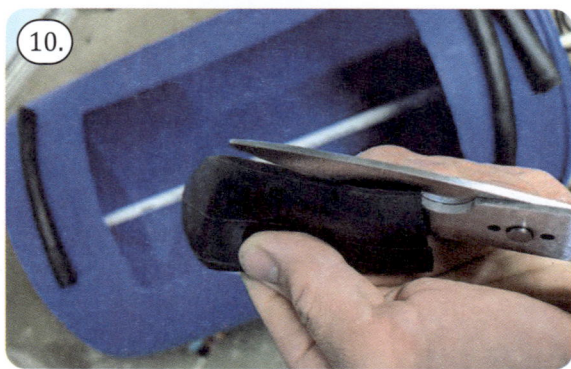

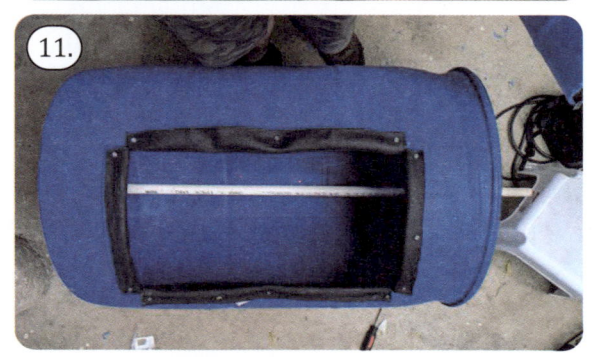

# How to Use the Bicycle Operated Washing

1. Load the drum with dirty clothes, fresh water and detergent.
2. Secure the drum door and pedal the bicycle for five to ten minutes.
3. Allow the laundry to soak for half an hour or so.
4. Repeat this procedure several times.
5. Drain the water.
6. Fill the drum with fresh water and do a cycle or two so that you can rinse the clothes of residual soap.
7. Remove the clothes, wring out the excess water, and hang to dry.

Don't let a trivial matter like the grid going down be an excuse not to do the laundry. With a small amount of effort and some materials you may have lying around, you can devise either or both of these grid-down washing machines. When the world around you is crumbling into chaos and bedlam, you can rest easy knowing that you are going into each post-apocalyptic day with clean underwear.

OTHER PROJECTS TO DO IN YOUR BACKYARD

# How To Build Your Own Aquaponics System

**MATERIAL COST** $ 382.00    **COMPLEX DIFFICULTY**    **4 HOURS**

Aquaponics is a food producing system that is built on a symbiotic relationship between fish and plants. The plants will filter the water naturally and this will create a clean environment for the fish to grow and thrive. At the same time, the fish will produce waste that will organically fertilize the plants.

The result of this symbiotic relationship are large, prolific plants and fish that can be harvested and eaten. Fish like tilapia, trout and catfish can all be grown in an aquaponics system.

The carcasses of these fish can even be used in the soil based garden so that your system creates virtually zero waste. This is why the aquaponics system holds such appeal to the homesteader.

We are going to build a DIY aquaponics system using a simple hydroponics setup as the base. This build is amazingly simple and once you begin to understand how it works and build your routine, you can make this system work anywhere.

The costliest part will be your large basin so look for one that is second hand or shop your local thrift stores to see if something is laying around that can be had for cheap.

This system will produce food outside in the sunlight or you can bring the whole system indoors, under grow lights, to produce food all year long.

## Quick Setup Aquaponics Tip

When you are setting up your aquaponics system, the germination of seeds and the development of seedlings will have you waiting weeks to get your system up and running.

You can bypass this long wait using a simple trick. Soil potted seedlings, like those at your local hardware or garden center, can be easily transferred from their pots to your new system. It is simply a matter of removing them from the plastic container and soaking them in a 5 gallon bucket filled with water.

After a few minutes of soaking, you will be able to shake loose most of the dirt from the root system. Once the root system is bare then you can simply plant them into your aquaponics system. It is that simple and it saves you weeks.

## Materials and Cost

- 52 Plant Hydroponics PVC System by VIVO SUN $ 89.00 USD (includes cups, water pump, seed starters)
www.amazon.com/dp/B08GPZVR26/

- Large Basin $200 USD
www.amazon.com/Tuff-Stuff-Products-KMT50-50-Gallon/dp/B0000W8S80/

- Clay Pebbles $11 USD
www.amazon.com/Clay-Pebbles-2qt-1-6-8mm-12mm/dp/B097C5ZP1B/

◆ Seeds $4 USD
www.amazon.com/Gaeas-Blessing-Seeds-Open-Pollinated-Germination/dp/B08L4NDSH3/

◆ PH Test $18 USD
www.amazon.com/General-Hydroponics-pH-Control-Kit/dp/B000BNKWZY/?th=1

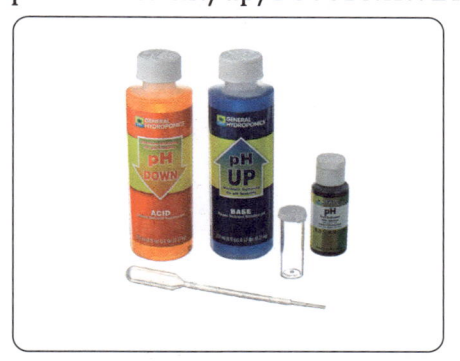

◆ Plant Nutrient $30 USD
www.amazon.com/AeroGarden-Liquid-Nutrients-1-Liter/dp/B004M5NGJG/

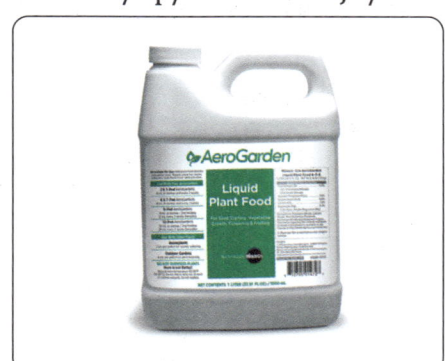

◆ Fish Food $30 USD
www.amazon.com/Natural-Waterscapes-Resealable-Bluegill-Floating/dp/B07YBJX6JH/

## Process

### Assembling the PVC System

1. Whether you decide to buy the VIVOSUN or cut your own PVC you will need to assemble the hydroponics portion first.
2. If you are assembling your system from scratch do not forget to drill 2" inch holes evenly spaced the length of your growing pipe. These holes will house your growing cups.
3. Connect all of your growing pipes before adding a reducer for your pump hose. This should go on one end of the connected pipes.
4. On the other end you should connect your outflow pipe.
5. Your PVC frame can be built next to hold your system in place.
6. Using your basin or a small 5 gallon bucket you can test inflow and outflow of your system.

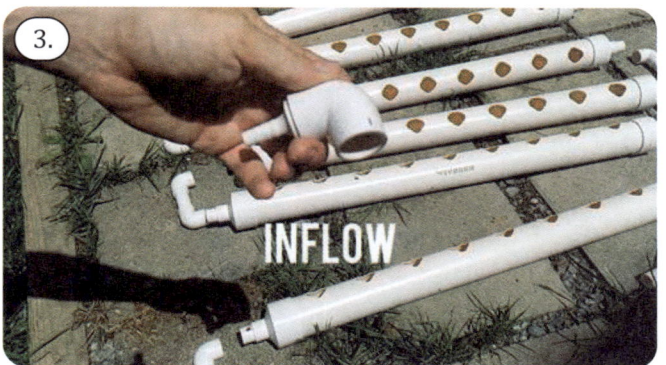

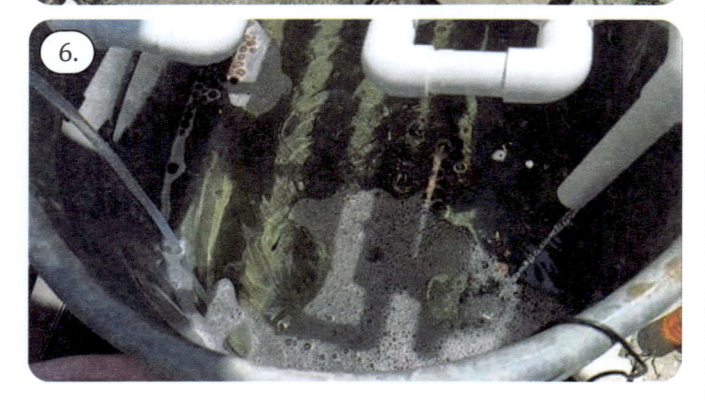

that you are adding to the system.
7. Seedlings potted in dirt can have their roots rinsed clean and transplanted into a hydroponics system. They cannot go back into the dirt after this, but they can go from dirt to water without issue.
8. Test the PH of your water, and adjust if necessary, using a PH Test kit and then add your plants.

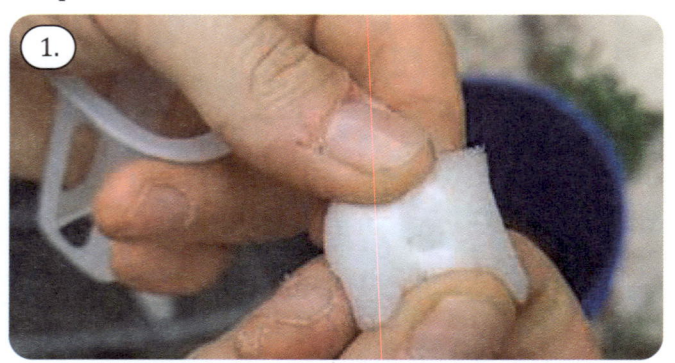

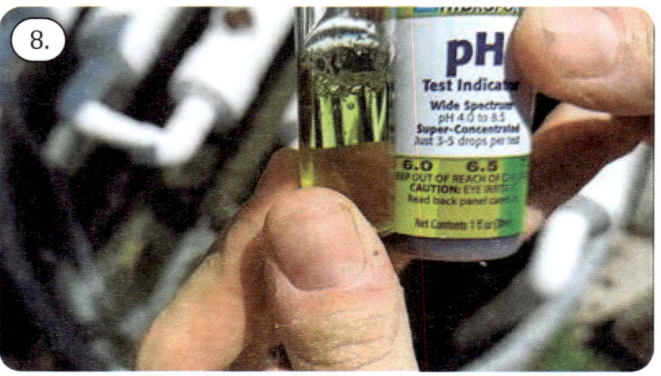

## Starting Seeds

1. Seed starters like rock wool or even foam are great ways to get seeds started. Start by placing a seed or two at the center of each.
2. Place these in an area that can hold a shallow bit of water and allow the seeds to sprout.
3. Place the sprouts outside or under a grow light.
4. Meanwhile open your clay pebbles and soak them in a 5 gallon bucket. Shake them around a bit and then drain them. These will protect the roots of the plants in your system.
5. Once they become seedlings they can be transferred to your system.
6. Read the directions on your growing nutrient and make sure you have enough nutrient in your water to support the seedlings or plants

## Adding Fish

1. Fill your basin with water. If it is from the hose you will have to treat it for the chlorine. This is toxic to your fish and will kill them almost instantly. Water from rain barrels is much better.
2. Water from the hose will be cold and your fish can also die from shock if you do not allow them to acclimate to the temperature.
3. You can sit the bag in the basin water to allow the fish to get comfortable and acclimated in the new temperature.
4. Finally release them into the water. Some may die and that is ok.
5. We started our system with some minnows and goldfish to keep it cheap and easy. I suggest you do the same so if you have loss, you aren't out $100 or more for fingerling trout.
6. Feed the fish daily and keep an eye on PH for your plants and your fish.

This system will require you to keep and eye on it but little more than a daily check in is required and the annual cleaning out of the whole system.

OTHER PROJECTS TO DO IN YOUR BACKYARD

# How To Hide From Thermal Vision

Modern surveillance technology can be scarily effective and it's getting better all the time.

The first night vision device I ever used was an old Individual Weapon Sight, a huge starlight scope that cost as much as a pretty good car and weighed more than the L1A1 battle rifle it was mounted on. Now, a few hundred dollars will buy you a much more effective night sight that weighs a few ounces, or a good set of night vision goggles – but night vision is old technology now.

The state of the art in surveillance is thermal imaging, and that's a lot harder to hide from.

**Night Vision vs Thermal Vision**

Thermal imaging is also called passive infrared. It works by picking up the infrared radiation – basically heat – radiated by objects, and displaying the different temperatures. It doesn't matter how expertly camouflaged something is – if it's warmer or cooler than its background, it will show up.

The effective range of a thermal imager is from a few dozen yards for the smallest handheld units, up to thousands of yards for large military surveillance systems and weapon sights.

And, while imagers were once heavy and incredibly expensive systems that needed to be cooled with refrigerated gas, they've become a lot smaller and more affordable.

Less than $2,000 will buy you a rifle scope that let's you shoot out to more than 300 yards in complete darkness. For $600 you can get a hand-held imager with a range of over 100 yards.

You can even get a $249 plug-in module for your smartphone that will pick up a hidden object a few yards away by its thermal emissions.

These days, if someone's looking for you it's smart to assume they have a thermal imager to help them.

Does this sound like bad news? It is.

Unlike standard night vision devices, thermal imagers don't need any light at all to pick you up. They can see through mist and smoke.

They penetrate rain and falling snow, although those can reduce their range by more than half. If a thermal imager is scanning for you it's a lot harder to hide.

But it isn't impossible, and if you know what you're doing you have a good chance of evading detection. Here's how to do it.

### Remember the basics

Hiding from a thermal imager follows the same basic principles as hiding from anything else.

Your challenge is to avoid standing out in the sensor display. If your pursuer has a conventional scope you do that with camouflage; if he has a thermal imager you'll need to adapt your techniques, but the basic aim is the same.

Hiding from a thermal imager follows the same basic principles as hiding from anything else. Your challenge is to avoid standing out in the sensor display.

If your pursuer has a conventional scope you do

that with camouflage; if he has a thermal imager you'll need to adapt your techniques, but the basic aim is the same.

## Hide Behind Things

A thermal imager is like any other sensor; it can't see you if you're hiding behind something that blocks the signal it detects. The thermal radiation you give off can penetrate some things that would hide you from visual detection, but it can't penetrate everything.

If you're moving across country, use the ground. No imager can see through a hill or rolling ground, so if you can put terrain between you and it, you're invisible. Solid walls will conceal you, too.

Stud partitions or drywall won't reliably block your body heat, and some military systems can see through a single layer of brick, but a brick cavity wall or masonry is enough to hide you.

Be careful with vegetation. Light brush or grass won't block your body heat, but heavy undergrowth will. If you're deep enough in the woods you're also safe from detection – from ground level, at least.

An airborne thermal camera, looking down, can see through a light forest canopy. On the other hand, old trees with a dense canopy can conceal you from all but the most sophisticated military imagers.

## Block Your Body Heat

If you trap heat, the imager can't detect it. Unfortunately, if you trap all your body heat, you're at risk of overheating and becoming a casualty. However, the less heat you're radiating the closer the imager has to be before you stand out enough to be detected. Just wearing a field jacket instead of short sleeves can cut the imager's range by five to ten percent, and every little helps.

Bare skin stands out more clearly than clothing, so minimize it.

Some people have suggested that wearing a wetsuit will hide you from a thermal imager. It won't. The problem is that the suit will quickly warm up until it's at the same temperature as your body.

An oversuit made of space blankets won't hide you either, but these lightweight sheets do have some uses.

They reflect heat, and any that's reflected back towards you won't reach the imager to reveal your position. Turning the blankets into clothing has the same problem as a wetsuit; they'll quickly warm up. If you use them as a liner in your shelter, however, they'll cut down the heat that escapes and can slice a good chunk off the imager's range. Think about where and how you shelter. Under a tent or shelter half you'll stand out clearly on thermal; in a cave you won't. If you're in the woods, a shelter with a roof of branches and dense brush will dramatically reduce the range you can be detected at; if you can put a layer of soil on top you'll cut it even more.

In winter thermal imagers are extremely effective, because they're scanning for warm objects on a uniform cold background – but you can turn that against them. Snow is a great insulator, so if you dig a snowhole in a drift, then shelter inside that, you'll be very well concealed.

## Match Your Background

It's very difficult to precisely match your background as a thermal imager sees it; different materials radiate heat in different ways, and you'll never be able to disguise yourself as a rock.

However, temperature contrasts make things a lot more obvious. If your background is close to body temperature you'll be much less obvious, and while you won't be invisible the detection range will fall.

On sunny days look for backgrounds that absorb heat, like brick walls or bare earth, and try to stay between those and locations where you think an imager is likely to be.

Use sources of heat. If you need a place to hide, and a nearby building has an air vent that's pumping out hot air, sit under it. The whole area will be above ambient temperature, and that can help mask your body heat.

Stay near water, especially in warm weather. If there's a lot of moisture in the air it will hold a surprising amount of heat, and this will help to reduce your contrast.

Your best chance of hiding in the open is against a confused background. On a uniform background like snow or an empty parking lot you'll stand out clearly.

If there are lots of different materials, all radiating heat at different rates and wavelengths, the imager's picture will be more confused and you stand a much better chance of blending in. Thermal imagers aren't magic; they just look at the world in a different way. If the picture the operator is looking at is a mess you're going to be much harder to pick out.

In an emergency, set things on fire. Multiple heat sources will confuse the picture and give you a chance of slipping away. And, while smoke generally won't block the picture, if you burn the right things it can help.

The military use white phosphorous or rubber-impregnated smoke shells to block thermal pictures, because they fill the air with burning particles and create a wall of heat that's opaque to the imager. If you can burn stuff that throws off lots of soot and burning particles, that will seriously cut down the imager's range.

Old tires can fill the air with dense, hot black smoke. Shredded paper will put up burning fragments. The fires themselves will be very obvious, but the messy picture they create might give you the chance you need to slip away.

## Use the Crossover

There are two times in the day when thermal imagers don't work very well; just after sunrise, and again just after sunset. These periods are called *thermal crossover*, and the change from day to night conditions dramatically reduces contrast in a thermal imaging view.

It's very hard to predict how long thermal crossover will last. On a bright sunny day it can be a few seconds, which is useless to you, but if the weather's overcast it can last several minutes.

High humidity will extend the length of crossover, and so will wind. If you have your own thermal imager you can check to see if crossover is having an influence – but be aware that military imagers will overcome the effect faster than commercial ones.

## A few Don'ts

- Wetsuits, drysuits, and Arctic clothing won't work
- Lining your clothes with space blankets won't work either
- Thermal imagers aren't like infrared security lights; moving very slowly won't hide you
- Hiding behind glass is not effective – and many military systems combine thermal and optical imaging, so they can see through glass anyway.

There's no doubt that hiding from a thermal imager is difficult.

Don't give up, though; with some knowledge you can reduce the sensor's detection range, and that can give you the edge you need to stay concealed. A thermal imager isn't an all-seeing, Godlike adversary; it's just a camera with some special tricks, and it can be fooled.

OTHER PROJECTS TO DO IN YOUR BACKYARD

# How To Make A Mini Root Cellar In Your Backyard

**MEDIUM DIFFICULTY    2 HOURS**

When it comes to off grid food storage the root cellar is really hard to beat. You are using the naturally consistent temperature of the earth to turn a simple hole in the yard into a climate-controlled food storage area.

In the past root cellars would have been dug out of the ground or a hill side. These large, often framed, cellars served as a great place to store produce, grains, curing meats and aging cheeses.

Thanks to modern technology we no longer have to dig giant holes in our yard to create a root cellar. Using plastic barrels or galvanized steel barrels you can dig a much smaller hole and bury your produce for as long as 6 months!

In this chapter we are going to walk you through the process of making your own mini root cellar in your backyard in less than 2 hours!

### Understanding the Frost Line

When temperatures drop below freezing plants die. We all watch in horror as our gardens go limp and the growing season ends after that first frost. However, at a certain depth the world remains unfrozen. This frost line is mapped out across the nation because it is also an important bit of information for builders and engineers.

If you store food below the frost line of your area, then you will be able to store that food for the long term without refrigeration.

## How the Root Cellar Works

You will layer your vegetables or fruits between layers of straw or sand. These layers are what will keep your vegetables from touching each other and will keep them cool and delicious for months at a time. Since the storage area is below the frost line, you will keep a consistent temperature and that is great for shelf life. Below the frost line you will not be able to freeze your vegetables which would ravage the food in the root cellar.

The root cellar works off a consistent temperature range that exists below the frost line in your area.

## Materials

To make your own root cellar, you'll need these materials:
- Barrel (galvanized steel or plastic)
- Drill and screws or hammer and nails
- Shovel
- Rocks
- Straw
- Plywood

### Process

1. Start by identifying the frost line for your area. This way you will know how deep you are going to dig your holes.
2. Locate an area that will not be bothered by digging, dogs or little kids.
3. Begin digging a hole that is large enough in width to accommodate your barrel.
4. I would recommend galvanized for dry areas and plastic barrels for wet areas near the water table.
5. Dig the hole deep enough that the lid to your barrel is at or below the frost line.
6. Place a layer of flat rocks at the bottom of your hole to set the barrel on top of.
7. Once the barrel is installed you can place a thick layer of sand or straw.
8. Your first bunch of vegetables will be layered on top of this and then you can continue to add layers of straw or sand followed by produce.
9. Once your barrel is full you are simply going to cover everything with a layer of straw or sand and then the lid.
10. Bury the entire root cellar.
11. If you want this to be a convert food source you might consider seeding the ground with grass. Otherwise come back to your root cellar as more food is needed.

Beyond temperature we must also consider humidity when it comes to storing produce. Different fruits and vegetables will take to humidity differently. Heat rises, even in small spaces, so variability will exist in your barrels.

If you find you have issues with humidity you can store a small sack of rice in the top of your root cellar to absorb the moisture.

### Onions

Store onions in a cool, dry root cellar with temperatures of 32—35°F (0—1°C) and 60—70% humidity after you shock them. Shock them by bending or snapping the green stems one month before harvest. You can store peas with onions.

### Potatoes

Regular potatoes and sweet potatoes need to be stored separately. Regular potatoes should be kept at 38—40°F (3—4°C) and 80—90% humidity. Sweet potatoes should be kept at 50—55°F (10—13°C) with 80—90% humidity.

### Dried Beans

Dried beans need to be kept cool and dry, at temperatures between 32—50°F (0—10°C) 60—70% humidity.

### Pumpkins and Squash

Pumpkins and squash can be stored together in a warm, dry root cellar. Temperatures should be kept between 50—55°F (10—13°C) with 60—75% humidity.

### Apples and Pears

Store apples and pears in a cold, moist root cellar with temperatures of 32—40°F (0—4° C) in 80—90% humidity.

STORE FRUITS AND VEGETABLES IN SEPARATE CONTAINERS BECAUSE FRUITS CONTAIN ETHYLENE WHICH WILL CAUSE VEGETABLES TO ROT.

The root cellar is ancient technology. It's time tested. Of course, we can improve upon it with an understanding of the process and modern technologies like plastics and metal. These micro root cellars are both easy to set up and can be employed in any sized backyard.

Self-sufficiency is not only for people on 40 acres! With processes like this you can quickly expand your ability to store more of the food you grow each year. Give this project a try and you might wind up with a backyard full of food both above and underground!

## How Long Will Food Keep in the Root Cellar

The fruits and vegetables you store will all vary in shelf life. Root vegetables are going to store the longest and greens are going to store for the shortest duration.

In some areas root vegetables can be stored for the entire winter season.

- Beets: 3—5 months
- Brussels sprouts: 3—5 weeks
- Cabbage: 3—4 months
- Carrots: 4—6 months
- Cauliflower: 2—4 weeks
- Celery: 2—3 months
- Endive: 2—3 weeks
- Kale: 10—14 days
- Leeks: 1—3 months

OTHER PROJECTS TO DO IN YOUR BACKYARD

# How To Make Bio Fuel At Home From Leaves And Manure

**COMPLEX DIFFICULTY**

This project is one that will surely help you with your savings and, of course, will also help the environment in several ways.

You will learn how to produce flammable gas from dry leaves and manure.

### What Is Biogas?

Biogas is a mixture of methane ($CH_4$) and carbon dioxide ($CO_2$); it is a renewable source of energy.

13.15hold waste.

Some feedstock like cow dung (manure) is also required to initiate the process, as it builds the methanogenic bacteria that convert this organic matter into biogas.

This biogas production also gives a byproduct called *digestate* or *slurry*, which is a type of organic manure for plants.

### Reasons for Making Your Own Fuel

Here are some of the most important reasons why you should add this project to your list:

- It helps you save money, because you no longer need to depend on the regular LPG cylinders or gas pipelines for cooking.
- It makes it easy for you to handle household waste, like food scraps, fallen leaves, and other organic materials.
- It provides you with free organic and nutrient-rich manure for your garden.
- It gives you the chance to be part of solving environmental issues like global warming, soil erosion because you would not be sending your household waste to the landfill sites.

We will be building a simple miniature biogas plant for your home.

## Materials Required

You will need:
- a plastic barrel or a plastic bucket along with a lid;
- 1-inch wide/4-inch long PVC pipe;
- 1-inch wide/10-inch long PVC pipe;
- 5 inch wide/18 inches long PVC pipe;
- 25-inches wide elbow pipe;
- a reducer, a hose barb, a hose barb tee;
- 12-inches + 20-inches long gas tube (can be transparent too);
- a gas valve, a plastic bottle, Teflon tape, clay (or hardener and resin);
- 4-pipe clips;
- PVC solvent cement.

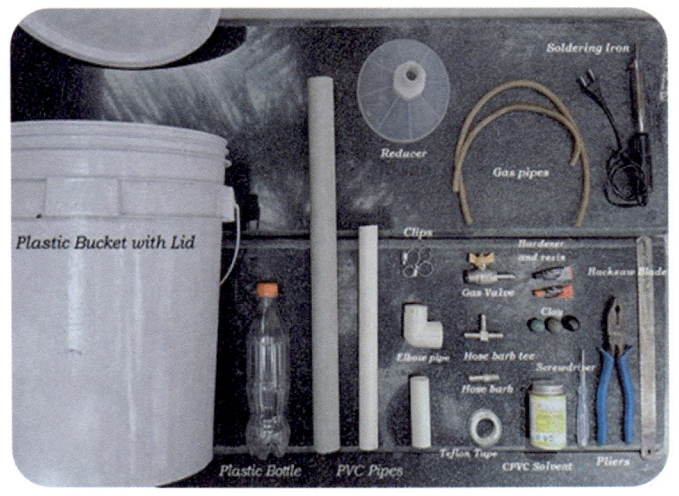

**Extras:** For soaking the dry leaves and mixing manure with water, we will need two more buckets.

And if you live in a place where the temperature is not between 75oF and 95oF, then you need black paint to paint your digester.

It will help to trap the heat, which is required to produce a good amount of gas.

## Tools Needed

As far as tools go, you will need:
- Hacksaw blade;
- Pliers;
- Screwdriver;
- Soldering iron.

## Making Your Own Bio Fuel

Before we begin to build this project, here is a basic diagram of a biogas plant.

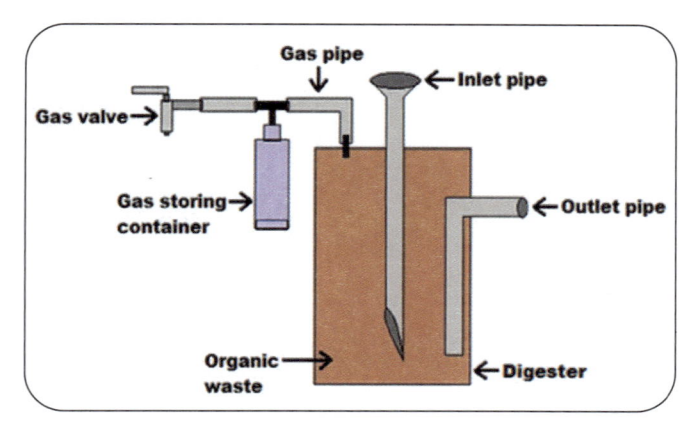

### Step 1: Making the Inlet Pipe

First, let's make the inlet pipe, from where we will add the raw materials and the feedstock. To build this intel pipe, follow the steps below:

- Take a 1.5 inch wide/18 inches long PVC pipe and cut one of its ends using a hacksaw blade. 
- Then make a hole a little bit more than 1.5 inches in the lid of the bucket with the help of soldering iron.
- Now, insert this pipe into this hole. Keep the pipe about 2-3 inches above the bottom of the bucket. 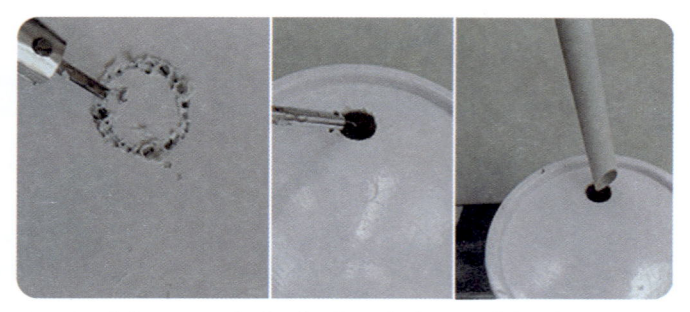
- And fix it with the help of clay and PVC cement.

### Step 2: Making the Outlet Pipe

The outlet pipe is that pipe from where the digestate or the slurry will come out. To build this outlet pipe, follow the steps below:

- First, make a 1.30-inch wide hole on the side of the bucket (2-3 inches below the bucket's brim) with the help of the soldering iron.
- Then insert a 1.25-inch elbow pipe in this hole. 
- Now fix a 1-inch wide/10-inch long PVC pipe in this elbow pipe's inner side (inside the bucket).
- Then put a 1-inch wide/4-inch long PVC pipe on the other end of the elbow pipe (outside the bucket). 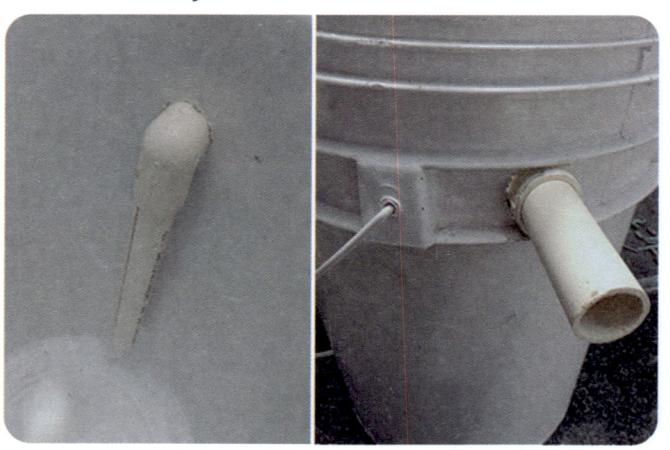
- And fix both joints with the PVC cement.

### Step 3: Making the Gas Outlet Setup

In this step, we will make the setup for taking out the produced gas.
To build this gas outlet setup, follow the steps below:

- First, make a small hole on the bucket's lid with the help of soldering iron.
- Then wrap some Teflon tape around the neck of the hose barb.
- Then insert this hose barb in the hole using pliers.
- Finally, fix this hose barb using clay and PVC cement.

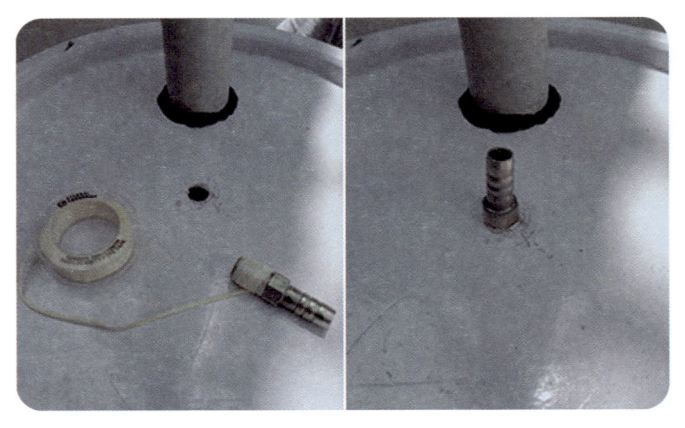

### Step 4: Making the Setup for Storing the Gas

Now we will make the setup for storing the produced gas. For this setup, follow the steps below:

- First, wrap some Teflon tape around the bottle's neck and then close the cap.
- Then apply some clay and PVC cement around the bottle's neck.
- After that, make a small hole on the bottle's cap using the soldering iron. 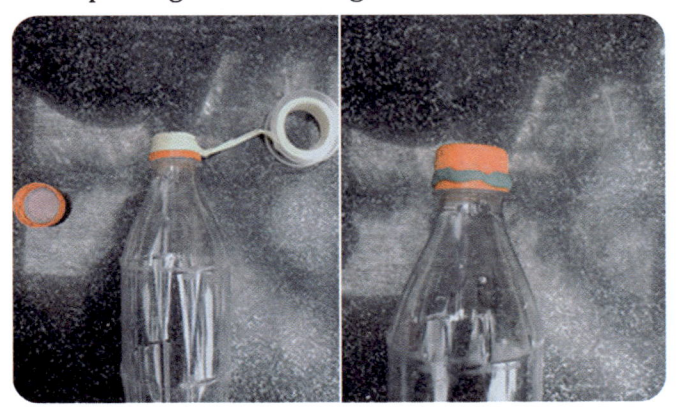
- Then wrap Teflon tape around the hose barb tee.
- Then fix this hose barb tee in the hole at the bottle's cap using clay and PVC cement. 
- Now connect a 12-inch gas tube at one end of the hose barb tee. And the other end to the hose barb (on the bucket's lid).
- Then fix both the connections using pipe clips and a screwdriver. 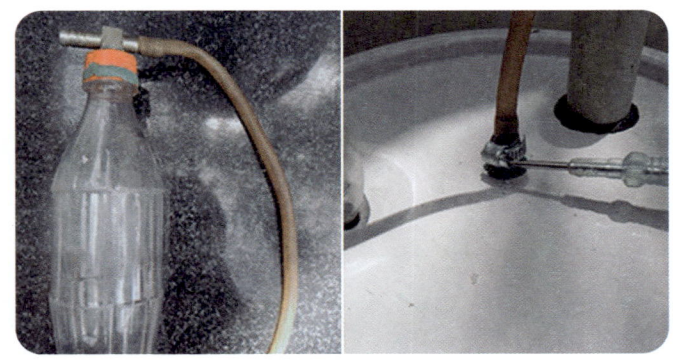
- After that, add some clay balls at the bottom of the bottle.
- Now fix this bottle on the bucket's lid.
- Finally, take a gas valve and connect it with a 20-inch gas tube using a clip.
- Then connect another end of this gas tube to the hose barb tee with a clip.
- Now close the bucket's lid. And apply some clay and PVC cement to make it airtight.

The miniature biogas plant setup is ready now, and it's time to bring it to work.

## The Process of Making Gas

Follow the steps below to start producing your homemade biogas:

- First, put a small basket of dry leaves in a half-filled bucket of water.
- Then put ⅓ part of manure in ⅔ portion of the water in another bucket of about 10 liters. And then mix well.
- After two days, they will look similar to the pictures below.

Soaked leaves

Cow dung mixture in water

♦ Then pour these soaked leaves with water and the mixture of manure into the digester.

**When Will the Biogas Be Produced?**

Usually, it takes about 3 to 30 days to produce gas, depending upon the type and the richness of the feedstock used.

After a day or two, you may see some vapors in the bottle. And in about 3-5 days these vapors will get collected in the bottle. And as soon as vapors reach up to 2-3 inches, you may use it.

But for a constant and abundant supply, you need to wait until the bottle is at least half-filled or fully filled. If the bottle gets completely filled, use a bigger bottle. So you may stock gas for later use.

## SAFETY AND PRECAUTIONS

For the proper building and functioning of this project, you need to take several required precautions:

- ♦ Risk of fire: Biogas contains about 50% to 70% methane gas, which is odorless, colorless and highly flammable. Therefore, you should not keep any electric or fire equipment near the biogas plant. 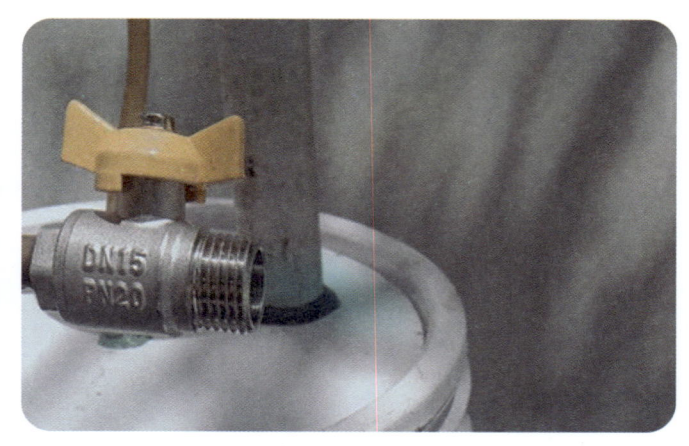
- ♦ Suffocation: Methane is a suffocating gas, which means it may suffocate you in an enclosed place. Therefore, you should keep the biogas plant in a well-ventilated area.
- ♦ Disease: Manure contains bacteria and germs that may infect you. So, you should wear safety equipment like gloves and a mask while handling it.
- ♦ Keep the whole setup away from the reach of children and animals.
- ♦ Do not use greywater for the biodigester. It may kill the methanogenic bacteria that produce biogas.
- ♦ Do not directly use the slurry from the outlet pipe as manure for plants, because it might contain bacteria or pathogens. Instead, reuse it as a feedstock for the digester or put it in the compost bin for further decaying. And then you can use it.
- ♦ Make sure that all joints are well sealed. If you smell any gas around the biogas plant, immediately repair it using clay or PVC solvent.

OTHER PROJECTS TO DO IN YOUR BACKYARD

# How To Make Your Own Toilet Paper

**MEDIUM DIFFICULTY**

The year 2020 is going to go down in history as one of the most difficult years that our combined generations have lived through.

We have yet to see what the final death toll from COVID-19 is going to be.

But there's another toll that will have to be tallied as well; that's the effect that months of a shutdown are going to have on the national and global economy. Are we going to end up in a global depression?

But probably the most memorable thing that the year 2020 will be known for, more than even the pandemic, is as the year of the Great American Toilet Paper Shortage.

For some unknown reason, the panic associated with the COVID-19 pandemic has sparked a run on toilet paper, even though it is a respiratory disease and not a gastrointestinal one.

We may never know what has caused the Great American Toilet Paper Shortage; but we're going to have to live with it.

That either means getting up at a ridiculous hour of the morning, in order to stand in line outside the grocery store, watching the sun rise and hoping that the store will have received some toilet paper overnight.

If luck is with you, you'll only have to do that once; but if not, you may have to do it several days in a row, in order to get your hands on some of those precious rolls.

That almost sounds a bit like a craps game; you pay your money and you take your chances. On the other hand, you can go with one of the other options out there.

Some people are touting the idea of using cloth and leaves, in place of toilet paper.

After all, we haven't always had toilet paper to use and people had to use something.

I decided to take matter into my own hands and make my own toilet paper.

### What's it Going to Take?

If you're someone who collects newspapers for recycling, you're in great shape. You already have the number one ingredient you need, so that you can make your own toilet paper.

While you can use other kinds of paper to make your TP, newsprint will break down easier and produce a softer paper.

## Materials Needed

Besides newspapers, you're going to need:
- More newspapers;
- Water;
- Bucket;
- Paper shredder;
- Electric mixer;
- Plastic storage bin;
- Frame to fit in the storage bin;
- Screen material;
- Staple gun;
- Putty knife;
- Something to cut your TP with;
- Something to roll your TP on.

## Making Your Own Toilet Paper

The first thing we need to do, in order to turn that newspaper into toilet paper, is to break the newspaper down.

This can be easily done with water, especially if you give that water a little mechanical help.

1. Shred the newspaper with a paper shredder. The smaller your paper shredder shreds the paper, the better.
   If you don't have a paper shredder, you can cut or tear the newspaper into strips; but it might need to soak in water longer.

2. Place your shredded newspaper in the bucket and cover it with water. You only need enough water to barely cover the shredded newspaper. Any more is a waste.
3. Allow the newspaper to sit in the water for 24 hours.
4. Using an electric mixer, chop up the wet newspaper, making it into pulp.

While your newspaper is soaking, it's a good time to make your screen frame. It needs to be as big as possible, but still sit in the bottom of your plastic storage bin.

I used 1"x 2" pine for this, but you can use wider boards if you want to.

There are a number of different ways you can assemble this frame, but the easiest way is to make butt joints in the corners and pin them with dowels, as I show in the video.

The reason I chose to dowel the corners of the frame was that glue doesn't stick well to end grain. This frame is going to sit in water and I don't want the joint to loosen up.

Screws don't work well into end grain either, although nails do. So you could choose to nail it, but it's just as easy to use dowel pins.

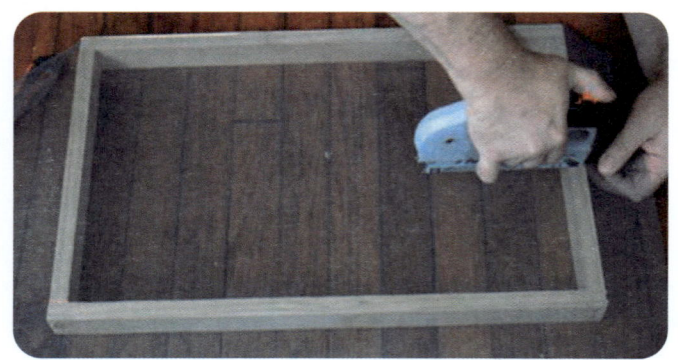

To dowel a joint of this type, first clamp the two parts making the corner of the frame, so that they are positioned properly, with the edges flush.

Then drill two holes of the appropriate size for the dowel being used. I used 3/8" dowels, so I drilled my holes with a 23/64" drill bit, drilling through the lap board, into the end grain of the other board. I made sure to drill the holes deeper than the length of the dowels.

With the holes drilled, I spread glue into the splines cut into the sides of the dowel pins with my finger. I then placed them in the holes and drove them flush with a wood mallet. Once all the corners were properly pinned together, I set the frame aside to dry.

Finally, staple screening material onto one side of the frame, working from the center outwards.

It doesn't need to be as tight as what you would do for a window, but it should be flat and smooth. If your staples don't go all the way in, hammer them flush with the top of the wood, so that they will grip the screening properly.

Now that your newspaper pulp and your frame are ready, it's time to make the toilet paper.

5. Place your frame into the bin and fill it with water. Ideally, the water should come to just below the top of the frame.
6. Scoop up a portion of the newspaper pulp, roughly equal to two cups (the quantity isn't exact, as your bin might be a different size than mine) and put it in the water, mixing it with the water and spreading it out to fill the entire area.

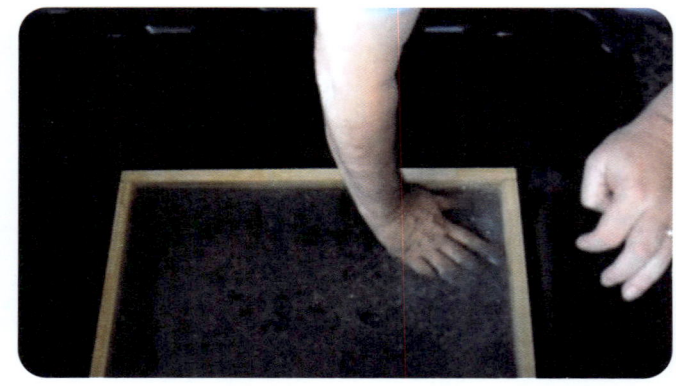

7. Slowly lift the frame out of the water, looking to see, as the water drains out, that the shredded newspaper pulp is evenly spread across the entire are of the screening.
8. Allow as much water as possible to drain out of the newspaper pulp.

Now we need to dry the pulp, allowing it to bond back together and turn into paper.

9. Set up an ironing board and cover it with a piece of absorbent cloth. An old towel will work. Place the frame, screen side down, on top of this cloth. 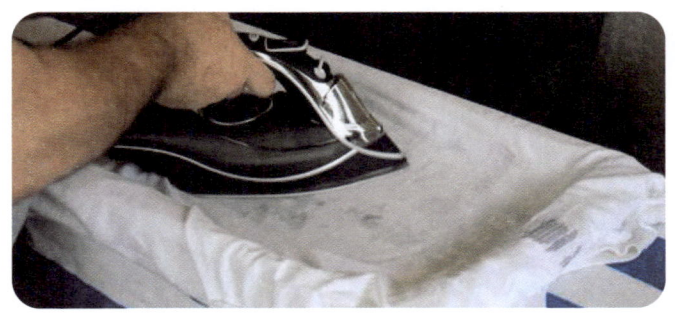
10. Place another absorbent, but smooth cloth on top of the newspaper pulp inside the frame. An old T-shirt will work.
11. Using a clothes iron, set for ironing cotton, iron the cloth, heating the newspaper pulp and drawing the moisture out of it. You're trying to do two things here; one is to draw the moisture out, and the other is to flatten the surface of the paper. If you don't iron it, you're going to end up with some rather scratchy paper.
12. Place the frame in the sun to finish drying. You could try drying it all the way with the iron, but that will take a long time.

With the paper dry, we're ready to make it usable in the bathroom.

13. Take a wide putty knife, preferably a plastic one, and use it to break your sheet of toilet paper free of the frame around the edges. Be careful not to cut through the screen, so that you can reuse it. 
14. Flip the frame over so that the screen side is up and push down gently on the screen, all around the edges. This should break the paper free from the screen. Continue through the middle of the paper as well.
15. Flip the frame back over, paper side up and work one corner of your paper free, then pull up the rest, taking care not to tear it. 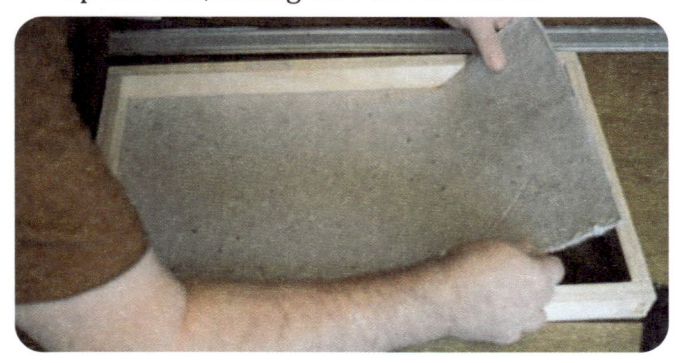
16. Measure the paper, marking it to the width of a toilet paper roll. If you don't have any toilet paper rolls to put your homemade TP on, you can cut paper towel or wrapping paper rolls down to four-inch segments.
17. Roll the paper onto the cardboard tube, overlapping pieces over each other.

Your finished toilet paper is going to be thicker than store-bought, even though it is only one single ply.

That means you can use less of it, which I'd recommend, considering that it's a bit harder to make than just going to the store and buying a four-pack of Charmin. But then, if you could do that, you wouldn't need to make your own.

PROJECTS ON SEEDS, HERBS, AND NATURAL REMEDIES

# DIY Mason Jar Soil Test

**EASY** DIFFICULTY **10 MINUTES**

Have you ever wondered what the structure of your garden soil is? It would help when making decisions on what and where you might plant, as well as amending the structure of your soil.

This test is so easy that I recommend doing it each year before creating a garden plan.

The results of the test could determine how much fertilizer you use or what changes you should make to the soil, depending on what you plan to grow in your garden.

It comes down to the number of various particles and components that make up your soil. The shapes and sizes of each group of particles determine the soil's structure and how well it will work for growing your garden. A good understanding of the soil and its components will lead to a more successful year of growth.

## Understanding the Basic Components of Soil

Most soil contains 3 components: sand, silt, and clay. Each region and area will have a different structure of these 3 components. In fact, different areas within your own property could vary quite a bit from one area to another.

### Clay

This is the smallest of the 3 mineral components. It consists of tiny and flat particles that fit together and often creates the biggest area of soil in many areas.

Clay consists of necessary nutrients and works well for storing water. So, having a large amount of clay can work in your favor, unless you have an abundance of rain in a season.

It's also a cooler soil that takes longer to warm up in the spring.

### Sand

The largest particle making up soil is sand. These particles are round, which allows more space between particles. As a result, water will drain more quickly from sandy soil than one of more clay. Another downside is that the nutrients drain right along with it. For gardens with a large amount of sand, it will require more fertilizer and water than soil consisting of more clay.

### Silt

The size of silt particles is between clay and sand, but closer to clay. Soil that consists of a large amount of silt is typically found along riverbanks. This soil feels smooth while moist, yet powdery when it's dry.

A good combination of all 3 of these particles is referred to as loam soil. And, it's the best type of soil for gardening. To obtain loam, you need to know what you currently have, so you can make adjustments. So, grab a mason jar!

## The Mason Jar Soil Test

Start with a clean and empty jar, such as a mason jar, including the lid.

It could be either quart or pint size. You just need a jar with lid, soil, and water.

1. Fill the jar halfway with soil.
2. Add water. Fill to about 1" from the top and put the lid on.
3. Shake the contents for a few minutes.
4. Set the jar aside for a few hours. As the content settles, it will separate into layers of silt, sand, and clay.

What you should see in a few hours:

- At the bottom, you will see the heaviest layer, consisting of sand and rocks;
- The next layer will consist of silt;
- Next will be the layer of clay.

You should also see some organic matter floating at the water's surface. Also, keep in mind that the color of the soil is indicative of the amount of organic material within it.

The lighter it is, the less there will be. Dark soil holds more organic matter and will warm quicker in the spring.

### Reading the Results

Once you have done the test, you need to know what it all means and if you have the desired loam soil.

- Loam – 40% sand, 40% silt, and 20% clay;
- Silty Clay Loam – 60% silt, 30% clay, and 10% sand;
- Sandy Loam – 65% sand, 20% silt, and 15% clay;
- Silty Loam – 65% silt, 20% sand, and 15% clay.

So, knowing that loam soil is ideal, what amendments could you do to achieve it?

### Sandy Soil

A good way to amend a sandy soil is to add compost or manure. This is probably the fastest way to get it to a loamy state.

However, both compost and manure contain significant amounts of salt, and high levels of salt can be damaging to plants.

So, if you already have high levels of salt in the soil, such as seaside gardens, use a plant-only based compost.

### Silty Soil

You can amend silty soil by tilling in 1" Cocopeat to break up clay particles to help with aeration, 2" of Perlite to help with drainage, and 4" of compost to help with water retention.

### Clay Soil

For the same reasons as above with silty soil, till in the same ingredients, but adjust the amount to 1" Cocopeat, 4" of Perlite, and 6" of compost.

My test resulted in about 50% sand, 40% silt, and maybe 10% clay. So, I have fairly good soil in that area. But, to get my perfect soil, I would do a combination of the sandy and silty soil amendments listed above. Or, because it's so close to the desired loam, I could just add fertilizer and water more often.

However, the area I tested is where we normally put a few annuals. We plan on planting a large produce garden on the other side of the house next year, and that will most likely have a completely different test result.

Therefore, it's important to do a different test for every area you intend to plant a garden.

Hopefully, this helps in getting you closer to the perfect soil for your garden. No more excuses! Well, except for maybe pesky critters that you will need to keep at bay.

PROJECTS ON SEEDS, HERBS, AND NATURAL REMEDIES

# DIY Survival Garden

No matter if you're planning to start a survival garden out of necessity, prepare for the worst times, or become more self-reliant, you'll love the security these gardens offer.

Homegrown produce boasts better flavors and is more nutritious than grocery store fruits and vegetables. History shows that people have planted survival gardens during the war, economic instability, and famine. Survival gardens assure you that you and your family can easily make it through hard times.

Survival gardens provide access to healthy, readily available food at budget-friendly prices. Do you know how to start growing your survival garden? Here's an easy-to-understand guide to starting your survival garden in your backyard.

## Why You Should Grow a Survival Garden

Homeowners often worry about day-to-day shopping for essentials and amenities. Going per week or even monthly can be too troublesome for some people. That's why Survival Gardens are the perfect solution.

The ability to harvest fresh produce from your backyard is an ideal way of filling up your pantry so that you can enjoy delicious and fresh food. On top of that, a survival garden provides access to organic and nutritious veggies and fruits. Typically, these are superior in quality to week-old, conventionally grown store-bought food.

One advantage of survival gardens is that you can grow a diverse variety of delicious veggies that extend the life of the stored food supply. Moreover, gardening is a great way to connect with nature and spend meaningful time with your family. Plus, gardening helps you relieve stress, as well as ensures you stay fit and healthy. Enjoy breathing fresh air as you enjoy fresh greens rich in starchy carbohydrates and necessary vitamins and minerals.

## Design Your Survival Garden

Designing the structure of your survival garden is just as crucial as buying garden seeds. When it comes to deciding what type of garden seeds you should plant, it's always a better idea to seek open-pollinated seeds. These allow you to save your seeds and, ultimately, ensure that you always have stock for the year to come.

Keep in mind that a survival garden is more than simply a garden; it is the thin line keeping you healthy and happy during tough times. Plus, you need to consider more than merely eating crops. From preservation to trading, excess crops are beneficial.

There's always a chance that your crops may fail due to a disease or drought. Thus, you need to learn to think diversely. For this reason, you should plan perennials, as well as annuals. Consider planting trees, canes, bushes, herbs, and weeds. Moreover, add sun and shading loving plants to enjoy delicious veggies regularly.

### HOW BIG SHOULD IT BE?

When it comes to how big should your survival garden be, you'll have to consider a variety of different factors such as:

- The number of people in your family
- What kinds of crops will you be growing in your garden- some require more space than others
- What kind and quality of soil does your backyard boast?
- Also, what is your climate?
- Your gardening skills and experience
- The amount of time you must spend on gardening and, in turn, feeding your family.

While it's not possible to provide you with an exact number, you'll likely need a minimum of ¼ acre land for starting your survival garden. Depending on your family size and vegetable preferences, chances are, you may end up with a 2-acre expansive survival garden.

**PICK A SITE WITH LIGHT**

One additional tip to keep in mind when designing your survival garden is the location. Apart from factoring in the area and size, you'll have to make sure the garden allows adequate sunlight to enter. No matter if you're planting in the ground or pots, your spot should enjoy at least 8 to 12 hours of uninterrupted sunlight per day. A tree's shadow or structure can prevent the sprouting of certain plants.

The fact is that light is critical for the healthy growth of plants. Moreover, most plants are sensitive to interruptions in light. When designing your garden, test the spot from different angles and at a different time to ensure ideal light exposure.

**BE MINDFUL OF THE SEASON**

No need to grow tropical vegetables in early spring. Instead, focus on frost-tolerant plants. If you're not growing your plants indoors, you'll want to find out the date of your area's 'last frost. The garden elevation plays a significant role in determining frosts, freezes, and nighttime temperatures. Plants native to warm places such as peppers, tomatoes, and eggplants are not cold tolerant. Even the slightest frost will kill them.

That's why you must grow your tropical seedlings during comparatively warmer months or in a warm indoor space. Here's a small guide:

### Seeds to Sow During Early Spring
- Greens: lettuce, spinach, swiss chard, and kale
- Root crops: turnips, carrots, radishes, and beets
- Peas: snow peas and early peas

### Live plants to Sow during Early Spring
- Onion sets
- Hardy herb: thyme and rosemary
- Cruciferous vegetable seedlings: cabbage, broccoli, and cauliflower

# Important Crops for Your Survival Garden

Here's a list of plants to consider growing in your survival garden:

- Corn
- Spinach
- Potatoes
- Onions
- Beans
- Peas
- Tomatoes
- Cucumbers
- Winter Squash
- Lettuce
- Sunflower Seed
- Cilantro.

When growing crops is near impossible during the colder months, you'll have to preserve and store produce. For this reason, you'll have to learn how to cook, keep, and store vegetables for later use. Freezing, dehydrating, and canning are the top couple of ways to preserve your favorite foods for the colder months.

When drought or food insecurity hits you, the first thought that pops into your mind is providing your family with proper food, shelter, and water. That's exactly what a survival garden offers. However, keep in mind that a survival garden isn't all sunshine and rainbows. You may face failure, limited space, limited resources, and difficulty protecting it from critters and plant diseases. However, keeping your goal at the forefront ensures you're always motivated and level-headed. Allow your dreams to inspire you always to keep moving forward.

PROJECTS ON SEEDS, HERBS, AND NATURAL REMEDIES

# DIY Wall-Hanging Herb Garden

MATERIAL COST $ 68.00   MEDIUM DIFFICULTY   3 HOURS

Gardening is primarily dependant on the amount of space that you have for your garden. With food security being top of mind, establishing a garden to grow your food is a critical component of off-grid living. The problem is that you will be limited by the amount of available ground available for planting.

The solution is to build a garden vertically, utilizing the unused space above the ground. One of the easiest and best places to do this is to use the backyard fences surrounding most people's backyards.

The location you choose for building a hanging herb garden will depend largely on what herbs you want to plant. Each plant has different sunlight and shade requirements along with soil types and watering. The first step is to formulate a list of herbs and other plants you want to grow as a part of your long-term food security plans. Following this, you must research each herb and determine the precise requirements for them.

After this research, you can plan where on your property would be best for each plant and from there, you can come up with a plan for where you will build a hanging herb garden and what you will be planting in it. You may need to create multiple hanging herb gardens to accommodate each plant.

## What to Plant in a Hanging Herb Garden

There are many herbs that you could plant in a hanging herb garden. But, of course, what you decide to plant is largely dependant on your area, tastes, and medical requirements. Still, the following herbs are being included as a starting point in designing your hanging herb garden:

◆ **Cilantro**
- It is a digestive aid and possibly removes heavy metals and other toxins from the body
- Been shown to have anticonvulsant properties, contains antioxidants, and has anti-inflammatory properties
- It also has antimicrobial properties.

◆ **Lemon Balm**
- Antispasmodic effect on the stomach
- It may help reduce stress and treat insomnia
- It has some anti-inflammatory properties.

◆ **Peppermint**
- Relieves indigestion
- It helps to treat colds and flu symptoms
- It can be used to treat headaches and migraines.

◆ **Cayenne**
- Rich in vitamins, minerals, and antioxidants
- Helps with blood clotting
- It can ease cold symptoms
- It might help with pain relief.

◆ **Aloe Vera**
- It helps to accelerate wound healing, especially helpful with burns
- Antioxidant and antibacterial.

◆ **Basil**
- Antioxidant
- It has been used to treat colds, especially inflammation in nasal passageways
- It may reduce high blood sugar.

◆ **Cloves**
- Clove oil is fantastic for treating toothaches
- When used as a mouth rinse, it can reduce inflammation and bacteria.

◆ **Lavender**
- It can improve sleep
- It may be effective at reducing pain
- Lavender can help reduce stress.

◆ **Garlic**
- It may reduce blood pressure and improve cholesterol levels
- Garlic may be effective in treating the common cold
- It has been used for centuries in the treatment of a variety of ailments.

- ◆ **Ginger**
  - It has been shown to help with relieving nausea
  - Ginger may help treat cold and flu symptoms
  - It may help reduce inflammation
  - A good source of antioxidants.
- ◆ **Sage**
  - Contains antioxidants
  - Possibly helps control blood sugar.
- ◆ **Feverfew**
  - It helps to treat migraines
  - o It May help ease the pain caused by arthritis.
- ◆ **Parsley**
  - It can be used to help with eye health because it is a source of vitamin A
  - Freshens breath
  - It may help to prevent heart disease
  - Parsley could be used to treat UTI's.
- ◆ **German Chamomile**
  - It can be used to treat anxiety
  - Often used as a sleep aid when made into tea.
  - It may have anti-inflammatory properties
  - It has been traditionally used to treat a wide variety of conditions.

## How to Use Herbs from Your Garden

Each herb that you will plant will be best utilized in specific ways, and it is essential to understand the methods for preparing them for use either medicinally or in recipes. Knowing which parts of the herb to use for different applications is also critical to effectively using a backyard hanging herb garden. There are multiple ways to prepare an herb for medicinal use.

A few examples of preparation methods are:
- ◆ Poultice – A paste made from the herb which is spread on the body using a moist cloth to promote healing.
- ◆ Tincture – A concentrated extract made from the herbs through soaking in alcohol or vinegar.
- ◆ Infused oil – Are made by infusing a carrier oil with an herb. These can be used in cooking, as the base for salves or balms, in soaps, or directly on the skin.
- ◆ Salves and Balms – Are made by combining herb-infused oil with a wax such as beeswax. These can then be applied directly to the skin.
- ◆ Teas – Are usually made from the dried leaves of your herbs steeped in hot water until you get the desired concentration.

It may seem daunting to make medicinal herbal products, but with a bit of research and practice, you will be able to treat a wide variety of ailments while also being able to spice up your cooking or baking.

## Building the Hanging Herb Garden

The construction of a hanging herb garden is not complicated but will depend on your fencing and the amount of space you have to work with. The dimensions that I have listed here are what worked for me and the area that I had available. You will need to adjust the sizes to suit your space and needs.

## Tools

You will need:
- ◆ Staple gun and staples
- ◆ Drill with bits and drivers
- ◆ Tape measure
- ◆ Level
- ◆ Saw
- ◆ Square

## Materials

As far as materials go, I used:
- ◆ Four pieces of 2 x 8 x 8' pressure treated lumber which is available at Home Depot for $ 12.68 USD.

www.homedepot.com/p/2-in-x-8-in-x-8-ft-2-Ground-Contact-Hem-Fir-Pressure-Treated-Lumber-549000102080800/206931771

- ◆ 5/8" x 5 ½" x 8' Cedar Fence picket, which you can find at Home Depot for $ 5.24 USD each.

www.homedepot.com/p/Alta-Forest-Products-5-8-in-x-5-1-2-in-x-8-ft-Western-Red-Cedar-Flat-Top-Fence-Picket-63028/205757691

- ◆ A roll of landscape fabric can be found at Home Depot for $ 29.98 USD per 100' roll.

www.homedepot.com/p/Vigoro-4-ft-x-100-ft-Polypropylene-Landscape-Fabric-Weed-Barrier-2239RV/311040977

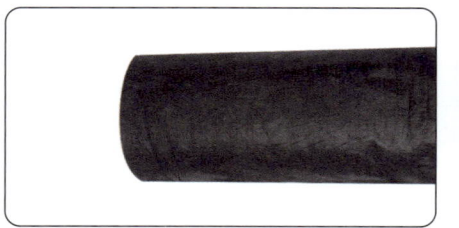

- #8 x 1 ½" Screws which are $ 8.78 USD per pack of 100 at Home Depot.
www.homedepot.com/p/Everbilt-8-x-1-1-2-in-Zinc-Plated-Phillips-Flat-Head-Wood-Screw-100-Pack-801842/204275487

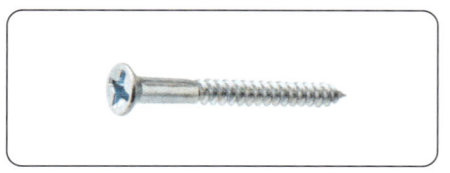

- Potting soil, which is $ 9.97 USD for a 25qt bag at Home Depot.
www.homedepot.com/p/Miracle-Gro-25-qt-Potting-Soil-Mix-72781431/206457033

## Instructions

Putting the garden together is a straightforward process. Still, as I stated earlier, the dimensions depend on the space you have available, so you will have to adjust the measurements that you see here for your area. I designed this hanging garden to make the best use of the lumber with minimal crops.

1. Measure the space and determine how you would like the hanging herb garden to be arranged. In my case, I chose one fence panel and arranged the garden beds in a checkerboard fashion.
2. Once you have determined the number of herb garden beds you need, you'll have to figure out how big each bed will be. In my case, I decided to build them 24 inches long by about 6 inches wide with a height of one board width. Depending on what you plan to grow, you may want to build your beds larger or deeper.
3. Cut the lumber for the beds. For the garden beds that I will use, I cut three pieces at 24 inches and two pieces at 6 7/8 inches.
4. If you are using nails, lay one of the 24" boards down and get a few nails started along one of the long edges.
5. Arrange a second 24" board underneath the first, with its edge directly underneath the nails, so they form an 'L' shape.
6. Repeat for the other side so you form a 'U' shape.
7. Nail the end caps on each end.
8. Repeat this for all of the required garden beds.
9. Cut some landscape fabric and line the inside of each of the beds, stapling them in place.
10. Trim the excess.
11. Cut the four pieces of pressure-treated lumber to the height of the fence.
12. Level and screw these pieces to the fence panel, keeping an appropriate spacing to achieve your desired pattern. In my case, I chose a 24-inch centre to centre spacing for each of the boards.
13. Layout where the planters will be mounted by drawing a line with your level at the heights you want the planters' top to be.
14. Mount each bed by drilling pilot holes then screwing them in place.
15. Fill the beds with soil and plant the herbs.

## Variations

There are a couple of variations that you could consider employing depending on the situation you find yourself in.

- Instead of installing the hanging herb garden on a fence, you could cut two boards so that they can lean against a fence or wall at an angle. Then, the planters can be screwed into the boards so that they form a ladder.
- The same style of hanging herb garden could be built and used indoors as well. The only issue would be dealing with any water that may be leaking out from the planters. In this instance, plastic planters with no drain holes may be more appropriate.
- Each of these planters can also be covered to form a mini greenhouse in the environmental situation warrants it.

A DIY hanging herb garden is a fantastic way to utilize the vertical space around your backyard, expanding your ability to grow herbs and vegetables, and take a further step towards food self-sufficiency.

# How To Make Cabbage Bandages To Treat Inflammation And Joint Pain

EASY DIFFICULTY

When I was a child, I didn't stay indoors much. I used to play with other kids in my neighborhood all day long. Of course, this meant injuries were an almost daily occurrence.

But I didn't care. I was just a kid doing things that every other kid did back then. Whenever I'd come back home, my mother would look at me and sigh, "Christ, not again…"

She would then prepare some cabbage leaves and wrap them around my wounds, using bandages to keep them in place.

After a time the swelling would go away, the bruises would be significantly reduced, and cuts would be almost completely healed. And that happened much faster than normal.

We weren't a wealthy family, so we couldn't afford to go to the doctor for every minor thing.

However, my parents were very knowledgeable about the natural remedies passed on by my grandfather.

For centuries, people all over the world have used cabbage leaves to successfully reduce swelling, pain, and strains.

It is high in vitamins and phytonutrients, as well as anthocyanins and glutamine; both of which have anti-inflammatory properties.

Furthermore, modern science shows that cabbage contains 2.6% to 5.7% sugars, 1.1% to 2.3% proteins, fixed oil, and mineral salts, including sulfur and phosphorus.

The plant also contains vitamin C and S-Methylmethionine, also known as vitamin U, which is antiulcer.

This makes it a very powerful and convenient tool against joint pain, arthritis, and most injuries.

## What You'll Need

Here is a list of everything you'll need:
- A cabbage (obviously);
- Bandages;
- Cellophane;
- A cup, hammer or rolling pin (basically anything that gets the job done);
- A cutting board.

## How to Make Cabbage Bandages

1. Place cabbage leaves (green or red) on a cutting board and cut out the hard stem.
2. Hammer the leaves with any kitchen utensil to gently bruise the leaves in order to release some of the cabbage juices.
3. Layer the cabbage leaves around the knee or ankle joint until it is completely encased with the leaves.
4. Hold the leaves in place by wrapping them with bandages.
5. Wrap all of this up with cellophane in order to hold the warmth and cabbage juice around the skin.
6. Leave the cabbage leaves wrapped around the joint for at least one hour.
   If no skin sensitivity is noted, the leaves can be left on overnight.
7. Unwrap the cabbage leaves when cool and discard.

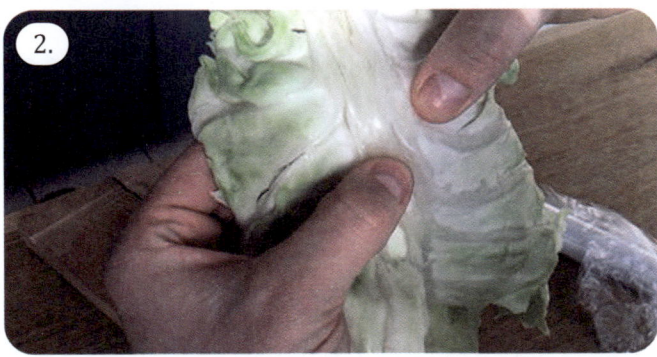

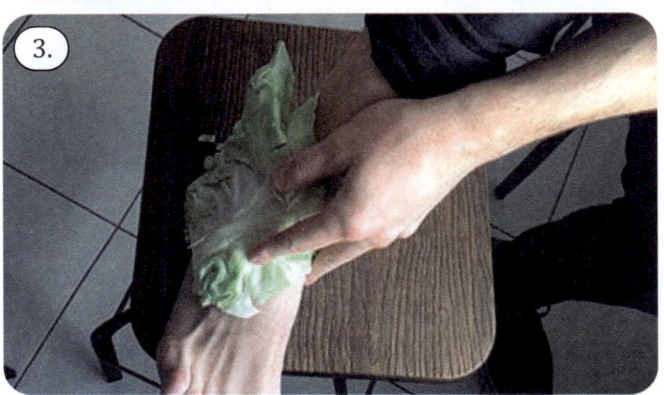

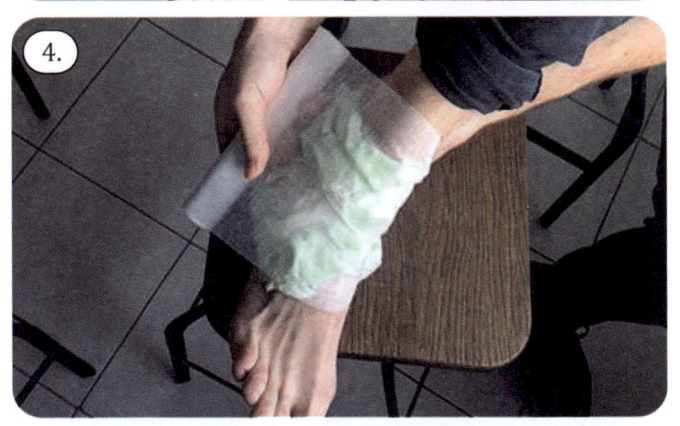

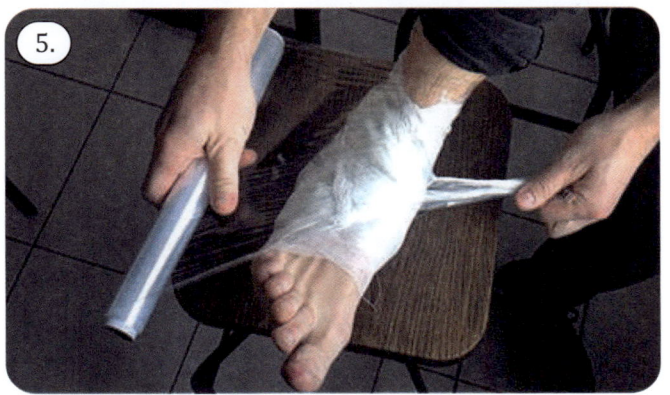

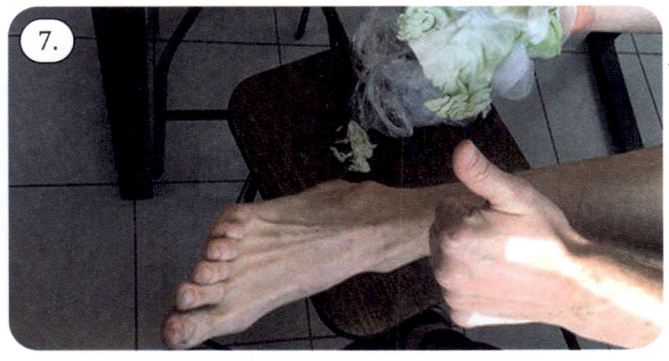

Here are some of the things cabbage bandages can help you out with:

**Eczema**

Use cabbage leaf bandages for about one hour.

**Asthma**

Apply four cabbage leaf bandages on the chest or shoulders for at least four hours.

**Arthritis**

Pound the cabbage leaves with any kitchen utensil you have on hand (even a simple cup) and apply it directly to the affected area.

Wrap it up in a bandage and cellophane to make sure it stays tight so that the skin absorbs the vital nutrients.

Leave it on for several hours and repeat this process until you see a huge improvement.

With all of these benefits, how can you not love cabbage? God has indeed blessed us and we can gain so much simply by studying his creation.

PROJECTS ON SEEDS, HERBS, AND NATURAL REMEDIES

# How To Make Moringa Powder

EASY ◁ DIFFICULTY

Numerous studies have already been conducted regarding the medicinal properties of moringa and it has been found to be beneficial for many conditions, ranging from skin diseases to hypertension, diabetes, kidney stones, tuberculosis, and even tumors.

In Ayurvedic medicine, moringa is cited to have the ability to treat more than 300 illnesses and diseases.

Aside from vitamins, moringa is also rich in minerals, antioxidants, and antibacterial and tissue protective properties.

The number of nutrients it contains is staggering: 92 nutrients, 46 antioxidants, 36 anti-inflammatories, 18 amino acids, and 9 essential amino acids!

So what does that mean for you? It means if you choose to incorporate moringa into your daily diet, your body will be able to:

◆ **Fight Free Radicals**

Free Radicals cause oxidative stress and cell damage. By fighting these, your organs will stay healthy and function optimally.

◆ **Fight Inflammation**

Moringa helps treating chronic diseases such as diabetes, arthritis, respiratory problems, and cardiovascular diseases while even reducing or avoiding obesity.

◆ **Protect Your Brain from Alzheimer's**

Moringa's antioxidants and neuro-enhancers improve cognitive function and support brain health.

◆ **Ward Off and Fight Infections**

Moringa's natural antimicrobial and antibacterial properties are effective against a host of microbes, bacteria, and fungi that are responsible for all kinds of infections.

◆ **Protect Your Liver**

Moringa's high concentrations of polyphenols and other antioxidants can protect your liver against toxins and oxidative damage.

◆ **Keep Your Skin Youthful and Radiant**

The antioxidants in moringa not only fight toxins and free radicals, but also shield your cells and tissues.

◆ **Improve Your General Health**

Indeed, nothing comes close to moringa when it comes to providing your body with nutrition, health, and beauty. The most convenient and enjoyable way to take moringa is by its powder form.

## Step-by-Step Guide on How to Make Moringa Powder

### 1. Harvest

If you have moringa trees in your backyard, simply harvest a bunch of stalks (about two pounds). You can also buy some at the market. Always opt for the mature, rich green leaves.

### 2. Sanitize

Sanitize a basin, pan, bowl, or any vessel that you can use to wash the leaves.

Sprinkle a few tablespoons of baking soda into the water to clean the dust and other impurities off the moringa leaves.

### 3. Cleanse

Wash the moringa leaves, removing dead and yellow leaves and any infected parts.

### 4. Hang

Shake the excess water off the leaves, tie the ends of the stalks together, and hang them upside down in an enclosed place that doesn't get direct sunlight, to preserve the nutrients.

### 5. Air Dry

Leave the leaves hanging for three to four days until they are brittle to touch.

### 6. Separate

Separate the leaves from the stalks and stems. The fewer stems there are, the smoother the powder will be.

### 7. Grind

You can use a blender to grind the moringa leaves into powder form.

Run from 30 seconds to a full minute or till you achieve the desired texture.

### 8. Store

Keep the moringa powder in an airtight container to preserve the nutrients and store it in a cool, dry place. Keep the container closed at all times to keep moisture out and to preserve a longer shelf life. The powder will last up to six months without preservatives. Now you're ready to try your moringa powder and experiment with a myriad of ways to enjoy it! You can make hot tea, cold tea, or iced tea out of it, or you can add it to your smoothies, shakes, and salads.

To make moringa tea, just add a teaspoon of moringa powder to hot water. You can also add peppermint leaves and lemon for flavor and sugar or honey to taste.

Here are some other ways to enjoy your moringa powder:

### Mangosteen Moringa Tea

A combination of mangosteen tea and moringa powder will yield a very strong antioxidant and antibacterial concoction. Mangosteen is an exclusive source of xanthones, which can inhibit cancer cell growth.

Simply add a teaspoon of moringa powder, along with some lemon and honey, to mangosteen tea, and you will have a very refreshing and healthy beverage.

### Moringa Chicken Soup

What you will need:
- ½ lb. cut chicken;
- 2/3 small slices of Fresh Ginger;
- Lemongrass leaves;
- Bell pepper;
- Table salt;
- 1 Tbsp. moringa powder.

1. Sautee the cut chicken on a few slices of ginger.
2. Add a cup or two of water and salt to taste; throw in the bell pepper and a few lemongrass leaves.
3. Bring to a boil until chicken is tender, then sprinkle moringa powder.

### Moringa Fish Soup

What you will need:
- 1/2 lb. fish;
- 2/3 small slices of Fresh Ginger;
- 1/2 cup coconut milk;
- 1 bell pepper;
- 1 tomato;
- 1 onion;
- Table salt;
- Moringa powder.

1. Fry fish and set aside.
2. Slice the onion, tomato, bell pepper, and ginger.
3. Boil two cups of water.
4. Add onion, ginger, bell pepper, fried fish, and salt to taste.
5. Boil for ten minutes more then add moringa powder and coconut milk.
6. Boil for 15 seconds more, then serve. Never boil coconut milk longer than 15 seconds or it will start to turn into oil.

### Moringa Lentil Curry Soup

What you will need:
- 2 teaspoons edible oil;
- 1/4 lb. pork, in cubes;
- 1 medium onion, diced;
- 1/2 Tbsp. grated fresh ginger;
- 1 Tbsp. curry powder;
- 1 cup baby carrots, grated;
- 1 cup lentil;
- salt to taste;
- a pinch of black pepper powder;
- 1 cup coconut milk.

1. Soak the lentil in some water an hour or two before cooking to reduce cooking time.
2. Preheat pan, then add oil.
3. Sautee onion till golden brown.
4. Add ginger and curry powder and stir for 30 seconds.
5. Add pork and salt to taste, stir for one to two minutes.
6. Add just a little water (about 1/4 cup) to keep the meat from being burnt.
7. Cook in slow fire, till meat is tender.
8. Add 2 cups water, bring to a boil.
9. Add lentils, more salt if needed, and pepper. Keep adding a little water as necessary.
10. When lentil is soft, add carrots and moringa powder.
11. Simmer for 2 minutes, then add coconut milk, then simmer for 30 seconds.

PROJECTS ON SEEDS, HERBS, AND NATURAL REMEDIES

# How To Make Your Own SHTF Medicinal Garden

There are several ways you can start your SHTF garden. It all depends on how much money you want to spend, how much space you have to work with, and how much work you want to put into it. The first thing you should do is assess your property and determine a good spot to place your garden. You will need a spot for plants that require full sun, plants that require partial sun, a few medicinal bushes, and plants that require shade. You should also look for a spot to plant invasive plants so you don't compromise other important plants in your garden. If you are planning on a food garden, make sure you leave enough room for this as well.

## How Much Space Do You Need?

You do not need a huge yard or farm to create an effective and useful medicinal plant garden with the plants discussed further in this chapter. Building a few raised beds that are roughly 4x12 (48 square feet) will suffice. This can easily be accomplished on plots of land no bigger than ⅙ to ⅛ of an acre. With that much space, you can have several large raised beds in various areas of sun, while also allowing a spot for the medicinal bushes and potentially invasive medicinal plants to thrive.

## Materials Required

While it is entirely possible to create a SHTF garden by tilling up areas of your yard and sowing seeds/planting seedlings directly in the soil, your best bet for the survival of your potentially life-saving plants is in raised beds. As you are probably already aware, all gardens need weeding. Weeding gardens can take up a huge amount of time and leave you down in your back if you aren't careful. Putting in a little extra work at the beginning of this endeavor will save you countless hours weeding in the future!

Consider saving money by chopping down cedars to place on the ground for your raised beds. Cedar is an excellent choice because it is a natural pest repellent. When you chop the cedars down, trim off all the limbs and dig a small groove in the ground to lay the logs flat. Trim the logs to be somewhat flush as you lay them down in your desired areas. You can either buy dirt to fill the raised beds with, or you can use a tractor to move dirt from another area of your property to the raised beds.

If you have livestock, consider mixing in manure with the soil for a natural fertilizer. Horse manure is optimal, but you can also use chicken, sheep, cow, or other types of manure. Don't go overboard, however, or you can burn up your crops. A little will go a long way.

Make sure you have a good place indoors for that gets plenty of sunlight. Perhaps a sunroom or an area with several windows would be the perfect spot. Set up a table to place your seedlings on and keep them moist and warm so they can thrive.

Another option, if you have the money is to build a small greenhouse outdoors near your garden area. This makes it much more convenient when you want to move some of your seedlings outside but don't want to plant them in the garden right away. If you have heat to your greenhouse, you can also start your seedlings in there. Some people heat their outdoor greenhouses with wood heat; just make sure you have good ventilation. Again, using cedar along the bottom and for the beams can help repel pests in your greenhouse. Keep in mind that a greenhouse is preferred, but not required.

Access to a water source is important. Make sure you have a spigot or a source of water nearby. If you are off-grid and do not use electricity, consider placing a rainwater collection barrel near your garden so you can water plants easily.

Gardening tools like a spade or trowel for digging small areas to plant seedlings, small trays for planting seeds, a device for tilling soil, a hoe, a rake, a pruner for your bushes, and scissors for trimming and harvesting herbs are all very handy to have in this endeavor. If you are off-grid, a chainsaw is almost essential for chopping down cedars and being able to make your own raised beds without purchasing lumber. A way to drag or haul the cedars is also important. There are several ways to do this: you could use a mule or two if you have them, a tractor, a truck, or a utility vehicle/four-wheeler. It all depends on how far you need to haul the cedars and how independent you are.

Handy but optional tools like a moisture content reader, weeding tool, seed distributor, and gas-powered tiller are also something to consider, depending on the funds you have set aside for your garden.

Pest control is an issue in any garden. There are several things you can do to stay on top of this problem, such as using cedar for your raised beds or bordering your garden with plants that repel insects naturally, like lavender and peppermint (they serve a dual purpose, as they are medicinal as well).

Diatomaceous earth is a natural and safe alternative to commercial insecticides, which are not recommended for use in a medicinal plant garden. Another natural pest control method is neem oil. Simply add a few drops to a spray bottle of water and spray your plants as needed.

## Plants Required

The best way to create a true SHTF medicinal garden is to think about all the different systems of the body and try to choose plants that help with conditions for these systems. You never know what kinds of issues you will run into in a SHTF situation, so you want to be ready for anything. Choose plants that target these systems specifically and help treat common ailments of these systems. Below are systems of the body and plants you can grow to target ailments of each system:

### 1. Medicinal Plants to Have at Hand for Your Circulatory System

Common issues with the circulatory system include high blood pressure and blocked arteries from high cholesterol. If these remain untreated (and in a SHTF scenario these will likely get worse) damage to the heart, or even death, can occur.

a. **Lavender (*Lavandula angustifolia*) for blood pressure**

A great plant to grow for treating high blood pressure is lavender. It is such a low-maintenance plant once it is established! It does not require much watering and does best in full to partial sun. It grows in a variety of growing zones, but does best in USDA zones 5-9. It prefers well drained soil. Avoid planting lavender in acidic soils. Try planting lavender seeds indoors in early spring and achieving a strong seedling before planting in your garden. Lavender has been proven through scientific research to lower blood pressure and help promote calm and peace.

To prepare lavender for medicinal use, harvest by clipping the plants in full bloom. Next, chop the plants finely and place the chopped plant matter in a glass jar. Cover the plant material completely with at least 80 proof alcohol and let this infuse for four to six weeks, shaking daily. When it is fully infused, strain out and bottle the liquid. Take one to two 5 ml doses daily to help manage blood pressure issues. You may increase or decrease as needed.

**b. Garlic for cholesterol**

Common garlic has been shown to lower cholesterol. It is an easy-to-grow plant that many gardeners include in their gardens. It is a wonderful addition to any meal! Garlic can be grown in almost all growing zones. Since garlic is so common, it can easily be grown by breaking the cloves out of a bulb of garlic and planting them in well-draining soil about two inches down and eight inches apart. Make sure when you are breaking the bulb into cloves that you try to leave as much of the papery substance that surrounds each clove intact. The best time to plant is said to be in the fall, around six weeks before the ground freezes. Cover the cloves with a thin layer of compost and fertilizer. Water them daily or as needed, depending on the weather and the dryness of the soil. If you planted in the fall, the most common time to harvest is in late July.

The best way to use garlic is to use it as often as possible in meal preparation. If you don't think you are getting enough garlic in your diet by adding minced cloves to meals, you can chop up cloves and add them to a jar of raw honey and let it ferment. Honey-fermented garlic is highly medicinal. It is a great way to treat a variety of infections and a great way to keep cholesterol in check.

## 2. Medicinal Plants to Have at Hand for Your Digestive System

Common complaints of the digestive system include gas/bloating, diarrhea, and constipation. While gas and bloating are usually minor, diarrhea can be life-threatening if it is not treated soon. Below are plants you can grow to manage these issues.

a. **Peppermint (*Mentha piperita*) for gas/bloating, upset stomach, nausea, and indigestion**

Peppermint has long been utilized for its ability to soothe a variety of digestive woes. One of the best things about peppermint is how easy it is to grow! You can start peppermint seeds indoors in early spring by shaking a few into separate trays. When they have sprouted and are strong enough to transplant outdoors, you can plant them (after the first frost) in your raised bed, or pretty much anywhere on your property. Water them as needed and watch them take over the area you planted them. Make sure to keep an eye on them, as they can spread fast and take over other plants. Peppermint can grow in almost all USDA zones. Harvest peppermint by clipping as needed and drying the plants (laying on a drying rack or hanging in small bundles will work).

When it is dried, use the dried leaves to infuse in a cup of hot water (using reusable tea bags or a tea infusion ball) and drink as needed to relieve stomach issues.

b. **Agrimony (*Agrimonia eupatoria*) for diarrhea**

Agrimony is a gentle and effective way to help calm the stomach and treat diarrhea. The first thing to do if you have diarrhea is to make sure you are drinking more water than normal. You want to avoid dehydration, which can come on quick if you have diarrhea.

Agrimony is native to many areas in North America, but it can also be grown in a medicinal garden if you don't have the time to go looking for it. Agrimony is best grown in USDA zones 6-9. Plant agrimony seeds indoors in early spring and then transplant seedlings in your garden after any danger of frost has passed. Make sure then are planted around twelve inches apart in well-draining soil. Clip the above ground parts of the plant when it is mature and dry them to make tea to help treat diarrhea. Drink peppermint tea as well to further calm the stomach.

c. **Licorice root (*Glycyrrhiza glabra*) for constipation, heartburn, and ulcers**

Licorice is surprisingly tolerant of a variety of conditions, but grows best when it is watered regularly and planted in well-draining soil. It prefers full sun and optimal growing zones are USDA zones 9-11. Plant seeds indoors and transplant to optimal conditions in your garden when they are well-established. Harvest the full plant when it is mature.

The root is what is needed for medicinal purposes. Before harvesting, you may want to clip a cutting off the plant and put it in water in the sunlight, as it can grow new plants from cuttings! Chop the roots well and dry them to drink in tea to relieve chronic constipation.

# 3. Medicinal Plants to Have at Hand for Your Endocrine System

The thyroid seems to be one of the most affected organs of the endocrine system. It is highly susceptible to environmental toxins. Issues with the pituitary and ovaries are also common. Adaptogenic herbs like ashwagandha are perfect for restoring balance to all parts of the endocrine system, but especially the thyroid. For the pituitary and ovaries, Vitex is extremely helpful.

a. **Ashwagandha (*Withania somnifera*) for thyroid support and overall endocrine health**

Ashwagandha is what herbalists refer to as an adaptogen. Adaptogens are amazing plants because they can do what many plants cannot: target what needs fixed in the body and restore balance/health. Ashwagandha is known for its ability to calm how the body reacts to stress. As a result, the endocrine system is greatly affected in a good way. It can be cultivated in a medicinal garden for its powerful roots. It can be grown as an annual in USDA zones 3-10, but it does best in warmer, drier zones. It prefers growing in temperatures between 70 and 90 degrees Fahrenheit. It also prefers sandy, rocky soil and full sun. Start seeds indoors and plant strong seedlings in your garden (with suitable conditions) after the first frost. Water as needed, but try not to overwater. If you live in a cooler zone, you may want to consider growing this plant indoors in a large pot.

When the plant is fully mature, harvest its roots, which will have a smell described as "sweaty." Chop them well and place them in a glass jar. Completely cover the chopped roots with at least 80 proof alcohol. Let this sit and infuse for four to six weeks, shaking the jar (lid closed) daily. Strain out the extract when it is ready and bottle the liquid for medicinal use. Take 2.5 mil twice daily for thyroid and endocrine support.

### b. Vitex (*Vitex agnus-castus*) for hormonal balance and restoration

Vitex, or chaste tree berry, is also an adaptogen. It is known for restoring balance to hormones and helping treat conditions of the pituitary and ovaries. For the pituitary, it can restore normal hormone levels, reducing prolactin levels as needed. For the ovaries, it can reduce symptoms of Poly Cystic Ovarian Syndrome. This is not an herb, but rather a bush. Plant this in an area of your property that would accommodate a medium-sized bush, and not in your garden bed. The easiest way to grow a chaste tree bush is to grab a cutting. They grow roots rather easily when submerged in water for a while. Once you have good suckers established on your cutting, plant the shrub in a large pot with well-draining soil and water it as needed. When it is established well, transplant it (after the last frost) to a part of your property that has full to partial sun. Make sure the soil drains well. Fertilizing this bush every few years is recommended. The berries can be harvested to make a medicinal preparation. Collect berries and place them in a jar. Fill the jar with at least 80 proof alcohol, making sure the berries are fully submerged. Place a lid on the jar and store it in a cool, dark place for four to six weeks, shaking it daily. Strain out the liquid when the time is ready and store your extract in a bottle. Take 2.5 ml twice daily to manage symptoms of PCOS or other hormonal and pituitary issues.

## 4. Medicinal Plants to Have at Hand for Your Integumentary System

Your skin is your largest organ-and your first line of defense when it comes to foreign objects and bacteria entering your body and causing destruction! Some common issues of the skin are rashes/irritation and wounds. There are several plants you can use to promote wound healing and calm a variety of rashes and irritations.

### a. Lavender (*Lavandula angustifolia*) for calming redness, irritation, burns, and rashes:

Lavender is one of those multipurpose plants you can use for all kinds of issues. It has already been discussed for use in calming anxiety and lowering blood pressure. However, this amazing plant has been used for centuries for calming inflamed skin. Whether the inflammation and redness is caused by a rash, chapped skin, or a burn, lavender has you covered. Growing instructions have already been provided under the circulatory system section of this chapter, but using lavender for skin issues requires a different preparation after it is harvested. First, harvest the aerial parts when the plant is in full bloom. Next, hang or lay your lavender flat on a screen to dry. When it is dried, crumble it into a glass container. Finally, cover the plant material completely in olive oil (or a different skin-nourishing oil like jojoba, rose hip, coconut, etc.). Let this sit and infuse for four weeks, shaking the jar daily. Strain the oil out when it is ready and apply this to irritated skin, burns, or chapped skin to heal it.

### b. Yarrow (*Achillea millefolium*) for cuts and scrapes

Yarrow is known for its ability to help the blood clot, as well as its ability to cleanse a minor wound. This comes in handy in a SHTF situation where it is important that a wound does not get infected. While yarrow can be found growing in the wild in most of the United States, it can also be cultivated in a medicinal garden. Make sure you get seeds from the white variety of yarrow, *Achillea millefolium*. To grow yarrow, plant seeds indoors in early spring. They need plenty of light to germinate, and sometimes they may take a while to germinate. Give them patience and anywhere from two weeks to three months. Transplant the seedlings to your garden as soon as they sprout. They require loamy soil that drains well. Yarrow grows best in USDA zones 3-9. They do well in full sun and do not require a lot of water once they are established. You may need to trim them back every now and then. To use medicinally, harvest the aerial parts of the plant and dry them. For minor cuts and scrapes you can apply the yarrow straight to the area after mashing it into a poultice with your fingers. Leave it on the area until the bleeding stops. You can also harvest yarrow and dry the aerial parts to grind into a powder that acts as a styptic powder for wounds.

# 5. Medicinal Plants to Have at Hand for Your Immune System

There are many reasons for a SHTF situation, but one obvious reason is a pandemic. The whole world knows about Covid and how it spread quickly, sparing some and killing others. Before you find yourself worrying about any virus, keep in mind that most of the battle is keeping yourself healthy so your immune system can fight battles like it is supposed to. This requires keeping it healthy with a balanced, healthy diet first and foremost. As the saying goes, "the best defense is a good offense." Another thing you can do to keep your immune system strong and ready for anything is to grow these plants in your medicinal garden.

a. **Astragalus for preventing overactive immune response and nourishing the immune system**

One big reason why so many people succumb to a virus (other than serious underlying health conditions) is an overactive immune response to the virus. Astragalus can help keep the immune system strong, while balancing its response to unwelcome viruses and pathogens. Astragalus is an adaptogenic plant, so it can help keep your immune system working like it should, despite what your body is confronted with. There are many species of astragalus, but the Chinese version, *Astragalus membranaceus*, is best. It prefers full sun and soil that drains well. Start seeds inside by first rubbing them gently with sandpaper to scrape off some of that tough outer membrane that may prevent germination. Don't scrape too hard because you can damage the seed. Next, soak the seeds in water overnight. The next day they should look swollen. There may be some that are not swollen. To make sure they germinate, poke them with a needle lightly without disturbing the inner portion of the seed. Plant your seeds in small containers indoors in a 2:1 mixture of soil and sand. Keep the soil moist, but don't over water. Transplant the seedlings to a bigger pot with the same soil/sand ratio as the plants grow. They can be planted outdoors in early spring, after the last frost. Be careful with their roots, as they can be tender. Do not over water your plants; just make sure the soil stays moist. USDA zones 6-9 are optimal for growing this plant. It will take around three to four years for your astragalus roots to be big enough to harvest for medicinal use.

When it is ready, harvest the root, wash it off, and chop it into pieces. Place the pieces in a glass jar and cover them completely with at least 80 proof alcohol. Let this sit and infuse for four to six weeks, shaking it daily. Store it in a cool, dark place during this time. Strain out the liquid at the end of the infusion period and bottle it. Take 2-5 ml up to three times daily if you have a virus. For maintenance, take 2-5 ml once daily.

b. **Chinese Skullcap (*Scutellaria baicalensis*) for killing viruses**

Another way to stay on top if you have a virus is to target the virus itself and not just the immune system. Chinese skullcap is antiviral and can be of great help when taken in conjunction with astragalus when you are ill. This Chinese relative of native US skullcap species can grow in North America quite readily. It requires full sun in USDA zones six or higher. It can tolerate partial sun in zones 7-8. It does best when started indoors and can be transplanted in your medicinal garden after the last frost. It does not tolerate clay soils and prefers well-draining soil.

Harvest aerial parts when the plant is mature. Chop them up well and place them in a glass jar. Cover the plant material with 80 proof or greater alcohol. Let this infuse for four to six weeks before straining the liquid out. Take 2.5-5 ml up to twice daily to target a virus.

c. **Elderberry (*Sambucus* spp.) for antiviral and immune support**

Elderberry has long been used for its ability to nourish the immune system and fight viruses. It is native to many parts of North America, but can easily be grown from cuttings as well. If you wish to grow elderberry in your garden, find a bush and trim cuttings while the bush is dormant. In many states, the local conservation agency actually offers elderberry plants each spring that they grow in their native plant nurseries. This is another option if you wish to avoid looking for an elderberry bush to get a cutting. Make sure your cuttings are slanted as you gather them. Pull off the bottom two leaf buds with your fingers. Some people sit the bottoms of the stems in willow tea for six hours before placing them in water to root because willow tea contains constituents that may act as a root hormone. When you place your cuttings in water, it usually takes around six weeks to see suckers if you sit your plants in the sun. Once they have grown nice roots, transplant them to well-draining soil directly in your garden or in a bigger pot. It is probably best to try planting them somewhere in your garden rather than indoors. These are bushes and can get rather big. Choose a place in your garden that is in full or partial sun. Make sure not to place it too close to your other plants because it will likely grow to a place where it blocks out the sun for them.

Harvest the berries in early fall. You have several options with what to do with them for a medicinal preparation, but the best way for a SHTF situation is to make a tincture (the method already described that entails soaking the plant in alcohol). Tinctures have a better shelf life than other preparations. Dry the berries first by sitting them on a screen (still attached to the stems) in a well-ventilated area with great air flow. Once they are dry, place them in a glass jar and cover them with at least 80 proof alcohol. Let this infuse for four to six weeks, shaking them daily. Strain them out and bottle the deep magenta liquid to take when you want to fight a virus. Take 5 ml up to twice daily for this purpose.

# 6. Medicinal Plants to Have at Hand for Your Muscular System

Common ailments of the muscular system include pulled muscles and muscle pain from overwork. In a SHTF situation, this is likely to occur because you will be working harder outdoors. Be sure to do your best to be mindful of your body and don't attempt to lift heavy objects by yourself! Below are plants you can grow in your garden to treat muscle aches and pains.

a. **Cayenne for blocking pain at the site**

Growing cayenne in your garden has double the benefits because it is already a common fixture in many gardens for food. Cayenne contains a constituent that can help to block pain when applied externally. Growing cayenne isn't hard either. Start seeds indoors in early spring and transplant them to well-draining soil in your garden when there is no danger of frost. Water them as needed. Not surprisingly, cayennes are used to hot conditions and prefer heat from the sun to grow. Plant them in a sunny area of your garden. Cayenne does not tolerate high nitrogen levels in the soil. Cayenne do best in USDA zones 8 and above. In zones below 7, you may want to grow cayenne in pots indoors, as it requires heat to grow.

To use cayenne medicinally, harvest them when the peppers are mature and red. Dry them and grind them down. Infuse a tablespoon of flakes into a cup of olive oil in a double boiler for up to five hours, or you can combine the cayenne and oil in a glass jar and sit it on the "warm" spot on your stove (if your stove has this option) all day. Strain the flakes out and bottle the oil infusion. Rub this into sore muscles liberally as needed. Avoid rubbing it onto open skin. Avoid touching your mucus membranes after application and make sure to wash your hands well.

b. **Rosemary (*Rosmarinus officinalis*) for muscle pain, muscle relaxation, and inflammation reduction**

How fortunate that one of the world's most common garden herbs is useful as medicine in addition to flavoring food! Rosemary packs quite a medicinal punch and has been used for a variety of ailments. It contains a constituent that can bring relief to sore muscles, as well as reduce inflammation if you have pulled a muscle. Rosemary is grown in gardens across the globe and is generally easy to grow. It does grow best in USDA zones 9 or higher, where it will be an evergreen. In all other zones, it will likely come back each year as the temperatures warm up. Rosemary seeds can be sowed outdoors, but to give them their best chance at germination, many gardeners start them indoors first. They seem to take longer to germinate than other herbs. Plant your seeds up to four months before the growing season starts. After danger of frost has passed, plant your rosemary seedlings in an area of your garden that gets full sun. Since rosemary is native to the Mediterranean region, it is used to dry conditions. Do not overwater this plant. Make sure it is planted in well-draining soil with little risk of standing water.

To use this plant medicinally, clip some and hang it to dry somewhere. When it is sufficiently dried, crumble it up and place what you have in a glass jar. Cover the plant material with a carrier oil like olive oil. Let this infuse in the jar for four weeks, shaking it daily, before straining it out. Apply this oil infusion to pulled and sore muscles as needed. Use with cayenne oil for expedited results.

# 7. Medicinal Plants to Have at Hand for Your Nervous System

Ailments of the nervous system could involve stress, anxiety, and depression, since these things are the result of the activation of the sympathetic nervous system. It could also involve nerve issues that cause pain in certain regions of the body. There are plants you can have on hand and ready to use should you experience any issues of the nervous system:

a. **Valerian (*Valeriana officinalis*) for anxiety and stress**

Valerian may be more famous for its ability to help you get to sleep, but because it directly affects the central nervous system, it can provide positive benefits for those dealing with stress and anxiety as well. This plant does best in USDA zones 4-9 as a perennial. It is somewhat hardy, and will usually grow well in most gardens. It prefers full to partial sun and well-draining soil. Start seeds indoors in early spring, or sow seeds in an area of your garden that meets its sun needs. If sowing directly in your garden, sow seeds after all danger of frost has passed. Plant seeds around ½ inch deep in the soil and thin plants out to eighteen inches apart when they begin to grow well. The roots are the medicinal part of this plant. Try letting your plants grow a few seasons before harvesting the roots. They will have a distinctive smell that people usually describe as "sweaty feet." Don't let this deter you, though!

This plant contains potent medicine! fter harvesting the roots, chop them well and fill a glass jar. Cover the root material completely in at least 80 proof alcohol and let this infuse in a cool, dark, place for four to six weeks before straining out the liquid to bottle. Take 2.5 ml up to two times daily for anxiety, or 5 ml one hour before bedtime if you want to fall asleep fast.

### b. St. John's Wort (*Hypericum perforatum*) for nerve pain and mild depression

St. John's Wort grows wild over most of North America, so it is no surprise that it is an easy-to-grow garden plant with all kinds of medicinal benefits. USDA zones 5-10 are best for growing this plant, but it can thrive in many conditions once it is established. In fact, you may have to keep an eye on this plant and put it somewhere where it cannot encroach on other plants, because it can become invasive in the right conditions. It does not like wet soil, and would prefer soil on the drier side. Be sure the soil you plant it in is well-draining. You can start seeds indoors and then plant them in your garden after the last frost. Try not to overwater these plants and plant them in an area with full to partial sun. Clip the aerial portions of the plants when they are in full flower.

If you are looking for a remedy for nerve pain, wilt the plants and then chop them (make sure you get as many flowers as possible in this remedy). Fill a glass jar with the plant material and cover it completely with olive oil, or a carrier oil of your choice. Let this infuse for four weeks, shaking it daily, before straining it out. Massage a liberal amount of this oil in areas where you are experiencing nerve pain and discomfort. If you want to use this plant for depression, follow the same steps as previously mentioned, but instead of using oil, use 80 proof or higher alcohol. Take 2.5 ml three to four times daily for management of seasonal affective disorder or mild depression.

# 8. Medicinal Plants to Have at Hand for Your Renal System

It is important to take care of your kidneys and drink plenty of water. This becomes even more important in a SHTF situation, because you certainly don't want to risk becoming dehydrated or giving yourself a kidney/bladder/urinary tract infection. Below are common plants you can employ to take care of kidney ailments and nourish the renal system.

### a. Dandelion (*Taraxacum officinale*) for cleansing

This may be one of the easiest plants to grow in your garden because it will often "volunteer" in your garden without you lifting a finger! Most people think dandelion is a weed, but it is quite the opposite. Firstly, all parts of the plant are incredibly useful. You can eat the flowers and leaves for optimum nutrition. Second, the roots have potent cleansing properties and can act as a tonic for the kidneys. One simple way to get this plant to grow in your garden is to find the dandelion seed heads and scatter them where you would like to see them grow. You could also just harvest them as you find them in your yard, since they grow in yards across the world! Just make sure you don't spray your yard with toxic substances so you can have healthy yard "weeds."

Harvest the root, which is a somewhat large taproot. You will need a good spade to do this. Once you have collected a few roots, wash them off good and chop them up. Lay the chopped roots on a towel to dry. When they are sufficiently dry, bag them up and use them as needed in tea. Simply fill a reusable tea bag or tea ball with the root pieces and infuse it in a cup of hot water for several minutes. Drink one to three cups a day if you are in need of renal cleansing. Make sure to drink plenty of water, as the roots act as a diuretic and pull water out of the body to aid in cleansing.

### b. Celery root for nourishment and cleansing

Celery is a common garden plant because it can provide a healthy snack, but it also has medicinal properties. Celery roots are diuretic and can help to eliminate waste from the body, especially the renal system! To grow celery from seeds, soak the seeds overnight. Next, plant the seeds in little trays of soil and place them in a window sill or sunny area of your home. A great idea is to cove the trays with plastic wrap after watering to trap in moisture and warmth. Remove the wrap when the seedlings begin to sprout. Keep the area moist and make sure they are getting sun as much as possible. Transplant them in your garden when the seedlings are stronger and the ground is warmer (at least 50 degrees Fahrenheit). Plant the seedlings at least eight inches apart and keep them well-watered.

Harvest the mature plant, root and all, for medicinal purposes. Don't waste the above ground parts – eat them! To prepare the root, chop it up good. Next, put the chopped root in a jar and cover everything with at least 80 proof alcohol. Let this infuse for four to six weeks before straining out and bottling the liquid. Take 2.5 ml up to three times daily for kidney cleansing. Drink more water than usual to counteract any chance of dehydration from the diuretic effects of the plant.

## 9. Medicinal Plants to Have at Hand for Your Reproductive System

Ailments of the reproductive system can be extensive, so it pays to pay attention to your body and what it is telling you. If you notice anything "off" don't take a chance and ignore it. Symptoms of hormonal issues in both women and men include acne on the jawline, mood swings, and pain in the reproductive regions. There are plants you can have on hand to nourish your reproductive system and balance hormones, should you feel they are off kilter.

### a. Vitex (*Vitex agnus-castus*) for balancing female hormones

Vitex, or Chaste Tree, has already been mentioned in the "endocrine system" section of this chapter. However, since it is an adaptogen, it is especially handy for balancing hormones. It is popular among many women for its ability to restore balance to whatever hormones are off in their body. As a result, women who take Vitex often discover that their cycles return to normal (if they were abnormal) and their mood swings begin to dissolve. Follow the growing and medicinal preparation instructions in the endocrine system section. Take 2.5 to 5 ml of Vitex tincture up to three times daily, depending on the severity of the hormonal issues. You can slowly start to take less as you notice improvement. Give this medicinal preparation several months to work, because although it works well, the results may be slow in coming initially.

### b. Ashwagandha (*Withania somnifera*) for male hormones

Ashwagandha is another adaptogenic plant already mentioned in the endocrine system section of this chapter for its ability to support the thyroid. In addition to what it can do for the thyroid, it is also a great supplement for men who wish to boost their stamina, energy, and balance hormones. Growing and medicinal preparation instructions can be found in the endocrine system section. Take 2.5-5 ml of ashwagandha tincture twice daily for any issues afflicting the male reproductive system. When combined with a healthy diet and plenty of exercise, ashwagandha can also significantly reduce sluggishness and low sex drive.

## 10. Medicinal Plants to Have at Hand for Your Respiratory System

Having a bad cough or dealing with a lot of drainage are never fun, but when you are experiencing a SHTF situation, this can be quite worrisome. There is always the chance that if it is not taken care of soon it may develop into pneumonia. Staying on top of drainage and mucous is important, so make sure at the first sign of these things you are ready with the following plants from your garden:

a. **Oregano (*Origanum vulgare*) for preventing infections and clearing mucous**

Oregano may be one of the most important herbs you can grow in your medical garden, and thank goodness it will also be one of the easiest to grow! It has long been hailed for its bacteria-killing abilities. It also contains constituents that help to loosen up mucous and get it out of the body. Oregano doesn't need much water to grow thick and healthy. It also isn't picky about the soil; just make sure to avoid really wet soil. Plant it in full sun for best results. Sow seeds in an area of your garden that will have plenty of room for this fast-spreading plant. Seeds should be sown six weeks before the last frost. Keep them watered, but do not over-water them. It can grow in nearly all USDA zones, but in zones that are prone to very hot, harsh summers, you may think about allowing the plant some afternoon shade to take the edge off. In no time you will have a garden full of this wonderful plant!

Clip the aerial parts of the plant to harvest for medicinal purposes. Hang small bundles to dry or place them on a drying rack. Store your dried oregano in a glass jar and keep it in a cool, dark place in your house. To use for respiratory issues, one easy and effective way is to create a steam using this herb. Boil a small pot of water on the stove and add a few tablespoons of dried oregano. Let this boil for a few minutes and then put your head over the steam (not too close, you don't want to get burned). Take deep breaths and inhale the steam coming from the pot. Put a towel over your head to help trap in more steam as you finish this breathing treatment. Make sure the towel does not come into contact with the hot burner or pot. Breathe in this steam for 10-20 minutes and up to twice daily for best results and to prevent any respiratory infection from forming. Keep doing this until symptoms are gone.

b. **Horehound (*Marrubium vulgare*) for wet coughs and mucous clearing**

Years ago, candy made from this popular herb was a favorite of boys and girls all over North America. While horehound may be known for its interesting flavor in candies, it is also a very handy herb for clearing mucous and calming a wet cough. It grows wild in many areas of North America and is very easy to grow in a garden! Use horehound for ailments like bronchitis, chest congestion, asthma, and allergies. Sow seeds in your garden around three weeks before the last frost. Cover the area with a dusting of soil to prevent the wind blowing the seeds away. Horehound does best in dry, poor soil. Do not over water this plant. It will not take long for horehound to take off once it is established. Be sure you keep an eye on it so it doesn't crowd other plants in your garden.

Harvest the aerial parts of the plant when you want to make medicine. You can dry some of what you harvest to make tea, or you can fill a jar with the plant, cover it in alcohol, and let this infuse for four to six weeks before straining out the liquid and bottling it. Take horehound in tea or in the tincture described at the first signs of congestion for best results. Drink two to three cups of the tea daily, or take 5 ml of the tincture up to twice daily for congestion. Do oregano steam treatments described above in addition to the horehound for expedited healing.

# 11. Medicinal Plants to Have at Hand for Your Skeletal System

Some common skeletal issues one may experience include sprains, fractures, and joint pain. Sprains and fractures can be very problematic in a SHTF situation, so you want to make sure you do not use the affected area and give it plenty time to heal.

You need your body in top shape to survive. There are several useful plants you can have ready in your garden to heal these ailments:

a. **Comfrey (*Symphytum officinale*) for sprains and fractures**

Comfrey is a great plant to have on hand in first-aid situations. This is because the leaves can be plucked and applied straight to a sprain, helping to relieve inflammation and pain in the immediate area. It was a staple in gardens for centuries for this reason. It is harder to grow from seed, so many gardeners use root pieces (comfrey grows easily even when small root pieces are planted in the ground). However, it may be hard to find root pieces, so if you wish to plant from seeds, you will need to stratify them first. To do this, place the seeds in a moist paper towel. Place this into a glass jar and close the lid. Place this in a cold place, like a refrigerator, for up to sixty days. Now your seeds should be ready to plant. Start them indoors if the temperatures outdoors are under sixty degrees Fahrenheit. Start them in well-draining soil and keep the soil moist but not soaked. Place your seeds in a sunny area of your house and let them get strong. When the weather is warm, place them in a sunny area of your garden. Plant them in an area where they won't encroach on your other plants, as they can become very invasive. They will come back every year.

To use them, pluck a leaf and apply to the affected area. It helps to wrap the area so the leaf stays on. Keep it wrapped for several hours and reapply leaves as needed until the swelling goes down. Stay off the area until further assessment determines what should be done.

b. **Cabbage (*Brassica oleracea*) for inflammation and pain**

This is another amazing plant that is usually thought of as food, and rightfully so!

Cabbage is nutritious and even more nutritious when it is fermented and full of beneficial probiotics. However, this unassuming plant also boasts impressive anti-inflammatory properties. Controlling major inflammation means controlling pain, as the two go hand-in-hand. Cabbage has long been used by nursing mothers who wish to wean without pain.

The same concept can be used with sprains, fractures, and sore joints. To grow cabbage, plant seeds indoors around six weeks before the last frost. Place them two inches down and keep the area moist and in full sun. Get your seedlings used to the cold by sitting them outside when they are established (before planting them outdoors). After the last frost, place seedlings in your garden 12 to 24 inches apart.

To utilize this plant, simply break off a large leaf and apply it to the sore joint or sprain. Wrap this area with plastic wrap or another material to keep it in place. Leave it on for up to three hours before repeating with a fresh leaf. When placed on engorged and painful breasts, cabbage leaves help bring down inflammation and dry up the milk fast.

# 12. Medicinal Plants to Have at Hand for Infections

One of the most dangerous medical situations in a SHTF situation will likely be an infection. Antibiotics will likely not be available. You will have to rely on highly antimicrobial plants to prevent and treat any issues that arise from bacteria invading the body and causing issues.

a. **Garlic for UTI, yeast infection, MRSA, and more**

Garlic has already been mentioned in the "circulatory system" section of this chapter, so make sure you check out how to grow it there. It has many uses, and treating infections is at the top of the list. Garlic has been shown to treat many infections, ranging from deadly to common. If you are injured and wish to avoid infection in the area, you can apply poultice garlic cloves to the area daily to keep bacteria at bay. For internal infections, you can dehydrate and powder garlic and place it in capsules to take. Taking five to six capsules a day may be just what is needed to clear up a UTI. For yeast infections, place the garlic clove (after removing the outer paper) directly in the vagina for several hours daily until the infection clears.

- b. **Oregano (*Origanum vulgare*) to fight respiratory infections, staph infections, and parasites**

Oregano and garlic can both be used to combat infections, and using them together just speeds up healing even more. Growing and using oregano has already been mentioned in the "respiratory section" of this chapter, but there are other ways to use it for infections in other areas of the body. For UTI's and internal infections, you can chop garlic and place it in a glass jar, covering it in at least 80 proof alcohol to infuse for four to six weeks. Strain it out when the time is up and bottle your oregano tincture. Take 3-5 ml (depending on what your stomach can handle) every three to four hours until the infection is gone. It can be infused the same way as previously mentioned but in olive oil for external infections like wounds. Apply the oregano-infused oil to wounds daily. Another great use for this oil infusion is ear infections. Do not put this inside the ear, but rather massage around the outer ear and lymph area down the neck. This will help drainage in the ear, as well as treat infection.

*Another great infection-fighting substance you should consider having on hand is raw honey. Start looking into beekeeping now so you are prepared with plenty of honey if and when the time comes. Honey is highly antimicrobial and can be smeared on wounds to prevent and treat a variety of infections.

# 13. Medicinal Plants to Have at Hand for Pain Management

If you are one of those people who find yourself grabbing for the Tylenol or Ibuprofen, you will want to make sure you have alternative sources of pain management in your medicinal garden. These pain-relieving plants also have the bonus of less liver and kidney-ruining side effects, unlike the drugs previously mentioned.

- a. **Toothache plant (*Acmella oleracea*) for numbing and general anesthetic**

You might be shocked at the numbing sensation that occurs when you place even the smallest toothache plant bud in your mouth and chew it a bit. The numbing is so profound that you may even find yourself drooling!

The plant comes by its name honestly and is a must-have for pain management. It is generally easy to grow, and an added bonus is that the leaves are edible and tasty in salads! To grow toothache plant, start seeds indoors or in a greenhouse in early spring. Make sure they are kept in a warm, sunny environment as often as possible. Keep the soil moist and it shouldn't take long for them to germinate. You can transplant them in your garden after the last frost, but be aware that they are not cold tolerant at all. Once cold weather hits, your plants will likely die. They will start producing lots of buds in late summer, so harvest buds daily when you are working in your garden.

The sphere-shaped buds are the medicinal portion of the plant. Set the buds on a towel to dry as you continue to collect them. Once you have a fair amount of buds, fill a glass jar and then top them with 80 proof alcohol, completely covering the plant material. Store it in a cool, dark place and shake daily. Strain out your new numbing solution and bottle it. Using a dropper, place 5-10 drops as needed in your mouth on any areas where you have a toothache or sore. It may even numb other areas of the body, depending on how strong your tincture is!

- b. **Valerian (*Valeriana officinalis*) for pain relief**

Valerian may be famous for its ability to get you to sleep, but it is also an effective pain reliever. This is because it acts directly on the central nervous system. An added bonus is that valerian can also help to provide a sense of relief and calm to an unsettled mind. Instructions for how to grow valerian, as well as how to create valerian tincture, can be found in the "Nervous System" section of this chapter. For pain management, take 5 ml of valerian tincture every three to four hours as needed. Avoid operating any heavy machinery or partaking in any dangerous activity after taking valerian, as it may impair your ability to move quickly.

Many of the medicinal plant preparations in this section entailed creating an alcohol extract called a tincture. This is because tinctures have a very long shelf-life. Many tinctures will last up to seven years, and even as long as ten. This means that if you are able to grow many of the plants mentioned in this book in your garden and have a good harvest, you may be able to create enough tinctures to last you for years just in case your garden doesn't do as well later on! The alcohol acts as an effective preservative, as well as an optimal solution for extracting the medicinal portions of the plants. Of course, you can always harvest and dry your plants, making sure you store them in a cool, dark place in airtight containers afterwards. Then they will be on hand when you need them for teas and poultices. However, keep in mind that dried herbs have a shelf life of around one year.

It might be a good idea to start looking into moonshine stills and learning how to make your own alcohol for tincturing purposes.

## Estimated Cost

Costs for creating your own medicinal plant garden are going to vary greatly depending on many factors. Lumber and soil prices will be different in different states and may even vary depending on where you are purchasing them. If you are the do-it-yourself, self-sufficient type, you are going to save a lot of money in lumber (by cutting your own) and on soil (by using soil from your property). You will also save on construction by building the beds yourself and not paying to have them built.

If you wish to purchase lumber for your beds, understand that the price of lumber has gone up in the past year and you will likely be paying more than you normally would. You have several options when it comes to lumber for your beds. You could go for longevity and purchase plastic lumber that will hold up for years and not rot away. It would cost you anywhere from $200-$250 per bed if you go this route. The pro is that it is durable and will last a while. The con is that it is more expensive than using untreated lumber.

It will cost roughly $100 per bed if you use untreated lumber. A pro is the affordable price, but the con is that untreated lumber may not last too many years before it begins to rot. You can buy treated lumber of course, but it is highly unadvisable to use chemically treated lumber for a medicinal plant garden. Those chemicals can leach into the soil and do more harm than good with your plants and your health.

Aside from lumber, soil will be your next big expenditure. If you cannot get soil from another area of your property to add to your beds, you can order a dump truck of soil to be poured in the beds. Prices vary, but you should be able to order what is called a "tandem dump truck load" of topsoil delivered to your house for around $45 to $60 per raised bed. This is roughly 10,000 cubic feet of topsoil. This option is absurdly cheaper than going out and buying bags of topsoil and trying to fill your beds. If you were to attempt this, you would be spending hundreds of dollars more than just getting topsoil delivered.

For essential tools and pest control (mentioned earlier in this chapter), you can safely budget $100 to $200 to get what you need to dig up the beds, plant seedlings, control pests, and weed your garden.

Here are some useful links to where you can purchase the needed materials from:

◆ Pruning Shears:
www.amazon.com/Fiskars-91095935J-Bypass-Pruning-Shears/dp/B00002N66H/

◆ Trowel:
www.amazon.com/Mr-Garden-Trowel-Stainless-Gardening/dp/B08FHN6WSP/

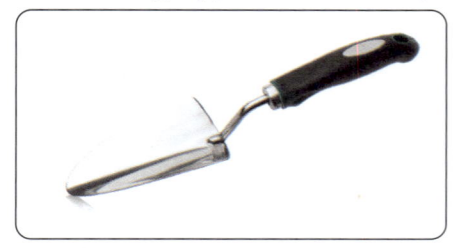

◆ Weeder:
www.amazon.com/Grampas-Weeder-CW-01-Original-Remover/dp/B001D1FFZA/

- Garden Tool Set:
www.amazon.com/Aluminum-Lightweight-Gardening-Anti-Skid-Ergonomic/dp/B08C7HXJR9/

- Rake:
www.amazon.com/Martha-Stewart-MTS-TELR-Comfort-Handle/dp/B086FG3XR7/

- Hoe:
www.amazon.com/Berry-Bird-Stainless-Weeding-Cultivating/dp/B08C4KTSS5/

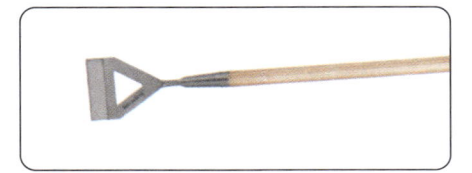

- Moisture Meter:
www.amazon.com/SURENSHY-Gardening-Hygrometer-Humidity-Required/dp/B0895QM8S9/

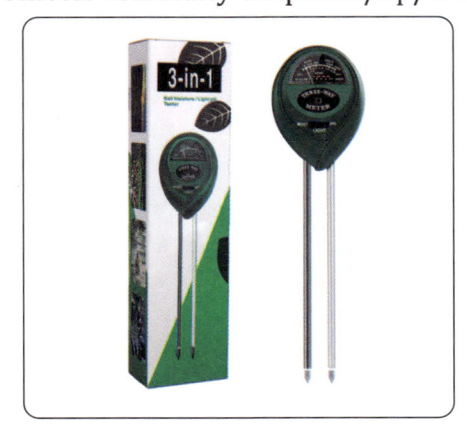

- Seed Dispenser Kit:
www.amazon.com/Batino-Adjustable-Transplanter-Spreaders-Dispenser/dp/B07X23YRXS/

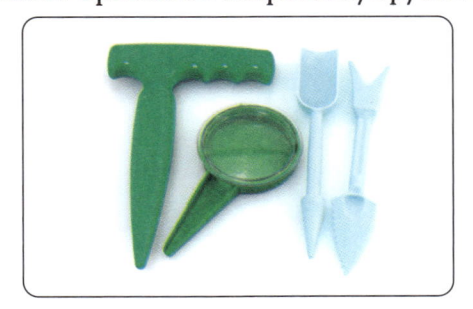

- Seed Trays:
www.amazon.com/9GreenBox-Seedling-Starter-6-Cells-Labels/dp/B0149L72CE/

- Diatomaceous Earth for Pest Control:
www.amazon.com/Harris-Diatomaceous-Earth-Food-Grade/dp/B07RV67ZNL/

- Neem Oil for Pest Control:
www.amazon.com/Harris-Pressed-Unrefined-Cosmetic-Grade/dp/B07732SVD3/

- Lumber:
www.homedepot.com/b/Lumber-Composites/N-5yc1vZbqpg?catStyle=ShowProducts&NCNI-5&search

*Top soil will be locally sourced, so you will need to contact a company in your area that delivers topsoil by the truckload.

Seeds may be the third largest expenditure, after lumber and soil. You want to make sure you are purchasing non-GMO, preferably heirloom seeds from a reputable seed company that specializes in medicinal seeds. There are several great companies that you can purchase seeds from. You may also choose to give your business to your local nursery. Prices vary, but plan on spending anywhere from $150 to $250 if you want to purchase all the seeds mentioned in this chapter. This may seem pricey, but keep in mind that you can easily save seeds from the plants you grow the first year so you don't have to keep buying them every year thereafter.

# How Much Work to Put Into it

Your garden can take a lot of work to get started, but keep in mind that the more work you put in, the less money you are going to spend creating it. If you can put in the work to chop down your own cedars, build your own beds, and get your own topsoil, you are cutting out hundreds and hundreds of dollars. If you put your mind to the task and have the whole day to work on it, it will probably take you no more than a week to get things built and ready to go.

You will not be able to avoid the work that goes into starting seedlings indoors or in a greenhouse. This requires time and patience. It will also take time transplanting seedlings into your raised beds. If you have back issues, take your time with this part because it will require you to be hunched over planting for a while. Rest in between plants and walk a few circles around the bed before getting back to it. If you have bad knees, consider getting a mat to kneel on as you plant.

Reserve time to visit your garden daily to keep up with the weeding and pest control. It will not take long for weeds to take over an unattended garden. If you can, purchase a weeder so you don't have to bend down and pick weeds all the time. Make sure you keep your plants watered, but many of the plants mentioned in this chapter do not need watered daily unless it is extremely hot and dry in your local climate. Going a day or two between watering can actually help the roots grow stronger and deeper as they search for water.

# How to Tend Your Garden in Winter and How to Use Plants in Winter

If you plant the plants mentioned in this chapter, many of them will die back in the winter but come back in the spring. Make sure you take notes on which plants will come back and which will not so you know what to plant the next year and what not to plant.

When the weather begins to cool down before the first frost of the year, go out and harvest all of your remaining plants before the frost kills them. Remember to check back to the plants section of this chapter to know which parts to harvest and which to leave. Some plants will only need to be trimmed down, while other plants will need dug up because the root is the medicinal portion of the plant. Also keep in mind that a few of the plants mentioned in this chapter require more than one year's growth before harvesting. In that case, leave them be until they come back next year.

Let some of your plants go to seed. Harvest those seeds to plant next year. This will ensure that you will always have medicinal plants to use on your homestead, as well as save you a lot of money on seeds. Set your saved seeds on a towel to dry before storing them in a container in a cool, dark place until they are ready to plant.

The majority of your harvested plants do not need to be processed immediately, although if you are tincturing them in alcohol, they can be processed right away if you want. If you don't have a lot of time on your hands to tincture a bunch of plants that you just harvested, you can hang them somewhere to dry, and then when they are fully dry store them in an airtight container in a cool, dark place until you are ready to create a tincture or make tea. If at all possible, try to tincture all of the plants that need tinctured (see plant section of this chapter for instructions) because this will extend the shelf life and give you medicine on hand to use as soon as you need it. Remember that tinctures and oil infusions take time to make.

As spring comes back around, keep an eye on emerging plants coming back after the long winter. If you start to notice any plants sprouting and are expecting another frost soon, cover them with a tarp to keep them from being killed. With a little attention and love, you will likely find your garden rewarding in more ways than you imagined.

PROJECTS ON SEEDS, HERBS, AND NATURAL REMEDIES

# How To Stockpile Seeds

During the height of the Covid-19 pandemic, gardeners were in for quite a shock as they walked into some retail stores and found the seed aisle blocked off. Many big retail chains that remained open during the pandemic seemingly decided that seeds weren't important enough to allow the public access to buy. In fact, it's one year later and some retailers are still not allowing access to seeds. Is it really because they are deemed "non-essential"? Could there be other motives behind this insanity?

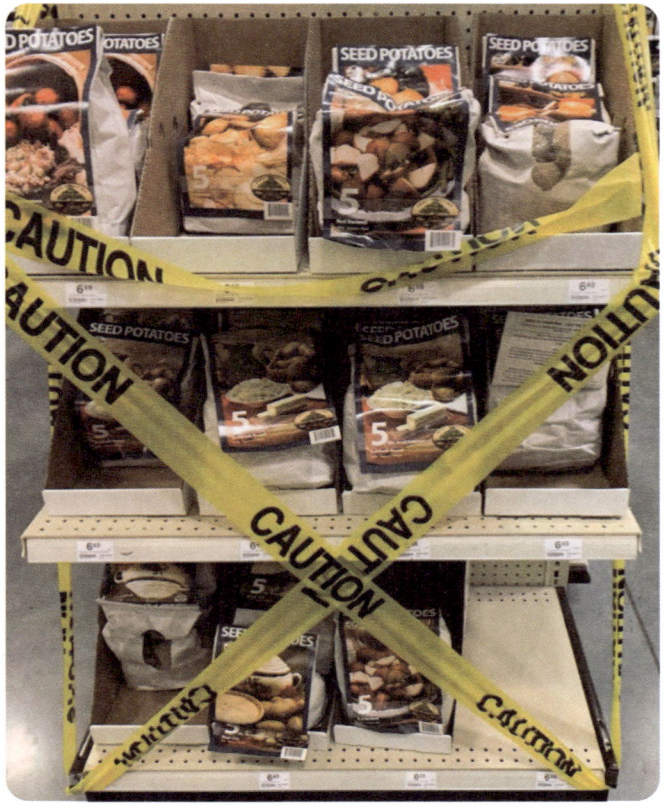

The sight of caution tape strung all over the seed aisle made a lot of free-thinkers stop and think. Why deny access to seeds? Have we forgotten where our food comes from? Have we reached a point in society where one cannot grow their own food, but instead must rely on grocery stores to supply what we need? This is a dangerous precedent.

Things were not always this way during times of crisis. During times of war, specifically WWI and WWII, the government actually encouraged the public to grow a garden. They were termed "Victory Gardens" and were planted at both private residences, as well as public parks throughout the United States, United Kingdom, Australia, Canada, and Germany. These gardens were encouraged because of a serious food shortage. Those who worked in the agricultural field were called into the service to fight. This put a strain on manpower to maintain enough crops to feed the country.

All land not being used was suddenly worked and turned into gardens. Self-sufficiency was highly encouraged with the slogan "Grow your Own, Can your Own". A victory garden was even planted on the White House lawn. This attitude of self-sufficiency and growing your own food to care for your family has faded away over the years to the point where the current generation has little to no knowledge or skill when it comes to seeds, gardening, and how to survive in a crisis.

There may come a time when grocery stores don't have what you need to survive. Working now to be as self-sufficient as possible will pay off exponentially in the future. Seeds are your ticket to provision for yourself and your loved ones.

## Why You Should Stockpile Seeds Now

Seeds can and should be stockpiled now more than ever. When the powers that be are telling the public not to buy seeds, that is when you should buy as many seeds as you can. Start your collection now and keep collecting at every opportunity. One of the biggest incentives to start stockpiling seeds is what has come to light during our recent time of crisis. A pandemic hit the world in 2020 and we had the opportunity to see how people reacted to this time of turmoil. What did most people do? They stockpiled things like toilet paper. Toilet paper is something that is nice to have, but we can see where people's priorities were by the empty shelves in the toilet paper aisle. What about basic necessities like food and water? Those were also stockpiled in many cities around the world. Even today, the shelves in some produce and meat aisles are surprisingly scant.

This mass drive to buy things that are not necessary to our survival goes to show that the public can react fast and irrationally in a crisis. While people are out buying all the bread and milk, you can take comfort in the fact that you have access to a bounty of nutritious food in your backyard for years to come, all without ever leaving your home. Most food items at grocery stores have a shelf life. By the time you purchase the food and bring it home, you have a few weeks at best. When you have your own survival garden with the seeds you collect, you have fresh food year-round just a few steps away. The time to stockpile seeds has certainly come and the importance of being prepared with plenty of seeds cannot be ignored as we face an uncertain future.

# The Best Way to Stockpile Your Seeds

Believe it or not, most seeds have a decent shelf life. Their survival all depends on the conditions in which you choose to store them. You can very realistically collect enough seeds to last your whole life.

Temperature and humidity are everything. Make sure that wherever you choose to keep your seeds, the humidity is low to non-existent. The temperature needs to be cool to room temperature. High humidity can negatively impact seeds because it increases the chance they are exposed to some moisture. Seeds should not be exposed to any moisture until they are ready to be planted. Temperatures too hot or too cold can damage seeds as well, although some seeds don't mind.

Make sure you store your seeds in a container that is completely water proof. Water is their enemy until they are ready to be planted. Another thing to keep in mind is that the container should be as airtight as possible. Most seeds come in individual envelopes. This is completely fine and there is no reason to remove them from these if they are dry. These envelopes can be stored in an airtight container with a lid for safe keeping. Containers like waterproof five gallon buckets with securely-fitting lids are perfect.

Do you ever notice little silica gel packets in products you buy? Save them! These packets are placed in products to keep moisture from ruining them. You can place some of these packets inside your containers to keep moisture at bay. They can also be purchased online.

Store your seeds in a place with consistent, non-fluctuating temperatures. Make sure the area is dry and dark. Sometimes, sunlight can damage products and it may also heat up the container and damage seeds.

Label your containers. This is very important. This saves you from having to constantly open the containers and rifle through seeds to try and find what you need. Seeing what you have will also allow you to take stock of what you have and what you still need to collect. Write the date you purchased the seeds, as well as the type of seed, on the outside of the container. This will help you keep track of which seeds need to be used first. Always plant the oldest seeds first.

Seeds can be stored in the refrigerator or freezer for safekeeping and to extend shelf life. These are best stored in envelopes inside glass mason jars. Fill a jar (write all information on the outside of the jar) and place it in the freezer until you are ready to plant. There is a process to removing these seeds and planting them. First, carefully sit the jar out at room temperature for at least twelve hours. Remove the lid and let the air circulate in the jar so it can prevent any moisture that may occur from the temperature change. Let this jar sit in the open air several days before planting the seeds.

# Seed Shelf Life

There are some seeds that last longer than others. Seeds that last up to two years before their germination rate decreases include: sweet corn, onions, parsley, peppers, parsnips, and okra. Keep an eye on the dates you purchased these particular seeds and try to use them in a timely fashion.

For all seeds you purchase, try to buy heirloom seeds. These are the best seeds for growing food that you can then collect more seeds from to save. For the seeds with a shorter shelf life, like the ones mentioned above, plant them each year and try to have enough for one or two more years in your collection. Each year, collect seeds from the vegetables you grow and save them by harvesting them, cleaning them, and drying them thoroughly. When they are completely dry, place them in labeled envelopes and store them in a container. Always plant your oldest seeds first.

Seeds with a shelf life of up to four years include: carrots, celery, peas, leeks, eggplants, broccoli, kohlrabi, cauliflower, Brussels sprouts, beets, beans, watermelons, pumpkins, turnips, spinach, tomatoes, turnips, and squash. Try to have around four years' worth of these seeds on hand and use the oldest seeds each year during planting time. It is not a bad idea to collect these heirloom seeds each year to process and store for emergencies in case something happens to your collection.

Some seeds have a shelf life up to six years, or even longer, when stored properly. These include cucumber, radish, and lettuce seeds. Try to always have up to six years' worth of these seeds on hand in your stockpile.

There may come a time when you are no longer able to purchase seeds. If this happens, you should already be prepared with all the heirloom seeds you have grown and processed for storage. Each year, whether you have ample purchased seeds in storage or not, collect seeds from your garden to dry and store just in case. If you can keep doing this through the years, you will start a self-sufficiency cycle that can last a lifetime.

## The Best Seeds to Stockpile

The best seeds to stockpile in terms of shelf life include cucumber, radish, and lettuce seeds because they last longer than most other seeds. Under the right conditions, they can last much longer than the six year shelf-life they are generally given.

In terms of optimal nutrition, the best seeds to stockpile include amaranth, spinach, alfalfa, kale, broccoli, peas, and beets. These are packed full of vitamins and minerals your body needs to flourish. They may come in especially handy when you can no longer purchase vitamins to take daily.

In addition, consider making sure you have an ample amount of starches, such as sweet potatoes, potatoes, carrots, pumpkin, squash, and corn. These are not only nutritious, but they contain fiber that can help keep your digestive system healthy.

Always have seeds on hand that produce vegetables that supply ample protein to the body. Protein is important for the body to function. It also helps the body maintain healthy muscle mass. Some healthy sources of protein include chickpeas, lentils, asparagus, pinto beans, lima beans, and fava beans. Quinoa, chia seeds, and Brussels sprouts also contain protein.

### Stockpiling Seeds for a Brighter Future

While the future is uncertain, don't let fears or anxiety about the future steal your joy. While things may look bleak at times, it is within us as human beings to forge on and blaze a path to victory. Stockpiling seeds give you peace of mind, optimal nutrition, and the ability to survive most any crisis without depending on help from the outside world. This independence and self-sufficiency is one of the most precious gifts you can give yourself and your family.

PROJECTS ON SEEDS, HERBS, AND NATURAL REMEDIES

# Natural Remedies To Make At Home Using Local Plants

Did you know that there are numerous plants growing near you that can be used to make natural remedies for all kinds of ailments? The plants in this chapter are familiar and some are even invasive. They can often be found growing right outside your door in many parts of North America. Below, you will discover what plants you can use, as well as how to use them for common ailments.

## 1. Natural Remedies to Fight Viruses

### Japanese Honeysuckle, *Lonicera japonica*

Japanese honeysuckle is a vining plant that has become an aggressive and invasive plant in many parts of the world. However, this "weed" has a surprising medicinal use for killing viruses. All aerial parts of the plant can be utilized to create a tincture to target a variety of viruses. Tinctures are plant extracts that use a liquid solvent like alcohol to pull the medicinal properties out of plants.

To create a tincture with this plant, rip it out (vine and all) and chop what you have collected into small pieces. Make sure to harvest the plant when it is flowering. Fill a glass jar with the vine, flower, and leaf pieces and then cover the plant material completely with at least 80 proof alcohol. Let this sit in a cool, dark place for four to six weeks. Place a lid on the jar and shake it daily to help the tincture infuse better. After four to six weeks, strain out the liquid and bottle it. Since they are made with alcohol, tinctures have a long shelf life and can last for up to seven years if stored out of sunlight and in a cool place. Take 5ml every few hours as needed if you feel you have a virus.

### Elderberry, *Sambucus nigra* or *Sambucus canadensis*

Elderberries are a powerful antiviral. So many people are unaware of just how common elder is in North America. It flourishes in the wild all around us. It can easily be spotted in midsummer because the big umbels where the berries will emerge are clusters of white flowers. Look for bushes with these large white flower clusters and take note of where you saw them. Go back to those spots in early fall and check for berries. The berries are ripe when they are a dark purple color. Collect the berries by trimming the stems and then lay the stems in a dehydrator to dry the berries. Once they are dried, they will fall off the stems easily and will be much easier to prepare. Fill a glass jar with the dried berries and then cover them completely in 80 proof (or higher) alcohol. Let this infuse for four to six weeks, shaking the tincture daily to help it infuse. It will eventually turn a deep crimson or purple color. Strain it out when it is ready and bottle the liquid. Take 5ml two to three times a day at the onset of a virus. The sooner you begin taking it the speedier your recovery will be.

## 2. Natural Remedies to Treat Wounds

### Yarrow, *Achillea millefolium*

Yarrow is commonly found in early to late summer. It is usually found growing in fields and pastures. It can be identified by its white flower cluster on top. It is an uneven shape, unlike Queen Anne's lace, which is more round. Another characteristic that makes yarrow easy to identify is its medicinal and herbaceous aroma, unlike Queen Anne's lace which as a carrot-like aroma.

Yarrow is known for its ability to heal wounds; specifically, wounds that are bleeding. It can act as a styptic and help the blood to clot. Additionally, yarrow can help cleanse a wound with its antiseptic properties. Yarrow can be used in several ways, but one popular way is straight from the plant to the wound. Pluck a leaf and mash it up. Then place it on the cut. You can also collect yarrow and dry it for later use. Once it is dry, grind it into powder and apply the powder to wounds.

### Witch Hazel, *Hamamelis vernalis*

Witch hazel is native to many parts of North America. This tree may not be easy to spot during the spring, summer, and fall months. However, it is easy to spot in the winter due to its bright yellow blooms that emerge when few other colors are visible in the forest! Take a walk in the woods on a winter's day and look out for witch hazel trees with their yellow, ribbon-like flowers. You may even notice a pleasant aroma before you get to the tree itself.

This tree has been utilized for ages for its astringent, wound cleansing properties. It is also known for reducing inflammation and redness on the skin. It can help calm angry skin and promote healing. Harvest a few small branches and let them dry in your apothecary. When you need them, you can break off some to infuse in hot water to make tea. This tea, when cooled, is useful for wound cleansing. This tea is very soothing when applied to hemorrhoids and postpartum wounds as well.

## 3. Natural Remedies to Treat Allergies

### Purple Deadnettle, *Lamium purpureum*

One of the first plants to emerge in the spring, besides dandelions, is purple deadnettle. It is a member of the mint family, but does not have a minty smell. It can take over a yard from March to May. It has tiny purple flowers emerging from the top of a square-stalked plant. It does not grow too big, maybe up to five inches in height. The leaves are toothed and pointed at the top. They may have a purple color the closer to the top they are.

This plant contains flavonoids that can help suppress histamine production in the body. Collect plants from an unsprayed yard and chop them well. Fill a glass jar with the plant parts and then cover them completely with alcohol or apple cider vinegar. Let this infuse for four to six weeks before straining out. Take 5ml as needed to help with seasonal allergies.

## Stinging Nettle, *Urtica dioica*

Stinging nettle also contains flavonoids that help to suppress histamine production, thus lessening allergy symptoms. It can be found in the summer and fall months. Harvesting these plants means wearing gloves to protect your hands from the little stingers these plants possess. If these stinging hairs make contact with your skin, they can cause a lot of irritation. They can usually be found growing in fields and waste areas. They can become aggressive in many areas, so they usually aren't hard to find.

Dry the nettles by hanging them in an area of your house and when they are sufficiently dry fill a tea infusion ball or tea bag with crumbled leaves. Let this infuse in a cup of hot water for several minutes and then enjoy. Drink a cup of stinging nettle tea as needed for allergies.

## 4. Natural Remedies to Treat Sore Throat

## Echinacea, *Echinacea* spp.

This native pink flower is a powerful remedy against a sore throat caused by a bacterial infection. There are several species of Echinacea that grow throughout North America, with *E. purpurea* being the most popular for medicinal use. *E. angustifolia* has also been used for similar purposes. This plant is easily identifiable in the summer because it has bright pink flowers with a spiny black center. The plants are often on the taller side, ranging from three to five foot tall. When harvesting in the wild, be mindful and only take what you need. Do not harvest roots unless there are many flowers around.

Use all parts of this plant, from the flowers to the leaves to the roots. Chop everything well and fill a glass jar with the plant material. Next, cover it with at least 80 proof alcohol and let this infuse for four to six weeks. Strain everything out and bottle the liquid when it is ready. For strep, gargle for one minute in the back of your throat and then spit it out. Do this every other hour for a week until the strep is gone. You may also consume 5ml up to three times a day to help boost the body's immune system to help combat strep throat.

## Bee Balm, *Monarda fistulosa*

This native plant contains a constituent called thymol, which is highly antibacterial. It is even used commercially in some sanitizing products to kill germs. Bee balm also goes by the name wild bergamot in many parts of North America. There are several species, with some being lavender in color and others a dark magenta. They can be identified in the summer months by their wild-looking flower heads that are comprised of many small, tubular stalks coming from a central head.

Use the aerial parts of this plant to create a tincture to use for killing bacteria that cause throat issues. It can be gargled or taken internally in 5 ml doses (up to three times daily). It is extremely effective against throat infections when used along with Echinacea.

## 5. Natural Remedies to Treat Ear Infections

### Mullein, *Verbascum Thapsus*

It is a popular anti-inflammatory and pain-relieving remedy that can be found growing in the summer months and can be identified by its fuzzy, large leaves. A stalk comes from the center of the basal rosette of leaves. The yellow flowers can be collected from these stalks.

Once you have enough yellow flowers collected, fill a glass jar and then cover the flowers in olive oil. Let this infuse for four weeks. For extra antibiotic strength, you can add a dried and chopped garlic clove. When the time is up, strain out the oil and keep it refrigerated. When you have an ear ache or ear infection, take the bottle of oil and gently warm it by placing it in a bowl of hot water until the oil is melted and warm. Place a few drops into the affected ear and let this sit for several minutes. Do this as needed throughout the day to combat infection and inflammation.

### Oregano, *Origanum vulgare*

Oregano-infused oil is another effective natural remedy for ear ailments. Oregano is a very common garden herb, but contains powerful medicinal properties. There is a wild native plant called American dittany, *Cunila origanoides*, that contains a very similar chemical profile to oregano and can be used the same way. It smells identical to oregano and has a woody stem, lance shaped leaves, and small purple flowers that emerge in the fall.

Collect the oregano or dittany and let dry by hanging it somewhere with good air flow. Next, chop the aerial parts well. Fill a jar and cover them in olive oil. Let this sit for a month before straining it out. Apply this infused oil to the area around the ear (not inside the ear!) and massaging the lobes, around the ear, and the lymph area down the neck from the ear. Do this multiple times a day to help with drainage, kill infection, and provide pain relief.

## 6. Natural Remedies to Treat Bronchitis and Respiratory Ailments

### Mullein, *Verbascum Thapsus*

Mullein leaves also have a medicinal purpose. These thick and fuzzy leaves are an excellent remedy for mucous expulsion and to help clear bronchial passages. You can make a tincture from the leaves by collecting them from a clean area, chopping them, and covering them in alcohol in a glass jar. Let this infuse for four to six weeks before straining it out. The liquid should be a medium to dark green color. Take 5 ml every few hours to help your body get rid of mucous and clear the airways.

## Pleurisy Root, *Asclepias tuberosa*

Another name for this familiar plant is "butterfly weed" or "chigger weed." It can be spotted in the summer months by its bright red, vibrant clusters of flowers. It is a great pollinator plant, so you will often notice butterflies surrounding it. It only stands a foot or two high and can be spotted in fields and pastures throughout North America.

The root of this plant has been used as a lung remedy for centuries. It can help to clear the airways, expel mucous, and calm irritated lungs. Tincture the roots by harvesting them mindfully, chopping them, and covering them in alcohol in a glass jar. Let this sit for four to six weeks before straining it out. Take two to five ml every three to four hours if you are suffering from a respiratory issue. You can use this in conjunction with mullein leaf for additional healing.

## 7. Natural Remedies to Treat Urinary Tract Infections

### Oregano, *Origanum vulgare*

Because oregano contains potent antibacterial properties, it can be used to kill a variety of bacterial issues in the body. One such issue is a urinary tract infection. This results when bacteria get in the urinary tract and cause irritation. Drinking tea made from dried oregano leaves can flush out the bacteria, as well as kill it. You can infuse the leaves using a tea bag or tea infusion ball in a cup of hot water for five to seven minutes. Drink as many cups as you can throughout the day to target the infection and flush it out.

## Aloe Vera

Aloe vera is native in many southwestern states, but those who don't have it growing wild will often have it growing in their house. Aloe vera is a very common house plant because it is so easy to grow and requires little maintenance. It spreads easily and can propagate from little "babies" that spring up around the plant.

If you have this plant, you can use it to your benefit by slicing open the leaves and scraping out the inner gel-like substance. Drink a tablespoon of this in a smoothie or a glass of water up to three times a day. This will help to relieve inflammation in the urinary tract, as well as kill the infection. Using this in conjunction with oregano tea is optimal.

## 8. Natural Remedies to Treat Gastrointestinal Issues

### Mints, *Mentha* spp.

Not just one mint species is best for helping relieve gastrointestinal discomfort like gas, bloating, upset stomach, stomach cramps, etc. All members of the mint family can help. Some great examples to look for include include peppermint, *Mentha piperita*, catnip, *Nepeta cataria*, spearmint, *Mentha spicata*, and horsemint, *Mentha longifolia*. You can get a good idea whether or not you have a mint by looking at the stalk of the plant (which should be square) and by smelling the crushed leaves. Avoid germander, which is a member of the mint family that grows in the summer months and has light pink flowers atop stalks. It can be potentially dangerous. Harvest aerial parts of the mint plant and hang them to dry. When they are sufficiently dried, store your mint in a glass, airtight jar in a cool, dark place. When you need relief from gastrointestinal issues, simply take some dried leaves and infuse them in a cup of tea to drink as needed. You will find that this can help relieve bloating, gas, upset stomach, and constipation.

## Agrimony, *Agrimonia eupatoria*

This common and native plant can help provide relief from diarrhea and promote gastrointestinal healing. Agrimony can be found at the wood's edge in the late summer months. It can be distinguished by its long stalks with small yellow flowers at the top of the spiked stalks.

Harvest the aerial parts and dry them for use when you need them. You can infuse the plant parts in a cup of hot water to drink for diarrhea. Drink as needed when you need relief.

# 9. Natural Remedies to Treat Pain

## Willow, *Salix* spp.

Willow bark is known for its ability to combat pain and treat headaches, body aches, and inflammation. There are several species of willow that can be used because they contain salicin, a medicinal compound. The most popular species of willow used medicinally is the white willow tree, *Salix alba*. However, there are other species that can be found all over North America and be used medicinally.

The bark is what contains the compound. Cut into the inner bark of the tree to get what is behind the firs layer. Do not cut a ring completely around the tree or you could kill it. You can use this bark to infuse in water to drink as a tea for pain or make a tincture with alcohol for pain. For tea, drink a cup every few hours as needed. For a tincture with alcohol, take 5-8 ml every four to five hours for pain from headaches, body aches, or tooth aches.

## Poplar, *Populus* spp.

Like willow, the bark from the poplar tree also contains salicin. This tree can be found all over the world, primarily because there aren't many locations it can't grow. Harvest the inner bark from this tree much the same way you would willow bark. It can be used in the same ways, whether in a tea or tincture for pain.

# 10. Natural Remedies to Treat Circulation/ Heart Ailments

## Motherwort, *Leonurus cardiaca*

It can be found growing wild in many areas of North America, and is also a lovely garden plant. It is a member of the mint family and can be identified in the summer by its stalks with protruding, lobed leaves and purple flowers going up to the top. It has a pleasant, minty smell. It is known for its ability to nourish the heart and circulatory system. It can help lower blood pressure and strengthen the heart tissues. In addition, if blood pressure spikes are caused by stress, motherwort can help to provide calm and peace, thus lowering blood pressure as well.

Harvest aerial parts and chop them well. Cover the plant material in alcohol in a glass jar and let this infuse for four to six weeks before straining it out. Take 5 ml if you are feeling stressed or anxiety. This can help lower your blood pressure if you are worried it may spike as a result of the stress. Take 2.5 ml twice daily for heart and circulatory health.

## Hawthorn, *Crataegus laevigata* and *Crataegus pruinose*

It can be found all over Europe and North America. The berries from this tree are used to help with heart and circulatory issues. Hawthorn is known to help lower blood pressure and nourish the heart muscle.

Harvest the berries anywhere from mid spring to early fall. You can tincture them and take 5 ml up to twice daily for heart and circulatory health and maintenance.

# 11. Natural Remedies to Treat Liver Issues

## Dandelion, *Taraxacum officinale*

There may not be a more common, yet underrated, plant than dandelion. All parts of this plant can be used for both food and medicine. The root however, is known for its ability to tonify the liver and kidneys. You can find this plant almost anywhere, and it grows throughout the year. You may even be able to harvest it in the winter if the winter is mild. Use a good spade to dig up the plant, taking care to get the entire (sometimes large) taproot. Make sure you collect your dandelion roots from areas you know have not been sprayed with pesticides or other harmful chemicals. Wash the roots and chop them well. Let them dry and store them in an airtight jar for use in tea. Drink one to two cups of dandelion root tea daily for liver nourishment and healing.

## Yellow Dock, *Rumex crispus*

This common plant flourishes in pastures and fields throughout the United States. It can be identified by its large leaves with curled edges and tops that go to seed in the summer and fall months, appearing dark red to dark brown in color. While the seeds are a fiber-rich and nutritious snack, the roots are the part used for liver health.

Dig up the roots in the fall and make sure you have a good spade because they can be very large and deep in the ground. When sliced open, the roots are yellow inside. They are thick and meaty. Wash the roots and dry them. Infuse the chopped and dried roots in hot water to make tea for liver health. Enjoy this daily to help flush the liver and keep it healthy.

## 12. Natural Remedies to Treat Kidney Issues

## Cleavers, *Galium aparine*

They are common in the spring months. They are identified by their small, lobed leaves circling the stalk. One of the most common identification characteristics is the sticky nature of the plant. It will stick to almost anything, thus giving it the name "cleaver."

This plant is an excellent lymphatic cleanser, as well as an effective diuretic. Diuretic plants help to flush the body of toxins by promoting the removal of water from the body. If you wish to utilize cleavers for kidney flushing, simply harvest them and infuse them in alcohol while they are still fresh. Strain out the tincture after four to six weeks and take 5-10 ml of this up to three times in a day to cleanse the kidneys. Always drink extra water when you are taking a diuretic herb to avoid dehydration.

## Goldenrod, *Solidago* spp.

It is common in the fall months and is characterized by its blazing golden flowers atop a stalk. It is a favorite for bees and other pollinators during the autumn months.

Goldenrod is excellent for inflammatory conditions in the kidneys because it can help to reduce inflammation and promote healing. In addition, goldenrod is a diuretic and can help flush out toxins. Gather the aerial parts in the fall and infuse them in at least 80 proof alcohol for four to six weeks before straining out the tincture. Take four to six ml of the tincture up to three times daily for kidney ailments like kidney infections or kidney stones. Drink plenty of extra water when taking this remedy to flush out the infection or stone. There are many species of goldenrod, but some popular medicinal species include *Solidago virgaurea*, *Solidago canadensis*, *Solidago gigantea*, and *Solidago odora*.

# 13. Natural Remedies to Treat Insomnia, Depression, and Anxiety

## St. John's Wort, *Hypericum perforatum*

You may notice the bright yellow flowers of St. John's Wort in mid-June. It prefers sunny areas like open hillsides and pastures. You can even find it along roadsides. It grows in groups and can get up to three feet tall. It is a bushy native plant. You can tell it is the "real thing" if you smash one of the yellow flowers and your fingers become stained with a red-purple tint. This is proof the flowers contain hypericin, a chemical constituent in St. John's Wort responsible for its medicinal properties.

Harvest the flowering tops and tincture them in alcohol as soon as possible. The alcohol tincture will turn a bright red due to the hypericin. This plant has been shown to help relieve mild to moderate depression, as well as anxiety. Take 5 ml twice daily (morning and evening) to help manage these, as well as Seasonal Affective Disorder.

## Skullcap, *Scutellaria lateriflora*

This is a beautiful wildflower that can be found in the summer months. It prefers well-drained fields and meadows. The flowers are a lovely blue-purple color and have a distinctive "hood." This may be one reason they were named "skullcap." They are a member of the mint family, so the stalk is square.

Harvest the aerial parts of this plant and tincture it in at least 80 proof alcohol for four to six weeks. Strain it out when the time is up. You should have a vivid green tincture. Take three to five ml of this as needed for anxiety and stress. Skullcap has been used for hundreds of years to help calm the body and mind. It acts on the nerves, helping to provide peace amidst frustration and agitation.

PROJECTS ON SEEDS, HERBS, AND NATURAL REMEDIES

# The Only 7 Seeds You Need To Stockpile For A Crisis

If you have ever visited the seed store, you may have noticed the sheer variety of seeds available to purchase. There are so many seeds available that it may seem overwhelming when trying to decide which seeds are the best to purchase for your needs. Don't stress! The research has been done for you. Below you will discover the seven best seeds you need to stockpile for a crisis. They have been chosen for their nutrition content, ease of growing, and versatility of use. You will learn about why these seeds are superior, what they can do for you, and how to grow them.

## A Staple Since the Dawn of Times

Corn has been a staple in the diets of indigenous people since the dawn of time. Its importance in some indigenous cultures is sacred. Known as maize, almost every tribe grew corn and consumed it at nearly every meal. South American tribes were among the first to cultivate corn and are thought to have created it from wild grasses hybridized over time. Corn wasn't just their main source of food; it was a part of their spiritual practice. Today, corn has evolved into many different species. Some species are better for feeding livestock, some for their sweet taste, and some are even grown for decoration.

Look for heirloom varieties when searching for corn seeds. One of the best heirloom varieties of corn available is called *Golden Bantam*. It is a traditional corn that can be described as sweet, but not too sweet. This variety of corn grows up to six feet tall and will produce anywhere from eight to ten inch ears if it is given the right growing conditions. This variety was first introduced over a century ago. When storing your corn seeds, you can safely have up to two years' worth on hand. Corn seeds may even store longer than that if they are stored properly.

Heirloom varieties of corn are often easier to grow and delicious. You will need a few things to ensure a successful harvest. First, make sure the seeds are planted in well-draining soil. Corn is very picky about the soil and will not thrive in soil that doesn't drain well. Try to plant seeds around two weeks before the last frost. Prepare the soil with plenty of nitrogen by adding manure and blending it into your corn row well. Space your seeds up to 36 inches apart and plant them in a row where they can be exposed to plenty of sunlight. Many heirloom varieties are draught resistant, which may come in handy if you live in an area that doesn't get much rain. Try to plant them in an area of your property where they can be watered if they go too long without rain.

Why is corn so important? For starters, it is a great source of antioxidants, B vitamins (great for energy), and fiber. It is a nourishing crop that sustained indigenous people for centuries. Another reason corn is one of the best crops to grow is that it is versatile. So much can be done with corn besides just eating it off the ear (although boiled ears of corn are delicious). Corn kernels can be dried and processed into flour. Flour is an invaluable staple and can be used to make many other foods like tortillas, corn fritters, batter, and breads.

The corn silk that surrounds the kernels has a valuable use as well. It is diuretic and cleansing to the body. It has been collected, dried, and infused into water to make tea to treat ailments like urinary tract infections and gout.

## A Nutrition-Packed Root Vegetable

Carrots are an excellent choice for a hearty root vegetable to add to your survival garden. Carrots come in many varieties, just make sure to purchase heirloom seeds. Carrots are an excellent source of vitamin A, boasting a whopping 428 % of your daily vitamin A value. They are also a rich source of the antioxidant beta-carotene. Beta-carotene is the compound that gives carrots their vibrant color. It is known for its impressive health benefits like preventing cancer. Carrots are also a good source of vitamins C and K, as well as potassium.

In addition to the nutrition factor, carrot seeds are some of the easiest root vegetables to grow. One great thing about carrots is that they tolerate cold weather well. If you are concerned about what crops you may have available in the winter months, you might feel better to know that carrots may still be harvested during this time. Many gardeners actually plant carrot seeds sixty days before the first frost so they can have carrots through the winter. This makes them valuable for year-round nutrition.

Carrot seeds have a moderate shelf life of around two years, but may last longer if stored properly. Remember to let some of your carrots go to seed every year so you can harvest these seeds to add to your stockpile.

Carrots require loose soil without any rocks to inhibit their growth. They do well in a variety of temperatures, ranging from the 40s to the 80s. If you grow carrots in a raised bed, you can grow them just about any time of the year. Make sure you give them plenty of water as they grow. After planting seeds, you can expect to harvest your first carrots in around seventy to eighty days.

## The Two Great Grains

Wheat is a classic grain grown for use in a huge range of products from cereals to breads. Wheat has been cultivated since at least 9600 BCE.

It is a rich source of fiber, protein, B vitamins, and minerals like iron, magnesium, copper, selenium, folate, and phosphorus. This alone makes it vital for use in a survival garden.

If wheat seeds are given the right conditions, they can last many years in your seed stockpile. They need to be kept away from any moisture that might cause damage. One of the most effective ways to store wheat seeds is in the freezer. This can extend its shelf life by four to five times.

A variety of heirloom wheat called Emmer wheat (*Triticum turgidum*) is a very good option if you are considering growing wheat.

This is one of the oldest varieties of wheat, often called "pharaoh's wheat" because it was cultivated in ancient Egypt.

This wheat variety is said to be hearty and easy to grow in bad soil. It is also surprisingly disease resistant.

It is great for making anything from bread to beer. If you happen to be one of the millions of people who are sensitive to gluten, this variety of wheat is thought to have less gluten than most others and might be tolerated better than other varieties.

As previously stated, growing Emmer wheat is not as difficult as one might expect. This lies in the fact that it can grow in poor soil and is disease resistant. Start by planting seeds in the spring after the last frost.

They will require well-draining soil, but not soil that dries out too quickly. They do best in full sun. Wait to harvest until there is no longer any milky substance when grains are cut open.

Amaranth is another grain grown since ancient times, having been cultivated for at least 8,000 years.

It is arguably one of the most nutritious crops in the world. It is rich in fiber and protein, which are vital to healthy survival.

However, it also contains a large amount of micro nutrients that are vital to health, such as iron, magnesium, selenium, phosphorous, and copper.

It is packed with antioxidants that help to destroy disease-causing free radicals in the body.

This super food has been studied for its ability to lower inflammation in the body, reduce cholesterol that could lead to heart disease, and even aid in weight loss.

It does not contain any gluten, making it even more beneficial for those sensitive or unable to have any gluten in their diet.

Amaranth grows best in soil rich in nitrogen and phosphorous, but will still grow well (up to six feet tall) in the average garden soil. If given the right soil combination, amaranth plants can grow very tall, up to eight feet in height.

Try planting amaranth seeds in well-draining loam. They will need at least five hours of sunlight each day to thrive.

Although they seem to tolerate somewhat drier soils, they do better with regular watering. Do not plant seeds until danger of frost has passed.

Once amaranth starts to grow, you can use it in two different ways. After fifty days, you can use the nutritious greens in salads.

After ninety to one hundred days, you can begin to harvest its nutrient-dense grains to use.

Amaranth grains can be processed into flour for baking or added to virtually any meal as a valuable source of sustenance and nourishment.

# The Grandiose Greens

Green may not be your favorite color, but in the vegetable world, green is synonymous with "great".

Plants like spinach, peas, and asparagus are nutritional powerhouses that virtually all contain beta-carotene, vitamin A, vitamin C, vitamin K, magnesium, potassium, and iron, to name a few. In addition to these benefits, all three of these plants are relatively easy to grow.

Spinach is a leafy green that is a favorite among nutritionists around the world. This is because for every three cups of spinach you consume, you are getting roughly 300% of your daily vitamin K intake, 160% daily vitamin A, and 40% of the vitamin C you need each day.

You are also getting at least 45% of your daily intake of folate. It is a good source of antioxidants and has been studied for its ability to support brain health, lower blood pressure, and support healthy eyes.

Spinach actually grows better in cooler weather, so you can plant in early spring and then again in the fall. This way you will have spinach to enjoy twice a year. Sow the seeds in thin rows and try to space rows at least twelve inches apart. Lightly cover the seeds with soil. Plant seeds in a location that has plenty of shade, because spinach does not do well in the full sun.

Keep the soil moist until the leaves germinate, then water as needed. Once you see leaves begin to emerge, try to thin out your rows to keep plants six inches apart. Harvest all of your spinach leaves before they go to seed. After they go to seed, the leaves are too bitter. Let a few go to seed so you can harvest seeds to stockpile. Spinach seeds will keep up to four years, and perhaps longer if stored properly.

For a crop rich in fiber, protein, and plenty of vitamins and minerals, stock up on peas. Peas can be an important source of plant-based protein, making them valuable for survival gardens.

Their fiber content makes them a wise choice for gut and digestive health.

Another benefit of this crop is the shelf life of the seed, which is around three years. However, they may last longer than this if they are stored properly.

The simplicity of growing peas is another reason why they are a valuable seed to have in stock.

Peas can be planted as soon as the ground is workable. They require a growing temperature between 55 degrees and 65 degrees Fahrenheit for the most success. They prefer soil that is loamy and has a pH between five and seven.

Create a shallow trench around 22 centimeters wide and set seeds down inside. When placing seeds in the trench, place them down 3 centimeters deep and space them out around ten centimeters apart.

They will do well in full sun and will require a trellis to climb, as they are vining plants.

Asparagus is the gift that keeps on giving in the vegetable world. This is because it is a perennial vegetable that can produce crops for twenty years or more!

Additionally, asparagus is packed with nutrition and health benefits.

This useful crop has been studied for its ability to lower blood pressure, reduce allergy symptoms, and even protect against some diseases.

It is a mild diuretic, so it has been used traditionally to help flush out toxins from the body and promote a healthy urinary tract.

Asparagus can be planted in the spring after any danger of frost has passed. Start by digging a trench around six to twelve inches wide and six to twelve inches deep.

Choose an area of your garden that gets plenty of sun and has well-draining soil. Space seeds around twelve inches apart.

Lightly cover them with dirt. Water daily until germination, but avoid over watering.

Once these plants start growing, they are not as picky about their growing conditions.

Plant plenty of seeds your first go-around, because they take time to grow enough to harvest for food.

It generally takes about four years before you will have good-eating asparagus to harvest.

If you planted a lot of seeds the first year, you will have many plants to harvest in the following years since these plants come back yearly and last for many years.

The seeds have a relatively good shelf life of around three to four years.

A good garden is worth the time and effort you put into it.

With the seven seeds discussed in this article you can create a lot from a little and support yourself, as well as your family, through any crisis.

With the right seed storage and cultivation knowledge, you will be well on your way to having the ultimate survival garden setup with optimal sustenance for years to come.